THE ULTIMATE ENCYCLOPEDIA OF
SOCCER

CARLTON

THE ULTIMATE ENCYCLOPEDIA OF
SOCCER

The definitive illustrated guide to world soccer

Fourth Edition

General Editor: Keir Radnedge
Editor of World Soccer magazine

Foreword by Gary Lineker

THIS IS A CARLTON BOOK

This book published by
Carlton Books Ltd, 1997

Copyright © Carlton Books Ltd
1994, 1995, 1996, 1997

10 9 8 7 6 5 4 3 2 1

Fourth edition 1997

A CIP catalogue record for this book is
available from the British Library

ISBN 1 85868 415 3

Project editor: Martin Corteel
Project art direction: Russell Porter
Production: Sarah Schuman
Design: Stephen Cary

Printed and bound in Spain

To Aidan, Lyndon, Noel and Christy

GENERAL EDITOR

KEIR RADNEDGE is the editor of
the magazine *World Soccer*, the
acknowledged authority on the international game. He has also worked
on the *Daily Mail* sports desk since
1975, and broadcasts regularly on
international football for BBC Radio.
He has scripted World Cup and many
other football videos, includes the
acclaimed *World Club Directory*
among previous publications and
was the 1990 British Sports Magazine
Writer of the Year.

OTHER CONTRIBUTORS

COLIN BENSON is well known
around the British game for his work
in myriad media activities, including
club programmes, soccer videos, local
radio commentaries and freelance
contributions to many magazines.

IAN CRUISE, a self-confessed
Luton Town fan, began his career in
journalism with Hayters Sports
Agency in London in 1986. Four
years later he moved on to *Shoot!* magazine where he spent seven years as
a feature writer and sub-editor.

KEN GOLDMAN, has been edi-
tor of *Soccer Coach Magazine* for 27
years and editor of *Normidian*, the
North Middlesex referee's magazine, for 13 years. He has held
coaching qualifications for 30 years
and has been a qualified referee
since 1971.

JAMES HOOLEY joined the *Daily
Mail* sports staff in London in 1976
and is now Chief Sub-Editor. He
also reports on Premier League
matches and basketball and has contributed to other soccer books,
including *The Official History of
Arsenal FC*.

MARK IRWIN is a past editor of
Shoot! magazine, who became, in
1993, a partner in the Teamwork
Sports Agency of London before
joining the *Daily Mirror*.

JOHN KELLY is a London-based
soccer writer, statistician and
researcher. He is a regular contrib-
utor to *World Soccer* magazine and
helps compile its comprehensive
results and tables service. He worked
as a consultant for one of the biggest
play-by-mail football games. He also
contributes to other soccer magazines around the world and claims
Portman Road as his spiritual home.

DAVID PROLE was a veteran of
what used to be known as Fleet Street
before retiring from his position as
a pools specialist on *The People*.
Born on Merseyside and later a graduate of the *Hampstead and Highgate
Express*, he is the author of seven
books on soccer, including *Football
in London* and *Come On The Reds*,
an original history of Liverpool FC.

GENERAL EDITOR'S ACKNOWLEDGEMENTS

Thanks are due to all those, seen
and unseen, who worked so hard
and with such enthusiasm to bring an
ambitious project to fruition. Particular thanks to all my fellow writers
for their contributions on the many
and varied aspects of football considered in these pages. Thanks also
to Steve Dobell, Peter Arnold and
David Ballheimer for their work on
the text; Sharon Hutton and Gina
Wardrop for picture research; to
special photographer Christine Don-
nier-Valetin; and to Nick Cooper
and John Lucas for their help with the
illustrations. To Ian Cook and Mark
Wylie, curators of the Arsenal and the
Manchester United Museums respectively, for their assistance with special
photography. Last, but not least, to
Martin Corteel, Executive Editor
of Carlton Books, for keeping the
show on the road from initial plan-
ning meeting to final print run.

Previous pages (left): **ROMARIO** *Brazil's
star of the 1994 World Cup Finals;*
(right) **CUP-WINNING KICK** *World Footballer
of the Year, Ronaldo, converts the
penalty which was to clinch the 1997
European Cup-winners' Cup Final for
his former club Barcelona*

CONTENTS

COMPETITIONS *Dortmund Champions Cup*

STADIUMS *Stadio Giuseppe Meazza*

PLAYERS *Carlos Valderrama*

FOREWORD
BY GARY LINEKER

So far as I'm concerned, the best thing about football is playing it. But there are other pleasures to be had from football – and watching it, reading about it, talking about it and arguing about it are some of them. I suggest anybody who reads this encyclopedia will not only enjoy it for its own sake, but will be much better informed afterwards for those discussions and friendly arguments. What I like particularly about it is its international perspective.

My footballing career has been centred mainly on three English cities, Leicester, Liverpool and London, on a great Spanish city, Barcelona, and on Nagoya, a major port and key area for Japan's car industry.

At Leicester, my family were so keen on football they even moved house to ensure that I attended a football school rather than a rugby one. Nobody thought this odd, and nobody thought my first footballing move – from Filbert Street to Goodison Park – was odd either. Everton rivalled Liverpool as the strongest side in the country, and it certainly was a good opportunity for me. Moving to Barcelona was different. Some shook their heads and said it was a mistake to leave "the strongest league in the world".

I don't agree with this assessment. It is the hardest league in the world, perhaps. But I think there are leagues where sharper, more skilful football is played. This is no reflection on British players. The game is more demanding than ever now, and with a 20-club Premier League and two Cup competitions, playing in England at the top level is very tiring. By comparison, the players in Serie A, the top Italian division, can more consistently produce their best form, and play better football, because they are fresher. There are fewer pressure games – this is true in Spain, too – and players can rise to the big occasion more readily. I hope the situation will improve in Britain as we go through the rigours of qualifying for the World Cup in 1998, especially since the Home nations missed out in 1994.

I undoubtedly enjoyed one of my best club footballing memories with Barcelona – winning the European Cup-winners' Cup in 1989, an experience that compares with the two unforgettable games at Wembley in 1991 where Spurs beat Arsenal and then Forest to win the FA Cup.

I knew there was no danger that this book would take the blinkered view that many English soccer followers have in undervaluing overseas football compared to our domestic game. The general editor, Keir Radnedge, is not editor of the magazine *World Soccer* for nothing, and I recall talking to him when he was invited by the J-League to study the boom in Japan, where I finished my playing career. He shared my enthusiasm about the prospects there.

In fact, this book covers the world game in such depth, that I don't mind admitting that a number of the 200 or so international footballers in the Great Players section were relatively new to me. There's a great deal of new and fascinating information about equipment, stadiums, culture, and all aspects of football. For me, it certainly is the "ultimate" encyclopedia of football. I hope you get as much pleasure from it as I do.

THE EARLY HISTORY OF FOOTBALL

The precise origin of Association football is unknown. Its modern format of 11 players against 11 in a confined area can be attributed to the British in the nineteenth century, but there is evidence of a form of football being played in China long before Julius Caesar brought the Roman game of harpastum to Britain.

AN ANCIENT BALL GAME

China provides history's first football report, in the writings of the Han Dynasty 2000 years ago. Then Japan supported their bid to win hosting rights for the 2002 World Cup by noting 14-century-old records of a local game called kenatt. The rules may have changed down the centuries but the pursuit of what we term a football has remained one of man's most consistent entertainments.

It was just so for the Greeks and the Romans. Pollux describes the pastime of harpastum in the following terms: "The players divided themselves into two bands. The ball was thrown upon the line in the middle. At the two ends behind the places where the players were stationed there were two other lines (which would seem to be equivalent to modern goal-lines), beyond which they tried to carry it, a feat that could not be done without pushing one another backward and forward." This suggests that harpastum was the origin of both rugby football and association football.

Ball games in Britain seem to have started as annual events staged over Shrovetide. As a rule these contests began in the market-place and involved two teams of unlimited numbers trying to propel a ball into the opposite side's goal, which was usually some convenient spot not too remote from the centre of town.

It was very hostile, violent, and extremely dangerous. Householders had to barricade their lower windows as the mobs did battle along the streets. The hero was the lucky player who eventually grounded the ball in goal. Not that it was always a ball. The followers of the rebel leader Jack Cade kicked a pig's bladder in the streets of London. In Chester the object of the boot was a little more distasteful. There the game originated as a celebration of victory over the marauding Danes, and the head of one of the vanquished army was

AN ANCIENT SPORT *This early drawing confirms that a game similar to football was played in a confined area as early as the 16th century*

BLOWING UP THE BALL FOR PALLO *It is assumed that Pallo was a forerunner to football*

used as a football. Later generations were content to boot a leather ball at their Shrove Tuesday festivals.

There is a record of London schoolboys playing organized football before Lent in 1175, and so popular had the game become in the streets of London in the reign of Edward II that the merchants, fearing this most robust and violent activity was affecting their trade, petitioned the king to prohibit the game. On April 13, 1314, Edward II issued the following proclamation forbidding the practice as leading to a breach of the peace: "Forasmuch as there is great noise in the city caused by hustling over large balls, from which many evils may arise, which God forbid; we command and forbid on behalf of the King, on pain of imprisonment, such game to be used in the city in future."

This was just one of many attempts to stamp out this popular activity. In 1349 Edward III tried to put an end to football because he felt the young men of the day were spending more time playing football than practising archery or javelin throwing. He commanded his sheriffs to suppress "such idle practices". Similar orders were issued by Richard II, Henry IV and James III, without any lasting effect. One such Royal proclamation in 1491 forbade the people to participate in football and golf: it was to be an offence if "in a place of the realm ther be used futeball, golfe, or other sik unprofitable sports."

Despite these spoilsport measures the game flourished in the Tudor and Stuart epoch. It took Cromwell to effectively suppress the activity, after which the game did not come back into vogue until the Restoration. Samuel Pepys, writing a hundred years after the event, describes how, in the great freeze of January 1565, "the streets were full of footballs." There were still no rules, the game basically being an excuse for an uninhibited ruck. Sir Thomas Elyot, in a well-known book entitled *The Governour*, published in 1564, waxes wroth against football, which he dismisses as "beastlike furie and extreme violence deserving only to be put in per-

A SPLASH FROM THE PAST *The men of Ashbourne continue their tradition of the annual Shrove Tuesday game. The game dates back to the 16th century, but this encounter took place in 1952 with the rules almost entirely unchanged*

petual silence". But the lusty men of England were not to be denied their vigorous activity. During the reign of Elizabeth I football was played widely, and, in the absence of rules and referees, there were frequent and sometimes fatal accidents.

In the seventeenth century, football appears to have had various titles. In Cornwall it was termed "hurling", a name subsequently applied to hockey; while in Norfolk and parts of Suffolk it was known as "campynge" or "camping".

Carew, in his *Survey of Cornwall*, suggests that the Cornish were the first to adopt regular rules. He records that no one was permitted to "but or handfast under the girdle", which presumably meant that tripping, charging, or grabbing below the waist was prohibited. He goes on to state that it was also not allowed "to deal a foreball", which suggests that it was forbidden to pass forward, another similarity with Rugby football.

Such rules were obviously not in general use. Strutt, in his *Sports and Pastimes*, describes football thus: "When a match at Football is made, two parties, each containing an equal number of competitors, take the

ROYAL DISPLEASURE *Football in the streets of London at the time of Edward II*

field and stand between two goals, placed at the distance of eighty or one hundred yards the one from the other. The goal is usually made with two sticks driven into the ground about two or three feet apart. The ball, which is commonly made of blown bladder and cased with leather, is delivered in the midst of the ground, and the object of each party is to drive it through the goal of their antagonists, which being achieved, the game is won.

"The abilities of the performers are best displayed in attacking and defending the goals, and hence the pastime was more frequently called a goal at Football than a game at Football. When the exercise becomes exceeding violent, the players kick each other's shins without the least ceremony, and some of them are over-thrown at the hazard of their limbs."

It seems that "hacking" was as keenly relished in those days as it was when the game's modern renaissance began in the mid-19th century. By the end of the 20th century, of course, the very idea of "hacking" for its own sake would be considered with horror.

CODIFICATION OF ASSOCIATION FOOTBALL

Football's sometime image as the "working man's game" overlooks one salient piece of history: it was the public schools, and Oxford and Cambridge Universities in particular, which brought shape and order out of the almost aimless fury of multitudinous violence.

Nearly all the schools and numerous clubs which had mushroomed in the wake of the Industrial Revolution had their own sets of rules. Some catered for the ball to be handled, some did not; some limited the number of participants on each side, some did not. Some favoured hacking and tripping and grounding opponents by hand, while others barred these things.

The overall situation was chaotic to say the least so, in 1846 the first serious attempts to unify a code of rules was instigated at Cambridge University by Messrs H. de Winton and J.C. Thring. They met representatives from the major public schools with a view to formulating a standardized set of rules.

Their deliberations took seven hours 55 minutes and were published as the Cambridge Rules. These were well accepted and years afterwards, with very few alterations made, became the Association Rules. Unfortunately there is no copy of the original regulations, and the earliest set of rules to which those of the Football Association may be traced are those issued by Mr Thring in 1862 when he was the Assistant

Rules — THE SIMPLEST GAME

1. A goal is scored whenever the ball is forced through the goal and under the bar, except it be thrown by hand.
2. Hands may be used only to stop a ball and place it on the ground before the feet.
3. Kicks must be aimed only at the ball.
4. A player may not kick the ball whilst in the air.
5. No tripping up or heel kicking allowed.
6. Whenever a ball is kicked beyond the side flags, it must be returned by the player who kicked it, from the spot it passed the flag line, in a straight line towards the middle of the ground.
7. When a ball is kicked behind the line of goal, it shall be kicked off from that line by one of the side whose goal it is.
8. No player may stand within six paces of the kicker when he is kicking off.
9. A player is "out of play" immediately he is in front of the ball, and must return behind the ball as soon as possible. If the ball is kicked by his own side past a player, he may not touch or kick it, or advance, until one of the other side has first kicked it, or one of his own side has been able to kick it on a level with, or in front of him.
10. No charging allowed when a player is out of play; that is, immediately the ball is behind him.

C.W. ALCOCK *One of football's first and best administrators*

Master at Uppingham. These were the rules for what he termed "The Simplest Game," and as they are so important to the development of Association football as we know it today they are worthy of reproduction (above).

The Football Association came into being in October 1863 following a meeting at the Freemasons' Tavern, Great Queen Street, London, "for the purpose of forming an Association with the object of establishing a definite code of rules for the regulation of the game".

Representatives of all the major clubs were present and they appointed Mr A. Pember as president and Mr E.C. Morley as honorary secretary. Mr Morley was asked to write to the captains of the leading schools inviting them to co-operate in the movement but at a second meeting, held a few days later, it was revealed that replies from Harrow, Charterhouse and Westminster indicated they preferred to cling to their own rules.

At a third meeting a letter of acceptance was read from Mr Thring of Uppingham School and considerable progress was made with the laws, which were published on December 1, 1863. At the sixth meeting held that month the first committee of the Association was appointed.

It consisted of: Mr J.F. Alcock (Forest Club) — an elder brother of C.W. Alcock who came upon the scene later — Mr Warren (War Office); Mr Turner (Crystal Palace); Mr Steward (Crusaders) and the treasurer Mr Campbell (Blackheath); together with Pember and Morley.

It was at this meeting, however, that the "split" between the Rugby Unionists (as they were now termed) and the Associationists occurred. Blackheath withdrew their membership, though Campbell agreed to stay in office as treasurer.

Although there were no further major upsets it seems there was still some uneasiness about the way the game should be played.

At the Association's annual meeting in February, 1866, a representative of the No Names (from Kilburn, north London) complained that only Barnes and Crystal Palace were playing strictly to Association rules. All present, apart from the Lincoln club who withdrew, agreed that no member clubs should ever play under any other rules.

The Association and the game grew steadily in public favour following the introduction of the FA Cup and international fixtures but the comparatively peaceful progress enjoyed until 1880 was followed by a decade of drastic reforms.

The number of the rules of the Association had by now increased from 10 to 15. Scotland still refused to adopt the English throw-in, or the English understanding of the offside rule; apart from that the two Associations were on friendly terms with each other.

But there loomed another crisis which was to become as significant as that which separated the Associationists from the Rugby followers. It was the advent of the paid player — the first professionals.

By now the membership of the FA, including clubs and affiliated associations, amounted to 128, of which 80 belonged to the South of England, 41 to the North, six to Scotland and one to Australia.

Amid persistent rumours that many of the northern contingent were paying men to play for them the following new rule (No 16) was added in 1882: "That any member of a club receiving remuneration or consideration of any sort above his actual expenses and any wages actually lost by any such player taking part in any match, shall be debarred from taking part in either cup, inter Association, or International contests,

OPIUM OF THE PEOPLE *Hampton scores for Aston Villa in the 1905 FA Cup Final against Newcastle at Crystal Palace*

and any club employing such player shall be excluded from this Association."

The liberty to pay "wages lost" was extensively abused and this falling away from amateurism was seen by those in the south as a reflection of an unsportsmanlike spirit spreading through Northern and Midlands clubs.

Football had flourished with far greater rapidity in Scotland than in the rest of the UK and English clubs looked north of the border to strengthen their teams.

The FA at first turned a blind eye, but its hand was forced by the Sheffield, Lancashire, and Birmingham Associations, each of which held inquiries into charges of professionalism. In January 1883 an FA commission was appointed to look into the allegations. It consisted of: C.W. Alcock, N.L. Jackson, J.H. Cofield, T. Hindle and J.R. Harvey. They proved nothing. Yet the disquiet amongst the best amateur clubs continued and there was a veiled threat by some to boycott the

FA Cup at the commencement of the 1883–84 season.

The row came to a head early in 1884 when the Upton Park Club lodged a complaint against Preston North End on the grounds of professionalism. The case attracted wide publicity and when William Sudell, the president of the Preston club and in effect the manager, admitted that they did pay their players and that he could prove that nearly every other important club in Lancashire and the Midlands did likewise, the cat was out of the bag.

Preston were disqualified from that season's FA Cup but the frankness of Sudell's confession brought home to the FA councillors the need to face reality. At their next committee meeting C.W. Alcock proposed "that the time has come for the legalization of professionalism". This was seconded by Dr Morley but was by no means a unanimous decision and a concerted battle to repress the move raged until July 1885 when the football professional was at last legalized.

The amateur/professional dispute rumbled on for years and affected other countries as well. In Argentina in the late 1920s amateur and professional leagues existed briefly in competition and it was the growth of professionalism which helped lead to the foundation of the World Cup, while the amateur-based Olympic Games lost credibility as a representation of the true strengths of each nation.

Simultaneously, British opposition to broken-time payments — the practice of making up players' wages for pay lost while playing football — provoked the departure of the four Home Countries from FIFA. This cost them the right to participate in the first three World Cups, prior to the outbreak of World War II. And, as the Hungarians proved in 1953, it also hindered seriously the technical development of the British game.

Yet, only 13 years later, England were celebrating victory in the World Cup. The modern football had, apparently, rolled full circle.

FOOTBALL DIASPORA

The British were the original missionaries of modern, organised football. As communications and travel developed, so sailors, soldiers, merchants, engineers, teachers, students and other professional classes took their sports — cricket and football — around the world.

Local people joined in and football, consequently, gained universal popularity. Towards the end of the nineteenth century the game invaded Austria. There was a sizeable British colony in Vienna and their influence is manifest in the names of the two oldest clubs, the 1st Vienna FC and the Vienna Cricket and Football Club, from which FK Austria descended.

One of Vienna Cricket's keenest members was a little inside-forward named Hugo Meisl, who was to become an influential secretary of the Austrian Football Association. He recalled that the first ever game staged in Austria proper was between the Cricketers and Vienna on November 15, 1894. Cricketers won 4–0. In 1897 M.D. Nicholson was posted to the Vienna office of Thomas Cook and Sons and he became the most prominent English player in Austria's soccer history and the first president of the Austrian Football Union.

It was Meisl, though, who did most to spread the game on the continent. It was he who provided the driving force behind the launch of the Mitropa Cup — forerunner of today's European club events — and the Nations Cup competitions which popularized the game in central Europe.

Football has flourished in Hungary for longer than in almost any other European country. A young student returning from England imported the first football in the 1890s and two Englishmen, Arthur Yolland and Ashton, were included in the first Hungarian team. Before the First World War English teams had visited and impressed.

In Italy too the English played a great part in developing the game, as the names of some of the clubs reflect: Genoa Football and Cricket Club (founded by Englishmen in 1892) and Milan (not Milano). The game was introduced to Italy by a Turin businessman, Edoardo Bosio, in 1887, but Genoa were the first great club.

English boys at boarding school are claimed to have brought a rough type of football to Germany as early as 1865, though German football owes much to the enthusiasm of the two Schricker brothers. They actually borrowed money from their mother to help finance the first foreign tour ever made by a Football Association team, in 1899, which was a mixture of amateur and professional players. Steve Bloomer, the England and Derby County inside-right, went to Germany to coach and was interned during the First World War as was the highly influential coach, Jimmy Hogan.

Hogan was also to play a big part in the development of Dutch football. By 1908 Holland had 96 clubs and a competent national side under the direction of former England international Edgar Chadwick.

Football was introduced to Russia in 1887 by two Englishmen, the Charnock brothers, who ran a mill at Orekhovo near Moscow. They acquired equipment from England but had insufficient money for boots. Clement Charnock overcame the problem by getting a strap piercer at the mill to attach studs to the players' ordinary footwear. The Russians took to the game eagerly and by the late 1890s a Moscow League was in operation — the Charnocks' team, now called Morozovisti, winning the championship for the first five years.

The first continental country to master football was perhaps Denmark. Coached by English professionals the Danes were the outstanding continental side in Europe in the early part of the twentieth century and reached the Final of the Olympic Games in 1908, where they lost, unluckily, 2–0 to Great Britain.

It had all started when an English boy studying at Soro Akademi, a famous Danish public school, received a football from home. There were other links too. The English "Football Club" was formed in Copenhagen in 1879 and two Englishmen, Smart and Gibson, were instrumental in popularizing the game.

Football was exported to all four corners of the world. In Brazil, British sailors were the first to play on their shores in 1874, and in 1878 men from the ship *Crimea* allegedly put on an exhibition match for Princess Isabel. But Charles Miller, born in São Paulo, the son of English immigrants, who came to England to study and returned ten years later with kit and two new footballs after playing for Southampton, is acknowledged as the true inspiration of the game in Brazil. Miller encouraged the British workers in establishments such as the Gas Company, the London Bank and the São Paulo Railway and the founders of the São Paulo Athletic Club — which was then exclusively concerned with cricket — to form football teams. The first real match was staged in April 1894 with the Rail team beating the Gas team 4–2.

The first club comprising mainly Brazilians was established in 1898: the Associaciao Athletica Mackenzie College in São Paulo. Thus the game in South America is as old as it is on the European continent. The British influence is seen clearly in the names of some of the club sides: Corinthians in Brazil; Liverpool and Wanderers in Uruguay; and Everton and Rangers in Chile, while Argentina boasts Newell's Old Boys and River Plate.

In Argentina although football was begun in the last century by British residents of Buenos Aires, it was slow to catch on with the locals. The national side of 1911 was full of Englishmen, though one, Arnold Hutton, a star forward, declined to play in one match because he had agreed to play rugby for his club. But it was Italian immigrants who really triggered the game's popularity there, as indeed they did through much of Latin America.

In Africa not only the English but the French and, to a lesser extent, German and Portuguese colonial movements played predominant roles in introducing football. For Portugal, the investment paid off spectacularly: their outstanding team at the 1966 World Cup drew its finest players, Eusebio and Mario Coluna, from the colony of Mozambique.

Independence movements in Africa and Asia changed the balance of international football power. The traditionalist powers of Europe and South America now find themselves in a political minority within FIFA, the world governing body. Asia has 45 members and Africa 52 compared with Europe's 51 and South America's 10. Indeed, Europe has swollen in size in the early 1990s since the fragmentation of the former Soviet Union and Yugoslavia.

GOLD RUSH *Great Britain beat Denmark in the 1908 Olympic Games Final*

THE MAJOR COMPETITIONS

The international football programme has grown in piecemeal fashion since the first match between Scotland and England in November 1872. Some competitions, like the Mitropa Cup, faded and disappeared. But the strongest, like the World Cup for nations and the Copa Libertadores and the European club cups, flourished as a world-wide competitive structure developed.

First there was the British Home Championship, the South American Championship and the Mitropa Cup for continental Europe's top clubs, then the World Cup itself ... by the start of the 1930s the foundations of today's international competitive structure had been laid. The 1950s brought a further expansion, with the success of the European club cups and the launch of the European Championship. Each developing geographical region copied the competitive structures of Europe.

Now the sheer weight of the international fixture list has led football's world governing body, FIFA, into designing a worldwide fixture schedule around which the game can organize into the next century.

To qualify for the World Cup, many nations play around a dozen matches. When the various club competitions are added, top players can face around 70 games year with very little let-up.

THE WORLD CUP

The World Cup was conceived by FIFA's founders, but the driving force behind its launch was Frenchman Jules Rimet, the president of both FIFA and the French federation in the 1920s. The British had shunned FIFA's first meeting in Paris in 1904, and by the time the inaugural World Cup tournament was introduced in 1930 they had both joined and then withdrawn from the world governing body over the question of broken time payments for amateurs.

Italy, Holland, Spain, Sweden and Uruguay all applied to stage the tournament, but the European countries withdrew after an impassioned plea from the Latin Americans, who in 1930 would be celebrating a hundred years of independence. Uruguay were to build a new stadium in Montevideo and would pay all travelling and hotel expenses for the competing nations. However, faced by a three-week boat trip each way, the Europeans were reluctant to participate, and two months before the competition not one European entry had been received. Meanwhile, Argentina, Brazil, Paraguay, Peru, Chile, Mexico and Bolivia had all accepted, as well as the United States.

The Latin American federations were bitter and threatened to withdraw from FIFA. Eventually France, Belgium, Yugoslavia and, under the influence of King Carol, Romania, all relented and travelled to Uruguay.

URUGUAY 1930
Triumph for ambitious party-throwers

Because of the limited response the 13 teams were split into four groups, with Uruguay, Argentina, Brazil and the USA the seeded nations.

On the afternoon of Sunday, July 13, France opened the tournament against Mexico, and in the 10th minute lost goalkeeper Alex Thepot, who was kicked on the jaw. Left-half Chantrel took over between the posts (there would be no substitutes

HOW SWEET IT IS *Romario hugs the World Cup after Brazil's fourth triumph in 1994*

for another forty years), but even with 10 men the French proved too good. Goals by Laurent, Langiller and Maschinot gave them a 3–0 advantage before Carreno replied for Mexico. Maschinot then grabbed a second to complete a 4–1 victory for France.

Two days later France lost to Argentina through a goal scored by Monti, nine minutes from time. The game had ended in chaos when Brazilian referee Almeida Rego blew for time six minutes early as Langiller raced through for a possible equalizer. In their next match, against Mexico, Argentina brought in young Guillermo Stabile, known as "El Infiltrador". He scored three goals in Argentina's 6–3 victory – in a game of five penalties – and finished as the top scorer of the tournament.

Argentina topped Group 1, while from Group 2 Yugoslavia qualified with victories over Brazil and Bolivia. The USA were most impressive in Group 4, reaching the semi-final without conceding a goal. However, their hit-on-the-break tactics were no match for Argentina, who cruised into the Final 6–1. In the other semi-final Uruguay dispatched Yugoslavia by the same margin to set up a repeat of the 1928 Olympic Final.

On this occasion Pablo Dorado shot Uruguay into a 12th-minute lead but Peucelle equalized and Argentina forged ahead in the 35th

minute with a disputed goal by Stabile – who the Urugayans claimed was offside! Excitement grew when Pedro Cea made it 2–2 just after the break. In the 65th minute outside-left Santos Iriarte made it 3–2 for Uruguay, who underlined their victory with a fourth goal, smashed into the net by Castro in the closing seconds.

ITALY 1934
Tetchy Europeans battle it out

RESPITE *Italy prepare for extra time*

Uruguay are the only World Cup winners in history who did not defend their title. Upset by the Europeans' reluctance to participate in 1930, and plagued by players' strikes, they stayed at home.

No fewer than 32 countries – 22 from Europe, eight from the Americas and one each from Asia and Africa – contested a qualifying series in which even hosts Italy had to take

part, and before the competition proper got under way the USA beat Mexico in Rome, but then crashed 7–1 to Italy in Turin.

Of the 16 finalists, Italy and Hugo Meisl's "Wunderteam" were the clear favourites, though the Austrians, who were just past their peak, were taken to extra time by a spirited French side in the first knockout round. Belgium led Germany 2–1 at half-time, then crumbled as Conen, Germany's centre-forward, completed a hat-trick in a 5–2 win.

Brazil, beaten 3–1 by Spain, and Argentina, defeated 3–2 by Sweden, had travelled 8,000 miles to play one solitary game.

Spain forced Italy to a replay in the second round after a physical 1–1 draw was not resolved by extra time. In the replay, the following day, Meazza's 12th-minute header put Italy into the semi-finals. Austria, who led Hungary 2–0 after 51 minutes through Horwarth and Zischek, then found themselves in what Meisl described as "a brawl, not an exhibition of football". Sarosi replied for Hungary from the penalty spot, but the Magyars' comeback was spoiled when Markos foolishly got himself sent off.

Italy and Austria now faced each other in the semi-finals. A muddy pitch was not conducive to good football and Italy won when right-winger

Guaita capitalized on a brilliant set-play routine, following a corner, to score in the 18th minute. Czechoslovakia, the conquerers of Romania and Switzerland joined Italy in the Final after a 3–1 victory over Germany, with two goals by Nejedly.

In the Final, Puc shot the Czechs into a deserved 70th-minute lead, Italian keeper Combi reacting late to the shot from 20 yards. Sobotka then squandered a fine opportunity and Svoboda rattled a post as the Czechs impressed with their short-passing precision. With eight minutes left the Slavs were still 1–0 ahead. Then left-winger Raimondo Orsi left Czech defenders in his wake as he dribbled through on goal. He shaped to shoot with his left but hit the ball with his right boot. The ball spun crazily goalwards, and though Planicka got his fingers to it, he could not prevent a goal. Schiavio grabbed the Italian winner seven minutes into extra time. Italy were World Champions.

FRANCE 1938
Italians make it two in a row

Europe was in turmoil, Argentina and Uruguay were absent but the tournament welcomed for the first time Cuba, Poland and Dutch East Indies.

1930	Pool 1					Pool 2						P	W	D	L	F	A	Pts	Semi-finals				ARGENTINA Botasso, Della Torre,
	France	4	Mexico	1		Yugoslavia	2	Brazil	1		Uruguay	2	2	0	0	5	0	4	Argentina	6	USA	1	Paternoster, Evaristo J., Monti,
	Argentina	1	France	0		Yugoslavia	4	Bolivia	0		Romania	2	1	0	1	3	5	2	Uruguay	6	Yugoslavia	1	Suarez, Peucelle, Varallo, Stabile,
	Chile	3	Mexico	0		Brazil	4	Bolivia	0		Peru	2	0	0	2	1	4	0					Ferreira (capt.), Evaristo M.
	Chile	1	France	0															Final				
	Argentina	6	Mexico	3			P	W	D	L	F	A	Pts	Pool 4					Uruguay (1) 4	Argentina(2) 2	**Leading scorers:**
	Argentina	3	Chile	1		Yugoslavia	2	2	0	0	6	1	4	USA	3	Belgium	0		*Dorado, Cea,*	*Peucelle,*	8 Stabile (Argentina); 5 Cea
						Brazil	2	1	0	1	5	2	2	USA	3	Paraguay	0		*Iriarte, Castro*	*Stabile*	(Uruguay).
		P	W	D	L	F	A	Pts	Bolivia	2	0	0	2	0	8	0	Paraguay	1	Belgium	0			
	Argentina	3	3	0	0	10	4	6	Pool 3										P	W	D	L	F	A	Pts	URUGUAY Ballesteros, Nasazzi
	Chile	3	2	0	1	5	3	4	Romania	3	Peru	1		USA	2	2	0	0	6	0	4	(capt.), Mascheroni, Andrade,
	France	3	1	0	2	4	3	2	Uruguay	1	Peru	0		Paraguay	2	1	0	1	1	3	2	Fernandez, Gestido, Dorado,
	Mexico	3	0	0	3	4	13	0	Uruguay	4	Romania	0		Belgium	2	0	0	2	0	4	0	Scarone, Castro, Cea, Iriarte.

1934	First round				Second round				Semi-finals				Final				CZECHOSLOVAKIA Planicka (capt.),
	Italy	7	USA	1	Germany	2	Sweden	1	Czech.	3	Germany	1	Italy	(0) 2	Czech.	(0) 1*	Zenisek, Ctyroky, Kostalek,
	Czech.	2	Romania	1	Austria	2	Hungary	1	Italy	1	Austria	0	*Orsi, Schiavio*	*Puc*			Cambal, Kreil, Junek, Svoboda,
	Germany	5	Belgium	2	Italy	1	Spain	1*									Sobotka, Nejedly, Puc.
	Austria	3	France	2*	Italy	1	Spain	0®	**Third place match**				ITALY Combi (capt.), Monzeglio,				
	Spain	3	Brazil	1	Czech.	3	Switzerland	2	Germany	3	Austria	2	Allemandi, Ferraris IV, Monti,				**Leading scorers:**
	Switzerland	3	Holland	2									Bertolini, Guaita, Meazza, Schiavio,				4 Nejedly (Czechoslovakia),
	Sweden	3	Argentina	2									Ferrari, Orsi.				Schiavio (Italy), Conen (Germany).
	Hungary	4	Egypt	2													

BACK TO BACK *Vittorio Pozzo brandishes the World Cup in Paris*

In the first round only Hungary, who eclipsed the Dutch East Indies 6–0, and France – 3–1 winners over Belgium – came through in 90 minutes, all the other ties going to extra time or replays. Defending champions Italy were saved by their goalkeeper Olivieri, who made a blinding save from Norwegian centre-forward Brunyldsen in the last minute of the game to earn extra time, and Piola struck to see them through.

Brazil emerged from the mud of Strasbourg after an 11-goal thriller. A Leonidas hat-trick gave the South Americans a 3–1 half-time lead, but the Poles ran riot after the break to force extra time. Willimowski netted four times but by then Leonidas had

grabbed his fourth to help Brazil to a 6–5 win! The second round provided no shocks, though Brazil needed two games to eliminate Czechoslovakia and earn a semi-final joust with Italy, whose captain, Meazza, converted the winning penalty. In the other semi-final, Hungary beat Sweden, 5–1.

When Italy met Hungary in the final, Colaussi drilled Italy ahead in the sixth minute after a scintillating run almost the length of the field from Biavati, but Titkos equalized from close range within a minute. Then, with inside-forwards Meazza and Ferrari in dazzling form, Italy asserted themselves. Piola scored in the 15th minute, and Colaussi made

it 3–1 in the 35th. In the 65th minute Sarosi forced the ball over the Italian line, but a magnificent back-heeled pass from Biavati set up Piola to smash in the decisive goal.

BRAZIL 1950
Hosts upstaged in final act

The first tournament after the war – for what was now known as the Jules Rimet Trophy – was to prove a thriller. Argentina refused to play in Brazil, and the Czechs and Scots declined to take their places, but England were there for the first time.

The competition was arranged, as in 1930, on a pool basis. Brazil won Pool 1 despite a 2–2 draw with Switzerland, and Uruguay topped two-team Pool 4, where they thrashed Bolivia 8–0. The shocks came in Pools 2 and 3. Italy started well enough, Riccardo Carapellese shooting them into a seventh-minute lead against Sweden. But by the break they were 2–1 down to goals from Jeppson and Sune Andersson. Jeppson grabbed another midway through the second half and, though Muccinelli replied and Carapellese hit the bar, this was Sweden's day. It was a setback the Italians were unable to overcome.

The greatest shock of all time,

however, was to beset England. After a 2–0 victory over Chile, the game against the USA in Belo Horizonte seemed a formality. Instead it became a fiasco. England hit the bar and found goalkeeper Borghi unbeatable. Then in the 37th minute the impossible happened. Bahr shot from the left and Gaetjens got a touch with his head to divert the ball into the net. 1–0 to the USA!

There was no final in this competition, Brazil, Uruguay, Sweden and Spain qualifying for the Final Pool. The hosts were favourites as they faced Uruguay in the last game (a virtual final), a point ahead. A draw would make Brazil champions.

It proved a real thriller. Brazil's much-acclaimed inside-forward trio of Zizinho, Ademir and Jair, weaving gloriously through the Uruguayan defence, found goalkeeper Maspoli playing the game of his life. The giant Varela proved another stumbling block, as did Andrade. They cracked in the 47th minute, Friaca shooting past Maspoli. Uruguay's response was positive, and in the 65th minute Ghiggia's cross found Schiaffino unmarked – his thunderous shot gave Barbosa no hope. Brazil were shaken, the fizz went out of their game, and when Ghiggia ran in to shoot home in the 79th minute they were beaten. After 20 years the World Cup returned to Uruguay.

1938

First round

Switzerland	1 Germany	1*
Switzerland	4 Germany	2®
Cuba	3 Rumania	3*
Cuba	2 Rumania	1®
Hungary	6 Dutch E.Ind.	0
France	3 Belgium	1
Czech.	3 Holland	0*
Brazil	6 Poland	5*
Italy	2 Norway	1*

Second round

Sweden	8 Cuba	0
Hungary	2 Switzerland	0
Italy	3 France	1
Brazil	1 Czech.	1*
Brazil	2 Czech.	1®

Semi-finals

Italy	2 Brazil	1
Hungary	5 Sweden	1

Third place match

Brazil	4 Sweden	2

Final

Italy	(3) 4 Hungary (1) 2
Colaussi (2),	Titkos, Sarosi
Piola (2)	

ITALY Olivieri, Foni, Rava, Serantoni, Andreolo, Locatelli, Biavati, Meazza (capt.), Piola, Ferrari, Colaussi.

HUNGARY Szabo, Polgar, Biro, Szalay, Szucs, Lazar, Sas, Vincze, Sarosi (capt.), Szengeller, Titkos.

Leading scorers

8 Leonidas (Brazil); 7 Szengeller (Hungary); 5 Piola (Italy).

1950

First round Pool 1

Brazil	4 Mexico	0
Yugoslavia	3 Switzerland	0
Yugoslavia	4 Mexico	1
Brazil	2 Switzerland	2
Brazil	2 Yugoslavia	0
Switzerland	2 Mexico	1

	P	W	D	L	F	A	Pts
Brazil	3	2	1	0	8	2	5
Yugoslavia	3	2	0	1	7	3	4
Switzerland	3	1	1	1	4	6	3
Mexico	3	0	0	3	2	10	0

Pool 2

Spain	3 USA	1
England	2 Chile	0
USA	1 England	0
Spain	2 Chile	0
Spain	1 England	0
Chile	5 USA	2

	P	W	D	L	F	A	Pts
Spain	3	3	0	0	6	1	6
England	3	1	0	2	2	2	2
Chile	3	1	0	2	5	6	2
USA	3	1	0	2	4	8	2

Pool 3

Sweden	3 Italy	2
Sweden	2 Paraguay	2
Italy	2 Paraguay	0

	P	W	D	L	F	A	Pts
Sweden	2	1	1	0	5	4	3
Italy	2	1	0	1	4	3	2
Paraguay	2	0	1	1	2	4	1

Pool 4

Uruguay	8 Bolivia	0

	P	W	D	L	F	A	Pts
Uruguay	1	1	0	0	8	0	2
Bolivia	1	0	0	1	0	8	0

Final pool

Uruguay	2 Spain	2
Brazil	7 Sweden	1
Uruguay	3 Sweden	2
Brazil	6 Spain	1
Sweden	3 Spain	1
Uruguay	2 Brazil	1

	P	W	D	L	F	A	Pts
Uruguay	3	2	1	0	7	5	5
Brazil	3	2	0	1	14	4	4
Sweden	3	1	0	2	6	11	2
Spain	3	0	1	2	4	11	1

Deciding match

Uruguay	(0) 2 Brazil (0) 1
Schiaffino,	Friaca
Ghiggia	

URUGUAY Maspoli, Gonzales, M., Tejera, Gambetta, Varela, Andrade, Ghiggia, Perez, Miguez, Schiaffino, Moran.

BRAZIL Barbosa, Augusto, Juvenal, Bauer, Danilo, Bigode, Friaca, Ziziho, Ademir, Jair, Chico.

Leading scorers:

9 Ademir (Brazil); 6 Schiaffino (Uruguay); 5 Zarra (Spain).

*Notes: * After extra time ® Replay*

SWITZERLAND 1954
'Magic Magyars' found out by astute Germans

Hungary arrived in Zurich as the hottest ever World Cup favourites. The magic of Puskas, Hidegkuti and Kocsis had added a new dimension to the beautiful game and, what is more, had proved an unbeatable combination in the 1952 Olympic tournament.

No one was really surprised when the Magyars rattled in 17 goals in their opening pool matches against Korea and Germany. Kocsis scored four against the Germans but Hungary were left a significant legacy by their opponents, centre-half Werner Liebrich delivering a fateful kick on Puskas that caused him to retire from the match in the 30th minute. It was an injury from which he never fully recovered during the remainder

NOT SO FAST *Morlock gets one back*

of the tournament. Hungary of course cruised into the quarter-finals, where they dispatched Brazil 4–2, but Germany had to win a play-off with Turkey to earn the right to face Yugoslavia.

England began with a 4–4 draw with Belgium, yet secured a quarter-final place with a 2–0 win over Switzerland. The Scots were not so successful. They failed to score and were beaten by Austria and Uruguay, neither of whom conceded a goal in their pool. Stanley Matthews and Schiaffino took the individual honours as Uruguay beat England 4–2, but the competition was sullied by a notorious clash between Brazil and Hungary, which was dubbed "The Battle of Berne". Three players were sent off, and a shameful fight ensued in the dressing-rooms afterwards. If that was infamous, then the Austria-Switzerland tie was incredible. The Swiss scored three in 20 minutes, and Austria replied with three in three minutes. In one seven-minute period, there were five goals! Eventually Austria came out 7–5 winners.

Puskas returned for the Final, but it was a mistake. Although he scored the opening goal in a devastating start which saw Hungary score twice in eight minutes, his ankle was not fully recovered. Morlock replied for Germany in the 11th minute and Rahn blasted in two fine goals – the last only seven minutes from time – to win it for Germany.

SWEDEN 1958
Brazil teach the world a football lesson

Brazil enthralled the world in this competition, which was notable for the emergence of 4–2–4 and the outstanding individual talents of stars such as Didi, Garrincha, Vava and the teenager Pele. France too were to perform with style, Just Fontaine and Raymond Kopa providing the magic, while hosts Sweden provided their share of surprises.

West Germany headed Pool 1, where Northern Ireland, who had eliminated Italy in the qualifying rounds, caused an upset by beating Czechoslovakia in a play-off to earn a quarter-final tie with France, who headed Pool 2 with Yugoslavia. Likewise Wales also made the quarter-finals, following a play-off with Hungary, and did themselves proud

1954

Pool 1
Yugoslavia	1	France	0
Brazil	5	Mexico	0
France	3	Mexico	2
Brazil	1	Yugoslavia	1

	P	W	D	L	F	A	Pts
Brazil	2	1	1	0	6	1	3
Yugoslavia	2	1	1	0	2	1	3
France	2	1	0	1	3	3	2
Mexico	2	0	0	2	2	8	0

Pool 2
Hungary	9	Korea	0
W. Germany	4	Turkey	1
Hungary	8	W. Germany	3
Turkey	7	Korea	0

	P	W	D	L	F	A	Pts
Hungary	2	2	0	0	17	3	4
W. Germany	2	1	0	1	7	9	2
Turkey	2	1	0	1	8	4	2
Korea	2	0	0	2	0	16	0

Play-off
W. Germany 7 Turkey 2

Pool 3
Austria	1	Scotland	0
Uruguay	2	Czech.	0
Austria	5	Czech.	0
Uruguay	7	Scotland	0

	P	W	D	L	F	A	Pts
Uruguay	2	2	0	0	9	0	4
Austria	2	2	0	0	6	0	4
Czech.	2	0	0	2	0	7	0
Scotland	2	0	0	2	0	8	0

Pool 4
England	4	Belgium	4
England	2	Switzerland	0
Switzerland	2	Italy	1
Italy	4	Belgium	1

	P	W	D	L	F	A	Pts
England	2	1	1	0	6	4	3
Italy	2	1	0	1	5	3	2
Switzerland	2	1	0	1	2	3	2
Belgium	2	0	1	1	5	8	1

Play-off
Switzerland 4 Italy 1

Quarter-finals
W. Germany	2	Yugoslavia	0
Hungary	4	Brazil	2
Austria	7	Switzerland	5
Uruguay	4	England	2

Semi-finals
W. Germany	6	Austria	1
Hungary	4	Uruguay	2

Third-place match
Austria 3 Uruguay 1

Final
W. Germany (2) 3 Hungary (2) 2
Morlock,   *Puskas, Czibor*
Rahn (2)

WEST GERMANY: Turek, Posipal, Kohlmeyer, Eckel, Liebrich, Mai, Rahn, Morlock, Walter O., Walter F. (capt.), Schäfer.
HUNGARY: Grosics, Buzansky, Lantos, Bozsik, Lorant, Zakarias, Czibor, Kocsis, Hidegkuti, Puskas (capt.), Toth J.

Leading scorers
11 Kocsis (Hungary); 8 Morlock (W. Germany); 6 Probst (Austria), Hügi (Switzerland).

1958

Pool 1
W. Germany	3	Argentina	1
N. Ireland	1	Czech.	0
W. Germany	2	Czech.	2
Argentina	3	N. Ireland	1
W. Germany	2	N. Ireland	2
Czech.	6	Argentina	1

	P	W	D	L	F	A	Pts
W. Germany	3	1	2	0	7	5	4
Czech.	3	1	1	1	8	4	3
N. Ireland	3	1	1	1	4	5	3
Argentina	3	1	0	2	5	10	2

Play-off
N. Ireland 2 Czech. 1

Pool 2
France	7	Paraguay	3
Yugoslavia	1	Scotland	1
Yugoslavia	3	France	2
Paraguay	3	Scotland	2
France	2	Scotland	1
Yugoslavia	3	Paraguay	3

	P	W	D	L	F	A	Pts
France	3	2	0	1	11	7	4
Yugoslavia	3	1	2	0	7	6	4
Paraguay	3	1	1	1	9	12	3
Scotland	3	0	1	2	4	6	1

Pool 3
Sweden	3	Mexico	0
Hungary	1	Wales	1
Wales	1	Mexico	1
Sweden	2	Hungary	1
Sweden	0	Wales	0
Hungary	4	Mexico	0

	P	W	D	L	F	A	Pts
Sweden	3	2	1	0	5	1	5
Hungary	3	1	1	1	6	3	3
Wales	3	0	3	0	2	2	3
Mexico	3	0	1	2	1	8	1

Play-off
Wales 2 Hungary 1

Pool 4
England	2	Soviet Union	2
Brazil	3	Austria	0
England	0	Brazil	0
Soviet Union	2	Austria	0
Brazil	2	Soviet Union	0
England	2	Austria	2

	P	W	D	L	F	A	Pts
Brazil	3	2	1	0	5	0	5
England	3	0	3	0	4	4	3
Soviet Union	3	1	1	1	4	4	3
Austria	3	0	1	2	2	7	1

Play-off
Soviet Union 1 England 0

Quarter-finals
France	4	N. Ireland	0
W. Germany	1	Yugoslavia	0
Sweden	2	Soviet Union	0
Brazil	1	Wales	0

Semi-finals
Brazil	5	France	2
Sweden	3	W. Germany	1

Third place match
France 6 W. Germany 3

Final
Brazil (2) 5 Sweden (1) 2
Vava (2),   *Liedholm*
Pele (2), Zagallo   *Simonsson*

BRAZIL: Gilmar, Santos D., Santos N., Zito, Bellini (capt.), Orlando, Garrincha, Didi, Vava, Pele, Zagallo.

SWEDEN: Svensson, Bergmark, Axbom, Boerjesson, Gustavsson, Parling, Hamrin, Gren, Simonsson, Liedholm (capt.), Skoglund.

Leading scorers
13 Fontaine (France); 6 Pele (Brazil), Rahn (W. Germany); 5 Vava (Brazil), McParland (N. Ireland).

by limiting Brazil to one goal, inevitably scored by Pele. Brazil had comfortably emerged from Pool 4 without conceding a goal, but England were knocked out, when they lost 1–0 to Russia in another play-off.

The semi-finals pitted Sweden against West Germany and Brazil against France. Hans Schäfer blasted West Germany into the lead with a spectacular volley from 25 yards. Sweden's equalizer from Skoglund should not have been given – Liedholm blatantly controlling the ball with a hand before setting up the chance. Juskowiak was sent off in the 57th minute, and Sweden took full advantage to clinch their Final place with goals from Gren and Hamrin. Brazil took a second-minute lead against France thanks to a spectacular finish from Vava. Fontaine equalized within nine minutes, but Didi restored the lead for the South Americans, and in the second half young Pele ran riot with three more goals.

There was a sensational start to the Final, when Liedholm kept his poise and balance to shoot Sweden into a fourth-minute lead. It was the first time in the tournament that Brazil had been behind. Six minutes later it was 1–1. Garrincha exploded down the right, and cut the ball back for Vava to run on to and fire firmly past Svensson. This was proving a fascinating spectacle. Pele slammed a shot against a post, Zagallo headed out from beneath the bar. In the 32nd minute the Garrincha-Vava combination struck again, and when Pele made it 3–1 in the 55th minute with a touch of sheer magic, the game

LAP OF HONOUR *Brazil celebrate their first World Cup triumph in 1958*

was won. Bringing a dropping ball down on a thigh in a crowded penalty area, the youngster hooked it over his head, spun and volleyed thunderously into the net. Zagallo and Pele added further goals, either side of a dubious second Swedish goal from Agne Simonsson, who looked offside. There was no doubt that Brazil were the best in the world.

CHILE 1962
Brazil without Pele still can't be matched

Brazil retained their world crown as Garrincha took centre stage and 4–3–3 became the subtle change. But this was a World Cup marred by violence.

The Soviet Union and Yugoslavia comfortably overcame the Uruguayan and Colombian challenge in Group 1, while in Group 3 Brazil's only hiccup was a goalless draw with Czechoslovakia, who were to prove the surprise package of this tournament.

England got off to a bad start. Unable to break down the massed Hungarian defence after Springett was beaten by a thunderous long-range effort from Tichy, they equalized from a Ron Flowers penalty, but the impressive Albert clinched it for Hungary 18 minutes from time with a glorious individual goal. England did find some form to beat Argentina 3–1. Another Flowers penalty, a Bobby Charlton special and Jimmy Greaves clinched their first World Cup finals victory since 1954.

The Chile-Italy tie turned into a violent confrontation, with spitting, fighting, and two-footed tackles

intended to maim. That referee Ken Aston sent only two players off was amazing in a game that sullied the name of football. Brazil, however, continued to thrill, even without the injured Pele, who was to take no further part after the group match against Mexico. Garrincha mesmerized England to defeat, then took Chile apart in the semi-final, only to be sent off for retaliation.

In Vina del Mar a mere 5,000 watched Czechoslovakia earn their Final place at the expense of Yugoslavia, and the Czechs threatened to upset all the odds when Masopust cleverly gave them the lead over Brazil in the 16th minute. The equalizer, from Amarildo – Pele's replacement – was quickly registered but it was not until the 69th minute that Zito headed them into the lead. Vava made it 3–1 when goalkeeper Schroiff fumbled a lob.

SIMPLY THE BEST *Pele bides his time*

1962

Group 1

Uruguay	2	Colombia 1
Soviet Union	2	Yugoslavia 0
Yugoslavia	3	Uruguay 1
Soviet Union	4	Colombia 4
Soviet Union	2	Uruguay 1
Yugoslavia	5	Colombia 0

	P	W	D	L	F	A	Pts
Soviet Union	3	2	1	0	8	5	5
Yugoslavia	3	2	0	1	8	3	4
Uruguay	3	1	0	2	4	6	2
Colombia	3	0	1	2	5	11	1

Group 2

Chile	3	Switzerland 1
W. Germany	0	Italy 0

Chile	2	Italy 0
W. Germany	2	Switzerland 1
W. Germany	2	Chile 0
Italy	3	Switzerland 0

	P	W	D	L	F	A	Pts
W. Germany	3	2	1	0	4	1	5
Chile	3	2	0	1	5	3	4
Italy	3	1	1	1	3	2	3
Switzerland	3	0	0	3	2	8	0

Group 3

Brazil	2	Mexico 0
Czech.	1	Spain 0
Brazil	0	Czech. 0
Spain	1	Mexico 0
Brazil	2	Spain 1
Mexico	3	Czech. 1

	P	W	D	L	F	A	Pts
Brazil	3	2	1	0	4	1	5
Czech.	3	1	1	1	2	3	3
Mexico	3	1	0	2	2	3	2
Spain	3	1	0	2	2	3	2

Group 4

Argentina	1	Bulgaria 0
Hungary	2	England 1
England	3	Argentina 1
Hungary	6	Bulgaria 1
Argentina	0	Hungary 0
England	0	Bulgaria 0

	P	W	D	L	F	A	Pts
Hungary	3	2	1	0	8	2	5
England	3	1	1	1	4	3	3
Argentina	3	1	1	1	2	3	3
Bulgaria	3	0	1	2	1	7	1

Quarter-finals

Yugoslavia	1	W. Germany 0
Brazil	3	England 1
Chile	2	Soviet Union 1
Czech.	1	Hungary 0

Semi-finals

Brazil	4	Chile 2
Czech.	3	Yugoslavia 1

Third place match

Chile	1	Yugoslavia 0

Final

Brazil	(1) 3	Czech. (1) 1

Amarildo, Zito, Vava   Masopust

BRAZIL: Gilmar, Santos D., Mauro (capt.), Zozimo, Santos N., Zito, Didi, Garrincha, Vava, Amarildo, Zagallo.

CZECHOSLOVAKIA: Schroiff, Tichy, Novak (capt.), Pluskal, Popluhar, Masopust, Pospichal, Scherer, Kvasniak, Kadraba, Jelinek.

Leading scorers

4 Garrincha (Brazil), Vava (Brazil), Sanchez L. (Chile), Jerkovic (Yugoslavia), Albert (Hungary), Ivanov V. (USSR); 3 Amarildo (Brazil), Scherer (Czechoslovakia), Galic (Yugoslavia), Tichy (Hungary).

ENGLAND 1966
Victory for Ramsey's wingless wonders

For the first time in 32 years the host nation was to win the title. This was a series that had everything – passion, controversy, some fine football, and one of the greatest upsets of all time when North Korea knocked Italy out at Ayresome Park!

The tournament got off to a slow start, with England held 0–0 by Uruguay, but in Group 2 West Germany quickly displayed their potential with a 5–0 win over Switzerland. Brazil, alas, disappointed. Having beaten Bulgaria 2–0, they lost a classic encounter with Hungary, for whom Albert was the dominating factor, then succumbed to Portugal, whose striker Eusebio was to be one of the stars of the competition. The Soviet Union, efficient and technically sound, cruised through to the quarter-finals without alarm. For Italy, however, there was a rude awakening. Having lost 1–0 to the Soviets, they had to beat North Korea to stay in the competition, but what seemed a formality turned into a nightmare. In the 42nd minute Pak Doo Ik dispossessed Rivera, advanced and crashed a searing shot past Albertosi. It was the only goal. Italy were eliminated.

At Goodison Park there was a sensational opening to Korea's quarter-final with Portugal. There was a goal in the opening minute, followed by a second and a third – and all for Korea. It was then that Eusebio

IT'S ALL OVER NOW *Bobby Moore celebrates with England their extra-time victory over West Germany at Wembley*

proved his genius and, thanks to him and the towering Torres, the Portuguese clawed back the deficit to win a sensational game 5–3.

The England–Portugal semi-final produced an emotional classic, Bobby Charlton upstaging the mercurial Eusebio with what many felt was his greatest game for England. This, unlike the bad-tempered quarter-final shambles with Argentina, when Rattin was sent off and Geoff Hurst arrived as a new shooting star, was a

wonderful advertisement for the game.

West Germany had edged out the Soviet Union, in a disappointing tie, to secure their place in the Final, and there they struck the first blow through Haller. Hurst equalized and his West Ham colleague Martin Peters gave England the lead. But a scrambled goal from Weber just before time forced the game into extra time. In the 100th minute controversy raged. Alan Ball crossed, and Hurst coming in on the near post, ham-

mered his shot goalwards. It thumped against the underside of the bar and dropped – but which side of the line? Swiss referee Dienst was not sure, but the Soviet linesman Bakhramov was. 3–2 England! Any feeling of injustice felt by the Germans was quickly irrelevant. Bobby Moore swept a long ball upfield for Hurst to chase, and the big striker slammed his shot into the roof of Tilkowski's net to become the first player ever to score a hat-trick in a World Cup Final.

1966

Group 1

England	0	Uruguay	0
France	1	Mexico	1
Uruguay	2	France	1
England	2	Mexico	0
Uruguay	0	Mexico	0
England	2	France	0

	P	W	D	L	F	A	Pts
England	3	2	1	0	4	0	5
Uruguay	3	1	2	0	2	1	4
Mexico	3	0	2	1	1	3	2
France	3	0	1	2	2	5	1

Group 2

W. Germany	5	Switzerland	0
Argentina	2	Spain	1
Spain	2	Switzerland	1
Argentina	0	W. Germany	0
Argentina	2	Switzerland	0
W. Germany	2	Spain	1

	P	W	D	L	F	A	Pts
W. Germany	3	2	1	0	7	1	5
Argentina	3	2	1	0	4	1	5
Spain	3	1	0	2	4	5	2
Switzerland	3	0	0	3	1	9	0

Group 3

Brazil	2	Bulgaria	0
Portugal	3	Hungary	1
Hungary	3	Brazil	1
Portugal	3	Bulgaria	0
Portugal	3	Brazil	1
Hungary	3	Bulgaria	1

	P	W	D	L	F	A	Pts
Portugal	3	3	0	0	9	2	6
Hungary	3	2	0	1	7	5	4
Brazil	3	1	0	2	4	6	2
Bulgaria	3	0	0	3	1	8	0

Group 4

Soviet Union	3	North Korea	0
Italy	2	Chile	0
Chile	1	North Korea	1
Soviet Union	1	Italy	0
North Korea	1	Italy	0
Soviet Union	2	Chile	1

	P	W	D	L	F	A	Pts
Soviet Union	3	3	0	0	6	1	6
North Korea	3	1	1	1	2	4	3
Italy	3	1	0	2	2	2	2
Chile	3	0	1	2	2	5	1

Quarter-finals

England	1	Argentina	0
W. Germany	4	Uruguay	0
Portugal	5	North Korea	3
Soviet Union	2	Hungary	1

Semi-finals

W. Germany	2	Soviet Union	1
England	2	Portugal	1

Third place match

Portugal	2	Soviet Union	1

Final

England (1) 4   W. Germany (1) 2*
Hurst (3), Peters   Haller, Weber

ENGLAND: Banks, Cohen, Wilson, Stiles, Charlton J., Moore (capt.), Ball, Hurst, Hunt, Charlton R., Peters.

WEST GERMANY: Tilkowski, Höttges, Schülz, Weber, Schnellinger, Haller, Beckenbauer, Overath, Seeler (capt.), Held, Emmerich.

Leading scorers
9 Eusebio (Portugal); 5 Haller (West Germany); 4 Beckenbauer (West Germany), Hurst (England), Bene (Hungary), Porkujan (USSR).

*Note: * After extra time*

MEXICO 1970
Beautiful football secures the Jules Rimet trophy

Football triumphed again in Mexico, where the colourful free-flowing Brazilians delighted, overcoming the heat, the altitude and, in a dramatic Final, Italy – the masters of defensive caution.

There were no surprises in Groups 1 and 2 where the Soviet Union and Mexico and Italy and Uruguay qualified comfortably. The fixture between Brazil and England in Group 3 provided the outstanding tie of the series. In the 10th minute Jairzinho, a wonderful player of power and pace, delivered the perfect cross from the line. Pele timed his run and jump to perfection, and his header was hard and true, angled to bounce before passing just inside the left post. The shout of "Goal!" was already in the air when Gordon Banks, who had anticipated the ball going the other way, twisted athletically to pounce and incredibly push the wickedly bouncing ball over the bar. It was one of the greatest saves ever seen.

The only goal was scored in the second half by Jairzinho, who was to score in all of Brazil's six matches. England faltered in the quarter-final. Without Banks, because of an upset stomach, they squandered a two-goal lead to lose to West Germany in extra time.

The semi-final between Italy and

TOTAL FOOTBALL *But Johan Cruyff could not overcome West Germany in '74*

West Germany was dramatic. Having taken the lead through Boninsegna, Italy withdrew in the second half to protect their advantage. Given control of midfield, Germany took the initiative but did not equalize until the third minute of injury time through Schnellinger. In extra time, the goals came thick and fast: Müller for Germany, 1–2, Burgnich, then Riva for Italy, 3–2. Müller again, 3–3, before Rivera clinched it for Italy.

The Final proved a marvellous affirmation of attacking football. Pele opened the scoring and made two more after Boninsegna had made it 1–1, capitalizing on a dreadful error by Clodoaldo. Gerson drove in a powerful cross-shot in the 66th minute, and the match was sewn up with goals from Jairzinho and Carlos Alberto.

WEST GERMANY 1974
Pyrrhic victory for 'Total Football'

European teams dominated this series in which West Germany regained the World Cup after 20 years. It was another triumph for positive tactics, as Holland and Poland – who had surprisingly eliminated England – demonstrated to the full the attributes of skill and technique. The term "Total Football" crept into the football vocabulary, with Cruyff, Neeskens and Rep leading the Dutch masters who abandoned the rigidity of 4–2–4 and 4–3–3 to introduce the concept of "rotation" play.

Half of the 16 competing nations had been eliminated after the first

series of group matches. The two Germanys qualified for the second phase comfortably, as did Holland and Sweden, and Poland from Group 4, where Argentina just pipped Italy on goal difference thanks to a 4–1 victory over Haiti, whom Italy had beaten 3–1.

Group 2 proved to be the most competitive. Brazil, now sadly without the retired Pele, could only draw 0–0 with Yugoslavia and Scotland. Zaïre were to be the key factor. Scotland defeated them 2–0, but Yugoslavia overwhelmed them 9–0 to clinch pole position on goal difference. As they went into the final round Scotland needed victory over Yugoslavia to win the group. They could only draw 1–1, and Brazil squeezed through, by virtue of one goal, thanks to a 3–0 win over Zaïre.

Holland looked impressive. They topped Group A to qualify for the Final without conceding a goal. Brazil, a shadow of their former selves, bowed out leaving us with one magic memory, their winning goal against East Germany. Jairzinho, standing on the end of the German wall facing a free-kick, ducked as Rivelino crashed his shot towards him, the ball swerving past the bewildered goalkeeper Croy.

West Germany's passage was a little more uncertain. It hinged on their clash with the impressive Poles in the final game of Group B. On a waterlogged pitch they made their physical strength pay. Tomaszewski saved a Hoeness penalty, but the German atoned for his miss when his shot was deflected to "The Bomber",

1970

Group 1

Mexico	0	Soviet Union	0
Belgium	3	El Salvador	0
Soviet Union	4	Belgium	1
Mexico	4	El Salvador	0
Soviet Union	2	El Salvador	0
Mexico	1	Belgium	0

	P	W	D	L	F	A	Pts
Soviet Union	3	2	1	0	6	1	5
Mexico	3	2	1	0	5	0	5
Belgium	3	1	0	2	4	5	2
El Salvador	3	0	0	3	0	9	0

Group 2

Uruguay	2	Israel	0
Italy	1	Sweden	0
Uruguay	0	Italy	0
Sweden	1	Israel	1
Sweden	1	Uruguay	0
Italy	0	Israel	0

	P	W	D	L	F	A	Pts
Italy	3	1	2	0	1	0	4
Uruguay	3	1	1	1	2	1	3
Sweden	3	1	1	1	2	2	3
Israel	3	0	2	1	1	3	2

Group 3

England	1	Romania	0
Brazil	4	Czech.	1
Romania	2	Czech.	1
Brazil	1	England	0
Brazil	3	Romania	2
England	1	Czech.	0

	P	W	D	L	F	A	Pts
Brazil	3	3	0	0	8	3	6
England	3	2	0	1	2	1	4
Romania	3	1	0	2	4	5	2
Czech.	3	0	0	3	2	7	0

Group 4

Peru	3	Bulgaria	2
W. Germany	2	Morocco	1
Peru	3	Morocco	0
W. Germany	5	Bulgaria	2
W. Germany	3	Peru	1
Morocco	1	Bulgaria	1

	P	W	D	L	F	A	Pts
W. Germany	3	3	0	0	10	4	6
Peru	3	2	0	1	7	5	4
Bulgaria	3	0	1	2	5	9	1
Morocco	3	0	1	2	2	6	1

Quarter-finals

W. Germany	3	England	2*
Brazil	4	Peru	2
Italy	4	Mexico	1
Uruguay	1	Soviet Union	0

Semi-finals

Italy	4	W. Germany	3*
Brazil	3	Uruguay	1

Third place match

W. Germany	1	Uruguay	0

Final

Brazil	4	Italy	1

Pele, Gerson, Jairzinho, Carlos Alberto — *Boninsegna*

BRAZIL: Felix, Carlos Alberto (capt.), Brito, Piazza, Everaldo, Clodoaldo, Gerson, Jairzinho, Tostao, Pele, Rivelino.

ITALY: Albertosi, Cera, Burgnich, Bertini (Juliano), Rosato, Facchetti (capt.), Domenghini, Mazzola, De Sisti, Boninsegna (Rivera), Riva.

Leading scorers
9 Müller (West Germany); 7 Jairzinho (Brazil); 4 Pele (Brazil), Cubillas (Peru), Byscevietz (USSR), Seeler (West Germany).

*Note: * After extra time*

1974

Group 1

W. Germany	1	Chile	0
E. Germany	2	Australia	0
W. Germany	3	Australia	0
E. Germany	1	Chile	1
E. Germany	1	W. Germany	0
Chile	0	Australia	0

	P	W	D	L	F	A	Pts
E. Germany	3	2	1	0	4	1	5
W. Germany	3	2	0	1	4	1	4
Chile	3	0	2	1	1	2	1
Australia	3	0	1	2	0	5	1

Group 2

Brazil	0	Yugoslavia	0
Scotland	2	Zaïre	0
Brazil	0	Scotland	0
Yugoslavia	9	Zaïre	0
Scotland	1	Yugoslavia	1
Brazil	3	Zaïre	0

	P	W	D	L	F	A	Pts
Yugoslavia	3	1	2	0	10	1	4
Brazil	3	1	2	0	3	0	4
Scotland	3	1	2	0	3	1	4
Zaïre	3	0	0	3	0	14	0

Group 3

Holland	2	Uruguay	0
Sweden	0	Bulgaria	0
Holland	0	Sweden	0
Bulgaria	1	Uruguay	1
Holland	4	Bulgaria	1
Sweden	3	Uruguay	0

	P	W	D	L	F	A	Pts
Holland	3	2	1	0	6	1	5
Sweden	3	1	2	0	3	0	4
Bulgaria	3	0	2	1	2	5	2
Uruguay	3	0	1	2	1	6	1

Group 4

Italy	3	Haiti	1
Poland	3	Argentina	2
Italy	1	Argentina	1
Poland	7	Haiti	0
Argentina	4	Haiti	1
Poland	2	Italy	1

	P	W	D	L	F	A	Pts
Poland	3	3	0	0	12	3	6
Argentina	3	1	1	1	7	5	3
Italy	3	1	1	1	5	4	3
Haiti	3	0	0	3	2	14	0

Group A

Brazil	1	E. Germany	0
Holland	4	Argentina	0
Holland	2	E. Germany	0
Brazil	2	Argentina	1
Holland	2	Brazil	0
Argentina	1	E. Germany	1

	P	W	D	L	F	A	Pts
Holland	3	3	0	0	8	0	6
Brazil	3	2	0	1	3	3	4
E. Germany	3	0	1	2	1	4	1
Argentina	3	0	1	2	2	7	1

Group B

Poland	1	Sweden	0
W. Germany	2	Yugoslavia	0
Poland	2	Yugoslavia	1
W. Germany	4	Sweden	2
Sweden	2	Yugoslavia	1
W. Germany	1	Poland	0

	P	W	D	L	F	A	Pts
W. Germany	3	3	0	0	7	2	6
Poland	3	2	0	1	3	2	4
Sweden	3	1	0	2	4	6	2
Yugoslavia	3	0	0	3	2	6	0

Third place match

Poland	1	Brazil	0

Final

W. Germany (2) 2 Holland (1) 1
Breitner (pen),   *Neeskens (pen)*
Müller

WEST GERMANY: Maier, Beckenbauer (capt.), Vogts, Schwarzenbeck, Breitner, Bonhof, Hoeness, Overath, Grabowski, Müller, Hölzenbein.

HOLLAND: Jongbloed, Suurbier, Rijsbergen (De Jong), Haan, Krol, Jansen, Neeskens, Van Hanegem, Rep, Cruyff (capt.), Rensenbrink (Van de Kerkhof, R.).

Leading scorers 7 Lato (Poland); 5 Neeskens (Holland), Szarmach (Poland); 4 Müller (West Germany), Rep (Holland), Edstroem (Sweden).

Gerd Müller, who booked the date with Holland.

The Dutch produced the most dramatic opening to a Final in the history of the competition. Right from the kick-off the ball was fluently played into the German area, where Cruyff was brought down by Hoeness. Neeskens calmly converted the first penalty awarded in a World Cup Final to record the fastest Final goal ever. And the Germans had yet to play the ball.

After being outplayed, West Germany got off the hook. Hölzenbein was homing in on goal when he was tripped by Jansen, and Breitner duly rammed in the resultant penalty himself to make it 1–1. A 43rd-minute goal from Gerd Müller – his 68th, last and most important for his country – won the World Cup.

CLINCHER *Bertoni scores for Argentina*

ARGENTINA 1978
Tickertape triumph for hyper hosts

Ecstasy and euphoria greeted Argentina's eventual triumph on home soil, yet for neutrals the failure of Holland, as in 1974, to claim their rightful crown as the best team in the world left a void.

The home nation, backed by fanatical support and animated tickertape adoration in the River Plate Stadium, staged a colourful and dramatic tournament. Yet their passage to the Final was not without controversy. Their opening game proved a torrid affair. Hungary took the lead in 12 minutes through Zombori only for Leopoldo Luque to equalize three minutes later. The Hungarians were to have two players sent off before Bertoni fired the winning goal. Italy and Argentina had already qualified for the second stage when they met to decide the final Group 1 places. The Italians played it tight and snatched the win through Bettega in the 67th minute.

In Group 2 Poland carried on where they left off in Germany, with slick precise play. The shock result featured Tunisia, who held West Germany to a goalless draw and could have won. Brazil once again failed to inspire, and only a fortunate 1–0 victory over Austria, who topped their group, squeezed them into the second phase. Scotland, the United Kingdom's only representatives, suffered humiliation. Rocked by a 3–1 defeat by Peru, they received a further blow to morale when Willie Johnston failed a drugs test and was ordered home. A 1–1 draw with Iran added to the troubles, but they went out in style against Holland.

While Italy and West Germany played not to lose, Holland thrilled with their adventurous attitude. The "reprise" of the 1974 Final between them and Germany provided one of the best games of this series. The final score was 2–2 and Holland were back in the Final. Meanwhile Brazil's

---

1978

Group 1

Argentina	2	Hungary	1
Italy	2	France	1
Argentina	2	France	1
Italy	3	Hungary	1
Italy	1	Argentina	0
France	3	Hungary	1

	P	W	D	L	F	A	Pts
Italy	3	3	0	0	6	2	6
Argentina	3	2	0	1	4	3	4
France	3	1	0	2	5	5	2
Hungary	3	0	0	3	3	8	0

Group 2

W.Germany	0	Poland	0
Tunisia	3	Mexico	1
Poland	1	Tunisia	0
W. Germany	6	Mexico	0
Poland	3	Mexico	1
W. Germany	0	Tunisia	0

	P	W	D	L	F	A	Pts
Poland	3	2	1	0	4	1	5
W.Germany	3	1	2	0	6	0	4
Tunisia	3	1	1	1	3	2	3
Mexico	3	0	0	3	2	12	0

Group 3

Austria	2	Spain	1
Sweden	1	Brazil	1
Austria	1	Sweden	0
Brazil	0	Spain	0
Spain	1	Sweden	0
Brazil	1	Austria	0

	P	W	D	L	F	A	Pts
Austria	3	2	0	1	3	2	4
Brazil	3	1	2	0	2	1	4
Spain	3	1	1	1	2	2	3
Sweden	3	0	1	2	1	3	1

Group 4

Peru	3	Scotland	1
Holland	3	Iran	0
Scotland	1	Iran	1
Holland	0	Peru	0
Peru	4	Iran	1
Scotland	3	Holland	2

	P	W	D	L	F	A	Pts
Peru	3	2	1	0	7	2	5
Holland	3	1	1	1	5	3	3
Scotland	3	1	1	1	5	6	3
Iran	3	0	1	2	2	8	1

Group A

Italy	0	W. Germany	0
Holland	5	Austria	1
Italy	1	Austria	0
Austria	3	W.Germany	2
Holland	2	Italy	1
Holland	2	W. Germany	2

	P	W	D	L	F	A	Pts
Holland	3	2	1	0	9	4	5
Italy	3	1	1	1	2	2	3
W. Germany	3	0	2	1	4	5	2
Austria	3	1	0	2	4	8	2

Group B

Argentina	2	Poland	0
Brazil	3	Peru	0
Argentina	0	Brazil	0
Poland	1	Peru	0
Brazil	3	Poland	1
Argentina	6	Peru	0

	P	W	D	L	F	A	Pts
Argentina	3	2	1	0	8	0	5
Brazil	3	2	1	0	6	1	5
Poland	3	1	0	2	2	5	2
Peru	3	0	0	3	0	10	0

Third place match

Brazil	2	Italy	1

Final

Argentina (1) 3 Holland (0) 1*
Kempes (2),   *Nanninga*
Bertoni

ARGENTINA: Fillol, Olguin, Galvan, Passarella (capt.), Tarantini, Ardiles (Larrosa), Gallego, Kempes, Bertoni, Luque, Ortiz (Houseman). HOLLAND: Jongbloed, Krol (capt.), Poortvliet, Brandts, Jansen (Suurbier), Van de Kerkhof W., Neeskens, Haan, Rep (Nanninga), Rensenbrink, Van de Kerkhof R.

Leading scorers
6 Kempes (Argentina); 5 Rensenbrink (Holland), Cubillas (Peru).

*Note: * After extra time*

3–1 defeat of Poland left Argentina needing to beat Peru by at least four goals to make the Final. They beat them by six in a shambolic exercise that tarnished the image of the whole competition.

The Final, more dramatic than distinguished, saw Mario Kempes score twice as once more Holland fell at the final hurdle.

SPAIN 1982
Italy have the last laugh

Italy deservedly won the 1982 World Cup, after a slow start in which they drew all three games in Group 1 and qualified on the slenderest goal difference. West Germany, who were to finish runners-up, were on the wrong end of a shock 2–1 defeat in their opening tie against Algeria but, like Italy, got better as the tournament progressed.

England, in contrast, started with a bang then gradually eased up. Skipper Bryan Robson got them off to a dream start against France with a goal in 27 seconds, but although Ron Greenwood's team proved hard to beat, without the injured Keegan

CIAO BELLA *Marco Tardelli kisses the cup alongside Dino Zoff after Italy's triumph over West Germany in 1982*

and Brooking they had little guile. The outstanding game was that between Italy and the favourites, Brazil. Three times Italy took the lead, twice Brazil came back to level the score in a classic that would not be matched for quality. Paolo Rossi, back after a two-year suspension, was the hero with a brilliant hat-trick.

In the semi-finals Rossi scored twice more to beat the impressive Poles, while West Germany and France, who had grown in stature and confidence following that initial setback against England, were involved in a pulsating thriller. With Platini, Tigana and Giresse at their teasing best, many fancied France as winners. In a tense 90 minutes they carved out the better chances but

failed to make them count, then in extra-time fell victim on penalties after German keeper Toni Schumacher got away with an appalling foul on Battiston.

The less glamorous sides also had their moments. Algeria, Honduras and Kuwait caught the eye, and Northern Ireland – whose Norman Whiteside was, at 17, the youngest ever

1982

Group 1

Italy	0	Poland	0
Peru	0	Cameroon	0
Italy	1	Peru	1
Poland	0	Cameroon	0
Poland	5	Peru	1
Italy	1	Cameroon	1

	P	W	D	L	F	A	Pts
Poland	3	1	2	0	5	1	4
Italy	3	0	3	0	2	2	3
Cameroon	3	0	3	0	1	1	3
Peru	3	0	2	1	2	6	2

Group 2

Algeria	2	W. Germany	1
Austria	1	Chile	0
W. Germany	4	Chile	1
Austria	2	Algeria	1
Algeria	3	Chile	2
W. Germany	1	Austria	0

	P	W	D	L	F	A	Pts
W. Germany	3	2	0	1	6	3	4
Austria	3	2	0	1	3	1	4
Algeria	3	2	0	1	5	5	4
Chile	3	0	0	3	3	8	0

Group 3

Belgium	1	Argentina	0
Hungary	10	El Salvador	1
Argentina	4	Hungary	1
Belgium	1	El Salvador	0
Belgium	1	Hungary	1
Argentina	2	El Salvador	0

	P	W	D	L	F	A	Pts
Belgium	3	2	1	0	3	1	5
Argentina	3	2	0	1	6	2	4
Hungary	3	1	1	1	12	6	3
El Salvador	3	0	0	3	1	13	3

Group 4

England	3	France	1
Czech.	1	Kuwait	1
England	2	Czech.	0
France	4	Kuwait	1
France	1	Czech.	1
England	1	Kuwait	0

	P	W	D	L	F	A	Pts
England	3	3	0	0	6	1	6
France	3	1	1	1	6	5	3
Czech.	3	0	2	1	2	4	2
Kuwait	3	0	1	2	2	6	1

Group 5

Spain	1	Honduras	1
N. Ireland	0	Yugoslavia	0
Spain	2	Yugoslavia	1
N. Ireland	1	Honduras	1
Yugoslavia	1	Honduras	0
N. Ireland	1	Spain	0

	P	W	D	L	F	A	Pts
N. Ireland	3	1	2	0	2	1	4
Spain	3	1	1	1	3	3	3
Yugoslavia	3	1	1	1	2	2	3
Honduras	3	0	2	1	2	3	2

Group 6

Brazil	2	Soviet Union	1
Scotland	5	New Zealand	2
Brazil	4	Scotland	1
Soviet Union	3	New Zealand	0
Scotland	2	Soviet Union	2
Brazil	4	New Zealand	0

	P	W	D	L	F	A	Pts
Brazil	3	3	0	0	10	2	6
Soviet Union	3	1	1	1	6	4	3
Scotland	3	1	1	1	8	8	3
New Zealand	3	0	0	3	2	12	0

Group A

Poland	3	Belgium	0
Soviet Union	1	Belgium	0
Soviet Union	0	Poland	0

	P	W	D	L	F	A	Pts
Poland	2	1	1	0	3	0	3
Soviet Union	2	1	1	0	1	0	3
Belgium	2	0	0	2	0	4	0

Group B

W. Germany	0	England	0
W. Germany	2	Spain	1
England	0	Spain	0

	P	W	D	L	F	A	Pts
W. Germany	2	1	1	0	2	1	3
England	2	0	2	0	0	0	2
Spain	2	0	1	1	1	2	1

Group C

Italy	2	Argentina	1
Brazil	3	Argentina	1
Italy	3	Brazil	2

	P	W	D	L	F	A	Pts
Italy	2	2	0	0	5	3	4
Brazil	2	1	0	1	5	4	2
Argentina	2	0	0	2	2	5	0

Group D

France	1	Austria	0
N. Ireland	2	Austria	2
France	4	N. Ireland	1

	P	W	D	L	F	A	Pts
France	2	2	0	0	5	1	4
Austria	2	0	1	1	2	3	1
N. Ireland	2	0	1	1	3	6	1

Semi-finals

Italy	2	Poland	0
W. Germany	3	France	3*

(West Germany won 5–4 on pens)

Third place match

Poland	3	France	2

Final

Italy	(0) 3	W. Germany (0)	1

Rossi, Tardelli   *Breitner*
Altobelli

ITALY: Zoff (capt.), Bergomi, Cabrini, Collovati, Scirea, Gentile, Oriale, Tardelli, Conti, Graziani (Altobelli) (Causio), Rossi.

WEST GERMANY: Schumacher, Kaltz, Förster K., Stielike, Förster B., Breitner, Dremmler (Hrubesch), Littbarski, Briegel, Fischer (Müller, H.), Rummenigge (capt.).

Leading scorers

6 Rossi (Italy); 5 Rummenigge (West Germany); 4 Zico (Brazil), Boniek (Poland).

to play in the finals – distinguished themselves in a win over Spain.

The Final did not live up to its billing. There was not a shot on target in the opening 45 minutes including Cabrini's effort from a penalty. But in the second half the Germans paid, in fatigue, the price of their extra-time victory over France. Italy, inspired by the effort of Marco Tardelli and counter-attacking pace of Bruno Conti, were deserving winners – thus sealing a World Cup hat-trick.

MEXICO 1986
Divine intervention determines destiny of Cup

Mexico staged its second World Cup finals in the wake of a tragic earthquake, and set records all round with 52 matches played before 2,406,511 spectators.

West Germany continued their impressive World Cup record by reaching their fifth Final, once again eliminating France at the semi-final stage, while Argentina overcame the impressive Belgiums to make a third Final appearance. However, their 2-1 quarter-final victory over England had been soured by the infamous "hand of God" incident,

THEY SHALL NOT PASS *Karl-Heinz Rummenigge is stopped by Argentina's Oscar Ruggeri during the Final in 1986*

when Maradona knocked the ball past goalkeeper Peter Shilton with a hand to score the opening goal. There was no argument about Argentina's second goal, a brilliant solo run by the Argentinian ace taking him past three England defenders before he dispatched the ball into the back of the net.

Of the earlier games, the Soviet Union's 6–0 demolition of Hungary and Belgium's thrilling 4–3 victory over the Soviets in the second round were the most memorable. England muddled through after a desperate start, Carlos Manuel's lone strike giving Portugal a 1–0 win. Bobby Robson's team were then held 0–0 by Morocco. A Gary Lineker hat-trick against Poland revived England's flag-ging fortunes and earned them a place in the second round.

In a dramatic Final Argentina led 2–0 through Brown and Valdano before West Germany launched a remarkable recovery to equalize through Karl-Heinz Rummenigge and Völler. Burruchaga snatched the winner for Argentina's second World Cup title.

1986

Group A

Bulgaria	1	Italy	1
Argentina	3	South Korea	1
Italy	1	Argentina	1
Bulgaria	1	South Korea	1
Argentina	2	Bulgaria	0
Italy	3	South Korea	2

	P	W	D	L	F	A	Pts
Argentina	3	2	1	0	6	2	5
Italy	3	1	2	0	5	4	4
Bulgaria	3	0	2	1	2	4	2
South Korea	3	0	1	2	4	7	1

Group B

Mexico	2	Belgium	1
Paraguay	1	Iraq	0
Mexico	1	Paraguay	1
Belgium	2	Iraq	1
Paraguay	2	Belgium	2
Mexico	1	Iraq	0

	P	W	D	L	F	A	Pts
Mexico	3	2	1	0	4	2	5
Paraguay	3	1	2	0	4	3	4
Belgium	3	1	1	1	5	5	4
Iraq	3	0	0	3	1	4	0

Group C

Soviet Union	6	Hungary	0
France	1	Canada	0
Soviet Union	1	France	1
Hungary	2	Canada	0
France	3	Hungary	0
Soviet Union	2	Canada	0

	P	W	D	L	F	A	Pts
Soviet Union	3	2	1	0	9	1	5
France	3	2	1	0	5	1	5
Hungary	3	1	0	2	2	9	2
Canada	3	0	0	3	0	5	0

Group D

Brazil	1	Spain	0
N. Ireland	1	Algeria	1
Spain	2	N. Ireland	1
Brazil	1	Algeria	0
Spain	3	Algeria	0
Brazil	3	N. Ireland	0

	P	W	D	L	F	A	Pts
Brazil	3	3	0	0	5	0	6
Spain	3	2	0	1	5	2	4
N. Ireland	3	0	1	2	2	6	1
Algeria	3	0	1	2	1	5	1

Group E

W. Germany	1	Uruguay	1
Denmark	1	Scotland	0
Denmark	6	Uruguay	1
W. Germany	2	Scotland	1
Scotland	0	Uruguay	0
Denmark	2	W.Germany	0

	P	W	D	L	F	A	Pts
Denmark	3	3	0	0	9	1	6
W. Germany	3	1	1	1	3	4	3
Uruguay	3	0	2	1	2	7	2
Scotland	3	0	1	2	1	3	1

Group F

Morocco	0	Poland	0
Portugal	1	England	0
England	0	Morocco	0
Poland	1	Portugal	0
England	3	Poland	0
Morocco	3	Portugal	1

	P	W	D	L	F	A	Pts
Morocco	3	1	2	0	3	1	4
England	3	1	1	1	3	1	3
Poland	3	1	1	1	1	3	3
Portugal	3	1	0	2	2	4	2

Second round

Knock-out phase comprising the top two teams from each group plus the four best third-placed teams.

Mexico	2	Bulgaria	0
Belgium	4	Soviet Union	3*
Brazil	4	Poland	0
Argentina	1	Uruguay	0
France	2	Italy	0
W.Germany	1	Morocco	0
England	3	Paraguay	0
Spain	5	Denmark	1

Quarter-finals

France	1	Brazil	1*

(France won 4–3 on pens)

W.Germany	0	Mexico	0*

(W Germany won 4–1 on pens)

Argentina	2	England	1
Spain	1	Belgium	1*

(Belgium won 5–4 on pens)

Semi-finals

Argentina	2	Belgium	0
W.Germany	2	France	0

Third place match

France	4	Belgium	2

Final

Argentina (1) 3	W.Germany (0) 2	

Brown, Valdano, Burruchaga / *Rummenigge, Völler*

ARGENTINA: Pumpido, Cuciuffo, Olarticoechea, Ruggeri, Brown, Giusti, Burruchaga (Trobbiani), Batista, Valdano, Maradona (capt.), Enrique.

WEST GERMANY: Schumacher, Berthold, Briegel, Jakobs, Förster, Eder, Brehme, Matthäus, Allofs (Völler), Magath (Hoeness, D.), Rummenigge (capt.).

Leading scorers

6 Lineker (England); 5 Butragueño (Spain), Careca (Brazil), Maradona (Argentina); 4 Altobelli (Italy), Belanov (USSR), Elkjaer (Denmark), Valdano (Argentina).

*Note: * After extra time*

TOP OF THE WORLD *West German captain Lothar Matthäus celebrates victory over Argentina after the Final in Rome*

ITALY 1990
Penalties decide in a tear-jerking anti-climax

The 14th World Cup finals did not live up to the setting. There was a miserly shortage of goals, but perhaps the saddest failure of all was on the part of the established stars who failed to enhance their reputations. The occasion was saved by the Italians themselves, for this was the People's World Cup.

It started dramatically with Cameroon beating the champions Argentina – Omam Biyik scoring the only goal. The Africans topped their group, with Argentina trailing in third place, and were later to frighten the life out of England when they took a 2–1 lead over them in the quarter-finals. "Toto" Schillaci's tense expressions were to reflect the Italian mood. He scored the winner against Austria and the first against the Czechs as Italy comfortably headed Group A. Scotland were humili-

ated by Costa Rica, bounced back against Sweden, then crashed out to Brazil after taking them all the way. Scotland's gloom contrasted with the Republic of Ireland's popular success, their shoot-out win over Romania earning them a tilt at the hosts in the quarter-finals. Belgium emerged as an impressive combination, but their journey ended when David Platt thumped home a brilliant volley to see England to the last eight.

The highlights included the drama in Milan, when Littbarski's goal seemed to have ended Colombia's dream before one of the great characters of the tournament, Carlos Valderrama, who had been carried off, returned to lay on an equalizer for Freddy Rincon. There was the reckless stupidity of Colombian goalkeeper René Higuita, the grace of Tomas Skuhravy, the Czech striker and the magic of Yugoslavia's Dragan Stojkovic. There was also the sheer theatre of West Germany blasting England in a penalty shoot-out, with Gascoigne sobbing.

But the lasting impression of Italia '90 was of the villain of the piece, Argentina, who ousted Brazil, and spoilt the script by beating Italy on penalties to reach a Final they were to sully with their dour tactics and flagrant abuse of the rules. Two Argentines were sent off, before, ironically, they were beaten by a penalty.

1990

Group A
Italy	1	Austria	0
Czech.	5	USA	1
Italy	1	USA	0
Czech.	1	Austria	0
Italy	2	Czech.	0
Austria	2	USA	1

	P	W	D	L	F	A	Pts
Italy	3	3	0	0	4	0	6
Czech.	3	2	0	1	6	3	4
Austria	3	1	0	2	2	3	2
USA	3	0	0	3	2	8	0

Group B
Cameroon	1	Argentina	0
Romania	2	Soviet Union	0
Argentina	2	Soviet Union	0
Cameroon	2	Romania	1
Argentina	1	Romania	1
Soviet Union	4	Cameroon	0

	P	W	D	L	F	A	Pts
Cameroon	3	2	0	1	3	5	4
Romania	3	1	1	1	4	3	3
Argentina	3	1	1	1	3	2	3
Soviet Union	3	1	0	2	4	4	2

Group C
Brazil	2	Sweden	1
Costa Rica	1	Scotland	0
Brazil	1	Costa Rica	0
Scotland	2	Sweden	1
Brazil	1	Scotland	0
Costa Rica	2	Sweden	1

	P	W	D	L	F	A	Pts
Brazil	3	3	0	0	4	1	6
Costa Rica	3	2	0	1	3	2	4
Scotland	3	1	0	2	2	3	2
Sweden	3	0	0	3	3	6	0

Group D
Colombia	2	UAE	0
W. Germany	4	Yugoslavia	1
Yugoslavia	1	Colombia	0
W. Germany	5	UAE	1
W. Germany	1	Colombia	1
Yugoslavia	4	UAE	1

	P	W	D	L	F	A	Pts
W. Germany	3	2	1	0	10	3	5
Yugoslavia	3	2	0	1	6	5	4
Colombia	3	1	1	1	3	2	3
UAE	3	0	0	3	2	11	0

Group E
Belgium	2	South Korea	0
Uruguay	0	Spain	0
Belgium	3	Uruguay	1
Spain	3	South Korea	1
Spain	2	Belgium	1
Uruguay	1	South Korea	0

	P	W	D	L	F	A	Pts
Spain	3	2	1	0	5	2	5
Belgium	3	2	0	1	6	3	4
Uruguay	3	1	1	1	2	3	3
South Korea	3	0	0	3	1	6	0

Group F
England	1	Rep of Ireland	1
Holland	1	Egypt	1
England	0	Holland	0
Egypt	0	Rep of Ireland	0
England	1	Egypt	0
Holland	1	Rep of Ireland	1

	P	W	D	L	F	A	Pts
England	3	1	2	0	2	1	4
Rep of Ireland	3	0	3	0	2	2	3
Holland	3	0	3	0	2	2	3
Egypt	3	0	2	1	1	2	2

Second phase
Knock-out phase comprising the top two teams from each group plus the four best third-placed teams

Cameroon	2	Colombia	1*
Czech.	4	Costa Rica	1
Argentina	1	Brazil	0
W. Germany	2	Holland	1
Rep of Ireland	0	Rumania	0*
(Rep. of Ireland won 5–4 on pens)			
Italy	2	Uruguay	0
Yugoslavia	2	Spain	1*
England	1	Belgium	0*

Quarter-finals
Argentina	0	Yugoslavia	0*
(Argentina won 3–2 on pens)			
Italy	1	Rep of Ireland	0
W. Germany	1	Czech.	0
England	3	Cameroon	2*

Semi-finals
Argentina	1	Italy	1*
(Argentina won 4–3 on pens)			
W. Germany	1	England	1*
(West Germany won 4–3 on pens)			

Third place match
Italy	2	England	1

Final
W.Germany (0) 1 Argentina (0) 0
Brehme (pen)

WEST GERMANY: Illgner, Berthold (Reuter), Kohler, Augenthaler, Buchwald, Brehme, Littbarski, Hässler, Matthäus (capt.), Völler, Klinsmann.

ARGENTINA: Goycochea, Lorenzo, Serrizuela, Sensini, Ruggeri (Monzon), Simon, Basualdo, Burruchaga (Calderon), Maradona (capt.), Troglio, Dezotti.

Leading scorers
6 Schillaci (Italy); 5 Skuhravy (Czechoslovakia); 4 Michel (Spain), Milla (Cameroon), Matthäus (West Germany), Lineker (England).

*Note: * After extra time*

USA 1994
Brazil's glory in Final shoot-out

History was made twice over at the 1994 World Cup finals. Brazil secured a fourth title to add to their triumphs in 1958, 1962 and 1970. But to do so they needed to win the first-ever penalty shoot-out at the end of extra time after a goalless Final against Italy in the Rose Bowl in Pasadena.

FIFA introduced four radical measures in an attempt to improve the quality of the action: three points for a win instead of two in the first round group matches; a relaxation over the offside law by which play was to be stopped only if an attacking player was interfering with play; a crackdown on the tackle from behind in particular – for which a red card would be automatic – and violent conduct in general; and finally, injured players would be taken off the field immediately for treatment.

In simple statistical terms these changes added up to 15 sendings off and a record 235 bookings. But, on the positive side, they also computed to 141 goals in 52 matches, a match average of 2.71 and an improvement on Italia '90.

More Than a Game

The biggest shadow over the finals was cast by the death of Andres Escobar, the Colombian defender, who was shot dead a few days after returning back home to Medellin. The exact reason for his murder is not known – gambling losses, probably involving drug barons, is thought to be the cause – but what was certain was that the centre-back had, inadvertently, scored an own goal against the United States in Colombia's 2–1 defeat.

That victory for the US was probably the most significant single result in the finals because it virtually ensured the hosts a place in the second round. This success struck a chord with the domestic audience which helped carry the World Cup along on a wave of excitement and enthusiasm which surprised even the most optimistic of American soccer people.

However, the team of Group A were undoubtedly Romania, inspired by their attacking general Gheorghe Hagi. The well-organized Swiss team qualified in second place, but Colombia – among the pre-tournament favourites – played without conviction or pattern and were eliminated.

Group B offered clear favourites in Brazil and they did not disappoint their colourful, noisy and musical supporters. Brazil's strength was the striking partnership of Romario and Bebeto. Romario either scored or had a creative hand in 10 of Brazil's 11 goals. Brazil topped the group with Sweden second.

FIVE GOALS IN ONE MATCH *Russia's Oleg Salenko set an individual goalscoring record for the World Cup finals*

Group C included the formal Opening Match in which holders Germany beat Bolivia 1–0. The Germans appeared laboured, and Stefan Effenberg was expelled from the squad at the end of the first round for making a rude gesture towards jeering German fans in the narrow 3–2 win over South Korea. This was the other group which provided only two, rather than three, second round qualifiers. Germany finished top followed by Spain.

Maradona's Misery

In Group D Argentina's Diego Maradona was his team's attacking inspiration in the opening 4–0 win over Greece, and in the 2–1 follow-up defeat of Nigeria, but it was after this game that he failed a dope test which showed traces of the banned stimulant ephedrine. The tournament was over for Maradona and Argentina lost their next game, without him, 2–0 to Bulgaria. The Bulgarians thus qualified for the second round despite having crashed 3–0 to the entertaining World Cup newcomers Nigeria in the group's opening match.

Ten Men Fight Back

The tightest division was Group E, featuring Italy, the Republic of Ireland, Mexico and Norway, and the six matches produced only eight goals.

Ireland shocked Italy with a 1–0 victory in their opening match, and Norway appeared on the verge of inflicting a second defeat on the group favourites when goalkeeper Gianluca Pagliuca was sent off. Remarkably, however, Italy fought back to win, 1–0, when defeat would have resulted in almost certain elimination. Wasting that numerical superiority cost Norway dear. All four teams ended up on four points and zero goal difference, but Norway finished bottom of the group on goals scored and were thus eliminated.

Another favoured team who struggled in the first round were Holland. They beat Saudi Arabia only 2–1 in their first match then lost an exciting duel 1–0 to Belgium next time out and escaped early elimination by defeating Morocco 2–1 in their final match, to qualify along with Belgium and World Cup newcomers Saudi Arabia – who beat Belgium 1–0 along the way.

> ## " It's a death sentence. You can't have fun in this job. It will only be a pleasure if we win the World Cup. "
>
> *Carlos Alberto Parreira, Brazil coach*

The opening match of the second round saw Germany, as on the opening day, playing in Chicago. This time they defeated Belgium 3–2 in an exciting game which marked the successful two-goal return of veteran World Cup-winner Rudi Völler.

The Republic of Ireland committed defensive suicide against Holland, losing 2–0 on mistakes by full-back Terry Phelan and goalkeeper Packie Bonner. Spain had an easy time in beating Switzerland 3–0 and Sweden saw off Saudi Arabia 3–1. Brazil also spoiled the Americans' Independence Day holiday by defeating the hosts more easily than the 1–0 scoreline suggests. The other three second-round games were even more dramatic. Bulgaria defeated Mexico 3–1 on penalties – the first shoot-out of the finals – after an entertaining 1–1 draw, marred by two contentious sendings-off.

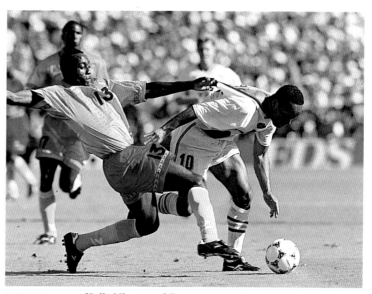

AFRICAN CHALLENGE *Kalla Nkongo of Cameroon tussles with Dahlin of Sweden*

A TANGO NOT A SAMBA *Romario and Baresi battle for supremacy in the Final at the Rose Bowl*

Hagi's Army March On

In Pasadena, Romania's Ilie Dumitrescu played the game of his life scoring twice and creating a third for Hagi in a 3–2 defeat of Argentina. Italy dramatically defeated Nigeria; with two minutes remaining the Italians were 1–0 down and had again been reduced to ten men by the dis-

missal, this time, of midfield substitute Gianfranco Zola. Roberto Baggio snatched an equaliser and as the Nigerians sagged in extra time, he scored again, from the penalty spot.

In the quarter-finals, Sweden, themselves down to 10 men after Stefan Schwarz was sent off, defeated Romania on penalties after a 2–2 draw.

Roberto Baggio confirmed his star rating with Italy's late second goal in their 2–1 victory over Spain. Another tight game saw Brazil defeat Holland 3–2, the first time an opposing team had put Brazil's defence under serious sustained pressure.

Completing the semi-final line-up were rank outsiders Bulgaria. Germany went ahead through a Lothar Matthäus penalty. But the holders conceded two last-gasp goals, from Hristo Stoichkov and Iordan Lechkov. It was Germany's earliest elimination since their quarter-final failure in 1962 and Bulgaria, who had played 16 matches at the finals without winning one before this tournament, were into the semi-finals.

That was to prove the end of the road. The two-goal brilliance of Roberto Baggio lifted Italy into their fifth Final while, in the other semi-final, Brazil encountered few difficulties in defeating a lacklustre and leg-weary Sweden 1-0.

Penalties in Pasadena

Italy gambled twice over, in playing superstar striker Roberto Baggio despite a hamstring strain and in recalling veteran sweeper Franco Baresi for his first appearance after a cartilage operation following his injury against Norway in the first round.

In fact, Baresi was Italy's man of the match. The game saw Brazil employing their technical brilliance to try to outflank Italy's defensive discipline while the Italians sat back and waited for the right moment to unleash their rapid counter-attacks.

It was a game of few chances, most of which fell to Brazil. Romario misplaced a first-half header and Mazinho couldn't quite capitalize on a half-chance when Pagliuca spilled a Branco free-kick. In the 75th minute Pagliuca also allowed a long-range Mauro Silva effort to slip through his hands, but the ball bounced off the post and back into his arms. Pagliuca kissed the post in gratitude. Italy's best chance ended with Taffarel saving from Massaro.

Roberto Baggio went close with one effort in each half of extra time while Brazil should again have taken the lead in the 109th minute when the industrious Cafu crossed to the far post and Romario put the ball fractionally the wrong side of the post from four

WE ARE THE CHAMPIONS *Dunga with the World Cup trophy*

yards out just beyond the far post.

In the penalty shoot-out, Taffarel benefited immediately when Baresi shot over. Baresi sank to his knees in despair. Pagliuca then saved from Marcio Santos and Italy went briefly ahead as Albertini scored from kick No 2. Romario squared for Brazil, Evani netted for Italy and Branco for Brazil. This was the point at which it fell apart for Italy as Taffarel saved from Massaro and Dunga shot what proved the vital Brazilian kick. Baggio needed to score with Italy's last kick of the five to keep his country alive. Instead, he scooped the ball over the bar. Brazil were back on top of the world.

1994

Group A

USA	1	Switzerland	1
Colombia	1	Romania	3
USA	2	Colombia	1
Romania	1	Switzerland	4
USA	0	Romania	1
Switzerland	0	Colombia	2

	P	W	D	L	F	A	Pts
Romania	3	2	0	1	5	5	6
Switzerland	3	1	1	1	5	4	4
USA	3	1	1	1	3	3	4
Colombia	3	1	0	2	4	5	3

Group B

Cameroon	2	Sweden	2
Brazil	2	Russia	0
Brazil	3	Cameroon	0
Sweden	3	Russia	1
Russia	6	Cameroon	1
Brazil	1	Sweden	1

	P	W	D	L	F	A	Pts
Brazil	3	2	1	0	6	1	7
Sweden	3	1	2	0	6	4	5
Russia	3	1	0	2	7	6	3
Cameroon	3	0	1	2	3	11	1

Group C

Germany	1	Bolivia	0
Spain	2	South Korea	2
Germany	1	Spain	1
South Korea	0	Bolivia	0
Bolivia	1	Spain	3
Germany	3	South Korea	2

	P	W	D	L	F	A	Pts
Germany	3	2	1	0	5	3	7
Spain	3	1	2	0	6	4	5
South Korea	3	0	2	1	4	5	2
Bolivia	3	0	1	2	1	4	1

Group D

Argentina	4	Greece	0
Nigeria	3	Bulgaria	0
Argentina	2	Nigeria	1
Bulgaria	4	Greece	0
Greece	0	Nigeria	2
Argentina	0	Bulgaria	2

	P	W	D	L	F	A	Pts
Nigeria	3	2	0	1	6	2	6
Bulgaria	3	2	0	1	6	3	6
Argentina	3	2	0	1	6	3	6
Greece	3	0	0	3	0	10	1

Group E

Italy	0	Rep of Ireland	1
Norway	1	Mexico	0
Italy	1	Norway	0
Mexico	2	Rep of Ireland	1
Rep of Ireland	0	Norway	0
Italy	1	Mexico	1

	P	W	D	L	F	A	Pts
Mexico	3	1	1	1	3	3	4
Rep of Ireland	3	1	1	1	2	2	4
Italy	3	1	1	1	2	2	4
Norway	3	1	1	1	1	1	4

Group F

Belgium	1	Morocco	0
Holland	2	Saudi Arabia	1
Belgium	1	Holland	0
Saudi Arabia	2	Morocco	1
Morocco	1	Holland	2
Belgium	0	Saudi Arabia	1

	P	W	D	L	F	A	Pts
Holland	3	2	0	1	4	3	6
Saudi Arabia	3	2	0	1	4	3	6
Belgium	3	2	0	1	2	1	6
Morocco	3	0	0	3	2	5	0

Second phase

Germany	3	Belgium	2
Spain	3	Switzerland	0
Saudi Arabia	1	Sweden	3
Romania	3	Argentina	2
Holland	2	Rep of Ireland	0
Brazil	1	USA	0
Nigeria	1	Italy	2*
Mexico	1	Bulgaria	1*

(*Bulgaria won 3–1 on pens*)

Quarter-finals

Italy	2	Spain	1
Holland	2	Brazil	3
Germany	1	Bulgaria	2
Sweden	2	Romania	2*

(*Sweden won 5–4 on pens*)

Semi-finals

| Brazil | 1 | Sweden | 0 |
| Italy | 2 | Bulgaria | 1 |

Third place match

| Sweden | 4 | Bulgaria | 0 |

Final

| Brazil | 0 | Italy | 0* |

(*Brazil won 3–2 on pens*)

BRAZIL: Taffarel, Jorginho (Cafu 20), Aldair, Marcio Santos, Branco, Mazinho (Viola 106), Dunga (capt.), Mauro Silva, Zinho, Romario, Bebeto.

ITALY: Pagliuca, Mussi (Apolloni 34), Maldini, Baresi (capt.), Benarrivo, Berti, Albertini, D. Baggio (Evani 94), Donadoni, R. Baggio, Massaro.

Leading scorers

6 Salenko (Russia), Stoichkov (Bulgaria).
5 K. Andersson (Sweden), R. Baggio (Italy), Klinsmann (Germany), Romario (Brazil)
4 Batistuta (Argentina), Dahlin (Sweden), Raducioiu (Romania)

*Note: * After extra time*

INTERNATIONAL COMPETITIONS

FIFA UNDER-17 WORLD CHAMPIONSHIP

FIFA have made no secret of their desire to encourage football at the grass roots level, and the Under-17 (Junior) and Under-20 (Youth) World Championships are crucial elements of that process. The Under-17 World Championship in particular has shown that skilful football is not confined to Europe and South America. Of the six tournaments held so far, Africa has won four times and Asia once.

FIFA Under-17 World Championship Finals
1985 Nigeria 2, West Germany 0.
1987 Soviet Union 1, Nigeria 1.
Soviet Union won 4–2 on penalties.
1989 Saudi Arabia 2, Scotland 2.
Saudi Arabia won 5–4 on penalties.
1991 Ghana 1, Spain 0.
1993 Nigeria 2, Ghana 1.
1995 Ghana 3 Brazil 2

FIFA UNDER-20 WORLD CHAMPIONSHIP

The World Youth Championship, as the Under-20 event is often known, reflects the gap between Europe and South America and the rest of the world which exists from this level up. The reasons for this are too numerous to list, but socio-economic problems and the strong club base in Europe and South America are certainly important factors. After 10 tournaments, Africa and Asia have yet to win, although Qatar, Ghana and Nigeria have been runners-up.

FIFA Under-20 World Championship Finals
1977 Soviet Union 2, Mexico 2
Soviet Union won 9–8 on penalties.
1979 Argentina 3, Soviet Union 1
1981 West Germany 4, Qatar 0
1983 Brazil 1, Argentina 0
1985 Brazil 1, Spain 0
1987 Yugoslavia 1, West Germany 1
Yugoslavia won 5–4 on penalties.
1989 Portugal 2, Nigeria 0
1991 Portugal 0, Brazil 0
Portugal won 4–2 on penalties.
1993 Brazil 2, Ghana 1
1995 Argentina 2, Brazil 0

NORWAY'S JOY *1995's World Champions*

WOMEN'S WORLD CHAMPIONSHIP

Introduced in 1991, the Women's World Cup has massive potential, with over half the world's population to cater for. FIFA are giving great encouragement to women's football and the first finals took place in China in 1991. Norway lost 2-1 to the United States in the Final in Guangzhou, but won the title two years later in Sweden. Their inspiration was Helge Riise, successor to American Michelle Akers-Stahl as the world's top woman player.

Women's World Championship Finals
1991 USA 2, Norway 1.
1995 Norway 2, Germany 0

OLYMPIC GAMES

Football has been part of the Olympic Games since 1908, but until the Olympic "revolution" of Juan Antonio Samaranch, the amateur ethos of the Olympics seemed at odds with senior football, which had long been predominantly professional. Trouble erupted as far back as the 1920s, when the four British Associations withdrew from FIFA in a row over broken time payments to players to compensate for loss of income from their regular jobs while they were away playing football.

Football was first played at the Olympics in 1896, when a scratch tournament involving select teams from Denmark, Athens and Izmir was organized. (The only recorded result was a 15–0 victory for the Danish XI against the Izmir XI.) In Paris in 1900, football was again included as a demonstration sport, with Upton Park FC, representing England, beating France 4–0 in the only game played. In 1904 in St Louis, three North American teams entered a demonstration event which was won by Galt FC from Ontario representing Canada.

Football finally arrived as an accepted Olympic sport with the 1908 Games in London. The England amateur team (not a United Kingdom team), containing many of the best players in the country, won the title, beating Denmark 2–0 in the Final at the White City Stadium. Vivian Woodward, one of the outstanding players of the day, scored the second goal at the White City, and led the England side four years later in Stockholm. Denmark, the best amateur side on the continent, were again England's Final opponents, and again they ended up with the silver medal. Berry, Walden and Hoare (twice) scored for England in a 4–2 win against a Danish side which contained Nils Middelboe, later to play for Chelsea – one of Woodward's clubs.

The 1920 Games in Antwerp are remembered for the bad-tempered Final between Belgium and Czechoslovakia. Trailing by two goals, the Czechs felt the referee was favouring the home side and walked off the pitch before the game had ended. They were duly disqualified by FIFA, and a tournament had to be quickly arranged to decide the silver and bronze medals. Spain, having won the consolation tournament, beat Holland 3–1 to claim the silver medal.

In 1924 the Games returned to Paris and a South American nation, Uruguay, appeared for the first time. The Uruguayans brought with them dazzling ball skills which most Europeans had never seen before. They fielded a side containing some of the greats of Uruguayan football: Nasazzi, Andrade, Vidal, Scarone, Petrone, Cea and Romano, and

GOLD GETTERS *France's 1984 Olympic-winning side*

TIGHT SQUEEZE *Spain's Albert Ferrar between Poles Dariusz Gestar (left) and Andrzej Kobylanski in the 1992 Final*

Switzerland were beaten 3–0.

Four years later the Uruguayans returned, along with their great rivals Argentina, to take part in the 1928 Amsterdam Games. They met in the Final and Uruguay won after a replay 2–1 to retain the title.

Uruguay's success in 1924 and 1928 confirmed the emergence of South America as a major footballing continent, and undoubtedly led to the idea of the World Cup. From 1930, the Olympic title assumed a less important role for the major players from Western Europe and South America. Italy were the next Olympic champions, when they beat Austria 2–1 in the 1936 Final – there was no tournament in 1932.

In London in 1948, the title went to Sweden. The Swedes, featuring the famous "Grenoli" trio forward line of Gunnar Gren, Gunnar Nordahl and Nils Liedholm (all of whom later joined Milan), beat Yugoslavia 3–1 at Wembley, with Gren scoring twice. Yugoslavia reached the Final again in Helsinki in 1952, but they came up against Hungary's "Magic Magyars". Ferenc Puskas and Zoltan Czibor scored in Hungary's 2–0 win – only major title.

The period from 1952 to 1976 was dominated by the "state amateurs" from the East where all players, officially "state amateurs" but indirectly professional, were allowed to compete; in the West, players were openly professional and thus ineligible.

A qualifying series was introduced for the 1956 Melbourne Games. Lev Yashin's Soviet Union won the gold medal, beating Yugoslavia 1–0 in the Final in front of an amazing 120,000 crowd at the Melbourne Cricket Ground.

Yugoslavia made it fourth time lucky in Rome, beating the Danes, 3–1, in the Final. Hungary clinched a hat-trick of titles when they beat Czechoslovakia in 1964 in Tokyo and Bulgaria in 1968 in Mexico City; Poland ended the Hungarians' run by beating them 2–1 in the Final in Munich in 1972; and East Germany made it seven in a row for Eastern Europe when they defeated Poland 3–1 in Montreal in 1976.

FIFA changed the rules for the 1980 tournament, preventing any European or South American who had played in a World Cup qualifier from taking part. Eastern European countries had a last hurrah in Moscow, where Czechoslovakia beat East Germany 1–0. But the new eligibility ruling, even if only an unsatisfactory compromise, did break the monopoly in 1984, when France won gold in Los Angeles.

The 1988 tournament in Seoul featured a host of top professional players and many emerging youngsters yet to play in the World Cup. Ironically, the Soviet Union again struck gold, beating Brazil 2–1 in the Final. The tournament also produced one of the biggest shocks in football history; Zambia beat Italy 4–0.

For 1992, the UEFA under-21 Championship became a qualifying competition. Hosts Spain won a splendid final, beating Poland 3–2 with goals from Kiko (two) and Abelardo. They were unable to hang on to their medals, however, four years later at the Atlanta Olympics.

Yet none of the football matches were played in Atlanta itself – a discourtesy which grated with FIFA, particularly after the world body had bent the rules again to permit each nation to field three over-age players. The hope was that this would encourage mainstream nations to send a handful of star names whose presence would contribute promotional support to US soccer.

In fact, it was not a mainstream nation who carried off gold at all but Nigeria who thus made history as first African winners of the Olympic title. No-one could say they did not deserve it. Relying on the experienced nucleus of their 1994 World Cup squad, the Nigerians beat favourites Brazil 4–3 in the semi-final and then Argentina 3–2 in the final.

Winners

Olympic Games Finals
1908 *London:* England 2 (Chapman, Woodward), Denmark 0
1912 *Stockholm:* England 4 (Berry, Walden, Hoare 2), Denmark 2 (Olsen 2)
1920 *Antwerp:* Belgium 2 (Coppee, Larnoe), Czechoslovakia 0
1924 *Paris:* Uruguay 3 (Petrone, Cea, Romano), Switzerland 0. Att: 41,000

1928 *Amsterdam:* Uruguay 1 (Ferreira), Argentina 1 (Petrone) – *Amsterdam* (replay): Uruguay 2 (Figueroa, Scarone H.), Argentina 1 (Monti)
1936 *Berlin:* Italy 2 (Frossi 2), Austria 1 (Kainberger, K.). Att: 90,000
1948 *London:* Sweden 3 (Gren 2, Nordahl G.), Yugoslavia 1 (Bobek). Att: 60,000
1952 *Helsinki:* Hungary 2 (Puskas,

Czibor), Yugoslavia 0. Att: 60,000
1956 *Melbourne:* Soviet Union 1 (Ilyin), Yugoslavia 0. Att: 120,000
1960 *Rome:* Yugoslavia 3 (Galic, Matus, Kostic), Denmark 1 (Nielsen, F.). Att: 40,000
1964 *Tokyo:* Hungary 2 (o.g., Bene), Czechoslovakia 1 (Brumovsky)
1968 *Mexico City:* Hungary 4 (Menczel 2, Dunai A. 2),

Bulgaria 1 (Dimitrov)
1972 *Munich:* Poland 2 (Deyna 2), Hungary 1 (Varadi). Att: 50,000
1976 *Montreal:* East Germany 3 (Schade, Hoffmann, Hafner), Poland 1 (Lato). Att: 71,000
1980 *Moscow:* Czechoslovakia 1 (Svoboda), East Germany 0. Att: 70,000
1984 *Los Angeles:* France 2 (Brisson, Xuereb), Brazil 0. Att: 101,000

1988 *Seoul:* Soviet Union 2 (Dobrovolski, Savichev), Brazil 1 (Romario) aet. Att: 73,000
1992 *Barcelona:* Spain 3 (Abelardo, Quico 2), Poland 2 (Kowalczyk, Staniek). Att: 95,000
1996 *Athens, Georgia:* Nigeria 3 (Babayaro, Amokachi, Amunike), Argentina 2 (C Lopez, Crespo). Att: 45,000

COPA AMERICA (SOUTH AMERICAN CHAMPIONSHIP)

The South American Championship is the oldest running international competition in the world. The Copa America, as the competition has been known since 1975, is contested by the 10 members of CONMEBOL, the South American Confederation, and is 50 years older than its European equivalent.

The first tournament, in 1910, was not an official championship ("extra-ordinario"). Argentinia decided to arrange a tournament involving themselves, Uruguay, Brazil and Chile. Brazil withdrew before the tournament began, but on May 29, 1910, Uruguay and Chile contested the very first South American Championship match at in Buenos Aires.

Penarol's José Piendibene scored the first goal in the Copa America as Uruguay ran out 3–0 winners. Seven days later Argentina had an even easier 5–1 victory over Chile.

Almost 40,000 crowded into the Gimnasia ground to see the great rivals, Argentina and Uruguay, battle it out for the inaugural title, but they were to be disappointed. The fans burned one stand and the match was abandoned before it started. A day later a rearranged match was staged at Racing Club's ground, where only 8,000 saw Argentina win 4–1. The second tournament, in 1916, was also unofficial, organized to celebrate

NO PLACE LIKE HOME *When Uruguay host the Copa America they always win it*

Argentina's centenary as an independent country. Argentina and Uruguay again clashed in the "decider", with Uruguay avenging their defeat of six years previously.

Between 1916 and 1959 the tournament was held, on average, every two years in one country. Uruguay won six of the first 11 tournaments.

Argentina then gained the upper hand winning 11 of the 18 tournaments from the 1920s to the 1950s. Brazil's four victories have all been on home soil but it was unlucky that, when they were at their peak, in the 1960s, only two tournaments were staged. Successes for the rest of the South American nations have

been few and far between. Peru won their titles in 1939 and 1975, Paraguay triumphed in 1953 and 1979. Most remarkably of all, Bolivia won in 1963 when they were hosts.

The tournament has, on all bar five occasions, been played on a group basis with no final match (there have been five championship play-offs). There is credence to the belief that the tournament had been held in disdain by some countries. Some countries entered weak or "B" teams or even youth sides. Indeed, 1975 was the first occasion on which all 10 CONMEBOL countries played.

Argentina has played host nine times, Chile seven, Uruguay six, Peru five and the indifferent Brazilians only four. The 1987 tournament was played in Argentina and won by Uruguay, repeating their 1983 triumph. Brazil hosted the 1989 event and won their first title in 40 years, while Argentina won in 1991.

In 1993, in Ecuador, the tournament underwent another face-lift. Mexico and the United States were invited to take part as guests, and three first round groups produced eight quarter-finalists. One of the invited guests, Mexico, almost spoiled the party by reaching the Final, where they lost 2–1 to Argentina. Mexico and the USA were invited again in 1995 in Uruguay and this time it was the US turn to embarrass their hosts, reaching the semi-finals before losing 1–0 to Brazil. But Brazil lost in the Final to hosts Uruguay, 5–3 in a penalty shoot-out, after a 1–1 draw.

Winners

South American Championship

1910 *Buenos Aires*: 1st Argentina, 2nd Uruguay*

1916 *Buenos Aires*: 1st Uruguay, 2nd Argentina*

1917 *Montevideo*: 1st Uruguay, 2nd Argentina

1919 *Rio de Janeiro* (play-off): Brazil 1 (Friedenreich), Uruguay 0. Att: 28,000

1920 *Vina del Mar*: 1st Uruguay, 2nd Argentina

1921 *Buenos Aires*: 1st Argentina, 2nd Brazil

1922 *Rio de Janeiro* (play-off): Brazil 3 (Formiga 2, Neco), Paraguay 1 (Rivas G.). Att: 20,000

1923 *Montevideo*: 1st Uruguay, 2nd Argentina

1924 *Montevideo*: 1st Uruguay, 2nd Argentina

1925 *Buenos Aires*: 1st Argentina, 2nd Brazil

1926 *Santiago*: 1st Uruguay, 2nd Argentina

1927 *Lima*: 1st Argentina, 2nd Uruguay

1929 *Buenos Aires*: 1st Argentina, 2nd Paraguay

1935 *Lima*: 1st Uruguay, 2nd Argentina*

1937 *Buenos Aires* (play-off): Argentina 2 (De la Mata 2), Brazil 0. Att: 80,000

1939 *Lima*: 1st Peru, 2nd Uruguay.

1941 *Santiago*: 1st Argentina, 2nd Uruguay*

1942 *Montevideo*: 1st Uruguay, 2nd Argentina

1945 *Santiago*: 1st Argentina, 2nd Brazil*

1946 *Buenos Aires*: 1st Argentina, 2nd Brazil*

1947 *Guayaquil*: 1st Argentina, 2nd Paraguay

1949 *Rio de Janeiro* (play-off): Brazil 7 (Ademir Menezes 3, Tesourinha 2, Jair R. Pinto 2), Paraguay 0. Att: 55,000

1953 *Lima* (play-off): Paraguay 3 (Lopez A., Gavilan, Fernandez R.), Brazil 2 (Baltazar 2). Att: 35,000

1955 *Santiago*: 1st Argentina, 2nd Chile

1956 *Montevideo*: 1st Uruguay, 2nd Chile*

1957 *Lima*: 1st Argentina, 2nd Brazil

1959 *Buenos Aires*: 1st Argentina, 2nd Brazil*

1959 *Guayaquil*: 1st Uruguay, 2nd Argentina

1963 *Bolivia*: 1st Bolivia, 2nd Paraguay

1967 *Montevideo*: 1st Uruguay, 2nd Argentina

1975 *Bogota* (1st leg): Colombia 1 (Castro P.), Peru 0. Att: 50,000
Lima (2nd leg): Peru 2 (Oblitas, Ramirez O.), Colombia 0. Att: 50,000
Caracas (play-off): Peru 1 (Sotil), Colombia 0. Att: 30,000

1979 *Asuncion* (1st leg): Paraguay 3 (Romero C. 2, Morel M.), Chile 0. Att: 55,000
Santiago (2nd leg): Chile 1 (Rivas), Paraguay 0. Att: 55,000
Buenos Aires (play-off): Paraguay 0, Chile 0. Att: 6,000 (*Paraguay won on goal difference*)

1983 *Montevideo* (1st leg): Uruguay 2 (Francescoli, Diogo), Brazil 0. Att: 65,000
Salvador (2nd leg): Brazil 1 (Jorginho), Uruguay 1 (Aguilera). Att: 95,000

1987 *Buenos Aires*: Uruguay 1 (Bengochea), Chile 0. Att: 35,000

1989 *Brazil*: 1st Brazil, 2nd Uruguay

1991 *Chile*: 1st Argentina, 2nd Brazil

1993 *Guayaquil*: Argentina 2 (Batistuta 2), Mexico 1 (Galindo pen.). Att: 40,000

1995 *Montevideo*: Uruguay 1 (Bengoechea 48), Brazil 1 (Tulio 30). (*Uruguay 5-3 on pens*). Att: 58,000

1997 *La Paz*: Brazil 3 (Edmundo 37, Ronaldo 79, Ze Roberto 90), Bolivia 1 (Irwin Sanchez 45). Att: 45,000

Notes: Details of finals or championship play-offs have been given where applicable. For all other tournaments, played on a league basis, only the first and second have been listed
* unofficial "extraordinarios" tournaments

EUROPEAN CHAMPIONSHIP

The European Championship, surprisingly, was the last of the continental tournaments to get under way, and was yet another French innovation. Proposed in the mid-1950s by Henri Delaunay, secretary of the French football federation, the European Nations Cup, as the event was previously known, was designed to bring together the various regional tournaments such as the British Home International Championship, the Nordic Cup and the Central European Championship for the Dr Gero Cup.

Delaunay, sadly, died before the tournament got under way, but the trophy still bears his name, and his idea has grown into the second most important international competition after the World Cup.

The first tournament was held in 1959–60, and was played on a straightforward home and away knock-out basis. A four-team final series followed, though the hosts for the final matches were not decided until the semi-finalists were known. The very first European Championship match took place in Moscow on September 28, 1958, when the Soviet Union beat Hungary 3–1 in a first round, first leg tie. Soviet winger Anatoly Ilyin scored the first ever European Championship goal after four minutes. There were many absentees from the tournament, including Sweden, Italy, West Germany, Switzerland, Holland and the four British nations.

The Eastern Bloc occupied three of the four semi-final slots in the 1960 finals, which France hosted. In the Final, Yugoslavia's all-out attack threatened to overrun the Soviets, but Lev Yashin responded with a string of fine saves. The Yugoslavs did take the lead, but the Soviets equalized almost immediately and made their superior physical strength count in extra time to win 2–1.

The 1964 finals tournament took place in Spain, where the hosts made good use of home advantage to win the trophy beating the Soviet Union in Madrid , 2–1.

The qualifying tournament was expanded to eight groups for the 1968 event. Hosts Italy beat the Soviet Union in the first semi-final, but only by the rather dubious method of tossing a coin. World champions England also reached the semi-finals, but were beaten 1–0 by Yugoslavia. The final went to a replay, where goals by Riva and Anastasi were too much for the exhausted Yugoslav players, who again had to be content with runners-up medals.

The Soviets reached their third final out of four in 1972, but were no match for the West Germans. The incomparable Gerd Müller was at his peak, and two goals by him in the Final set up a 3–0 victory, and confirmed the Germans as favourites for the World Cup to be held two years later on their home soil

The 1976 tournament threw up surprises from start to finish. England, Italy and France were eliminated in the qualifying round, and the semi-final line-up comprised surprising Czechoslovakia, 1974 World Cup winners West Germany and runners-up Holland and hosts Yugoslavia. Both semi-finals went to extra-time, the Czechs beating the Dutch 3–1 and the West Germans defeating the Yugoslavs 4–2, with a hat-trick from substitute Dieter Müller.

The Germans were clear favourites, but the Czechs had other ideas. Goals by Svehlik and Dobias gave them a 2–0 lead inside half an hour, but West Germany fought back, Holzenbein snatching an equalizer in the 89th minute. Extra time failed to separate the teams, and in the penalty shoot-out, Antonin Panenka chipped his penalty past Sepp Maier to win the trophy.

In 1980 the format for the final stages of the competition changed. The quarter-finals were abolished and the seven qualifying group winners proceeded straight to the finals along with the hosts, Italy, who received a bye direct to the final stage. The eight teams were divided into two groups of four, with the winners meeting in the final.

The Soviets failed to qualify for their "favourite" tournament, and the Yugoslavs also missed out, but there was a first ever finals appearance for Greece. Belgium proved the surprise package of the tournament, reaching the final after conquering England, Spain and Italy in the group matches. West Germany won the other group with a little to spare and became the only nation to win the trophy twice when they beat the Belgians 2–1 with two goals from Horst Hrubesch – one early in the game, the other two minutes from time. The Final was one of the few games to live up to expectations in a disappointing tournament marred by English hooligans.

The 1984 tournament was the best to date, with the flamboyant French in unstoppable form and playing at home, where new stadia were built and old ones refurbished. Semi-finals were introduced for group winners and runners-up, and although Holland, Italy, England and the Soviet Union failed to qualify, the quality of football was not diminished.

France had Michel Platini to thank for their success. His nine goals in five games was a superb achievement as the French swept aside Denmark, Belgium and Yugoslavia in the group matches. Unfancied Spain clinched the other group and then squeezed past the impressive Danes on penalties after a 1–1 draw in the semi-finals. The Final was more conclusive. Platini and Bellone scored the goals as the host country won for the third

time in seven events.

The 1988 finals in West Germany included all Europe's big names, bar the French, plus one new one: the Republic of Ireland. The Irish shocked lacklustre England in their first game and almost qualified for the semi-finals, but lost 1–0 to a late Dutch goal from Wim Kieft, a miscued header which spun past Pat Bonner into the Irish net.

The Soviet Union qualified with Holland to reach the semi-finals, where they met – and beat – Italy and West Germany respectively. With Rinus Michels in charge, the Dutch played irresistible football, beating the hosts 2–1 in the semi-final with a splendidly taken goal by Marco Van Basten two minutes from time. Van Basten did even better in the Final against the Soviet Union, crashing home a volley from an almost impossible angle to seal a 2–0 victory following Ruud Gullit's first-half opener.

Sweden hosted the 1992 finals. They and Scotland were making their debut in the finals and the now former Soviet Union played under the banner of Commonwealth of Independent States, but the biggest surprises were Denmark, last-minute replacements for the suspended Yugoslavia. They arrived with little time to prepare and walked off with the trophy!

Defending champions Holland impressed in the group matches, but were then victims of an old complaint: over-confidence. In the semi-final the Danes led twice in a 2–2 draw and then won 5–4 on penalties. In the other semi the Germans beat the hosts 3–2, having been two up, and looked set to claim their third European crown. But the hard-working, though injury-hit, Danish side confounded the experts by deservedly winning 2–0 with an outstanding display of counter-attacking football.

Finals

European Championship Finals

1960 *Paris:* Soviet Union 2 (Metreveli, Ponedelnik), Yugoslavia 1 (Galic). Att: 18,000
1964 *Madrid:* Spain 2 (Pereda, Marcelino), Soviet Union 1

(Khusainov). Att: 105,000
1968 *Rome:* Italy 1 (Domenghini), Yugoslavia 1 (Dzajic). Att: 85,000.
Replay – *Rome:* Italy 2 (Riva, Anastasi), Yugoslavia 0. Att: 85,000
1972 *Brussels:* West Germany 3 (Müller G. 2, Wimmer), Soviet

Union 0. Att: 65,000
1976 *Belgrade:* Czechoslovakia 2 (Svehlik, Dobias), West Germany 2 (Müller D., Holzenbein) (aet). Czechoslovakia won 5–4 on penalties. Att: 45,000
1980 *Rome:* West Germany 2

(Hrubesch 2), Belgium 1 (Vandereycken). Att: 48,000
1984 *Paris:* France 2 (Platini, Bellone), Spain 0. Att: 47,000
1988 *Munich:* Holland 2 (Gullit, Van Basten), Soviet Union 0. Att: 72,000

1992 *Stockholm:* Denmark 2 (Jensen, Vilfort), Germany 0. Att: 37,000

Euro 96
When Football
Came Home

Germany won the European Championship for a record third time when they beat the outsiders from the Czech Republic 2–1 at Wembley – the first time the controversial golden goal rule had settled a major event. Substitute Oliver Bierhoff was their two-goal hero. But hosts England were indirect winners as well for the staging of the most prestigious European event, mixing drama on the pitch with enthusiastic, welcoming support off it as well as a national team which rose to the occasion in magnificent style to reach the semi-finals.

Not that England's national team looked ready to party in the Opening Match against Switzerland. Perhaps it was the pressure of the nation's first serious competitive international since the autumn of 1993; perhaps it was the heat; perhaps it was the media fury provoked by the manner in which the players had let their hair down before the finals; perhaps it was the pressure of an occasion prefaced by a uniquely home-grown opening ceremony.

One of the tableaux – among the sky divers and the Red Arrows – was a pageant in which St George slew the dragon. To the disappointment of the Wembley crowd, England could not emulate their patron saint. A promising first half was followed by a weary stand-off in the second. To match the pattern of play England scored first, through Alan Shearer, and Switzerland crowned their comeback with a late penalty-spot equalizer from Kubilay Turkyilmaz.

England expects

Scotland opened their campaign with a rousing 0–0 draw against Holland but they were fortunate when Swedish referee Leif Sundell failed to spot a handled, goal-line clearance by John Collins in the opening exchanges. If Sundell had not been unsighted then Scotland would not only have conceded but been reduced to 10 men by Collins's virtually certain expulsion.

The Tartan Army had long been concerned by their favourites'

failure up front. It was to be their Achilles' heel in the so-called Battle of Britain against England at Wembley. Scotland's luckless skipper, Gary McAllister, even missed a penalty when his full-power spot-kick ricocheted over the bar off goalkeeper David Seaman's left elbow.

England, by contrast, crowned a spirited second-half display by scoring twice. First Shearer headed his second goal of the tournament then Paul Gascoigne, prime target of tabloid attack, flicked a pass from Darren Anderton skilfully past Colin Hendry before volleying perhaps the Goal of the Tournament.

. On the face of it, the last match day appeared to be a diplomatic straight jacket. A draw for England vs. Holland and both would qualify for the quarter-finals with Scotland and Switzerland comfortably eliminated. But that was to reckon without the rapidly increasing confidence filling the England team – and the fatal complacency which Holland brought into the Wembley clash. England's finest display since at least the 1990 World Cup earned a 4–1 victory. Remarkably, the humiliated Dutch still qualified thanks to a late consolation goal from substitute Patrick Kluivert which rendered null and void Scotland's 1–0 win over the Swiss at Villa Park, Birmingham.

A close run thing

Group B opened with a temperamental clash between Bulgaria and Spain at Elland Road, Leeds. Bulgarian defender Petar Hubchev and Spain striker Juan Pizzi were sent off in a 1–1 draw from which Spain snatched a point courtesy of a first-touch goal from newly arrived substitute Alfonso. Bulgaria fumed over the linesman whose mistaken flag denied them a superb "goal" by Hristo Stoichkov.

Spain qualified after a second 1–1 draw, against France, and a dramatic 2–1 win over Romania. The Balkans' third defeat in three matches was not the way in which midfield general Gheorghe Hagi had hoped to celebrate his 100th international appearance.

France finished top of the group. They opened with a 1–0 win

INSTANT HERO *Alan Shearer celebrates his semi-final goal against Germany*

presented to them on a plate by Romania's eccentric goalkeeper Bogdan Stelea. He knocked over his own central defender, Gheorghe Mihali, chasing a cross which bobbled into goal off the head of Milan-bound striker Christophe Dugarry. The subsequent 1–1 draw against Spain set France up for a 1–0 win over Bulgaria which avenged a string of humiliations at the eastern Europeans' hands.

Croatia impress

The confrontation of eastern European pride and western European fantasy was repeated in Group D where international newcomers Croatia cruised through with the electric-heeled Portuguese. The victims were Turkey and defending champions Denmark.

Croatia barely justified the popular belief that they were dark horses. They struggled to beat Turkey 1–0 in their first game thanks to a fine breakaway goal from Goran Vlaovic and, mistakenly shuffling the player pack, crashed 3–0 to Portugal in their group finale. The reason this did not prove fatal was down to a superb second-half display against Denmark second time out.

Even the great Peter Schmeichel was outgunned by the inspiration of Croat striker Davor Suker. He scored twice – once from a penalty – created the other Croat goal for Zvonimir Boban and produced one of the finals' most outstanding pieces of

individual virtuosity when he very nearly lobbed Schmeichel from the half-way line.

Even Croatia had to give way at the top of the group to Portugal. The so-called "Brazilians of Europe" entertained fans with a fascinating brand of delicate touch and bewildering positional inter-change. Their only weakness, going forward, appeared to be the lack of a killer touch in front of goal, which, ultimately, proved fatal.

Italian disappointment

It was not only Portugal who needed such a marksman in their team. Italy themselves were the shock first-round failures precisely because they could not score the goals they needed.

First-time out the Italians might have beaten Russia more easily than 2–1 had Fabrizio Ravanelli converted two easy chances in the closing 10 minutes after he arrived as a substitute. Second-time out Italy should have at least salvaged a draw from a thrilling match against the Czech Republic. Italy played more than half the game with 10 men after the expulsion of defender Luigi Apolloni and would have gained the draw they merited had Pierluigi Casiraghi not missed from point-blank range in the last minute.

Similarly, third time out. That shock defeat by the badly under-rated Czechs left Italy needing to beat group leaders Germany at Old Trafford while depending, simultaneously, on the outcome of the

Czechs' Anfield clash with home-ward-bound Russia.

Italy, boasting the greatest depth of natural talent in the finals, dominated the entire 90 minutes. But they fell victim to an incident reminiscent of France's gallant semi-final failure against these same Germans in 1982. Again the German goalkeeper was the centre of controversy because, having committed a blatant foul, he was not sent off. In 1982 it was Toni Schumacher; in 1996 it was Andy Köpke. Belgian referee Guy Goethals' failure to expel him for upending Casiraghi in the eighth minute had seismic consequences because Köpke then saved Gianfranco Zola's penalty.

Italy, for all their possession, for all their corners and free kicks around the German penalty box, failed to create any clear-cut chances. Ten minutes from time, when Russia went 3–2 ahead against the Czechs, Italy were in the quarter-finals. Two minutes from time, when Russia were pegged back to 3–3, Italy were out. Paolo Maldini may have been by far the greatest player on view at the finals. It mattered nothing. He – and Italy – were on their way home.

Cautious quarter-finals

Oddly, the quality of football on view nose-dived once the knock-out stages had been reached. Only one of the quarter-finals provided any serious entertainment and even that – England vs. Spain – had to be settled by one of the six penalty shoot-outs which were ultimately needed.

England started like a train and it took the sharpest of goalkeeper Zubizarreta's reflexes to deny Alan Shearer in the opening minutes. As the match wore on, however, Spain drew some pretty patterns in midfield and veteran striker Julio Salinas had a goal ruled out for offside by the linesman – wrongly as television replays proved. Spain grew even more upset with French referee Marc Batta when he twice refused penalty claims – once when Paul Gascoigne tripped Alfonso and once when Tony Adams cleared away Jose Luis Caminero's foot as well as the ball.

Ultimately the match became the first in the history of the European Championship to be subject to the Golden Goal regulation – without success. Neither team managed an extra-time winner and so the outcome went to penalties. Stuart Pearce fired in one kick for England to avenge his 1990 World Cup failure and then David Seaman saved, decisively, from Spain's Miguel Angel Nadal.

Penalties were also needed after France and Holland failed to provide the contest expected of two of Europe's most creative nations. This time Holland's Clarence Seedorf was the luckless shoot-out scapegoat as France scraped into the last four to meet a Czech Republic side who had surprisingly defeated Portugal 1–0 at Villa Park with perhaps the goal of the tournament. Karel Poborski, his shoulder-length hair twisting in the breeze, ran through the heart of the Portuguese defence then contrived a most delicate chip over Vitor Baia for the only goal.

The remaining quarter-final was the nastiest match of the tournament. Croatia, forgetting all their ambassadorial responsibilities, kicked Germany all over Old Trafford. Davor Suker did score one superb goal but Germany survived the loss of injury-battered Jürgen Klinsmann and Fredi Bobic to win 2–1.

Semi-final epic

Of the two semi-finals, only one mattered to the hosts: England vs. Germany, the latest episode in one

CHAMPIONS *German skipper Jürgen Klinsmann raises the trophy*

of international football's longest-running dramatic presentations.

Whoever won would be favourites for the Final – especially when the Czech Republic won another shoot-out to beat France after a 0–0 draw at Old Trafford. The French were toothless in the absence of injured centre-forward Christophe Dugarry. They leaned far too heavily on the creative talents of Youri Djorkaeff who came closest to a goal with a thundering drive which ricocheted off the Czech crossbar. That meant another penalty shoot-out in which Nantes' Reynald Pedros emulated the semi-final failures of Didier Six and Maxime Bossis in the 1982 World Cup.

England vs. Germany also went to a penalty shoot-out. But, unlike France vs. Czech Republic, it also provided a night of exciting intensity which a 76,000 crowd at Wembley and 26 million domestic television viewers will never forget. England secured a magnificent start, Shearer heading home in the third minute. Germany, with only one fit striker, responded with courage and invention and that lone raider, Stefan Kuntz, equalized in the 15th minute.

The game was an emotional roller-coaster and produced ultimately, one of the most thrilling extra-time spectacles Wembley has ever witnessed. Darren Anderton was an inch from the Golden Goal when his shot struck a post. Then Germany thought they had it as Kuntz headed past Seaman, only for referee Sandor Puhl to penalize the German for pushing. And so to penalties.

Both England and Germany converted their five regulation efforts. Then Gareth Southgate ran up for England ... and pushed his kick low into the grateful arms of German keeper Andy Köpke. Andy Möller ran up for Germany ... and shot them into the Final.

Germany lay Wembley ghosts to rest

Domestic euphoria might have been punctured like a toy balloon. Yet it said everything for the manner in which Euro 96 had gripped the public imagination that 73,611 turned out for the Final. The vast majority – English fans converted into honorary

Czechs for the night – were celebrating when Patrik Berger fired home a 59th-minute penalty.

Germany had lost to underdogs in the Final – against Denmark – four years earlier in Sweden and history appeared about to repeat itself. Then German coach Berti Vogts played his hidden ace, bringing on substitute centre-forward Oliver Bierhoff. Within four minutes Bierhoff had headed the Germans level then, in the fourth minute of extra time, he fired home the Golden Goal.

The Czechs protested that Kuntz had been standing in an offside position, but Italian referee Pierluigi Pairetto waved away their protests. An Italian linesman had proved a winner for Germany in the stadium where a Georgian had proved a loser in the World Cup 30 years earlier.

Unlike that World Cup, the hosts had not lifted the trophy. But they won just about everything else. Outgoing coach Terry Venables' last duty was to accept the UEFA Fair Play trophy and Shearer was crowned the tournament's five-goal top scorer. But, more than any individual, it was English football as a whole which was the winner. No game was blighted by hooliganism in or around the stadia. English football had been rehabilitated in the eyes of the world. What better time then, than the day after the Final for the FA to announce England's candidacy to host the World Cup itself in 2006?

Final
Czech Republic (0) 1   Germany (0) 2
(Berger 59 pen)   *(Bierhoff 72, 94)*
After extra time (1–1 at 90 min.)

CZECH REPUBLIC: Kouba, Rada, Kadlec, Suchoparek, Hornak, Nedved, Bejbl, Berger, Nemec, Poborski (Smicer 88), Kuka.
GERMANY: Köpke, Babbel, Sammer, Helmer, Strunz, Scholl (Bierhoff 69), Eilts (Bode 46), Hässler, Ziege, Klinsmann, Kuntz.

Att: 73,611 Ref: Pairetto (Italy)

Leading scorers
5 Alan Shearer (England).
3 Hristo Stoichkov (Bulgaria), Jürgen Klinsmann (Germany), Brian Laudrup (Denmark), Davor Suker (Croatia).
2 Pierluigi Casiraghi (Italy), Teddy Sheringham (England), Oliver Bierhoff (Germany), Matthias Sammer (Germany).

CLUB COMPETITIONS

WORLD CLUB CUP

The World Club Cup is not, as its name suggests, open to every side in the world. In reality it is a challenge match between the champions of Europe and the champions of South America. Asia, Africa and the rest of the world do not get a look in …yet. FIFA are now considering plans to expand the tournament to include the best sides from each of the continental confederations in an end-of-season event in years in between World Cups and European Championships. The idea is still in its infancy and may never come to fruition.

Henri Delaunay, UEFA general secretary, first suggested the idea of a challenge match between the champions of Europe and South America in a letter to CONMEBOL, the South American Confederation, in 1958. His idea provided the impetus for them to get the Copa Libertadores (the South American Club Cup) up and running because, at that stage, South America had no continental championship for its clubs, even though an event for national sides had been taking place since 1910.

Before 1980, matches in the World Club Cup, or Intercontinental Cup as it is sometimes known, were played on a home and away basis, and up until 1968 the result was decided by points, not the aggregate score. This meant that if the clubs won one match each or both were drawn, a decider had to be played. Until 1964 this decider had, for reasons never fully explained, to take place on the ground of the team who played at home in the second leg, giving them a massive advantage. Then for another four years the decider at least had to be played on that club's continent.

Despite these tortuous rules, the competition got off to a flying start in 1960, when Real Madrid met Penarol of Uruguay. Madrid had just won their fifth European Cup in a row, with a 7–3 demolition of Ein-tracht Frankfurt, while Penarol had become the first winners of the Copa Libertadores. The first leg, in Montevideo, produced a 0–0 draw, but in the return two months later Real Madrid pounded the Uruguayans 5–1. The Real forward line was one of the best ever, and contained Del Sol, Di Stefano, Gento and Puskas, who scored twice. A combined attendance of 200,000 saw the matches.

In 1961 it was Penarol's turn to chalk up five goals, this time against the emerging Portuguese eagles, Benfica. However, a solitary Coluna goal in the first leg meant a decider was necessary, and Penarol only just managed to win 2–1 at home against a Benfica side bolstered by a young Eusebio, who was specially flown in.

Benfica represented Europe again in 1962, but this time they ran head-long into Brazil's Santos …and Pele. The "Black Pearl" scored twice in Rio as Santos narrowly won 3–2, and then scored a breathtaking hat-trick in Lisbon as Benfica crashed to a 5–2 home defeat. Santos became one of only four sides to retain the trophy when they beat Milan in 1963. Both teams won 4–2 at home, but the decider provided a nasty taste of things to come, with a player from each side sent off and a penalty deciding the outcome, in favour of the Brazilians, who were without Pele for the second and third games.

The next two editions were contested by Internazionale of Italy and Independiente of Argentina, with Inter winning on both occasions. A goal by Corso in a decider in Madrid was enough in 1964, and the following year Inter drew 0–0 away and won the home leg 3–0 to retain the trophy. Among the famous names in the Inter line-up were Suarez, Mazzola and Fachetti.

In 1966 Penarol returned to win for the third time, beating Real Madrid 2–0 in both legs, with Spencer scoring three of the Uruguayans' goals. From this encouraging start, the World Club Cup ran into severe problems in the late 1960s and early 1970s, largely owing to different styles of play and behaviour.

The 1967 series paired Argentina's Racing Club with Scotland's Celtic. Feelings in Argentina were still running high over their 1966 World Cup quarter-final elimination by England, and the matches degenerated into a bad-tempered farce. After a 1–0 Celtic win in Glasgow, the return in Buenos Aires was chaotic. Celtic goalkeeper Ronnie Simpson was struck by a missile from the crowd before the kick-off, and could not play. Racing won 2–1 to set up a decider, in Montevideo, which was doomed before it began. Celtic lost their composure under extreme provocation and had four men sent off after Basile had spat at Lennox. Racing also had

WORLD'S BEST *Barcelona's Dane Michael Laudrup takes the ball away from São Paulo's Rai in Tokyo in 1992*

two men sent off but won 1–0.

It was extremely unfortunate, therefore, that the next team to represent South America – for three years running – were Estudiantes de la Plata of Argentina, a team who were solely interested in winning, and would stop at nothing to do it. At home in 1968 they battered Manchester United, who had Nobby Stiles sent off for a gesture to a linesman and Bobby Charlton taken off with a shin injury caused by a kick from Pachame. In the return at Old Trafford, Medina and Best were sent off for fighting as, under the competition's revised rules, the Argentinians completed a 2–1 aggregate win. The violence was so bad that FIFA president Sir Stanley Rous was prompted to write a letter of complaint to the Estudiantes hierarchy.

The following year, 1969, Milan came off even worse than United. After winning 3–0 at home, Milan were savaged in Buenos Aires, where Combin had his nose broken and Prati was kicked in the back while receiving treatment, but managed to hold on for a 4–2 aggregate victory.

Three Estudiantes players were imprisoned after the game for their outrageous behaviour and were given severe suspensions at the request of the Argentinian president.

Sadly, Estudiantes did not learn their lesson, and things were as bad in 1970 when they played Feyenoord, who came out on top after drawing the drawing the first leg in Buenos Aires. In the return in Rotterdam, Feyenoord's bespectacled Van Deale had his glasses smashed early in the game but still scored the winner. Feyenoord made it known that they would not have taken part in a decider if it had been needed, and the following year their countrymen, Ajax, went a step further by refusing to play against Nacional of Uruguay. Panathinaikos, beaten finalists in the European Cup, were appointed by UEFA to replace Ajax, and put up a brave performance before losing 3–2 on aggregate.

After such violent clashes, the value of the competition came into question, and it looked as if the World Club Cup would fade into history. Ajax did restore some credibility

with a fine 4–1 aggregate win over Independiente in 1972, despite some rough treatment for Johan Cruyff, but the trend they started the year before continued throughout the 1970s.

Rather than risk their valuable players being mangled by the South Americans, Ajax, Liverpool, Bayern Munich and Nottingham Forest refused to take part, reducing the competition to a side-show. On all bar two occasions, 1975 and 1978 (when the competition was not held), the beaten European Cup finalists substituted for the real champions – Atletico Madrid even managing a victory in 1974 against Independiente, who were making the fourth of their six appearances in the event. Clearly this situation could not continue and it is, ironically, Japan we have to thank for the event's survival.

In 1980 the format of the World Club Cup was changed. The two-legged tie was replaced by a single game at the National Stadium in Tokyo. The car manufacturers Toyota sponsor the competition.

The tournament has now regained much of its credibility, and since 1980

the European and South American champions have consistently taken part. The South Americans won the first five matches played in Tokyo, with the Europeans enjoying more success in the second half of the decade. In 1991 Red Star Belgrade became the first Eastern European side to win when they beat Chile's Colo Colo 3–0, with two goals from midfielder Vladimir Jugovic – whose European Cup-winning penalty in 1996 would earn Juventus another crack at the crown.

In the meantime, Barcelona and Milan (twice), however highly-rated in Europe, were successively dismissed by São Paulo (twice) and Argentina's Velez Sarsfield. While European commentators called Milan the world's best, their duel with São Paulo suggested otherwise. The Brazilians were coached by ex-World Cup boss Tele Santana and well-balanced through the experience of veterans Toninho Cerezo and Muller and new heroes Rai, Cafu and Juninho.

Not until 1995 did Europe regain the trophy and then they clung on to it. First Ajax needed a penalty shoot-out to defeat yet another contestant

---

Winners

World Club Cup Finals

1960 *Montevideo*: Penarol 0, Real Madrid 0. Att: 75,000
Madrid: Real Madrid 5 (Puskas 2, Di Stefano, Herrera, Gento), Penarol 1 (Borges). Att: 125,000
1961 *Lisbon*: Benfica 1 (Coluna), Penarol 0. Att: 50,000
Montevideo: Penarol 5 (Sasia, Joya 2, Spencer 2), Benfica 0. Att: 56,000
Montevideo (play-off): Penarol 2 (Sasia 2), Benfica 1 (Eusebio). Att: 62,000
1962 *Rio de Janeiro*: Santos 3 (Pele 2, Coutinho), Benfica 2 (Santana 2). Att: 90,000
Lisbon: Benfica 2 (Eusebio, Santana), Santos 5 (Pele 3, Coutinho, Pepe). Att: 75,000
1963 *Milan*: Milan 4 (Trapattoni, Amarildo 2, Mora), Santos 2 (Pele 2). Att: 80,000
Rio de Janeiro: Santos 4 (Pepe 2, Almir, Lima), Milan 2 (Altafini, Mora). Att: 150,000
Rio de Janeiro (play-off): Santos 1 (Dalmo), Milan 0. Att: 121,000
1964 *Avellanada*: Independiente 1 (Rodriguez), Internazionale 0. Att: 70,000
Milan: Internazionale 2 (Mazzola, Corso), Independiente 0. Att: 70,000

Milan (play-off): Internazionale 1 (Corso), Independiente 0 (aet). Att: 45,000
1965 *Milan*: Internazionale 3 (Peiro, Mazzola 2), Independiente 0. Att: 70,000
Avellanada: Independiente 0, Internazionale 0. Att: 70,000
1966 *Montevideo*: Penarol 2 (Spencer 2), Real Madrid 0. Att: 70,000
Madrid: Real Madrid 0, Penarol 2 (Rocha, Spencer). Att: 70,000
1967 *Glasgow*: Celtic 1 (McNeill), Racing Club 0. Att: 103,000.
Avellanada: Racing Club 2 (Raffo, Cardenas), Celtic 1 (Gemmell). Att: 80,000
Montevideo (play-off): Racing Club 1 (Cardenas), Celtic 0. Att: 65,000.
1968 *Buenos Aires*: Estudiantes 1 (Conigliaro), Manchester United 0. Att: 65,000
Manchester: Manchester United 1 (Morgan), Estudiantes 1 (Veron). Att: 60,000
1969 *Milan*: Milan 3 (Sormani 2, Combin), Estudiantes 0. Att: 80,000
Buenos Aires: Estudiantes 2 (Conigliaro, Aguirre-Suarez), Milan 1 (Rivera). Att: 65,000. Milan won 4–2 on aggregate
1970 *Buenos Aires*: Estudiantes 2 (Echecopar, Veron), Feyenoord 2 (Kindvall, Van Hanegem).

Att: 65,000
Rotterdam: Feyenoord 1 (Van Deale), Estudiantes 0. Att: 70,000. Feyenoord won 3–2 on aggregate.
1971 *Athens*: Panathinaikos 1 (Filakouris), Nacional (Uru) 1 (Artime). Att: 60,000
Montevideo: Nacional 2 (Artime 2), Panathinaikos 1 (Filakouris). Att: 70,000. Nacional won 3–2 on aggregate
1972 *Avellanada*: Independiente 1 (Sa), Ajax 1 (Cruyff). Att: 65,000.
Amsterdam: Ajax 3 (Neeskens, Rep 2), Independiente 0. Att: 60,000. Ajax won 4–1 on aggregate
1973 *Rome* (single match): Independiente 1 (Bochini 40), Juventus 0. Att: 35,000
1974 *Buenos Aires*: Independiente 1 (Balbuena 33), Atletico Madrid 0. Att: 60,000
Madrid: Atletico Madrid 2 (Irureta 21, Ayala 86), Independiente 0. Att: 45,000. Atletico won 2–1 on aggregate
1975 not played.
1976 *Munich*: Bayern Munich 2 (Müller, Kapellmann), Cruzeiro 0. Att: 22,000
Belo Horizonte: Cruzeiro 0, Bayern Munich 0. Att: 114,000. Bayern won 2–0 on aggregate
1977 *Buenos Aires*: Boca Juniors 2 (Mastrangelo, Ribolzi), Borussia

Monchengladbach 2 (Hannes, Bonhof). Att: 50,000
Karlsruhe: Borussia Mönchengladbach 0, Boca Juniors 3 (Zanabria, Mastrangelo, Salinas). Att: 21,000. Boca Juniors won 5–2 on aggregate
1978 not played.
1979 *Malmö*: Malmö 0, Olimpia 1 (Isasi). Att: 4,000
Asuncion: Olimpia 2 (Solalinde, Michelagnoli), Malmö 1 (Earlandsson). Att: 35,000. Olimpia won 3–1 on aggregate
1980 *Tokyo*: Nacional (Uru) 1 (Victorino), Nottingham Forest 0. Att: 62,000
1981 *Tokyo*: Flamengo 3 (Nunes 2, Adilio), Liverpool 0. Att: 62,000
1982 *Tokyo*: Penarol 2 (Jair, Charrua), Aston Villa 0. Att: 62,000
1983 *Tokyo*: Gremio 2 (Renato 2), Hamburg SV 1 (Schroder). Att: 62,000
1984 *Tokyo*: Independiente 1 (Percudiani), Liverpool 0. Att: 62,000
1985 *Tokyo*: Juventus 2 (Platini, Laudrup M.), Argentinos Juniors 2 (Ereros, Castro) (aet). Att: 62,000 (*Juventus won 4–2 on penalties*)
1986 *Tokyo*: River Plate 1 (Alzamendi), Steaua Bucharest 0. Att: 62,000
1987 *Tokyo*: FC Porto 2 (Gomes, Madjer), Penarol 1 (Viera) (aet). Att: 45,000

1988 *Tokyo*: Nacional (Uru) 2 (Ostolaza 2), PSV Eindhoven 2 (Romario, Koeman R.) (aet). Att: 62,000
(*Nacional won 7–6 on penalties*)
1989 *Tokyo*: Milan 1 (Evani), Nacional (Col) 0 (aet). Att: 62,000
1990 *Tokyo*: Milan 3 (Rijkaard 2, Stroppa), Olimpia 0. Att: 60,000
1991 *Tokyo*: Red Star Belgrade 3 (Jugovic 2, Pancev), Colo Colo 0. Att: 60,000
1992 *Tokyo*: São Paulo 2 (Rai 2), Barcelona 1 (Stoichkov). Att: 80,000
1993 *Tokyo*: São Paulo 3 (Palinha, Cerezo, Müller), Milan 2 (Massaro, Papin). Att: 52,000
1994 *Tokyo*: Velez Sarsfield 2 (Trott, Abad), Milan 0. Att: 65,000
1995 *Tokyo*: Ajax 0, Gremio 0 (aet). Att: 62,000 (*Ajax won 4–3 on penalties*)
1996 *Tokyo*: Juventus 1 (Del Piero), River Place 0. Att: 55,000

Notes:
From 1960 to 1979 the World Club Cup was decided on points, not goal difference. Since 1980 it has been a one-off match in Tokyo.

the Cup because, without the English clubs, who had such a fine record in the competition, winning it was less satisfactory. Meanwhile the hooligan problem still remained.

In 1986 Romania's Steaua Bucharest became the first Eastern European side to win the Cup, beating Barcelona – coached by Terry Venables – in Seville. The Final, however, was one of the worst in the tournament's history; still goalless after extra time, the penalty shoot-out produced only two successful kicks – both for the Romanian army club.

Portugal's FC Porto won in 1987 in Vienna with a fine 2–1 win over the favourites Bayern Munich, having been a goal down. PSV Eindhoven became Holland's third European champions when they beat poor old Benfica in 1988. A dull 0–0 draw in Stuttgart was followed by a 6–5 penalty win for the Dutch team.

Milan then returned to reclaim the trophy. Free from the restrictions on importing foreign players, and backed by media magnate Silvio Berlusconi's money, Milan bought the best and beat the rest. Their Dutch axis of Frank Rijkaard, Ruud Gullit and Marco Van Basten steered them to a crushing 4–0 victory over Steaua in 1989, Gullit and Van Basten both scoring twice, while a single goal from Rijkaard was enough to beat the perennial bridesmaids Benfica in 1990.

BACK ON TOP *Karlheinz Riedle celebrates his second goal in the 1997 Cup Final*

In 1991 English clubs were back in the running, but it was Yugoslavia's Red Star Belgrade and Marseille who met in the Final in Bari.

France, originators of the European Cup, were still hoping for a first ever victory … but the wait had to go on. Red Star abandoned their free-flowing, attacking style of play in favour of a blanket defence approach designed to stifle president Bernard Tapie's expensively assembled French champions. The plan worked. Red Star took the game to penalties and won the shoot-out 5–3, to become the second side from the East to be crowned European champions.

The format of the competition was radically changed in 1992, after direct pressure from Europe's bigger clubs who have made no secret of their desire to see a European Super League formed. The quarter-finals and semi-finals were replaced with two groups of four, playing home and away, to produce the two finalists. Johan Cruyff's Barcelona took the Cup for the first time – completing a hat-trick of European trophies – by beating Italy's Sampdoria 1–0 at Wembley with a rocket free-kick by Ronald Koeman.

Then, in 1993, came the biggest scandal the competition has ever witnessed. After 37 long years, the French drought in the European Cup seemed to have ended. Marseille beat Milan 1–0 in Munich, with a goal by centre-back Basile Boli, but the celebrations were cut short when it emerged that Marseille officials had allegedly paid three Valenciennes players to "take it easy" in a league game shortly before the Final. Chaos ensued, but in the end, Marseille were stripped of their European crown, their French title and the right to play São Paulo in the World Club Cup. Marseille's outspoken owner – socialist, millionaire and politician Tapie – threatened all sorts of lawsuits and legal actions, but in the end had to accept that Marseille's victory would be expunged from the record. So France still waits for its first European Cup, or any European trophy for that matter.

The format changed slightly again for the 1994 tournament, with the reintroduction of semi-finals for the winners and runners-up of the two Champions League groups. But nothing could stop Milan, their 4–0 defeat of Barceona was a stunning display.

Yet more tinkering with the format followed in 1994–95 as UEFA sought a compromise with the bigger clubs' desire for a TV-bankrolled European League.

The holders and top seeded teams went through directly to the Champions League, which was expanded to 16 teams in four groups of four; the eight other teams came from a preliminary round involving the teams ranked eight to 23 in the seeding list. All the other "minnow" national champions were off-loaded

---

---

into an expanded UEFA Cup. Basically, the European Cup, as we have known and loved it for almost 40 years, has ceased to exist.

Not all the seeded teams qualified; for the quarter-finals in 1994–95; Manchester United came third in a group topped by Swedish qualifiers Gothenburg and Barcelona, and a sluggish Milan, having had three points deducted in the wake of a bottle-throwing incident, needed a 1–0 victory against Casino Salzburg to go through.

The first redeveloped Champions League Cup Final – as it was clumsily repackaged – was won by Ajax of Amsterdam, who defeated Milan 1–0 in the Final in Vienna.

Ajax's success generated enormous interest in the Dutch club's youth development system. But big money spoke louder in 1996 when they lost in a penalty shoot-out to Juventus in Rome. The Italian club, just for good measure, thrashed Ajax in the 1997 semi-finals but were then themselves beaten, surprisingly decisively by 3–1, by Borussia Dortmund.

Two goals from Karlheinz Riedle and another by Lars Ricken, within 20 seconds of his appearance as a second-half substitute, shook Juventus out of their pretty patterns. Remarkably it was the first German victory in the European club game's most prestigious event since 1983 when Hamburg had also beaten Juventus.

EUROPEAN CUP-WINNERS' CUP

The European Cup-winners' Cup was originated by the organizing committee of the Mitropa Cup, and began in the 1960–61 season. Following the success of the European Cup, it seemed a logical step to introduce a competition for the winners of national knock-out competitions. However, many European countries did not have a knock-out competition and it was only in Britain, where the Cup dates back further than the League, that cup competitions fired the imagination of both the clubs and the public. Consequently, in many countries, new competitions were introduced, or old ones were revived.

Run along the same lines as the European Cup – home and away knock-out up to the Final, which was initially a two-leg, but is now a one-off match – the first Cup-winners' Cup attracted entrants from 10 countries. Vorwärts Berlin, Red Star Brno, Ferencvaros and Rangers contested the qualifying round to decide the quarter-final line-up. Rangers, having disposed of Ferencvaros, demolished West Germany's Borussia Mönchengladbach 11–0 on aggregate in the quarter-finals, before overcoming Wolverhampton Wanderers in an all-British semi-final. Italy's Fiorentina – European Cup finalists four years previously – beat FC Luzern 9–2 in the quarter-finals, before beating Dinamo Zagreb 4–2 on aggregate in the semi-finals.

The Final, played over two legs for the first and only time, saw Fiorentina at their best – defending solidly while always retaining the ability to break quickly, led by Swedish winger Kurt Hamrin. In the first leg, in Glasgow, Fiorentina frustrated the Rangers forwards, while Hamrin twice led the charge for Milani to score. In the return Hamrin again proved the match-winner, setting up Milani for the first and scoring the winner after Scott had equalized.

The success of the first tournament encouraged more clubs to get involved, and 23 entered the second in 1961–62. Swansea Town and Floriana of Malta were among them, clearly attracted by the prospect of money-spinning ties with some of Europe's biggest clubs and by the outside possibility of a "giant-killing". It was not to be, though, as both went out in the preliminary round – Swansea beaten 7–3 on aggregate by Motor Jena, Floriana trounced 15–4 by Ujpest Dozsa.

MERRY MILLER *The Aberdeen skipper leads the celebrations in 1983*

Fiorentina's impressive defence took them all the way again in 1962, where they met Atletico Madrid in the Final, now played as a one-off. The match, in Glasgow, produced a disappointing 1–1 draw, and when the replay took place – four months later – Atletico won the Cup with a straightforward 3–0 win.

In the 1963 competition the holders again reached the Final, and again they lost. Atletico faced Tottenham in Rotterdam and could not contain Bill Nicholson's international-packed side, who had won the FA Cup in successive seasons. Jimmy Greaves and Terry Dyson both scored twice as Tottenham won 5–1 to become the first English winners of a European trophy.

Tottenham's reign ended in the second round in 1964, when they were unfortunate to be drawn against Manchester United, who won 4–2 on aggregate. United fell in the quarter-finals to Portugal's Sporting Lisbon, who went on to win the Cup against MTK Budapest, although they needed a 1–0 replay win after a 3–3 draw in Belgium.

The Cup-winners' Cup had now established itself on the European scene, and 30 clubs entered the 1965 tournament. West Ham United, essentially novices at the European game, emulated Tottenham's success by beating TSV Munich 1860 in front of a full house at Wembley. The match was fast and open, but two goals in two minutes by reserve winger Tony Sealey won the Cup for the Londoners.

The following year, 1966, featured another England-West Germany Final, this time involving Liverpool and Borussia Dortmund. On a rain-lashed night in Glasgow, the Germans were slightly fortunate to win in extra time when a mis-hit lob by Libuda was deflected in by Yeats. Rangers returned for the 1967 Final, also against a German club, Bayern Munich – and were strangely out of sorts. Gerd Müller was well shackled but in the 18th minute of extra time Roth fired home the winner to keep the Cup in Germany. Another German club, Hamburg, contested the 1968 Final, but were no match for Milan, for whom Hamrin scored

2–2 draw at Stamford Bridge in the first leg of the Final, only for the Spaniards to win the return 6–0 – Suarez and Evaristo each scoring twice. Barcelona's win was the first of six in a row by Latin clubs in the competition, in keeping with the European Cup, which was also dominated by Latin sides in the early years of its existence.

The second tournament, 1958–60, drew 16 entrants, mostly club sides, and was played on a straight home-and-away knock-out basis. Barcelona, strengthened by the arrivals of Hungary's Sandor Kocsis and Zoltan Czibor, retained the trophy without losing a match. Their opponents were again English, but this time it was Birmingham and not London who made it to the Final. A 0–0 draw on a terrible pitch in Birmingham set Barcelona up for the 4–1 return win, with goals by Martinez, Czibor (two) and Coll.

Barcelona's attempt to win a hat-trick of Fairs Cups ended in the second round of the 1960–61

NO WAY *Butcher of Ipswich tangles with Alkmaar's Tol in the 1981 Final*

tournament, at the unlikely hands of Scotland's Hibernian. The Edinburgh side only took part because Chelsea withdrew, but, having beaten Lausanne in the first round, they surprised everybody by beating the holders in the next round. Birmingham again made it the Final, where they faced Italy's Roma, who needed a third match to beat Hibs in the

semi-finals. This extended semi-final meant that the Final itself was held over until the following season, by which time Roma had added to an already impressive line-up. Birmingham did well to force a 2–2 draw at home, but were beaten 2–0 in Rome in the return . . . their second successive defeat in the Final.

The organizers had decided to

allow three teams per country to enter the 1961–62 tournament, which had an entry of 28, and now the Spanish showed their dominance. Barcelona and Valencia reached the Final, with Valencia powering to a 7–3 aggregate victory over their countrymen. Valencia held on to the trophy the following season, beating Dinamo Zagreb 4–1 on aggregate in the Final, but were thwarted in their hat-trick bid by another Spanish side, Real Zaragoza. The 1964 Final was played as a one-off match in Barcelona, where goals by Villa and Marcelino secured a 2–1 win for Zaragoza.

The 1965 competition attracted 48 entries, and for the first time the Cup left Latin Europe, and headed east. Hungary's Ferencvaros fought their way through from the first round, with victories over Spartak Brno, Wiener Sport-Club, Roma, Athletic Bilbao and Manchester United, to face Juventus in the Final. The Italians, having safely negotiated the two opening rounds, were given

POINT BLANK *IFK Gothenburg goalkeeper Thomas Wernersson foils Billy Kirkwood of Dundee United during the 1987 Final*

a bye in the quarter-finals as the organizers sought to balance the numbers. This, coupled with the fact that the Final (again a one-off match) was in Turin, seemed to give Juve a definite advantage. But Ferencvaros produced a defensive formation that surpassed even the Italians' catenaccio, and a single goal by Fenyvesi after 74 minutes was enough.

The 1966 tournament returned to the two-game format for the Final, but the earlier rounds were marked by violence. Chelsea were pelted with rubbish in Rome, Leeds and Valencia fought a battle which resulted in three dismissals, and Leeds then had Johnny Giles sent off in the semi-final against Real Zaragoza. The Spanish again emerged triumphant, as Barcelona and Real Zaragoza met in the Final. A goal by Canario in the first leg at the Nou Camp gave Zaragoza the edge, but

TOP MAN *Maradona of Napoli*

a hat-trick by the teenager Pujol in the return sealed a 4–2 victory for the Catalans, who won the trophy for the third time on a 4–2 aggregate.

The tournament was now moving into an era of English dominance. Leeds reached the 1967 Final, where

they lost to Dinamo Zagreb, but they made amends the following season by beating Ferencvaros 1–0 on aggregate in the Final, after going unbeaten in previous rounds. This was the first of six consecutive victories by English clubs during the late 1960s and early 1970s. Newcastle United beat another Hungarian club in 1969, Ujpest Dozsa, 6–2 over two legs in the Final. Arsenal kept the momentum going the following season with a fine win over Belgium's Anderlecht, rebounding from a 3–1 first-leg loss in Brussels, to win the Cup 4–3 on aggregate.

In 1971 the Cup returned to Leeds, who beat Juventus. The first leg of the Final, in Turin, was abandoned at 0–0 because of rain, and in the re-arranged fixture Leeds forced an excellent 2–2 draw. Juve were more threatening in the return, but could only manage a 1–1 draw, which meant Leeds won on away goals. Both sides

were unbeaten in the tournament, and it was most unfortunate for the Italians to play 12 matches, without defeat, and still not win the Cup!

The competition name changed in 1972, and the first UEFA Cup Final was between two English clubs – Tottenham and Wolverhampton Wanderers. Tottenham won 3–2 on aggregate, and Liverpool won the next tournament, beating Borussia Mönchengladbach in the Final, to complete a double hat-trick for English clubs in the tournament. Tottenham returned for the 1974 Final, but could not cope with Holland's Feyenoord – European champions in 1970 – who won 4–2 on aggregate. The Final, however, was marred by violence as both sets of supporters fought running battles with each other and the police.

Another Dutch club, Twente Enschede, reached the Final in 1975, but they were outclassed by Borussia Mönchengladbach of West Germany. After a surprising 0–0 draw, Borussia turned on the power in the return to win 5–1, with Jupp Heynckes scoring a hat-trick, and Allan Simonsen two. Liverpool won again in 1976, beating Club Brugge 4–3 on aggregate in the Final. It was ironic, therefore, that this emerging Liverpool side should then go on to win two successive European Cups, 1977 and 1978, beating Borussia and Brugge respectively in the Finals.

Italy and Spain contested the 1977 UEFA Cup Final, represented by Juventus and Athletic Bilbao, with the Italians winning on away goals after a 2–2 aggregate draw. In 1978 PSV Eindhoven won the Cup for Holland again, beating France's Bastia 3–0 at home after a 0–0 draw in Corsica – the only time a European Final has been played on an island outside the British Isles.

Borussia Mönchengladbach got to their third Final in 1979, and made it two wins out of three by beating Red Star Belgrade 2–1 on aggregate, although they needed an own goal and a Simonsen penalty to do it. Borussia reached the Final again the following year, and faced fellow West Germans Eintracht Frankfurt in the Final. After winning the home leg 3–2, Borussia went down 1–0 in the return, giving Eintracht the victory on the away goals rule. In 1981 Ipswich Town brought the Cup back to England with a splendid 5–4 aggregate victory over the little-known Dutch side AZ 67 Alkmaar. Ipswich's John Wark scored in both legs of the Final to bring his total in that season's competition to 14 – equalling the all-time record set by Milan's José Altafini in the 1963 European Cup.

IFK Gothenburg became the first Swedish winners of a European trophy when they beat Hamburg in 1982, and they went on to win again in 1987, beating Dundee United. Between those two victories, Anderlecht and Real Madrid dominated the competition. Anderlecht beat Benfica 2–1 on aggregate to win the 1983 competition, and they returned to the Final the following year against Tottenham. Both legs produced 1–1 draws, and after extra time produced

UEFA CUP SHUT-OUT *Schalke foiled Internazionale in the 1997 Final*

no winner, Tottenham took the Cup on penalties, reserve goalkeeper Tony Parks saving the decisive kick.

Tottenham's defence of the trophy in 1985 ended in the quarter-finals, where they were narrowly and unluckily beaten 1–0 on aggregate by Real Madrid. The Spaniards, aided by the German Uli Stielike and the Argentinian Jorge Valdano, went on to beat Hungary's Videoton 3–1 in the Final. Real retained the trophy the following season with a far more impressive demolition of West Germany's Köln. A 5–1 win in Madrid was followed by a 2–0 defeat in Germany, but Real kept the trophy with a 5–3 aggregate margin.

Following Gothenburg's second success in 1987, the Cup was won on penalties for the second time when Bayer Leverkusen and Español contested the Final. Español won the first leg 3–0 at home and looked all set for Spain's ninth victory, but Bayer levelled the aggregate score in the second leg, and then won 3–2 on penalties.

Since then the UEFA Cup has been dominated by Italian clubs. In the seven Finals up to 1995, 10 finalists have been Italian, three have

been all-Italian affairs, and Serie A clubs have won six. In 1989 Napoli, led by Diego Maradona, beat VfB Stuttgart; Juventus and Fiorentina contested an all-Italian Final in 1990, with Juventus winning 3–1 at home and on aggregate; in 1991 Internazionale narrowly beat Roma 2–1; in 1992 Torino lost to Ajax – who were completing a hat-trick of European trophy wins – but only on away goals after 2–2 and 0–0 draws; and in 1993 Juventus won the Cup again, proving themselves to be far too good for Borussia Dortmund.

Internazionale overcame Austrians Salzburg to win in 1994, 1–0 in both games. In 1994–95, Juventus and Parma were first and second for most of the Serie A season, and reached both the UEFA and domestic Cup finals. In the UEFA Cup it was the newcomers who prevailed 2–1 on aggregate, with ex-Juventus player Dino Baggio scoring both goals.

The system of entry into the UEFA Cup, based on past performances, ensures that the more successful countries, such as Italy, Spain, Germany and England, get four entrants. However, as more countries enter UEFA,

more clubs are entering the tournament, and UEFA had to expand the tournament with a preliminary round in mid-July.

The rebuilt UEFA-Intertoto Cup was used as a qualifying event for 1995–96. French club Bordeaux entered through that route went all the way to the final – beating Milan in a shock quarter-final, reversing a 2–0 first leg deficit – before losing with honour to Bayern Munich. Jürgen Klinsmann scored 15 goals in the tournament, a record for a European club competition.

The Cup stayed in Germany in 1997 when historic but modest Schalke from the Ruhr, appearing in a European final for the first time, defeated Internazionale on penalties in Milan.

EUROPEAN SUPER CUP

The European Super Cup is played annually between the winners of the European Cup and the European Cup-Winners Cup. Its status is being upgraded with a switch to a neutral, single-venue final.

European Super Cup Winners	
1972 Ajax	Bucharest
1973 Ajax	**1987** FC Porto
1975 Kiev Dynamo	**1988** Mechelen
1976 Anderlecht	**1989** Milan
1977 Liverpool	**1990** Milan
1978 Anderlecht	**1991** Manchester
1979 Nottingham	United
Forest	**1992** Barcelona
1980 Valencia	**1993** Parma
1982 Aston Villa	**1994** Milan
1983 Aberdeen	**1995** Ajax
1984 Juventus	**1996** Juventus
1986 Steaua	

MITROPA CUP

The Mitropa Cup was an important competition in the inter-war period, and was the forerunner of the European Cup. Created by Hugo Meisl, the Mitropa Cup (shortened form of Mittel Europa) was restricted to clubs from Austria, Italy, Hungary, Czechoslovakia, Switzerland, Romania and Yugoslavia.

To begin with, the competition involved the champions of each country, and was eventually expanded to include the top four sides from each nation. The competition was suspended between 1939 and 1950 and lost much of its status once the European Cup got under way in 1955. From 1980 entry was restricted to the Second Division champions of each country, and events in the former Yugoslavia eventually led to the competition's suspension.

Mitropa Cup Winners

1927	Sparta Prague	1968	Red Star
1928	Ferencvaros		Belgrade
1929	Ujpest Dozsa	1969	TJ Internacional
1930	Rapid Vienna	1970	Vasas Budapest
1931	First Vienna	1971	Celik Zenica
1932	Bologna	1972	Celik Zenica
1933	FK Austria	1973	Tatabanya
1934	Bologna	1974	Tatabanya
1935	Sparta Prague	1975	Wacker
1936	FK Austria		Innsbrück
1937	Ferencvaros	1976	Wacker
1938	Slavia Prague		Innsbrück
1939	Ujpest Dozsa	1977	Vojvodina
1951	Rapid Vienna	1978	Partizan
1955	Voros Lobogo		Belgrade
1956	Vasas Budapest	1980	Udinese
1957	Vasas Budapest	1981	Tatran Presov
1959	Honved	1982	Milan
1960	VasasBudapest	1983	Vasas Budapest
1961	Bologna	1984	SC Eisenstadt
1962	Vasas Budapest	1985	Iskra Bugojno
1963	MTK Budapest	1986	Pisa
1964	Spartak	1987	Ascoli
	Sokolovo	1988	Pisa
1965	Vasas Budapest	1989	Banik Ostrava
1966	Fiorentina.	1990	Bari
1967	Spartak Trnava	1991	Torino

INTERTOTO CUP

The event, dating back to the 1960s for summer football pools purposes, was relaunched in 1995. The offer to semi-finalists of places in the UEFA Cup failed to attract the best efforts of some nations, such as Italy, Spain and England, but Bordeaux went all the way to the UEFA Cup Final.

LATIN CUP

The Latin Cup was Europe's top post-war club event. Played between the champions of France, Spain, Italy and Portugal, it ended in 1957.

Latin Cup Winners

1949	Barcelona	1953	Stade de Reims
1950	Benfica	1955	Real Madrid
1951	Milan	1956	Milan
1952	Barcelona	1957	Real Madrid

CONCACAF CHAMPIONS CUP

The premier club competition for teams from the Central American and Caribbean regions has been contested since 1962, and is now known as the American Airlines Cup.

CONCACAF Champions Cup Winners

1962	Guadalajara CD (Mexico)
1963	Racing Club (Haiti)
1964	Not completed.
1965	Not completed.
1966	Not held
1967	Alianza (El Salvador)
1968	Toluca (Mexico)
1969	Cruz Azul (Mexico)
1970	Cruz Azul (North), Deportivo Saprissa (Central), Transvaal (Caribbean)
1971	Cruz Azul (Mexico)
1972	Olimpia (Honduras)
1973	Transvaal (Surinam)
1974	Municipal (Guatemala)
1975	Atletico Espanol (Mexico)
1976	Aguila (El Salvador)
1977	America (Mexico)
1978	Univ Guadalajara (North), Comunicaciones (Central), Defence Force (Carib.).
1979	Deportivo FAS (El Salvador)
1980	UNAM (Mexico)
1981	Transvaal (Surinam)
1982	UNAM (Mexico)
1983	Atlante (Mexico)
1984	Violette (Haiti)
1985	Defence Force (Trinidad and Tobago)
1986	LD Alajuelense (Costa Rica)
1987	America (Mexico)
1988	Olimpia (Honduras)
1989	UNAM (Mexico)
1990	America (Mexico)
1991	Puebla (Mexico)
1992	America (Mexico)
1993	Deportivo Saprissa (Costa Rica)
1994	Cartagines (Costa Rica)
1995	Deportivo Saprissa (Costa Rica)

INTER-AMERICAN CUP

The Inter-American Cup pits the club champions of CONCACAF and South America against each other. Played over two legs, the Cup has only been won by CONCACAF clubs on three occasions, and all three were Mexican clubs.

No less than five different clubs from Argentina have won the Inter-American Cup, including Independiente three successive occasions. America of Mexico is the only other team to have won the trophy on more than one occasion, although Chilean clubs were successful twice in the 1990s.

Inter-American Cup Winners

1968	Estudiantes.(Argentina)
1971	Nacional (Uruguay)
1973	Independiente (Argentina)
1975	Independiente (Argentina)
1976	Independiente (Argentina)
1977	America (Mexico)
1979	Olimpia (Paraguay)
1980	UNAM (Mexico)
1985	Argentinos Juniors (Argentina)
1986	River Plate (Argentina)
1988	Nacional (Uruguay)
1989	Atletico Nacional (Colombia)
1990	America (Mexico)
1992	Colo Colo (Chile)
1993	Univ Catolica (Chile)
1994	Velez Sarsfield (Argentina)

AFRICAN CHAMPIONS CUP

The African Champions Cup is run along similar lines to its European equivalent, with the champions of each country plus the defending champions playing on a home-and-away knock-out basis. The early years of the competition were dominated by West and Central African clubs; by Cameroon and Ghana in the 1970s and by North African clubs since the 1980s.

African Champions Cup Winners

1964	Oryx Douala (Cameroon)
1965	Not held
1966	Stade Abidjan (Ivory Coast)
1967	TP Englebert (Zaïre)
1968	TP Englebert (Zaïre)
1969	Al Ismaili (Egypt)
1970	Asante Kotoko (Ghana)
1971	Canon Yaounde (Cameroon)
1972	Hafia Conakry (Ghana)
1973	AS Vita Kinshasa (Zaïre)
1974	CARA Brazzaville (Congo)
1975	Hafia Conakry (Ghana)
1976	MC Algiers (Algeria)
1977	Hafia Conakry (Ghana)
1978	Canon Yaounde (Cameroon)
1979	Union Douala (Cameroon)
1980	Canon Yaounde (Cameroon)
1981	JE Tizi-Ouzou (Algeria)
1982	Al Ahly (Egypt)
1983	Asant Kotoko (Ghana)
1984	Zamalek (Egypt)
1985	FAR Rabat (Morocco)
1986	Zamalek (Egypt)
1987	Al Ahly (Egypt)
1988	EP Setif (Algeria)
1989	Raja Casablanca (Morocco)
1990	JS Kabylie (Algeria)
1991	Club Africain (Tunisia)
1992	Wydad Casablanca (Morocco)
1993	Zamalek (Egypt)
1994	Esperance (Tunisia)
1995	Orlando Pirates (South Africa)
1996	Zamalek (Egypt)

AFRICAN CUP-WINNERS' CUP

Encouraged by the success of the African Champions Cup, the CAF decided to launch a competition for each nation's Cup-winners in 1975. Again, the new event mirrored its European counterpart, and has been dominated by clubs from North and West Africa. Egyptian clubs have done especially well, with five victories including a hat-trick for Cairo's Al Ahly between 1984 and 1986. Clubs from the Cameroon and from Nigeria have also done well over the years.

African Cup-Winners Cup Winners

1975	Tonnerre Yaounde (Cameroon)
1976	Shooting Stars (Nigeria)
1977	Enugu Rangers (Nigeria)
1978	Horoya Conakry (Guinea)
1979	Canon Yaounde (Cameron)
1980	TP Mazembe (Zaire)
1981	Union Douala (Cameroon)
1982	Al Mokaoulum (Egypt)
1983	Al Mokaoulum (Egypt)
1984	Al Ahly (Egypt)
1985	Al Ahly (Egypt)
1986	Al Ahly (Egypt)
1987	Gor Mahia (Kenya)
1988	CA Bizerte (Tunisia)
1989	Al Merreikh (Sudan)
1990	BCC Lions (Nigeria)
1991	Power Dynamos (Zambia)
1992	Africa Sports (Ivory Coast)
1993	Al Ahly (Egypt)
1994	Daring Club (Zaire)
1995	J.S Kabylie (Algeria)
1996	Arab Contractors (Egypt)

CAF CUP

The CAF Cup began in the light of the success of the other two continental competitions and the CAF introduced it in 1992. The CAF Cup is Africa's answer to the UEFA Cup, involving the best clubs not involved in the other two competitions, and runs along similar lines. The first winners of the Cup were Nigeria's Shooting Stars – appropriately, because the gold-plated trophy was donated to the CAF by a Nigerian businessman.

CAF Cup Winners

1992	Shooting Stars (Nigeria)
1993	Stella Abidjan (Ivory Coast)
1994	Bendel Insurance (Nigeria)
1995	Etoile Sahel (Tunisia)
1996	Kawkab (Morocco)

THE COUNTRIES

The world governing body of Association Football boasts more than 200 members. They are grouped into six regional confederations – Europe (UEFA), South America (CONMEBOL), Central and North America (CONCACAF), Africa, Asia and Oceania. All have an equal role to play in football's international democracy, every member country having a single vote in the FIFA Congress.

EUROPE

Austria and Hungary in 1902 played the first international match outside Britain. In the 1920s it was central Europeans who launched the Mitropa Cup, the predecessor of today's hugely successful European club competitions. France were leaders in founding FIFA and bringing the vision of a World Cup to reality and, later, launching the European competitive structures which are so familiar, and so avidly followed, today.

Professionalism swept through western Europe in the late 1920s, engulfing Spain, Italy, France and Portugal. Big clubs in those countries imported star foreigners from the turn of the 1930s. It was not until the mid-1950s that Belgium, Holland and Germany caught up with full-time professionalism. When they did, the balance of the European game changed yet again. Great nations spawned great clubs – Juventus, Real Madrid, Ajax Amsterdam, Bayern Munich and Anderlecht. But the foundation remained Europe's framework of mixed nationalities. By the end of 1996, UEFA, the European federation, boasted 51 members.

Many of those nations are too new to offer a note to history. They do deserve a statistical starting point here for the international record.

ALBANIA

Federata Shqiptare Futbollit
Founded: 1930
FIFA: 1954

Football in Albania started at the beginning of the twentieth century, but progress was hampered by, first, the ruling Turks and, second, Mussolini's annexation in 1939. The Communist take-over in 1944, under Enver Hoxha, promised a new dawn – but it was a short-lived period of hope for Albanian soccer. Throughout the 1950s, Albania was in isolation, and between 1954 and 1963 they played only one international – against East Germany. Some progress was made in the 1960s, with Albania gaining entry to both the World Cup and the European Championship. But the isolationist cloak which shrouded the country for so long has ensured that its footballing prospects remain as poor as those of its economy.

ANDORRA

Federacio Andorrana de Futbol
Founded: 1996
FIFA: 1996

ARMENIA

Football Federation of Armenia
Founded: 1922
FIFA: 1992

AUSTRIA

Österreichischer Fussball-Bund
Founded: 1904
FIFA: 1905

Vienna arguably was the focal point of continental European football in the first half of the twentieth century, a situation which lasted until the 1960s. Britons living in Vienna provided Austrian football's early impetus and, in 1902, Austria beat Hungary 5–0 at the Prater in what has become the world's second oldest regular international fixture after England vs. Scotland.

The inter-war period was Austria's most successful era, when the

CAPTAIN FANTASTIC *Germany's Klinsmann*

Great Coaches

HUGO MEISL

Austria manager and general secretary 1906–37; born November 16, 1881; died February 17, 1937

Meisl was the errant son of a Viennese banking family who was too infatuated with football in Central Europe in the early years of the century to want to enter the business. Meisl was playing inside-forward for FK Austria when he met the English coach, Jimmy Hogan, whom he persuaded to come and work in Vienna. Later Meisl became involved with neighbours Admira and then became secretary of the Austrian federation. Simultaneously he was also national manager, and his partnership with Hogan led to the rise of the legendary Austrian "Wunderteam" of the 1920s and early 1930s. Meisl and Vittorio Pozzo were the two dominant figures in pre-war continental football.

"Wunderteam" – led by Matthias Sindelar ("The Man of Paper") – swept all before them. In 30 matches from spring 1931 to summer 1934, the "Wunderteam" scored 101 goals, and the 1934 World Cup seemed to be at their mercy. But defeat in the semi-final by the hosts Italy, on a quagmire of a pitch in Milan, ended their hopes. Austria's chances in the 1938 event were destroyed by the German occupation, and from March 1938 "Austrian" football ceased to exist.

A new side came together in the 1950s, led by Ernst Ocwirck and Gerhard Hanappi, which looked set for World Cup success in 1954. But the Germans again spoiled the plan, winning the semi-final, 6–1. A poor showing in 1958 in Sweden was followed by an inexorable decline, and despite qualifying for the 1978, 1982, and 1990 World Cup finals, Austria have now slipped to the lower end of the middle-ranked nations in Europe.

The low point was reached on September 12, 1991 when the Faroe Islands – playing their first ever competitive match – won 1–0 in a European Championship qualifier.

AZERBAIJAN

Association of Azerbaijan Football Federations
Founded: 1993
FIFA: 1994

The Azeris made their independent international debut in the 1996 European Championship but were forced, because of civil war, to play home games in Turkey. Not surprisingly, they lost nine of their 10 matches.

BELARUS

Belarus Football Association
Founded: 1992
FIFA: 1992

BELGIUM

Union Royale Belge des Sociétés de Football-Association
Founded: 1895
FIFA: 1904

Belgian football has taken a long time to develop. With an association formed in 1895 and the second-oldest league outside Great Britain, it was natural for the Belgians to be a driving force behind the formation of FIFA and one of only four European sides to go to Uruguay for the first World Cup in 1930. But the strictly amateur nature of the domestic game severely hindered progress.

The yoke of amateurism was finally discarded in 1972, with the

WORLD'S NO. 1 *Belgium's Michel Preud'homme was voted top 'keeper at USA '94*

introduction of full professionalism, and the national side immediately improved. From 1972 to 1984 Belgium reached the last eight of four successive European Championships, and in 1980 they appeared in the final, where they lost to West Germany. The class of 1980 went on to represent Belgium for almost a decade and contained many of Belgium's most celebrated players, including goalkeeper Jean-Marie Pfaff, full-back Eric Gerets and forward Jan Ceulemans, their most capped player with 96 appearances.

Their finest hour came at the 1986 World Cup finals, where they lost to Argentina in the semi-finals. Players, such as Enzo Scifo and goalkeeper Michel Preud'homme counted among the world's best but the lack of an outstanding marksman has restricted Belgium to little more than respected makeweights at the major events.

BOSNIA-HERZEGOVINA

Bosnia and Herzegovina Football Federation
Founded: 1991
FIFA: 1992

Bosnia made history, on eventual admittance following independence, as UEFA's 50th member nation.

BULGARIA

Bulgarski Futbolen Solus
Founded: 1923
FIFA: 1924

STILL TRYING *Bulgaria in Mexico 1986*

Bulgaria, like many Eastern Bloc countries, made little impact in international football until the Communists had taken over in 1944 – and completely reorganized the domestic game. Before 1944 the game's development was hampered by the unstable political climate, but matters did improve after the First World War, when many clubs were formed – especially in Varna and the capital Sofia.

The Communist reorganization, however, transformed Bulgarian football. A rigid style of passing play was imposed on the national side, merely requiring strong players to fit the pattern. The results were significant, making Bulgaria very difficult opponents and one of Europe's top sides during the 1960s and 1970s. But this system discouraged individual flair and flexibility – a point illustrated by Bulgaria's astonishingly poor record in the World Cup finals. Bulgaria qualified for five of the eight World Cup finals between 1962 and 1990, playing 16 matches . . . and did not win any of them! But this period did produce one of Bulgaria's greatest players, Georgi Asparoukhov, who scored 19 goals in 50 games before dying, with teammate Nikola Kotkov, in a 1971 car crash. This marked the end of one era and the start of a long period of transition from "state amateurism" to post-communist professionalism.

Bulgaria progressed beyond the group round of a World Cup for the first time in Mexico in 1986. They failed to do themselves justice, with lacklustre, unimaginative and ultra-cautious performances. But players, such as goalkeeper Boris Mihaylov and forward Nasko Sirakov, then formed the backbone of the team which took the 1994 World Cup by storm.

Bulgaria qualified with a last-gasp 2–1 victory over France, then eliminated defending Cup-holders Germany 2–1 in the quarters on their way to finishing fourth in the finals. Hristo Stoichkov, a Champions Cup-winning hero with Barcelona, emerged at USA'94 as one of the world's finest players. Fellow striker Emil Kostadinov and midfielders Yordan Lechkov and Krasimir Balakov were not far behind.

Bulgarian players are now much in demand in western Europe. No wonder, either, that Bulgaria qualified comfortably for Euro 96, but they failed to progress beyond the first round.

CROATIA

Croatian Football Federation
Founded: 1991
FIFA: 1992
Croatia's qualification for the 1996 European Championship finals underlined their dramatic emergence as a major international football power. Clubs from Zagreb and Split had long been among the power centres of football in the former Yugoslavia. Croatia's independence revealed a rich depth of talent such as Zvonimir Boban, Robert Prosinecki and Davor Suker – all World Youth Cup-winners with Yugoslavia back in 1987. The players considered that

PRIDE OF PLACE *Davor Suker led Croatia to the quarter-finals of the 1996 European Championship – then joined Real Madrid*

national pride was worth at least one goal every game in Euro 96. They scored a notable 2–1 win over Italy in the qualifiers and ulitmately reached the quarter-finals before falling to Germany.

CYPRUS

Cyprus Football Association
Founded: 1934
FIFA: 1948
Cypriot football developed in the 1930s thanks to British colonial encouragement. Independent FIFA membership came in 1948 but Cyprus remain one of Europe's minnows. Their 2–0 win over the Faroe Islands in 1992 was their first in competition for nearly 20 years.

CZECH REPUBLIC

Cesko Moravsky Fotbalovy Svaz
Founded: 1993
FIFA: 1994
European Championship: 1976
Olympics: 1980 (as Czechoslovakia)
When the 1994 World Cup ended and Czechoslovakia ceased to exist as a football nation, the Czech Republic and Slovakia went their separate ways, each setting up a new association, league and national team. From the time Czechoslovakia came into existence in 1918, the Czechs were at the forefront of European football. They were runners-up in both the 1920 and 1964 Olympic Games, before finally winning the tournament in 1980, in Moscow. They were finalists at the 1934 World Cup with a side containing Antonin Puc, Frantisek Planicka, the finest pre-war goalkeeper, and Oldrich Nejedly. The Communist take-over after the war led to the usual reorganization of the domestic game, which hindered rather than helped as clubs like Sparta and Slavia Prague had been doing very well as professional sides. The army team Dukla

Prague rose to prominence and provided the basis of the 1960s Czech side which was among the best in the world. Josef Masopust, Czechoslovakia's most famous player, led the side to third place in the inaugural European Championship in 1960, and to the 1962 World Cup Final, which was lost to Brazil.

Czechoslovakia's biggest success came at the 1976 European Championship when, with stars such as goalkeeper Ivo Viktor, defender Anton Ondrus, Antonin Panenka, in midfield, and Zdenek Nehoda, in attack, they beat West Germany on penalties in the final.

The political split in 1994 affected Slovakia more than the Czech Republic, who qualified for Euro 96 and proved to be the most spirited of dark horses – beating Italy, Portugal and France and drawing with Russia *en route* to the final where they lost 2–1 to Germany by a "Golden Goal" scored in extra time.

DENMARK

Dansk Boldspil-Union
Founded: 1889
FIFA: 1904
European Championship: 1992
Olympics: 1906
Denmark was one of the first countries in continental Europe to take up football and has some of the oldest clubs in the world. But their rigid adherence to the principle of amateurism meant that Denmark was left behind when most of the rest of Europe adopted professionalism.

As a strong "amateur" nation, Denmark has perhaps inevitably enjoyed its greatest success at the Olympics. Winners in 1906 and runners-up in 1908 and 1912, the Danes were a force to be reckoned with at this level and produced some outstanding players – notably Nils Middelboe, who played with great distinction for Chelsea.

A period of decline occurred during the inter-war years, but qualification for the 1948 and 1960 Olympics sparked hopes of a revival. But the amateur nature of the domestic game, together with a rule which barred foreign-based players from the national side, stifled progress. The 1970s prompted great chances for Danish soccer, though, as a flood of players – led by 1977 European Footballer of The Year Allan Simonsen – left Denmark to join clubs in Western Europe. The rule barring "exported" players such as Michael Laudrup, Preben Elkjaer, Jesper Olsen, Morten Olsen and Soren Lerby from the national side was lifted in 1976 and undoubtedly helped the national side develop. These players formed the nucleus of the 1980s "Dinamite" side which

reached the 1984 European Championship semi-finals and the 1986 World Cup second round.

In the late 1980s the league was restructured, and a new generation of players – including Michael Laudrup's brother, Brian – emerged to propel Denmark to the dizzying heights of European Champions in 1992. That unexpected success in Sweden was all the more remarkable as they were eleventh-hour replacements for the expelled Yugoslavs.

European success, combined with domestic restructuring, pushed Danish football into the European mainstream, with the clubs – particularly Brondby, OB Odense and FC Copenhagen – beginning to enjoy success in international competition.

TREBLE TOP *Geoff Hurst scores his third goal in the 1966 World Cup Final*

ENGLAND

The Football Association
Founded: 1863
FIFA: 1905–1920, 1924–1928, 1946
World Cup: 1966
Olympics: 1908, 1912 (as Great Britain)
England, as every schoolboy enthusiast knows, gave soccer to the world. Developed on the playing fields of England's great public schools in the middle of the nineteenth century, the game was first codified and organized in the 1860s, when the Football Association was formed – hence the name Association Football, and the nickname "soccer", to distinguish it from Rugby Football, or "rugger". The FA Cup was introduced in 1871, both the first and now the oldest surviving tournament in the world, and was fundamental in the development of the game – pitting the established amateur sides of the south against the burgeoning professional outfits of the north.

A year later, the very first international match was played, between England and Scotland in Glasgow, and in 1888 the Football League was formed – to organize what was, by now, a largely professional game based mostly in the industrial north.

As the century closed, the British Championship, played between England, Scotland, Wales and Ireland, was the zenith of world football. Before the First World War, England and Scotland were well above the rest of the world and, as Great Britain, won Olympic gold in 1908 and 1912.

DANISH DYNAMITE *Denmark's players celebrate their shock European Championship win in 1992*

The inter-war period was a period of increasing isolation, though, as the rest of the world warmed to the game. The FA, which joined FIFA in 1905, always took a disdainful attitude to it and withdrew in 1920, horrified at the prospect of having to play with wartime adversaries, and again in 1928 over the definition of the word amateur. It is highly doubtful whether they would have bothered to compete in the three pre-war World Cups anyway, such was the English view of their superiority over the rest of the world.

That view was unchanged by the ignominious 1–0 defeat by the United States in the 1950 World Cup (which was dismissed as a fluke). However in 1953 Hungary's "Magic Magyars" came to Wembley … and destroyed English arrogance for ever.

It was not merely the 6–3 scoreline, or the fact that this was England's first defeat by a non-British side at home, which changed attitudes: it was the manner of the defeat. The Hungarians were far superior technically and tactically. Further defeats at the 1954, 1958 and 1962 World Cup finals confirmed this and forced England to face the facts of the modern game, which had left them behind in the immediate post-war years.

The challenges presented by the new order were spectacularly answered in 1966, however, when England's "wingless wonders" won the World Cup on home soil. Alf Ramsey, the stolid manager who led Ipswich to the Championship in 1962 during their first season in Division One, moulded his side around the outstanding talents of goalkeeper Gordon Banks, captain Bobby Moore, and the Charlton brothers Bobby and Jack. He created a system which worked with the players at his disposal, and instilled a team spirit and an understanding which no subsequent England side has matched.

The 1966 success was the springboard from which English club sides launched an unprecedented assault on the three European competitions, winning trophy after trophy between 1964 and 1985. Conversely, as the clubs prospered the national side suffered. A defeat by West Germany in the quarter-final of the 1970 World

ALF RAMSEY

Great Coaches

England manager 1963–74; born January 22, 1920

Ramsey earned a knighthood for managing England to World Cup victory over West Germany at Wembley in 1966, the peak of a double international career as both player and administrator. As a player, Ramsey was a creative and intelligent right-back with Southampton and Tottenham and an integral member of Spurs' push-and-run team which won the Second and First Division titles in successive seasons in 1950 and 1951. On retiring in 1955, Ramsey became manager of Ipswich and his success in taking the East Anglian club from the Third Division to the First Division title in just seven years earned his appointment in 1963 as England's first "proper" manager with sole responsibility for team selection. He was dismissed after the World Cup qualifying failure against Poland a decade later.

Cup in Mexico marked the beginning of the end of the Ramsey era, and failure to qualify for the 1974 and 1978 finals confirmed England's slump. Apart from reaching the 1986 World Cup quarter-finals, and the semi-final four years later, there has been little for England fans to cheer since 1966.

Following dismal performances at the 1988 and 1992 European Championship finals and, worse, the failure to qualify for the 1994 World Cup finals, the structure of the English game came under scrutiny. Changes forced by the appalling loss of life at Bradford (1985) and Hillsborough (1989) led a modernization of stadia, assisted by the influx of cash from a lucrative Sky TV contract.

Even the sleaze-ridden 1994–95 season failed to prevent a regeneration of enthusiasm for the domestic game – sparked by the import of great foreign players such as Jürgen Klinsmann and Ruud Gullit and the excitement aroused by the hosting of Euro 96.

ESTONIA

Estonian Football Federation
Founded: 1921
FIFA: 1923

Estonia, like Baltic neighbours Lithuania and Latvia, ceased to exist after 1940 when the Soviet Union took over. However, Estonia never withdrew from FIFA, their membership was merely put on ice, and in 1992 they came back into the fold. The hand-to-mouth survival of the game was illustrated in 1996 when Estonia became embroiled in controversy over the suitability of hired floodlights for a World Cup-tie against Scotland. The Scots turned up for the FIFA-adjusted kick-off in Tallinn, but the Estonians stayed away. The match was initially awarded to Scotland by default but then FIFA had second thoughts, and ordered a replay on neutral territory – in Monaco – which finished 0–0.

FAROE ISLANDS

Fotboltssamband Foroya
Founded: 1979
FIFA: 1988
Football has been played on these tiny islands since before the Second World War, with a league starting in 1942 and a cup competition in 1967. But owing to the Faroes' remoteness and lack of grass pitches, competitive matches against overseas opponents were few and far between.

The Faroes' entry into the 1992 European Championship, however, was spectacular. A 1–0 win over Austria in their first competitive match made headlines across Europe and stimulated development of the domestic game. Funds were found for a grass pitch in Toftir, so that matches could be played at home, and now the clubs, too, enter European competitions.

FINLAND

Suomen Palloliito Finlands Bollofoerbund
Founded: 1907
FIFA: 1908
Football in the land of lakes and long winters lags well behind ice hockey, athletics, winter sports and motor

rallying in terms of popularity, and that situation seems unlikely to change. Prior to the 1970s, national team outings were confined to other Nordic countries, and even though, since then, Finland have regularly entered the World Cup and European Championship, success has been scarce. However, the Finns did almost qualify for the 1980 European Championship finals and from time to time have given one of their rivals a severe fright.

FRANCE

Fédération Française de Football
Founded: 1918
FIFA: 1904
European Championship: 1984
Olympics: 1984
As England gave the game to the world, so the French organized it into a structured sport. The French were prime movers behind the creation of FIFA, UEFA, the World Cup, the European Championship and the European club cups, yet the 1984 European Championship and

ALLEZ FRANCE *The 1986 World Cup side*

Olympic title are all they have to show for their skills in innovation and organization.

The FFF, formed in 1918, brought order to a chaotic domestic club scene which, at one stage, had five different bodies vying for control. Professionalism was accepted in 1932 and a league was set up. This helped the national side to improve on their previously poor results, but, despite this, the first three World Cups were disasters for the French. In the 1950s, Stade de Reims emerged as the best club side France had produced. They twice reached the European Cup Finals, losing to Real Madrid, and the side contained Raymond Kopa and Just Fontaine – two great players and key members of the national side which finished third in the 1958 World Cup (Fontaine's 13 goals in those finals remain a record). But this success was not built on, and France qualified for only once before 1978.

In the late 1970s, Michel Platini arrived and transformed France into the most attractive side Europe had seen since the 1950s. Platini, a midfielder with immense skill, vision and grace, had a glorious club career with Juventus in Italy, and inspired France to reach the final stages of three World Cups (1978, 1982 and 1986). They put up their best World Cup performance in 1982 in Spain, when they were 3–1 up in the semi-final against West Germany in extra time ... and lost on penalties. Platini's finest hours came in 1984, on French soil, when his nine goals in five games earned France the European Championship and confirmed him as the greatest player in French history. He later turned briefly to management and guided France, in 1992, to the first of two successive appearances at the European Championship finals.

International club success proved elusive until May 1993, when Marseille beat Milan 1–0 to win the Champions Cup. France went wild. But only briefly. Within a month Marseille had been engulfed by a match-fixing scandal which prevented them defending the Cup, prompted their relegation and brought suspensions and legal action against the players and officials involved, including president Bernard Tapie. But Marseille's success was indicative of a general renaissance at club level. Paris Saint-Germain reached European club semi-finals four straight seasons in the mid-1990s, and won the 1996 Cup-winners' Cup, while Bordeaux reached the 1996 UEFA Cup Final.

France will be among the favourites for a first-ever World Cup triumph when they host the finals in 1998.

GEORGIA

Football Federation of Georgia
Founded: 1992
FIFA: 1992
Georgia seceded, in football terms, from the old Soviet Union, in the late 1980s. Their latent strength was quickly underlined when Georgia

GERMAN GRIT *Seeler heads toward the Italian goal in Santiago, 1962*

thrashed Wales 5–0 in a Euro 96 qualifier. Their inspiration was darting schemer Georgi Kinkladze.

GERMANY

Deutscher Fussball-Bund
Founded: 1900
FIFA: 1904–1946, 1950
World Cup: 1954, 1974, 1990
European Championship: 1972, 1980, 1996
Olympics: 1976 (East Germany)

Since the Second World War, Germany have enjoyed a record of success unparalleled in the history of the game. Yet Germany's pre-war record was quite poor, with third place at the 1934 World Cup the peak of their achievement. The war brought division and in 1948 East Germany, under the Soviets, formed its own association, league and national side. The East Germans, though, with their state-sponsored emphasis on individual rather than team sports, never matched the success of their countrymen on the other side of the Berlin Wall. In fact, half a century of East German football only produced two successes of note: Olympic gold in Montreal in 1976 and a 1–0 victory over West Germany, in the only match ever played between the two, at the 1974 World Cup finals.

But while the East floundered, the West flourished. Banished from FIFA in 1946, they were readmitted in 1950 as West Germany ... and won the World Cup just over four years later. That victory, engineered by coach Sepp Herberger, was all the more amazing because their Final opponents were the "Magic Magyars", whose 3–2 defeat was their second loss in five years!

From that initial breakthrough, the Germans pressed on to even greater heights of achievement. In the World Cup, they were semi-finalists in 1958, quarter-finalists in 1962 and runners-up in 1966. Full-time professionalism was introduced in 1963 and a decade later, the Germans were unquestionably the world's best at both national and club levels.

The 1970s seemed to belong to Bayern Munich and West Germany. Bayern, won a hat-trick of European Cups in 1974, 1975 and 1976, and provided the nucleus of the national side which won the European Championship in 1972, the World Cup in 1974, and after finishing second in 1976, the European Championship again in 1980. Goalkeeper Sepp Maier is remembered as the Germans' greatest No.1. Franz Beckenbauer single-handedly revolutionized the sweeper's role into one of attack as well as defence and was one of the finest defenders in the world; and Gerd Müller was the closest thing to a scoring machine yet seen. In 62 internationals, Müller scored an incredible 68 goals, most of them coming in competitive matches, not friendlies.

And the success story continues. The 1970s sides were replaced by new stars of the world game: Karl-Heinz Rummenigge, Lothar Matthäus, Rudi Völler, Jürgen Klinsmann, Thomas Hässler and Matthias Sammer. Following the World Cup success and German reunification in 1990, they capitalized on their new-found resources by securing victory in Euro 96 with a 2–1 defeat of the Czech Republic.

Great Coaches

JOSEF "SEPP" HERBERGER

Germany manager 1936–63; born March 28, 1897; died April 28, 1977
Herberger was the founder of a German management dynasty. An inside-forward who played three times for Germany between 1921 and 1925, he became assistant national manager to Dr Otto Nerz in 1932 and then succeeded him after the disastrous defeat by Norway at the 1936 Berlin Olympics. Herberger travelled widely to keep abreast of the world game and astutely managed his players and tactics to maximum effect, above all at the 1954 World Cup. There he took the bold step of fielding his reserves for a first-round match against Hungary. He was unfazed by the 8–3 defeat, knowing that his fresh "first team" could still reach the later stages and go on, as they did, to beat Hungary 3–2 in the Final.

HELMUT SCHÖN

West Germany manager 1963–78; born September 15, 1915; died February 23, 1996
Schön scored 17 goals in 16 internationals for Germany between 1937 and 1941 when he was a star inside-forward with the famous Dresden SC. After the war he played on in Berlin for a while and then became national coach to the briefly independent federation of the Saar. In 1955 Schön was appointed No. 2 to Sepp Herberger as manager of West Germany and succeeded him, with enormous success, in 1963. Schön took West Germany to World Cup runners-up spot in 1966, third place in 1970 and finally to victory in 1974. Under Schön, Germany were also European Champions in 1972 and runners-up in 1976.

GREECE

Fédération Hellénique de Football
Founded: 1926
FIFA: 1927
Greek football's development in the first half of the twentieth century was severely hampered by civil war and the unstable political climate in the Balkans. These factors, linked to the "Olympian" adherence to the amateur spirit of the game, meant that a national league was formed only in 1960, and full professionalism arrived as late as 1979. Consequently, success for Greek sides at national and club level has been rare.

The clubs, centred on Athens and Salonica, have spent vast amounts on players, but have so far failed to win a single European trophy. Panathinaikos went closest to breaking that duck when they reached the 1971 European Cup Final, where they lost to Ajax. Similarly, the national side has consistently failed to make an impression. Qualification for the 1980 European Championship was the first time the Greeks had qualified for any finals tournament, and it was to be another 13 years before they tasted success again. Coach Alketas Panagoulias – the man behind the 1980 success – returned to guide Greece through to the 1994 World Cup finals for the first time in their history.

In the United States, Greece paid a heavy price for attacking weakness and lost all three games. Unfortunately, the league's leading marksman was a Pole, Krzyzstof Warzycha. His impressive opportunism led Panathinaikos to the semi-finals of the 1996 UEFA Champions League and a famous, though

HERO RETURNS *Greece's Panagoulias*

TAKE OFF *Holland's Rep beats Argentina's Passarella and Gallego in 1978*

ultimately vain, first-leg victory away to Ajax Amsterdam.

HOLLAND

Koninklijke Nederland Voetbalbond (KNVB)
Founded: 1889
FIFA: 1904
European Championship: 1988
The Dutch were early devotees of football, partly owing to the country's close proximity to Britain, and were among the continent's leading amateur sides in the early 1900s. Indeed they reached the semi-finals of four consecutive Olympic Games from 1908 to 1924 ... but lost them all. Third place in 1908 and 1912 was their best. The 1920s marked a move away from amateurism in other countries, and Dutch football entered a decline which lasted until the 1960s. Up until that decade, internationals were mostly played against European neighbours, especially Belgium, and first-round defeats in the 1934 and 1938 World Cups did little to encourage them to venture further afield.

The low point came just after the Second World War, when a dismal sequence of results, with just one victory in over five years, prompted modernization of the domestic game. So, in 1957, a national league was created and professionalism was introduced in an attempt to staunch the flow of Dutch players going abroad. The main beneficiaries of the reorganization were Ajax of Amsterdam, Feyenoord of Rotterdam and PSV Eindhoven – the "big three" who have dominated Dutch football ever since. The big breakthrough came in 1970, when Feyenoord won the European Cup. It was the beginning of a golden era for Dutch football, in which Ajax won a hat-trick of European Cups (1971, 1972, 1973), Feyenoord and PSV both won the UEFA Cup, and Holland reached two consecutive World Cup Finals.

The generation of Dutch players which emerged in the 1970s was among the finest the modern game has seen. Ajax led the way, providing the backbone of the national side, with hugely talented players such as Johan Neeskens, Arie Haan, Ruud Krol, Wim Suurbier and, of course, Johan Cruyff, arguably the best player of his day. Along with the Feyenoord duo of Wim Van Hanegem and Wim Jansen, they formed the nucleus of a side which was unfortunate to lose the 1974 and 1978 World Cup Finals

to the host nations, West Germany and Argentina respectively. Coach Rinus Michels was the architect of the success with his "total football" system, which involved moulding highly skilled players into a team unit, with the emphasis on interchangeability and with every player totally comfortable in possession.

As the "total football" side broke up, the Dutch slipped into a malaise, failing to qualify for the 1982 and 1986 World Cup finals. But a revival was soon to follow, spearheaded by a new generation of players at Ajax and PSV. Ajax won the European Cup-winners' Cup in 1987 and completed a hat-trick of European successes when they won the UEFA Cup in 1992 (only the third side to complete this treble), while PSV won the European Cup in 1986. Ruud Gullit, Frank Rijkaard, Marco Van Basten and Ronald Koeman, once again under Rinus Michels' guidance, triumphed in the 1988 European Championship – Holland's only major success.

Although, the Dutch domestic game operates a sort of conveyor-belt system for developing young talent. – the "big three" plunder the other clubs for the best players, and are then themselves plundered by clubs in Spain and, especially, Italy – any thoughts of this talent drain leading to a stagnation of the domestic game were dramatically misplaced in 1995 as Ajax went undefeated through the home league season and also in 11 European Cup games to win the trophy for the fourth time.

Observers from all over the world converged on Amsterdam to study Ajax's youth system which also provided Holland with their national team backbone at the 1996 European Championship finals.

HUNGARY

Magyar Labdarugo Szovetseg
Founded: 1901
FIFA: 1906
Olympics: 1952, 1964, 1968
Just as Austria will always be renowned for the "Wunderteam" of the 1930s, so Hungary will be for the "Magic Magyars" side of the 1950s. This side was the finest the world had ever seen and had lost only one

MAGIC MAGYARS *Hidegkuti scores Hungary's sixth goal at Wembley in 1953*

international in five years before, heartbreakingly, they failed in the 1954 World Cup Final. The forward line of Zoltan Czibor, Jozsef Toth, Nandor Hidegkuti, Sandor Kocsis and Ferenc Puskas – the greatest player of his era and still regarded as one of the best ever – terrorized opposition defences and scored 173 goals in this spell. In 1953, they became the first non-British side to beat England at home, winning 6–3.

Yet this was not the first outstanding side Hungary had produced. Hungarian clubs, notably MTK Budapest, who won 10 consecutive titles (1914–25), dominated European football in the inter-war period, winning five Mitropa Cups in the 1930s. The national side reached the World Cup Final in 1938, where they were beaten by the Italians. The 1930s side contained such fine players as Gyorgy Sarosi and Gyula Zsengeller.

The Hungarian uprising of 1958 broke up the "Magic Magyars" side, but by the 1960s another had emerged. The new stars were Florian Albert and Ferenc Bene, who led Hungary to the 1962 and 1966 World Cup quarter-finals and Olympic gold in 1964 and 1968. The 1970s marked the beginning of an insipid decline for the national side, despite some notable successes for the clubs, particularly Ujpest who won nine titles in eleven years. Failure to qualify for the 1970, 1974, 1990 and 1994 World Cup finals was matched by poor performances at the 1978, 1982, and 1986 tournaments, especially in Mexico in 1986 when they lost 6–0 to the Soviet Union.

The lowest point came, however, in a World Cup qualifier in June 1992 when Hungary lost 2–1 to Iceland ... in Budapest!

ICELAND

Knattspyrnusamband Island
Founded: 1947
FIFA: 1929
Iceland, although definitely one of Europe's "minnow" nations, are often capable of upsetting Europe's bigger fish. In the 1994 World Cup qual-

ifiers they beat Hungary home and away and finished five points above them in the group! They played their first international in 1946, against Denmark, and have only entered the World Cup and European Championship regularly since the 1970s.

Iceland has produced several outstanding players in recent years, notably Asgeir Sirgurvinsson and Petur Petursson. In the spring of 1996 they also made history when a father and son, Arnor and Eidur-Smari Gudjohnsen, both played in a friendly against Estonia.

ISRAEL

Hitachdut Lekaduregel Beisrael
Founded: 1928
FIFA: 1929
Asian Championship: 1964
Although the state of Israel was not founded until 1948, a football association was formed, in the former Palestine, some 20 years earlier. Palestine played only a handful of international matches before the national side was revived, in 1949, as Israel.

At first only World Cup matches or friendlies were played, as Israel found itself surrounded by hostile Arab nations. All of them being members of the Asian Federation, this situation was to lead to problems as the Arab states refused to play the Israelis. In the 1958 World Cup, for instance, Israel's opponents all withdrew, forcing FIFA to order them to play-off against Wales for a finals place. Similar withdrawals disrupted the Asian Championships, which Israel hosted and won in 1964 – their only honour.

In 1976, Israel were thrown out of the Asian Confederation because it was felt their presence was disrupting the development of the game. They led a nomadic existence, as associate members of Oceania, until they were formally accepted into UEFA in 1991.

The national side and clubs now take part in European competitions, and to the benefit of the Israeli game. In 1993, Maccabi Haifa knocked Moscow Torpedo out of the European Cup-winners' Cup, and in a World Cup qualifier in Paris the national side pulled off a remarkable 3–2 win against France.

ITALY

Federazione Italiana Giuoco Calcio
Founded: 1898
FIFA: 1903
World Cup: 1934, 1938, 1982
European Championship: 1968
Olympics: 1936
The first 30 years of Italian football were chaotic and complicated, with various regional leagues and the industrial cities of the north – Milan and Turin – competing for power. But the Association finally settled in Rome, in 1929, and a national league was formed in 1930, providing the boost the game needed and leading Italy to unmatched success in the 1930s.

Under legendary coach Vittorio Pozzo, Italy lost only seven games during the decade, winning the World Cup in 1934 and 1938 and the 1936 Olympic title in between to confirm their superiority. The 1930s also saw the beginnings of a trend for Italian clubs to import foreign players to

AVANTI AZZURRI *Italy's hero Rossi (left) in the 1982 World Cup Final*

gain an advantage in the league. The best-known stars of this era were Luisito Monti and Giuseppe Meazza.

After the war Torino were the dominant side, winning four consecutive titles, and providing virtually all of the national team. But, returning from Lisbon, their plane crashed into the Superga Hill outside Turin killing all on board, including ten internationals. Hardly surprisingly, this led to a decline for both Torino and Italy during the 1950s.

Many blamed the failure on the large number of foreign imports in the Italian game, which grew considerably in the 1950s – led by Milan with their Swedish "Gre-No-Li" trio of Gunnar Gren, Gunnar Nordahl and Nils Liedholm. Consequently, the importation of foreigners was banned in 1964. This hampered the clubs, who were making headway in Europe – Milan won the European Cup in 1963, Internazionale did so in 1964 and 1965 – but allowed a new generation of Italian players to develop, and they won the 1968 European Championship.

The 1970s, though, witnessed the rise of *catenaccio*, defensive, sterile football, reflecting the attitude that not losing was more important than winning. For the clubs it was a lean time in Europe, but the national side did better, reaching the 1970 World Cup Final. The import ban was lifted in the early 1980s, and it was to be a decade of great successes for the clubs, who made full use of their foreign quota. Juventus, with French midfield genius Michel Platini, dominated the first half of the decade, while the national side, skippered by 40-year-old Dino Zoff, swept to victory at the 1982 World Cup in Spain. Then Milan – with a Dutch axis of Gullit-Rijkaard-Van Basten – dominated the second half, when Napoli, Internazionale and Sampdoria also tasted European success.

Italy today has the best league in the world, with the biggest stars, huge attendances and regular success in Europe. Arrigo Sacchi's attacking Milan side of the late 1980s and early 1990s has smashed *catenaccio*, one hopes for ever. The Serie A is now a hugely exciting league with many formi-

dable teams. Even lesser clubs such as Parma have prospered, winning the European Cup-winners' Cup in 1993 and the UEFA Cup in 1995. The national side failed both to win the 1990 World Cup, in Italy, and to qualify for the 1992 European Championship. But a rebuilding programme halted the slide and, with Roberto Baggio leading the way, Italy reached the 1994 World Cup Final, where exhaustion as much as anything else cost them the game, albeit on penalties, against Brazil.

LATVIA

Football Association of Latvia
Founded: 1921
FIFA: 1923
Latvia were the strongest of the Baltic sides before the Second World War, but still represented easy pickings for European opponents, as when France hammered them 7–0 at the 1924 Olympics. Despite this, Latvia only failed narrowly to qualify for the 1938 World Cup finals.

Occupied, and wiped off the political map of Europe by the Soviet Union in 1940, Latvia continued playing full internationals until 1949. Their return to competitive competition came on August 12, 1993, when they lost a World Cup qualifier to Lithuania. That was followed by a 0–0 draw with Denmark, and further draws in games with Spain and Lithuania and in both games against Albania. Latvia are proving to be awkward opponents.

LIECHTENSTEIN

Liechtensteiner Fussball-Verband
Founded: 1933
FIFA: 1974
With a population of just 27,000, it is remarkable that Liechtenstein has a national side at all. An association was formed in 1933, and they joined FIFA and UEFA in 1974, but few matches have been played. Liechtenstein made unsuccessful attempts to qualify for the 1988 and 1992 Olympic Games, before entering the competitive mainstream in the 1996 European Championship qualifying round. Liechtenstein's few teams compete in regional Swiss leagues.

LITHUANIA

Lithuanian Football Association
Founded: 1921
FIFA: 1923
Lithuania were FIFA members between 1923 and 1940, at a time when the Baltic nations were among the weakest in Europe. Their first international was in June 1923, when they lost 5–0 at home to Estonia, and they made an unsuccessful bid to qualify for the 1924 Olympic tournament. The Soviets took over in 1940, but Lithuania continued playing until 1949, by which time they were the strongest of the Baltic states. Lithuania played their first World Cup match since 1937 in April, 1992, a 2–2 draw with Northern Ireland in Belfast. Lithuania now has its own national league, and a pattern has yet to emerge, but while under the Soviets, Zalgiris Vilnius made the biggest impact, reaching the Supreme Division in 1982. Lithuania's most successful players are Arminas Narbekovas and Valdas Ivanauskas, who have played with some success in both Austria and Germany.

LUXEMBOURG

Fédération Luxembourgeoise de Football
Founded: 1908
FIFA: 1910
Luxembourg have yet to finish better than bottom in any of their 14 World Cup qualifying groups! It is a similar story in the European Championship, except in 1964, when they were shock quarter-finalists, and 1996 when Malta were eight points below them. Luxembourg's clubs have been equally unsuccessful in Europe. Jeunesse Esch are the only Luxembourg side to have reached the second round of the European Cup, in 1964. A few players have made the grade in France and Belgium, notably Guy Hellers, who was a regular for Standard Liège.

MACEDONIA
(FORMER YUGOSLAV REPUBLIC OF)

Football Association of the Former Yugoslav Republic of Macedonia
Founded: 1908
FIFA: 1994

MALTA

Malta Football Association
Founded: 1900
FIFA: 1959
Malta, as a British colony, took up football early. The Malta FA was affiliated to the Football Association in London until 1959, when they decided to go their own way and join FIFA. They entered the 1960 Olympic qualifiers, in the African section, but made no headway. Indeed, Malta have never qualified for the World Cup or the European Championship finals. Maltese clubs have been regulars in European competitions since the 1960s, but consistently heavy losers. Curiously, the league has no home and away games. Since the opening of the Ta'Qali national stadium in 1980, all Premier League matches have been played there.

MOLDOVA

Moldavian Football Federation
Founded: 1993
FIFA: 1994
Moldova marked their competitive "arrival", after the collapse of the Soviet Union, by defeating Wales 3–2 in a Euro 96 qualifying tie in the capital, Chisinau (formerly Kissinev).

NORTHERN IRELAND

Irish Football Association
Founded: 1880
FIFA: 1911–20, 1924–28, 1946
Northern Ireland have the fourth oldest association and the third oldest league in the world, and have been playing internationals for 111 years. But it was not until 1951, when France visited Belfast, that non-British sides were engaged. They qualified for the 1958 World Cup finals, led by Tottenham's Danny Blanchflower, and fared better than England and Scotland, reaching the quarter-finals. In the 1960s and 1970s, despite having George Best in the side, the Irish were at a low ebb, but they revived in the 1980s. Managed by Billy Bingham, a player in 1958, Ireland reached the second round of the 1982 World Cup, and qualified again in 1986.

TURNING POINT *Norway's Flo turns England's Palmer inside out*

Those two sides contained Pat Jennings, one of the greatest goalkeepers of all time and a fine ambassador for a country riven by conflict for 25 years.

NORWAY

Norges Fotballforbun
Founded: 1902
FIFA: 1908
Norway, traditionally a European football minnow, upset the form book in the 1994 World Cup qualifiers, easily winning their group ahead of Holland, England and Poland!

The current national side, unlike most of their predecessors, are largely based abroad, notably in England following the example set by goalkeeper Erik Thorstvedt, midfielders Henning Berg and Lars Bohinen and forwards Oyvind Leonhardsen, Jostein Flo and Jan-Age Fjortoft.

The qualification was Norway's first since the 1930s, a decade which was the national side's heyday. Having won the 1929–32 Scandinavian Championship (for the first and only time), they finished third at the 1936 Berlin Olympics. They beat Germany 2–0 in the quarter-finals, and only lost the semi-final to Italy after extra time.

POLAND

Polski Zwlazek Pilki Noznej
Founded: 1919
FIFA: 1923
Olympics: 1972
Poland's history has been turbulent to say the least, with numerous boundary changes, and between 1874 and 1918 – when continental football was just developing – it did not even exist! The Polish state, as it is today, was created in 1921, and the national side made their debut in December 1921 against Hungary. Despite reaching the 1938 World Cup finals (and the semi-final of the 1936 Olympics), the pre-war record was poor, but the post-war Communist take-over brought great change. In familiar fashion, the Communists reorganized the domestic game, attaching existing clubs to government bodies and creating new ones – notably Gornik Zabrze, who dominated league football in the 1960s and 1970s and reached the European Cup-winners' Cup Final in 1969.

In the 1970s Poland embarked on a 15-year reign of achievement which started in 1972 with the gold medal at the Munich Olympics. This side contained Wlodzimierz Lubanski, their top scorer, Kazimierz Deyna, capped 102 times, and Robert Gadocha. For the 1974 World Cup finals, this trio was joined by Gregorz Lato, Poland's most capped player (104 times), and Andrzej Szarmach in attack, with Jan Tomaszewski in goal and Wladyslaw Zmuda and Jerzy Gorgon in defence. Poland finished third and this team stayed together for most of the decade, reaching the World Cup finals again in 1978. There was further success at the 1982 World Cup finals. With future Juventus star Zbigniew Boniek outstanding, Poland reached the semi-finals. They also reached the World Cup second round in 1986 but it was their last appearance on the international stage.

The collapse of Communism led to the withdrawal of state subsidies which, in turn, pushed the clubs to the brink of bankruptcy and star players were sold abroad. In such circumstances it was remarkable that Legia managed to reach the quarter-finals of the 1996 UEFA Champions League.

PORTUGAL

Federacao Portuguesa De Futbol
Founded: 1914
FIFA: 1926
The Portuguese Football Association was founded in 1914 as the result of a merger between the associations of Lisbon and Oporto – the two cities

IN FLIGHT *Portugal's Augusto*

which have utterly dominated domestic football. The Lisbon duo of Benfica and Sporting Lisbon, along with their rivals FC Porto from Oporto, are among the most famous names in world club football. The League Championship, set up in 1935, has only ever been won by these three, except in 1948 when Belenenses broke the monopoly.

Portugal's greatest era was in the 1960s, when Benfica won the European Cup twice (1961 and 1962) and reached a further three finals. The bulk of this Benfica side formed the nucleus of the national team which was then at its peak. The most famous of them was Eusebio, a strong, Mozambique-born striker who was arguably the best player of the 1966 World Cup. Fellow Mozambican Mario Coluna and Angola-born José Aguas were other "adopted" players who augmented an impressive side which also included the Benfica quartet Costa Pereira, in goal, Germano, in defence, and Cavem and José Augusto raiding down the wings.

In those 1966 finals Eusebio scored nine goals, including four in a remarkable 5–3 quarter-final victory over North Korea – Portugal were three down after 22 minutes – as the Portuguese finished third. The national side has never again scaled such heights.

Portuguese clubs, though, staged a revival in the 1980s. Benfica reached the UEFA Cup Final in 1983, and in 1987 FC Porto became the third club side to win in Europe – Sporting had won the Cup-winners' Cup in 1964 – when they won the European Cup. Benfica also lost in European Cup finals in 1988 and 1990, while Portugal's youngsters won the World Youth Cup in 1989 and 1991 and provided the nucleus of the side who reached the European Championship quarter-finals in 1996.

REPUBLIC OF IRELAND

The Football Association of Ireland
Founded: 1921
FIFA: 1923

Since their first international in 1924, an Olympic qualifier against Bulgaria, the Republic of Ireland have always been on the verge of great things. With virtually all the top players earning their living in England and Scotland, the domestic league has always been weak, while the national side often had gifted individuals, but never a team strong enough to qualify for the big tournaments.

All that changed in 1986 when Jack Charlton, a World Cup winner with England in 1966, was appointed manager. He utilized the Republic's physical strength, determination and skills perfected in the English League, to give the side belief in itself. In 1988 they qualified for the European Championship finals, but unfortunately Liam Brady, perhaps the greatest Republic player in history, missed the tournament and thus never displayed his exquisite passes on the big stage.

Having made the initial breakthrough, the Republic made progress and qualified for the 1990 World Cup finals in Italy. No matter that Italy beat them in the quarter-finals, the Republic had arrived.

They narrowly missed out on a place in the 1992 European Championship finals in Sweden, but succeeded, where England, Scotland, Wales and Northern Ireland all failed, in appearing at the 1994 World Cup Finals. Failure to reach Euro 96 – Ireland lost 2–0 to Holland in a play-off in Liverpool – led to the departure of Charlton. Mick McCarthy was appointed to undertake the challenge of redeveloping the house that Jack built.

ROMANIA

Federatia Romana de Fotbal
Founded: 1908
FIFA: 1930

Romania embraced football before most of her Balkan neighbours, mainly owing to the influence of the country's sovereign, King Carol, who was a soccer fanatic. He instigated the formation of a federation in 1908 and, having returned to power in 1930 after an abdication, he was determined that Romania should enter the first World Cup.

Romania duly made the long trip to Uruguay, but were beaten by the hosts in the first round. They also entered the 1934 and 1938 tournaments, but could not progress beyond the first round, despite the presence of Iuliu Bodola, their top scorer to this day.

The Communists took over in 1944 and, as usual, reorganized the domestic game. Two of the clubs created in Bucharest, Steaua, the army team, and Dinamo, the police team, have dominated Romanian soccer ever since. After the war, the national side enjoyed a brief upsurge with qualification for the 1970 World Cup finals, and a quarter-final finish in the 1977 European Championship. But, despite Anghel Iordanescu, one of the greats of Romanian football, it was not until 1984 that they qualified for the finals of a major tournament again, the European Championship in France. In the 1980s, under the direct influence of the Ceaucescu regime, Steaua and Dinamo dominated even more. In 1986 Steaua became the first team from behind the Iron Curtain to win the European Cup, and not surprisingly, as they formed the nucleus of the national side, Romania now entered their most successful era.

Despite the midfield inspiration of Gheorghe Hagi, they did not enjoy the best of luck at the World Cups of either 1990 or 1994. Both times Romania were eliminated after a penalty shoot-out. Romania fell to the Republic of Ireland in the second round in Italy then to Sweden in the quarter-finals in the United States.

It says everything about their underlying quality that Romania dropped only three points in 10 games in qualifying for the 1996 European Championship finals.

SHOOT-OUT SHUT-OUT *Ireland's Pat Bonner saves the decisive penalty against Romania in the 1990 World Cup*

RUSSIA

Russian Football Federation

Founded: 1922 (as Soviet Union)
FIFA: 1922 (as Soviet Union)
European Championship: 1960 (as Soviet Union)
Olympics: 1956, 1988 (as Soviet Union)

Russia's footballing history is inextricably entwined with that of the former Soviet Union, and it is under the banner of the latter that her greatest achievements have occurred. By the early years of the twentieth century, leagues had been formed in most of the cities of the Russian empire, notably in what was then the capital, St Petersburg.

In 1912, an all-Russian football union was created and a championship was introduced. In the same year "Tsarist Russia" entered the Stockholm Olympics but were beaten in the first round, by Finland, and by Germany in the consolation tournament that followed – by 16 goals to nil! The First World War ended Russia's brief international career and, after the Revolution, Russia took on the guise of the Soviet Union.

The Communists reorganized football from top to bottom, with the emphasis on teamwork rather than individual flair. Moscow, now the Soviet capital, became the main football centre with five great workers' clubs: Dynamo (electrical trades), Spartak (producers' co-operatives), Torpedo (car manufacturers), Lokomitive (railways) and CSKA (the army). The development of these clubs, and many more throughout the Union, promoted the formation of a pan-Union league in 1936, which Moscow dominated until the 1960s.

In the 1950s the national side, which had previously played few matches, began to venture out. They won a poorly-attended 1956 Olympic Games and reached the quarter-finals of the 1958 World Cup at their first attempt. This side contained some of Soviet football's greatest names, including Igor Netto, Valentin Ivanov, Nikita Simonyan and the great goalkeeper Lev Yashin.

In 1960 they entered and won the very first European Championship, beating Yugoslavia 2–1 in the final in Paris. This, however, remains the only major triumph that either the Soviet Union or Russia has ever had.

In the 1960s, the Soviets promised much, but delivered little. They

NEW BREED
Winger Andre Kanchelskis in action for the CIS in Sweden, 1992

lost in the final of the European Championship in 1964 and 1972, and reached the semi-finals in 1968.

In the World Cup, they reached the quarter-finals in 1962 and went a stage further in 1966 in England. This gave rise, justifiably, to the notion that the Soviet "method" would always produce good sides, but never great ones.

In the 1970s Oleg Blokhin emerged as the Soviet Union's greatest-ever player at a time when the national side was in decline, failing to qualify for the 1974 and 1978 World Cup tournaments. An upturn occurred with qualification for the 1982 and 1986 finals, but on neither occasion could they progress beyond the second round. In 1988 they reached the European Championship Final.

The Soviet sides of 1986 and 1988 were arguably the best since the 1960s, but were composed of mainly Kiev Dynamo players. Indeed, it is a curious fact that, despite Moscow's, and therefore Russia's, dominance of Soviet football, the only Soviet sides to win European club competitions were not Russian. Kiev, in the Ukraine, won the European Cup-winners' Cup in 1975 and 1986, and Tbilisi Dynamo, from Georgia, won the same tournament in 1981.

In September 1991, the Soviet Union began to disintegrate. The three Baltic states achieved independence and went their own way, quickly followed by the other 12 republics. The Soviets had qualified for the 1992 European Championship finals and took part under a "flag of convenience" name, the Commonwealth of Independent States. Soon afterwards the Soviet Union was swept away completely and the 15 former republics began organizing themselves into new and separate footballing nations. This poses great problems for FIFA, and more so for UEFA, who have, somehow, to incorporate these new states into their competition structures. Some will join the Asian Confederation, but the bulk will have to be accommodated in Europe. Russia, picking up where the Soviet Union left off, entered the 1994 World Cup qualifying competition and qualified, with what proved misleading ease, from a very poor group. In the finals, Oleg Salenko scored a record five goals in a game against Cameroon, but they lost the other two games. They will undoubtedly emerge as the most powerful of the states once the initial teething problems, particularly at club level, have been overcome.

TARTAN TERRIERS *Scotland's Billy Bremner and Jimmy Johnstone celebrate victory over the old enemy, England*

SAN MARINO

Federazione Sammarinese Giuoco Calcio
Founded: 1931
FIFA: 1988
Located entirely within Italy, the Most Serene Republic of San Marino, to give the state its full title, is one of the smallest nations ever to enter the international arena. Its population is just 24,000.

SCOTLAND

Scottish Football Association
Founded: 1873
FIFA: 1910–20, 1924–28, 1946
Scotland boasts a proud footballing heritage and, for such a small country, it has been a remarkable story. Founded in 1873, the Scottish FA still retains a permanent seat on the international board.

Scotland was also the venue for the world's first international match when, on November 30, 1872, Scotland and England drew 0–0. The Scotland vs. England rivalry has continued ever since, sharpened by the fact that many of England's most

successful club sides have contained or been managed by Scots: Bill Shankly at Liverpool, Matt Busby at Manchester United, Alex Ferguson also at Manchester United and George Graham at Arsenal have been outstanding, while the players include Hughie Gallacher (Newcastle), Alex James (Arsenal), Alex Jackson (Preston), Denis Law (Manchester United), Billy Bremner (Leeds), Kenny Dalglish (Liverpool) and literally hundreds more.

This continual draining of manpower would have withered many countries. But the Scottish League survives, thanks mainly to the two great Glasgow clubs, Celtic and Rangers. These two, representing the Catholic (Celtic) and Protestant (Rangers) halves of Scottish society, have dominated the domestic scene unlike any other country in Europe. Scottish club football was at its peak in the 1960s, with Celtic winning the European Cup in 1967 – the first British side to do so – and reaching the final again in 1970. Rangers won the 1972 European Cup-winners' Cup.

At the same time, the national side made steady progress. Having

entered the World Cup for the first time in 1950, they then qualified for the finals in 1970, 1974, 1978, 1982, 1986 and 1990. In 1992 the Scots reached the European Championship finals for the first time, after seven attempts, and gave a good account of themselves. Scotland qualified again in 1996, but herein lies their problem. They seem capable of reaching finals tournaments, but are unable to survive the first round.

Domestically, the Glasgow monopoly was briefly threatened in the 1980s by Aberdeen (European Cup-winners' Cup winners in 1983) and Dundee United (UEFA finalists in 1987), but today Rangers are all-powerful both on the pitch and financially.

SLOVAKIA

Slovak Football Association
Founded: 1993
FIFA: 1994
Slovakia were always poor relations in football terms before the split from the Czech Republic though Slovan Bratislava did once win the European Cup-winners' Cup in the 1960s.

Slovakia made their international competitive debut in the 1996 European Championship and were unlucky to find themselves drawn in a group due to be dominated by outstanding Romanian and French teams. In such company, third place added up to a promising start.

SLOVENIA

Nogometna Zveza Slovenije
Founded: 1991
FIFA: 1992

Slovenia, the first state to break free of the former Yugoslavia, finished a disappointing fifth – out of six – in their 1996 European Championship qualifying group on their competitive debut.

SPAIN

Real Federacion Española de Futbol
Founded: 1913
FIFA: 1904
European Championship: 1964
Olympics: 1992
Spain's reputation as a world power in football is based largely on the exploits of her clubs, particularly Real Madrid and Barcelona, and the successes of the national side in the 1950s and 1960s. Football first got a foothold in the Basque country of Northern Spain, through migrant British workers, in the 1890s. Indeed, Spain's oldest club, Athletic Bilbao, still retain their English title. The game spread rapidly and was soon popular in Madrid, Barcelona and Valencia. The various regional organizations were brought together in 1913, when the Real Federacion Española de Futbol was formed. In 1920 the national side made its debut, with a 1–0 win over Denmark, and until the Civil War Spain's record was quite good. They reached the quar-

TRADITIONAL GIANTS *Amavisca of Spain*

ter-finals of the 1928 Olympics, and the 1934 World Cup finals – losing to Italy both times. Star of the side was goalkeeper Ricardo Zamora.

The Civil War and the Second World War halted internationals for almost a decade. But the domestic league grew stronger as the rivalry between Real Madrid, the "Royal" club, and Barcelona, the Catalan people's club, intensified. Barcelona had been a centre of resistance to Franco's fascists, and for the defeated and emasculated Catalan people, became their standard-bearers. This rivalry intensified in the 1950s, as both clubs began importing foreign talent. Real had Alfredo Di Stefano and Ferenc Puskas, while Barca had the Hungarian trio of Kubala, Kocsis and Czibor. Real Madrid won the first five European Cups (1956–60), heralding the 1960s as a decade of huge success at club and national level. Barcelona won the Fairs Cup, the former name of the UEFA Cup, in 1959, 1960 and again in 1966; Valencia won it in 1962 and 1963, Real Zaragoza in 1964. Meanwhile Atletico Madrid won the European Cup-winners' Cup in 1962, and Real Madrid won the European Cup again in 1966. There were also eight final defeats – shared among five clubs – in the three European competitions in this decade, a phenomenal record.

The national side qualified for the 1962 and 1966 World Cup finals and won the European Championship in 1964. A side containing Luis Suarez, possibly the greatest Spanish footballer ever, and one of the few Spaniards to play in Italy (with Internazionale), beat the Soviet Union 2–1 in Madrid to clinch Spain's first major trophy. The 1970s, however, marked a decline at both levels. A ban on foreign imports, imposed in 1963, was lifted in 1973 in order to improve the national side. But it had the reverse effect. Spain failed to reach the 1970 and 1974 World Cup finals and, after Real's 1966 European Cup success, it was not until 1979 that European success returned, when Barcelona won the European Cup-winners' Cup. Spain hosted the 1982 World Cup, but failed miserably. They qualified again in 1986 and

1990 but could do no better than the quarter-finals in Mexico. But the clubs continued to do well. Real won two UEFA Cups in the 1980s, while Barcelona won the European Cup-winners' Cup in 1982 and 1989 and completed a hat-trick of European trophies by winning the European Cup in 1992 – seven years after losing a final to Steaua Bucharest.

When the national side failed to qualify for the 1992 European Championship finals, the question was raised again of whether Spanish clubs' liking for foreign imports was damaging the national side's chances. When the import ban was lifted in the early 1970s, many of the world's top stars moved to Spain, including Cruyff, Neeskens, Breitner, Netzer and Rep. This influx coincided with a decline in the fortunes of the national team. Similarly, the 1980s saw top imports such as Diego Maradona, Bernd Schuster, Gary Lineker, Hugo Sanchez and Ronald Koeman playing in Spain while the national team stuttered.

However, the Under-23s success at the 1992 Barcelona Olympics and the continued successes of Barcelona and Real, domestically and in Europe, are reasons for hope. Several of the young Olympic victors were integrated into the full national side, which reached the quarter-finals of both the 1994 World Cup and the 1996 European Championship.

SWEDEN

Svensk Fotbollforblundet
Founded: 1904
FIFA: 1904
Olympics: 1948
Sweden have, since the 1920s, been Scandinavia's top national side and have a deserved reputation for producing quality players. An Association was formed in 1904 and joined FIFA the same year.

Gothenburg was, and still is, the centre of Swedish domestic football and the National League, instituted in 1925, has been dominated by Gothenburg's clubs, Orgryte, IFK and GAIS, along with AIK and Djurgardens of Stockholm. Sweden's national side made their debut in 1908 and entered the first four

IN TRIM *Liedholm (left) and Svensson*

Olympic tournaments – with mixed success. This era, however, produced the country's greatest striker, Sven Rydell, who scored 49 goals in 43 games. Sweden were at their best in the late 1940s when they boasted one of the most famous forward lines in history. Gunnar Gren, Gunnar Nordahl and Nils Liedholm – the "Gre-No-Li" trio – sparked Sweden to Olympic gold in 1948 and were promptly signed up by Milan, where they enjoyed great success. Swedes were regularly bought by European clubs but were then barred from the national side by the strictly-amateur rules of the association. Despite this handicap, Sweden finished third in the 1950 World Cup, with Nacka Skoglund the new star.

The import ban was lifted in time for the 1958 World Cup finals, which Sweden hosted, and with all their players available they reached the Final. A decline followed in the 1960s, but Sweden qualified for all three World Cup finals in the 1970s, with Bjorn Nordqvist clocking up a record 115 appearances between 1963 and 1978.

The clubs too began to make an

impact, and Malmo reached the European Cup Final in 1979. IFK Gothenburg enjoyed the greatest success, though, winning the UEFA Cup in 1982 and 1989 – as part-timers, because Sweden has not yet introduced full professionalism. Until it does, its top stars will continue to move abroad in droves.

Sweden's first appearance in the European Championship finals came in 1992, by virtue of being hosts, but they were beaten in the semi-finals by Germany. They followed up by finishing third in the 1994 World Cup and toppling Denmark as top dogs in Scandinavia.

SWITZERLAND

Schweizerischer Fussballverband
Founded: 1895
FIFA: 1904
Switzerland have always been at the forefront of world football without ever actually winning anything, because both FIFA and UEFA are based in the country.

The British helped develop the game in Switzerland in the late 1800s, and this can clearly be seen in the names of two of her top clubs: Grasshopper (Zurich) and Young Boys (Bern). They, along with Servette (Geneva), have dominated Swiss football without prospering in European competition.

The national side, however, have fared slightly better, particularly in the 1920s and 1930s when they were runners-up in the 1924 Olympics and quarter-finalists at both the 1934

HODGSON'S CHOICE *The Swiss celebrate a Chapuisat goal against Italy*

BACK IN ACTION *Sinisa Mihajlovic starred for Yugoslavia on both sides of his country's international suspension*

and 1938 World Cups. The most famous names of this era were the Abegglen brothers, Max and André, who scored over 60 goals between them.

The man responsible for this success was Karl Rappan – the father of Swiss football. He devised the "Swiss Bolt" system, which involved using a free man at the back as a sort of *libero*, and under Rappan the Swiss reached the finals of four of the first five World Cups played after the war. Their best performance was in 1954 when, as hosts, they reached the quarter-finals.

After 1966 the national side suf-fered a reversal of fortunes and failed to qualify for six consecutive World Cups and seven European Championships. But under English coach Roy Hodgson, they staged a come-back. They narrowly missed qualifying for the 1992 European Championship finals, but claimed a place at the 1994 World Cup finals after a fine qualifying programme that included a 1–0 win over Italy. They followed up by reaching the finals of the 1996 European Championship, where they drew 1–1 with hosts Eng-land in the Opening Match, but fell away, losing their other two games.

TURKEY

Turkiye Futbol Federasyono
Founded: 1923
FIFA: 1933

How Turkey have failed to develop into a top European football nation is a mystery. With a population of 55 million, a fiercely competitive and well-attended league and plenty of tal-ented players, one World Cup finals appearance in 1954 is a pretty sorry return. The British brought football to Turkey in the 1890s, and by 1910 the country's top clubs – Besiktas, Galatasaray and Fenerbahce – had been founded. The clubs attract fanatical support and have done better than the national side, with Gala reaching the semi-finals of the European Cup in 1989 and dismissing Manchester United from the same competition in 1993. The inter-national authorities may need to think again about Turkey's tradi-tional minnow rating after the man-ner in which they reached the finals of the 1996 European Championship. Centre-forward Hakan Sukur was their goalscoring hero.

UKRAINE

Football Federation of Ukraine
Founded: 1992
FIFA: 1992

Considering that Kiev Dynamo were one of Europe's top clubs, Ukraine's international competitive debut after the Soviet collapse was disappointing. They offered little threat to Croatia and Italy in the Euro 96 qualifying tour-nament. At club level mafia infil-tration and bribery problems have added to the difficulties.

WALES

Football Association of Wales
Founded: 1876
FIFA: 1910–20, 1924–28, 1946

Football has always come second behind Rugby Union in Wales, but the tide may be turning. In 1992, for the first time, the Welsh FA set up a National League, with a place in the Europe as an incentive for the "exile" clubs playing in England to join. Simultaneously, the national side is at its best since the inter-war period, when Billy Meredith led them to six British

Championships, and the 1950s when Wales reached the 1958 World Cup quar-ter-finals with a side containing the legendary John Charles.

Welsh hopes of a 1994 World Cup finals appearance rested on the stun-ning forward line of Ian Rush, the coun-try's top scorer, Mark Hughes, Dean Saunders and the "wonder boy" Ryan Giggs. They went very close but it was not to be. Further disap-pointment followed in the Euro 96 qualifiers when Wales changed man-ager three times in less than two years. Bobby Gould finally took on the challenge of building a new team which can no longer rely on the now-veteran skills of Rush, Hughes and Neville Southall.

YUGOSLAVIA

Fudbalski Savez Jugoslavije
Founded: 1919
FIFA: 1919
Olympic Games: 1960

Yugoslavia were often called the "Argentina of Europe" for the way – before the civil war in the Balkans – in which they exported hundreds of fine players and coaches all over the world. This was the Yugoslavia who were World Cup semi-finalists in 1930 and again in 1962, but never really achieved as much as they should have, although they did win the Olympic title in 1960.

In 1991, however, the old nation-alist tensions which have plagued the area for centuries erupted, and Yugoslavia violently disintegrated into several independent states. Yugoslavia's last international match was against Holland in the spring of 1992. Shortly afterwards, they were expelled from the European Championship finals and barred from the 1994 World Cup and Euro 1996. What seemed like a sad end to 70 years of united Yugoslav football proved premature as the country played friendlies in 1994 and 1995 against the likes of Brazil, Argentina and Russia.

"New" Yugoslavia are returning to competition in the 1998 World Cup. Hopes of a speedy revival of football fortunes rest on the shoulders of Milan's Dejan Savicevic and Real Madrid's Predrag Mijatovic as well as the veteran, Dragan Stojkovic.

SOUTH AMERICA

Wanderers and Liverpool in Uruguay, Rangers and Everton in Chile, Newells Old Boys in Argentina, Corinthians in Brazil . . . are all names which provide proof of the debt that football around South America owes to British soccer missionaries.

But the British were not alone in taking the round ball west. So did the French (namely Racing Club of Argentina), Italians (Boca Juniors of Argentina and Penarol of Uruguay), Spanish (Barcelona of Ecuador), and Portuguese (Vasco da Gama of Brazil).

The success of these missions is clear to see on the international stage. Uruguay won the Olympic Games in 1924 and '28, then the same nation hosted the inaugural World Cup in 1930, and won that too. The 1950s opened with Uruguay winning the World Cup in Brazil and ended with the Brazilians becoming the first South American nation to win the World Cup in Europe when they beat hosts Sweden in 1958. The star of that team was the legendary Pele, and he was at the heart of outstanding team of 1970. The 1970s and 80s belonged to Argentina, winners of two World Cups, in 1978 and '86 and to another footballing genius, Diego Maradona.

South American clubs have also dominated the World Club Cup, where success over European clubs has been at the rate of three to two since 1960.

ARGENTINA

Asociacion del Futbol Argentino
Founded: 1893
FIFA: 1912
World Cup: 1978, 1986
South American Championship: 1910, 1921, 1925, 1927, 1929, 1937, 1941, 1945, 1946, 1947, 1955, 1957, 1991, 1993
Of all South American nations, Argentina are the most consistently successful.

Football was brought to Argentina by the British in the 1860s, and although, at first, it was exclusive to the British residents in Buenos Aires, by the turn of the century numerous clubs had been formed.

The Argentine Football Association was founded in 1891 by an Englishman, Alexander Hutton, and a league was formed the same year. Although the championship was not a truly national competition, as it contained only clubs from Buenos Aires, La Plata, Rosario and Santa Fé, the intense rivalry of the clubs in Buenos Aires ensured that Argentina had a vibrant domestic scene from the outset.

The national side also made an early start, and in 1901 a representative side played neighbouring Uruguay, in the first international match to be staged outside Great Britain. The seeds were sown for a rivalry which has grown into one of the most enduring and

intense derby matches in the world.

Professionalism was adopted in 1931, and River Plate and Boca Juniors soon emerged as dominant forces in the new pro league. River's side of the 1940s was the greatest of them all, containing a forward line of Muñoz, Moreno, Pedernera, Labruna and Loustau which became known as *La Maquina* – the machine.

The national side were runners-up, to Uruguay, in the 1928 Olympics and met their deadly rivals again two years later in the 1930 World Cup Final. Although they lost 4–2 the impressive Argentine side was plundered by Italian agents – starting a draining process which continues today. To avoid a repeat of this poaching, a third-rate side went to the 1934 tournament, and Argentina did not make a serious attempt on the World Cup again until the 1950s.

Indeed, the 1950s saw the birth of an exceptional side, with another famous forward line of Corbatta, Maschio, Angelillo, Sivori and Cruz. They won the South American Championship twice during the 1950s and then made an unsuccessful bid to host the 1958 World Cup. Little progress was made in the 1960s and 1970s, despite Independiente and Estudiantes dominating the Libertadores Cup, and Argentina had to wait until 1978 for her first success in the World Cup.

On home soil, and with a side containing only one overseas-based player, Mario Kempes, Argentina deservedly won the tournament. They did so again in Mexico in 1986, when the side was led by Diego Maradona – who ranks as one of the greatest players the world has ever seen despite his drug abuse problems. In fact, Argentina featured in the final of three of the four World Cups from 1978 to 1990, they won the first two South American Championships of the 1990s, and they continue to produce extremely gifted footballers. The captain of the 1978 World Cup winning team, Daniel Passarella, became national coach in 1995.

BOLIVIA

Federacion Boliviana de Futbol
Founded: 1925
FIFA: 1926
South American Championship: 1963
Since their first international outing in 1926, Bolivia have been the perennial whipping boys of South American football – until now. In the 1994 World Cup qualifiers the Bolivians finished a close second in Group B to qualify for the finals for the first time in forty years, recording a notable 2–0 victory over Brazil along the way and knocking out Uruguay and Ecuador in the process. Prior to that, apart from World Cup qualification in 1930 and 1950, the 1963 South American Championship victory, played at home, was the only success of note.

BRAZIL

Confederacao Brasileira de Futebol
Founded: 1914
FIFA: 1923
World Cup: 1958, 1962, 1970, 1994
South American Championship: 1919, 1922, 1949, 1989
Brazilian football has a romantic air about it that sets it apart from other nations. Between 1958 and 1970 they won the World Cup three times, with a team packed full of star players, including arguably the greatest in history – Pele. Brazil remains the only country to have played in every World Cup finals tournament and the only four-time winner.

Brazilian football developed at the end of the nineteenth century, prompted by migrant British workers, and leagues were established in Rio de Janeiro and São Paulo by the turn of the century. The vast size of Brazil meant that a national league was impractical and until the 1970s these leagues dominated domestic football. The "classic" Rio derbies between Flamengo, Fluminense, Botafogo and Vasco da Gama regularly attracted massive crowds to the 200,000-capacity Maracana Stadium.

The national team were a little slower out of the blocks, and their first real international was not played until 1914 with a visit to Buenos Aires. In 1916 Brazil entered the South American

ARGENTINE ACES *The 1986 World Cup-winning side*

with a flourish and the global TV audience loved it. In attack, Pele was back to his best and he was superbly assisted by Jairzinho, Rivelinho and Tostao.

After 1970, it was 24 years before the national side again scaled such heights by winning the 1994 World Cup – albeit thanks to a penalty shoot-out. Their best showing along the way was in the 1982 World Cup, when a side containing Zico, Socrates, Junior and Falcao should have gone further than the second round in Spain, where they lost to the eventual winners Italy.

Ironically, in 1994's qualifiers, they lost to Bolivia, their first defeat ever in a World Cup qualifier, and scrambled through in an unconvincing and uncharacteristic fashion. At club level, Brazilian football is in a poor state, with too many meaningless competitions and games against mismatched opponents and continual rows between the various regional governing bodies.

Brazil having won the 1994 World Cup on a penalty shoot-out, then lost to Uruguay in the 1995 Copa America Final by the same method.

The legacy of the Pele years continues to weigh heavily, for any Brazil side, regardless of its capabilities, is expected to play what Pele himself called "the beautiful game".

CHILE

Federacion de Futbol de Chile
Founded: 1895
FIFA: 1912
Until Colo Colo's Libertadores Cup triumph in 1991, no Chilean side had ever won a major honour, and Chile have often been seen as the "nearly-men" of South American football.

Chile qualified for five of the 11 post-war World Cups, but have only once progressed beyond the first round, in 1962, when they reached the semifinals on home soil. Their best performances in the South American Championship came in 1979 and 1987, when they were runners-up. Chile, like many of its neighbours, is continually drained of its best players by European clubs, and it is unlikely that the Chileans will ever be able to improve on their third place in the 1962 World Cup.

ALL SQUARE *Aldair clashes with Italy's Nicola Berti in the 1994 World Cup Final at the Rose Bowl in Pasadena*

Championship, but this event has not been a rewarding one for the Brazilians, who have won it only four times – three of them on home soil.

The World Cup, however, is another matter. The first attempt on the trophy was made in 1930, when they went out in the first round. The 1934 campaign was equally bad, despite the presence of such fine players as Leonidas da Silva and Artur Friedenreich. In 1938, however, they showed the first signs of what was to come by reaching the semifinals, where they lost to Italy.

The golden age of Brazilian football was between 1950 and 1970, and it is the sides of this era that stick in the memory. In 1950 they were runners-up as Uruguay pipped them for the title in the deciding match. In 1954, with Nilton and Djalma Santos established at the back and Didi running the midfield, they reached the quarter-finals in Switzerland, where they lost to Hungary's "Magical Magyars".

In 1958 Brazil finally won the honour the nation's fans craved. With a forward line consisting of Garrincha, Vava, Zagalo and the 17-year-old Pele, they stormed to victory in Sweden, beating the hosts 5–2 in the Final. In Chile in 1962, an almost identical team – minus the injured Pele – triumphed again, beating Czechoslovakia 3–1 in the Final in Santiago.

In 1966, in England, the side was being rebuilt and Brazil fell in the first round. But the newcomers Tostao, Gerson and Jairzinho were present in Mexico four years later when Brazil clinched a hat-trick of World Cups, earning them the right to keep the Jules Rimet Trophy in perpetuity.

The 1970 side has been described as the best ever seen, and with some justification. The defence, marshalled by Carlos Alberto, was not all that strong, but this did not matter as the Brazilian approach at this time was all-out attack – and simply to score more goals than they conceded. This was football

SANTIAGO STRUGGLE *Chile vs. Switzerland in the first round of the 1962 World Cup, which the South Americans won 3–1*

COLOMBIA

Federacion Colombiana de Futbol
Founded: 1924
FIFA: 1936

Colombia is only now emerging as a challenger to Argentina and Brazil after years of internal disputes, disruptions and turbulence. The most notorious came in 1950, shortly after professionalism was introduced, when a break-away league outside FIFA jurisdiction, the DiMayor, was formed and Colombian sides began importing players from all over South America and from Britain. The huge salaries on offer led to the four years of its existence being known as the "El Dorado" period. The bubble burst in 1954, when Colombia were readmitted to FIFA and the league collapsed, leaving many clubs in desperate financial trouble.

The national side made its debut as late as 1938, and results at first were poor. Between 1949 and 1957 no internationals were played at all, and thereafter outings were infrequent. It was a huge surprise, then, when Colombia qualified for the 1962 World Cup in Chile, although to do so they only had to beat Peru. However, the best they managed on their World Cup debut was a 4–4 draw with the USSR.

In 1965 another breakaway federation was formed and confusion reigned once more. FIFA had to intervene and effectively ran Colombian football up until 1971, when the present administration was installed. A new league structure was introduced in 1968, careful controls on the number of foreign imports were implemented, and the national side soon benefited.

In 1989 Nacional Medellin won the Libertadores Cup, the country's only victory, and a year later the national side, coached by Francisco Maturana – who had led Nacional to their success – qualified for the 1990 World Cup finals.

But the best – and worst – followed. In the 1994 World Cup qualifiers, Argentina were thrashed 5–0 in Buenos Aires and consigned to a play-off. This performance led a number of people to consider the Colombians a good bet to win the whole competition.

At USA '94, Colombia's efforts foundered on poor morale, not helped by death threats against players and coach Maturana. Worst of all came after their surprise first-round elimination. Defender Andres Escobar – who had scored an own goal in the shock 2–1 defeat by the USA – was shot to death in Medellin. Drug and gambling cartels – believed to be behind the unsolved murder – still threaten to undermine all the good work achieved by outstanding players such as Carlos Valderrama.

ECUADOR

Asociacion Ecuatoriana de Futbol
Founded: 1925
FIFA: 1926

Ecuador are one of South America's weakest nations, and they have yet to qualify for any major tournament. The closest they have gone to reaching the World Cup finals was in 1966, when they lost a play-off to Chile. Between 1938 and 1975 the national side managed only eight wins, but there are signs of improvement. In 1990, Barcelona of Guayaquil were runners-up in the Libertadores Cup, and the semi-final in which they impressively beat River Plate is surely the country's proudest moment.

PARAGUAY

Liga Paraguaya de Futbol
Founded: 1906
FIFA: 1921
South American Championship: 1953, 1979

SPEED MERCHANT *Few players in world football can keep up with Colombia's striker Faustino Asprilla when he is in full flight*

Asuncion dominates Paraguayan football, and Olimpia dominate Asuncion. They are the country's most successful side and have won the Libertadores Cup twice, in 1979 and 1990, and have been runners-up three times.

The national side has also done well, for such a small and impoverished country. They won the South American Championship in 1953 and again in 1979 – a year in which Paraguayan teams won every trophy available to them. Paraguay have reached the World Cup finals four times, most recently in 1986, but in the search for honours, Olimpia will continue to lead the way.

PERU

Federacion Peruana de Futbol
Founded: 1922
FIFA: 1924
South American Championship: 1939, 1975.

Football in Peru has always been dominated by Lima, and the national association was founded there in 1922.

The local Lima League was the strongest in the country and, until a national championship was introduced in 1966, the winners were considered national champions. Lima's clubs, Alianza, Universitario and Sporting Cristal, have dominated at home, but none have achieved success in the Libertadores Cup. Sadly, the eyes of the world were focused on Peru in 1964, when 300 spectators died in a riot, and in 1988, when the Alianza team was wiped out in a plane crash.

Peru's international debut came in the South American Championship of 1927, and they won the event at home in 1939. The World Cup record was poor, however, until the 1970s, when a generation of notable players came together and made the decade the country's most successful ever.

Stars of the 1970s side were the highly eccentric and entertaining goalkeeper Ramon "El Loco" Quiroga, Hector Chumpitaz and midfield maestro Teofilo Cubillas, the greatest Peruvian player of all time. Coached by Brazilian World Cup winner Didi, this side reached the quarter-finals of the 1970 World Cup, won the 1975 South American Championship, and qualified for the 1978 World Cup, where they fell in the second round.

Peru qualified for the World Cup again in 1982, but the side was past its best and went out in the first round. Since then, Peru have slipped back into their familiar role of the "middle-men" of South American football. Political problems in the country have not helped.

URUGUAY

Asociacion Uruguaya de Futbol
Founded: 1900
FIFA: 1923
World Cup: 1930, 1950
South American Championship: 1916, 1917, 1920, 1923, 1924, 1926, 1935, 1942, 1956, 1959, 1967, 1983, 1987, 1995.
Olympics: 1924, 1928

Before the Second World War, Uruguay were undoubtedly the best team in the world, effectively winning three World Championships. Today they are no longer a world power, but they have a proud history and can still be dangerous opponents. Montevideo dominates the domestic scene and, as it is located just across the River Plate estuary from Buenos Aires, the two cities can rightly claim to be the centre of South American football. Montevideo's two great clubs, Penarol and Nacional, have dominated Uruguayan football, winning more than 80 championships between them. The clubs are fierce rivals and have both enjoyed great success in the Libertadores Cup; Penarol winning it five times, Nacional three. Both clubs have also won the World Club Cup.

The national side dominated world football in the first half of this century, but has faded since the 1950s. Early successes in the South American Championship were followed by victory in the 1924 Olympics in Amsterdam, at a time when the Olympic winners could justifiably claim to be world champions. Having amazed Europe with their skill at the 1924 Olympics, Uruguay repeated the trick in 1928 and two years later, as the host nation, swept to victory in the first World Cup.

The side of the 1920s and 1930s contained many of Uruguay's all-time greats: skipper Jose Nasazzi, the midfield "Iron Curtain" of Jose Andrade, Lorenzo Fernandez and Alvarez Gestido, and outstanding forwards Hector Castro, Pedro Cea and Hector Scarone.

In 1950 Uruguay pulled off one of the biggest World Cup finals shocks in history, coming from a goal down to beat Brazil 2–1 in the deciding match … in Brazil. The side contained strikers Juan Schiaffino, Uruguay's greatest player, and Omar Miguez, Victor Andrade, nephew of Jose, Roque Maspoli in goal and Obdulio Varela in defence. In Switzerland in 1954, the defence of their crown ended with a 4–2 semi-final defeat by Hungary in one of the best World Cup games ever.

Since then, Uruguay have enjoyed regular success in the South American Championship, but in the World Cup they have failed to matched their feats of the 1930s and 1950s. They finished fourth in the 1970, but elimination by Bolivia in the 1994 qualifiers showed just how far they had slipped.

Uruguay still produces outstanding players, like Enzo Francescoli and Carlos Aguilera, but they often go to Europe to further their careers. With so many foreign-based players, Uruguay developed a schizophrenic approach to the World Cup and South American Championship, often entering wildly different teams for tournaments staged less than a year apart. This unpredictability was shown in 1995, when Uruguay won the Copa America, beating 1994 World Cup winners Brazil after a penalty shoot-out in the Final.

VENEZUELA

Federacion Venezolana de Futbol
Founded: 1926
FIFA: 1952

Venezuela are the weakest of the 10 South American countries, but this is hardly surprising because the national sport is baseball. Originally members of CONCACAF, they made their international debut in 1938 and switched to CONMEBOL in 1958. The national record is awful, with just one match won in the South American Championship and only a handful more in World Cup qualifiers, even though they have entered both regularly.

The clubs are weak too, and three Libertadores Cup semi-finals are the best they have managed. A professional league was finally set up in 1956, but Venezuela have a long way to go if they are even to catch up with the other South American minnows.

MIDFIELD MAESTRO *Teofilo Cubillas, Peru's greatest ever player*

NORTH & CENTRAL AMERICA

Many central American nations may appear little more than a statistical dot in the world game's atlas. But CONCACAF (North and Central American confederation) is very quickly learning how to capitalize on the commercial value of football. The income is being used profitably for coaching schemes and administrative improvements. "American" soccer is much more now than merely those nations which have done well in the World Cup: Mexico's double staging of the World Cup finals in 1970 and 1986 proves the point. So, of course, did USA '94 ...

ANTIGUA AND BARBUDA

Antigua Football Association
Founded: 1928
FIFA: 1970

ARUBA

Arubaanse Voetbal Bond
Founded: 1932
FIFA: 1988

BAHAMAS

Bahamas Football Association
Founded: 1967
FIFA: 1968

BARBADOS

Barbados Football Association
Founded: 1910
FIFA: 1968

BELIZE

Belize National Football Association
Founded: 1980
FIFA: 1986

BERMUDA

Bermuda Football Association
Founded: 1928
FIFA: 1962

CANADA

Canadian Soccer Association
Founded: 1912
FIFA: 1912
Olympics: 1904 (Galt FC of Ontario)
Football in Canada has struggled to establish itself for two main reasons. First, the enormous size of the country makes a coherent structure difficult to implement and consequently a true, national league was only set up in 1987. Second, the sport trails badly in popularity behind ice hockey, baseball, gridiron and basketball – the big North American sports.

Football took hold in Canada at the turn of the century, and in 1904 Galt FC from Ontario entered the St Louis Olympic Games. Soccer was only a demonstration sport, but Galt won the event, still Canada's only major honour. The national side made a few outings in the 1920s, but went into hibernation until the 1950s when they entered the 1958 World Cup – their first attempt. Success eluded them, however, and even when Montreal hosted the 1976 Olympics, they were eliminated in the first round.

In the 1970s, three Canadian clubs, from Vancouver, Toronto and Edmonton, played in the North American Soccer League – as many of Canada's ice hockey and baseball clubs do. In 1976, Toronto won the NASL Soccer Bowl, as did Vancouver in 1979, and many of the Canadians playing in the NASL formed the backbone of the national side which reached the 1986 World Cup finals, their only appearance to date.

In the 1994 qualifiers Canada, with five British-based professionals in the side, reached a play-off with Oceania winners Australia, but lost on penalties. The side was coached by Bobby Lenarduzzi, who had been a member of the 1986 side.

BRIEF ENCOUNTER *Canada at Mexico '86, their only World Cup appearance*

CAYMAN ISLANDS

Cayman Islands Football Association
Founded: 1992
FIFA: 1992

COSTA RICA

Federacion Costarricense de Futbol
Founded: 1921
FIFA: 1921
CONCACAF Championship: 1941, 1946, 1948, 1953, 1955, 1960, 1961, 1963, 1969, 1989

Costa Rica are one of the better teams from Central America, and between 1940 and 1970 they won an impressive nine CONCACAF Championships. Despite this, Costa Rica struggled to make an impact in the World Cup – El Salvador and Honduras both qualified before them – but in 1990 the breakthrough came. Under coach Bora Milutinovic, they not only qualified for the finals, but also defeated Scotland and Sweden to progress into the second round. Costa Rica has a very healthy domestic scene too, and two clubs, Deportivo Saprissa and LD Alajeulense, have both won the CONCACAF Club Championship.

CUBA

Asociacion de Futbol de Cuba
Founded: 1924
FIFA: 1932

DOMINICA

Dominica Football Association
Founded:
FIFA:

DOMINICAN REPUBLIC

Federacion Dominicana de Futbol
Founded: 1953
FIFA: 1958

EL SALVADOR

Federacion Salvadorena de Futbol
Founded: 1935
FIFA: 1938
CONCACAF Championship: 1943

El Salvador's biggest claim to soccer fame is the 1969 "Football War" with Central American neighbours Honduras. The countries met in a World Cup qualifying group and rioting followed both matches, especially after the second game when El Salvador forced a play-off. El Salvador won it and, as tension mounted, the army invaded Honduras on the pretext of protecting expatriate Salvadorean citizens. The World Cup match was more an excuse than a cause for the war, but the conflict cost 3,000 lives before it was settled.

El Salvador have qualified for the World Cup finals twice, losing all three games in 1970 and again in 1982 – which included a 10–1 thrashing by Hungary.

GRENADA

Grenada Football Association
Founded: 1924
FIFA: 1976

GUATEMALA

Federacion Nacional de Futbol de Guatemala
Founded: 1926
FIFA: 1933
CONCACAF Championship: 1967

GUYANA

Guyana Football Association
Founded: 1904
FIFA: 1968

HAITI

Fédération Haitienne de Football
Founded: 1904
FIFA: 1933
CONCACAF Championship: 1957, 1973

HONDURAS

Federacion Nacional Automana de Futbol
Founded: 1935
FIFA: 1946
CONCACAF Championship: 1981
Honduras, like neighbouring El Salvador, is a country which has been plagued by insurgency and guerrilla warfare. Indeed, the two went to war in 1969, over the outcome of a foot-

ball match, as described in the entry for El Salvador. Honduras made their sole appearance in the World Cup finals in 1982, when they drew 1–1 with hosts, Spain, and Northern Ireland, before losing 1–0 to Yugoslavia and going out of the tournament.

Honduran clubs have enjoyed some success in the CONCACAF Club Championship, notably Olimpia, who won the event in 1972 and 1988, and were runners-up in 1985.

JAMAICA

Jamaica Football Federation
Founded: 1910
FIFA: 1962
Rapid progress was made after the Brazilian Federation loaned Jamaica coach Rene Simoes. Jamaica received a special award as the most improved team in the 1995 FIFA rankings and reached the final stages of the CONCACAF World Cup qualifiers in 1997.

MEXICO

Federacion Mexicana de Futbol Asociacion
Founded: 1927
FIFA: 1929
CONCACAF Championship: 1963, 1971, 1977, 1993
Mexico utterly dominate their Central American region, but this has hindered rather than helped their game. With no decent, local opposition for the national side or the clubs, Mexico have enjoyed their greatest moments in the World Cup.

The federation was formed in 1927, and a trip to the Amsterdam Olympics a year later ended after just one match. Two years later they entered the World Cup and have qualified for 10 of the 15 finals tournaments, a record which includes 1990, when they were barred by FIFA for breaches of age regulations in a youth tournament. Mexico's best World Cups were in 1970 and 1986, when they were hosts. They reached the quarter-finals of both and in 1986 were unlucky to lose on penalties to West Germany.

Star of the 1986 side was Hugo Sanchez, an agile forward who led Real Madrid to many honours in the 1980s. Famous for his exuberant, cartwheel-

ing celebrations when he scores, Sanchez is Mexico's greatest player since Antonio Carbajal, the goalkeeper who created a record by playing in all five World Cup finals tournaments from 1950 to 1966. Mexico won the CONCACAF Championship four times, but were shocked in 1991 when the United States beat them in the semifinals, though Mexico regained the upper hand in 1993. Many believe Mexico would benefit from joining the South Americans, and in 1993 they, and the USA, were invited to take part in the South American Championship.

Mexico embarrassed their hosts by reaching the final, losing narrowly to Argentina. Mexico then qualified for the 1994 World Cup finals with comparative ease, only to lose to Bulgaria in a second round penalty shoot-out.

NETHERLANDS ANTILLES

Nederlands Antiliaanse Voetbal Unie
Founded: 1921
FIFA: 1932

NICARAGUA

Federacion Nicaraguense de Futbol
Founded: 1931
FIFA: 1950

PANAMA

Federacion Nacional de Futbol de Panama
Founded: 1937
FIFA: 1938
CONCACAF Championship: 1951

PUERTO RICO

Federacion Puertorriquena de Futbol
Founded: 1940
FIFA: 1960

SAINT KITTS AND NEVIS

St Kitts and Nevis Football Association
Founded: 1992
FIFA: 1992

SAINT LUCIA

St Lucia National Football Association
Founded: 1988
FIFA: 1988

SAINT VINCENT & THE GRENADINES

St Vincent and the Grenadines Football Federation
Founded: 1988
FIFA: 1988

SURINAM

Surinaamse Voetbal Bond
Founded: 1920
FIFA: 1929

TRINIDAD AND TOBAGO

Trinidad and Tobago Football Association
Founded: 1906
FIFA: 1963

UNITED STATES

United States Soccer Federation
Founded: 1913
FIFA: 1913
CONCACAF Championship: 1991
The United States is viewed by many as a non-football country, yet US football has a long and interesting history. For example, the Oneida club of Boston was founded in 1862, making it the oldest outside England.

The national side entered the 1924 and 1928 Olympics and then travelled to Uruguay for the first World Cup in 1930 – where they reached the semifinals. Four years later they were represented at the finals again, but lost to hosts Italy in the first round. In 1950 the US caused one of the biggest World Cup shocks ever when they beat England 1–0, with Haiti-born Joe Gaetjens scoring the winning goal. It would be 40 years before the US qualified for the World Cup finals again.

Apart from the victory over England, US soccer was long famed for one other reason – the North American Soccer League. Founded in 1967, the NASL featured corporate-backed teams which enabled the clubs to pay huge wages and attract top foreign stars. such as Pele, Franz Beckenbauer, Johan Cruyff and George Best, but the NASL collapsed in the late 1980s.

With Mexico suspended, the US qualified for the 1990 World Cup finals, but their international naivety was clearly shown, losing all three matches. FIFA, bidding to promote the game world-wide, selected the US to host the 1994 finals. No one doubted that they would be well organized, the fears were all about the hosts' quality of play.

But, under coach Bora Milutinovic, the team became hard to beat and, in 1991 they won the CONCACAF Championship – their only honour to date. The US – containing a number of players with experience of club football in Europe – then produced one of the shocks of the 1994 World Cup when they defeated dark horses Colombia in the group stage and lost only 1–0 to Brazil in the second round. The 1995 Copa America, under a new coach – Steve Sampson – proved this success was not a fluke, as the US reached the semi-finals after defeating Argentina 3–0.

Major League Soccer, the first outdoor professional league since the demise of NASL began play in 1996. Some of the glitz of the former league may have been missing, but MLS did have one big advantage: as well as stars from around the world, the league boasted famous internationals who were home-grown.

OVER THE TOP *American Alexi Lalas tackles Colombian Ivan Valenciano*

OCEANIA

Oceania took a major step forward in 1996 when it was accepted by FIFA as a fully-fledged regional confederation. But that was still not enough to earn a guaranteed place for at least one of its nations at the World Cup finals. The best Oceania nation was still condemned to a qualifying play-off against one of the Asian nations.

AMERICAN SAMOA

American Samoa Football Association
Founded: 1975
FIFA: Associate member

AUSTRALIA

Australia Soccer Federation
Founded: 1961
FIFA: 1963
Soccer has struggled to gain a foothold in Australia, where cricket, Aussie Rules football and rugby are the most popular sports. The domestic league formed in 1977, has many ethnically linked clubs such as South Melbourne Hellas and Adelaide City Juventus

Australia's only World Cup finals appearance, in 1974, proved to be a disappointment. In the 1994 World Cup qualifiers, the "Socceroos" – as they are known – lost to Argentina for the last spot in the finals.

COOK ISLANDS

Cook Islands Football Federation
Founded: 1971
FIFA: 1994

FIJI

Fiji Football Association
Founded: 1938
FIFA: 1963

NEW CALEDONIA

Federation Neo-Caledonienne de Football
Founded: 1960
FIFA: Associate member

NEW ZEALAND

New Zealand Football Association
Founded: 1938
FIFA: 1963
New Zealand's only World Cup finals appearance was in 1982, when they were eliminated in the first round. Wynton Rufer was a member of that side, and won a German Championship medal with Werder Bremen in 1992–93 to establish himself as New Zealand's greatest-ever player.

PAPUA NEW GUINEA

Papua New Guinea Football Association
Founded: 1962
FIFA: 1963

SOLOMON ISLANDS

Solomon Islands Football Federation
Founded: 1988
FIFA: 1988

TAHITI

Fédération Tahitienne de Football
Founded: 1938
FIFA: 1990

TONGA

Tonga Football Association
Founded:
FIFA:

VANUATU

Vanuatu Football Federation
Founded: 1934
FIFA: 1988

WESTERN SAMOA

Western Samoa Football Association
Founded: 1968
FIFA: 1986

AFRICA

MOVING AHEAD *Algeria's Assad leaves a Chilean defender trailing*

FIFA has grown from the seven original members of 1904 through 73 in 1950 to more than 200 nations (including associate members). Africa is the largest of the regional confederations with 51 full members and one associate member state.

In the past 20 years FIFA has concentrated millions of dollars in educational programmes for coaches, referees, administrators and players in the developing world. Progress has been measured by World Cup finals entry: three African nations were present, for the first time, at USA '94, thanks to the feats of her entrants in 1990; the next World Cup, in France in 1998, will see expanded representation for the developing countries thanks to the enlargement of the event from 24 to 32 teams.

ALGERIA

Fédération Algérienne de Football
Founded: 1962
FIFA: 1963
African Nations Cup: 1990

The French brought football to Algeria in the late 1900s, and by the 1930s several Muslim Algerian clubs had been formed. The earliest was Mouloudia Challia (1920), and they won the African Champions Cup in 1976 at the first attempt.

Algeria gained independence in 1962, and since then the national side has improved considerably. In 1980 they reached the final of the African Nations Cup, where they lost 3–0 to hosts Nigeria, and two years later qualified for the World Cup finals in Spain. At the 1982 finals the Algerians pulled off one of the biggest World Cup shocks when they beat West Germany 2–1, and had it not been for a contrived result between the Germans and Austria, Algeria would have reached the second round. Rabah Madjer and Lakhdar Belloumi were the goalscorers against West Germany and they remain Algeria's greatest players. Madjer won a European Cup-winners' Cup medal with FC Porto in 1987, when he was also voted African Footballer of the Year.

Algeria were semi-finalists in the African Nations Cup in 1984 and 1988, and in between qualified for the 1986 World Cup finals. Then, in 1990 they won the African Nations Cup for the first time. In 1993 they qualified for the African Nations Cup finals, but were expelled for fielding an ineligible player in a qualifying game.

Algerian clubs have done well in African competitions, with MC Algiers (1976), J.S Kabylie (1981 and 1990) and ES Setif (1988), all winning the African Champions Cup.

ANGOLA

Federacao Angolana de Futebol
Founded: 1977
FIFA: 1980

BENIN

Fédération Beninoise de Football
Founded: 1968
FIFA: 1969

BOTSWANA

Botswana Football Association
Founded: 1970
FIFA: 1976

BURKINA FASO

Fédération Burkinabe de Football
Founded: 1960
FIFA: 1964

BURUNDI

Fédération de Football du Burundi
Founded: 1948
FIFA: 1972

CAMEROON

Fédération Camerounaise de Football
Founded: 1960
FIFA: 1962
African Nations Cup: 1984, 1988.

Of all the African nations to have reached the World Cup finals, Cameroon have made by far the biggest impact. In 1982, in Spain, they drew all three of their first round games – against Italy (eventual winners), Poland (third) and Peru – but went out at that stage. They qualified again in 1990, beat reigning champions Argentina in the opening match and reached the quarter-finals, losing narrowly to England. As a result of these performances FIFA agreed to grant Africa a third berth at the 1994 finals. This time, the "Indomitable Lions" were a major disappointment, torn apart by internal strife.

Cameroon's greatest player is undoubtedly striker Roger Milla, who played in the 1982, 1990 and 1994 World Cup teams. In 1994, he became the oldest player to appear in the finals. Milla was voted African

Footballer of the Year in 1976 and again in 1990, and delighted fans at Italia '90 with his goals and his celebratory wiggle which usually followed. Other Cameroon players to have won the award include Theophile Abega (1984), Thomas N'Kono (1979 and 1982) and Jean Onguene (1980). N'Kono is one of the greatest goalkeepers Africa has produced, and enjoyed a fine club career in Spain.

Cameroon also won the African Nations Cup twice to confirm their status as the top side of the 1980s. Cameroon clubs have also enjoyed success in African competitions: with five wins in the Champions Cup and three in the Cup Winners' Cup.

CAPE VERDE

Federacao Cabo-Verdiana de Futebol
Founded: 1982
FIFA: 1986

CENTRAL AFRICAN REPUBLIC

Fédération Centrafricaine de Football
Founded: 1937
FIFA: 1963

CHAD

Fédération Tchadienne de Football
Founded: 1962
FIFA: 1988

CONGO

Fédération Congolaise de Football
Founded: 1962
FIFA: 1962
African Nations Cup: 1972

DJIBOUTI

Federation Djiboutienne de Football
Founded: 1977
FIFA: 1994

EGYPT

All Ettihad el Masri Li Korat el Kadam
Founded: 1921
FIFA: 1923
African Nations Cup: 1957, 1959, 1986

Egypt were one of the four founder members of the Confédération Africaine de Football and were the first Africans to join FIFA, in 1923. Given this 20-year start on most of her neighbours, it is no surprise that Egypt became one of the great African powers , winning the first two Nations Cups in 1957 and 1959.

Egypt finished fourth in the 1928 Olympics and entered the World Cup in 1934. Having beaten Palestine in a qualifying play-off, they lost 4–2 to Hungary in the first round. Olympic semi-finalists again in 1964, Egypt entered only one of the World Cups played between 1938 and 1970.

A revival in the 1970s saw them finish third in the African Nations Cup in 1970 and 1974, fourth in 1976 and reach the Olympic quarter-finals in 1984. Two years later, as hosts, they won the African Nations Cup for the third time, and then qualified for the 1990 World Cup finals, where they did well to hold Holland and the Republic of Ireland to draws.

Allied to this success at national level, Egyptian clubs are among the most powerful in Africa. Well organized, wealthy and well supported, Egypt's clubs have won the African Champions Cup and the African Cup Winners' Cup ten times. Al Ahly, the most successful, have won the former twice and the latter thrice – in consecutive years from 1984 to 1986.

Al-Titsh, who played for Al Ahly in the 1920s, was one of Egypt's finest players, and Ahly's stadium still bears his name. Other great Egyptian players include Mahmoud Al Khatib, Ibrahim Youssef and Abu Zeid, Egypt's best striker during the 1980s.

EQUATORIAL GUINEA

Federacion Equatoguineana de Futbol
Founded: 1976
FIFA: 1986

ETHIOPIA

Yeithiopia Football Federechin
Founded: 1943
FIFA: 1953
African Nations Cup: 1962

DOWN AND OUT *Ireland's Moran is left grounded by Egypt's El Kass*

GABON

Fédération Gabonaise de Football
Founded: 1962
FIFA: 1963

GAMBIA

Gambia Football Association
Founded: 1952
FIFA: 1966

GHANA

Ghana Football Association
Founded: 1957
FIFA: 1958
African Nations Cup: 1963, 1965, 1978, 1982
Ghana achieved independence in 1957 and the "Black Stars" quickly established themselves as a powerful force in African football. They won the African Nations Cup in 1963, at their first attempt, retained the trophy two years later and in the following two events, 1968 and 1970, were beaten finalists. Ghana is the only nation to win the trophy four times.

In club football, Asante Kotoko have won the African Champions Cup twice and Ghana have produced some outstanding players. Mohamed Ahmed Polo and Adolf Armah were stars in the 1970s; Ibrahim Sunday, African footballer of the year in 1971, played for Werder Bremen in the German League; Abedi Pele won many trophies with Marseille in the 1980s; and Nii Lamptey, of PSV Eindhoven, led Ghana to victory in the 1991 World Youth Championship. Nevertheless, Ghana have yet to qualify for the World Cup finals.

GUINEA

Fédération Guinéenne de Football
Founded: 1959
FIFA: 1961

GUINEA-BISSAU

Federacao de Football da Guinea-Bissau
Founded: 1974
FIFA: 1986

IVORY COAST

Fédération Ivoirienne de Football
Founded: 1960
FIFA: 1960
African Nations Cup: 1992

The Ivory Coast are one of Africa's great footballing enigmas. Of the field, they have a stable government and a healthy economy; on it the Ivory Coast has a well-organized league – advantages which many African countries do not enjoy – and yet success at international level eluded them until 1992. In that year "The Elephants" won the African Nations Cup in Senegal, defeating Ghana on penalties in the final. They had previously been semi-finalists three times without going further.

The 1992 success confirmed the Ivorians as favourites to qualify for the 1994 World Cup finals for the first time ever, but they faded badly in the final round and finished second behind Nigeria.

KENYA

Kenya Football Federation
Founded: 1932
FIFA: 1960

LESOTHO

Lesotho Sports Council
Founded: 1932
FIFA: 1964

LIBERIA

Liberia Football Association
Founded: 1936
FIFA: 1962

LIBYA

Libyan Arab Jamahiriya Football Federation
Founded: 1962
FIFA: 1963

MADAGASCAR

Fédération Malagasy de Football
Founded: 1961
FIFA: 1962

MALAWI

Football Association of Malawi
Founded: 1966
FIFA: 1967

MALI

Fédération Malienne de Football
Founded: 1960
FIFA: 1962

MAURITANIA

Fédération de Football de la République de Mauritanie
Founded: 1961
FIFA: 1964

MAURITIUS

Mauritius Football Association
Founded: 1952
FIFA: 1962

MOROCCO

Fédération Royale Marocaine de Football
Founded: 1955
FIFA: 1956
African Nations Cup: 1976
Morocco qualified for the World Cup finals in 1970 – the first African side to do so – and have made steady progress since, even applying to host the finals in 1984 and 1998. In those 1970 finals they held Bulgaria to a draw and gave West Germany a terrible fright before losing 2–1. They qualified again in 1986 and won their first

SWERVING *Morocco's Lamriss*

round group ahead of England, Poland and Portugal. In the second round they lost to the Germans again, but only through an unfortunate free-kick in the last minute. The side contained an outstanding goalkeeper, Zaki, and Mohammed Timoumi and Aziz Bouderbala were fine ball players in midfield. In 1976 they won the African Nations Cup for the only time and their presence at their third World Cup finals in 1994 confirmed them, along with Cameroon, as one of the leading soccer-playing countries of the African continent.

Moroccan domestic football is untypical of Africa, inasmuch as the clubs are well spread throughout the country, rather than concentrated in one city. They have also been very successful. FAR Rabat won the Champions Cup in 1985, Raja Casablanca repeated the trick in 1989, followed by Wydad Casablanca in 1992.

Morocco has also provided several stars of French football. Probably the greatest was Larbi Ben Barek, the "Black Pearl", who won 17 French caps and had a distinguished career with Marseille and Stade Français in the inter-war years. Another French star born in Morocco was Just Fontaine, whose 13 goals in the 1958 World Cup finals remains a record.

MOZAMBIQUE

Federacao Moçambicana de Futebol
Founded: 1975
FIFA: 1978

NAMIBIA

Namibia Football Federation
Founded: 1992
FIFA: 1992

NIGER

Fédération Nigérienne de Football
Founded: 1967
FIFA: 1967

NIGERIA

Nigeria Football Association
Founded: 1945
FIFA: 1959
Olympic Games: 1996
African Nations Cup: 1980, 1994
Nigeria, with a huge population and over 500 registered clubs, emerged at last in the 1990s as one of the most powerful nations in Africa. Nigeria's youngsters had already proved well capable of winning trophies, and this continues to bode well for the future of the national side.

In 1985 Nigeria won the World Under-17 Championship, becoming the first African side to win a FIFA world tournament at any level, beating West Germany 2–0 in the final; in 1989, Nigeria were runners-up in the World Under-20 Youth Championship; and in 1993 the "Green Eaglets" won their second Under-17 title in only the event's fifth staging.

A World Cup breakthrough came in 1994 when Nigeria nearly sprang one of the greatest of all upsets. They topped their first-round group – ahead of Argentina, Bulgaria and

Greece – and came within a couple of minutes of eliminating eventual finalists Italy in the second round.

Sadly, political problems then prevented Nigeria from defending their African Nations title in South Africa in 1996. But they more than atoned later in the year by becoming the first African nation to win the Olympic tournament. They did it the hard way too – beating favourites Brazil in the semi-final and Argentina in the final. Sadly their hero, forward Nwankwo Kanu, was forced out of the game shortly afterwards. He had just been sold by Ajax to Italy's Internazionale when a routine medical showed up a heart defect for which he underwent major surgery.

REUNION

Ligue de la Réunion
Founded: 1985
FIFA: Associate member

RWANDA

Fédération Rwandaise de Football Amateur
Founded: 1972
FIFA: 1976

SAO TOME AND PRINCIPE

Federacion Santomense de Futebol
Founded: 1975
FIFA: 1986

SO NEAR *Emmanuel Amunike's goal almost knocked Italy out of the World Cup*

SENEGAL

Fédération Sénégalaise de Football
Founded: 1960
FIFA: 1962

SEYCHELLES

Seychelles Football Federation
Founded: 1976
FIFA: 1986

SIERRA LEONE

Sierra Leone Amateur Football Association
Founded: 1923
FIFA: 1967

SOMALIA

Somalia Football Federation
Founded: 1951
FIFA: 1961

SOUTH AFRICA

South African Football Association
Founded: 1892
FIFA: 1952 (suspended 1964–76), 1992
African Nations Cup: 1996
Football was the sport of the masses in South Africa, but for 30 years the top clubs, such as the Kaiser Chiefs and Orlando Pirates, were football outcasts in Africa, until the collapse of apartheid. Returning to the fold in 1992, South Africa not only hosted the 1996 African Nations Cup but shocked the world by winning it.

SUDAN

Sudan Football Federation
Founded: 1936
FIFA: 1948
African Nations Cup: 1970

SWAZILAND

National Football Association of Swaziland
Founded: 1964
FIFA: 1976

TANZANIA

Football Association of Tanzania
Founded: 1930
FIFA: 1964

TOGO

Fédération Togolaise de Football
Founded: 1960
FIFA: 1962

TUNISIA

Fédération Tunisienne de Football
Founded: 1956
FIFA: 1960

UGANDA

Federation of Uganda Football Associations
Founded: 1924
FIFA: 1959

ZAIRE

Fédération Zaïreoise de Football-Association
Founded: 1919
FIFA: 1964
African Nations Cup: 1968, 1974
Zaïre won their second African Nations Cup in 1974, the year in which they also became the first black African side to qualify for the World Cup finals. But the gulf in experience between the "Leopards" and their European and South American opponents was cruelly exposed. Since then, their best performances have been in the African Nations Cup.

ZAMBIA

Football Association of Zambia
Founded: 1929
FIFA: 1964
Zambia's national side have been semi-finalists in the African Nations Cup three times since 1974, and pulled off a remarkable victory over Italy in the 1988 Olympics in Seoul. The star was Kalusha Bwalya, who became a top professional with PSV Eindhoven in Holland.

Sadly, Zambia will always now be remembered for the plane crash in April 1993 which wiped out the entire national squad – bar the five overseas-based professionals who were not travelling with the rest to a World Cup qualifier in Senegal. Astonishingly, the Zambians rebuilt their squad around their five exports, and went on to reach the 1994 African Nations Cup Final. They reached to the second round of the African World Cup qualifiers but missed clinching a place in the finals losing the last game, 1–0 in Morocco.

Zambian clubs are also beginning to do well in the African club competitions. Nkana Red Devils were runners-up in the 1990 Champions Cup, and Power Dynamos won the 1991 Cup-winners' Cup.

ZIMBABWE

Zimbabwe Football Association
Founded: 1950
FIFA: 1965
Zimbabwe won independence as recently as 1983 and have been making steady progress ever since. They went within one game of reaching the 1994 World Cup finals, but lost the last group match 3–1 in Cameroon. Their emergence owed much to former Liverpool goalkeeper Bruce Grobbelaar, and another English based player, Peter Ndlovu.

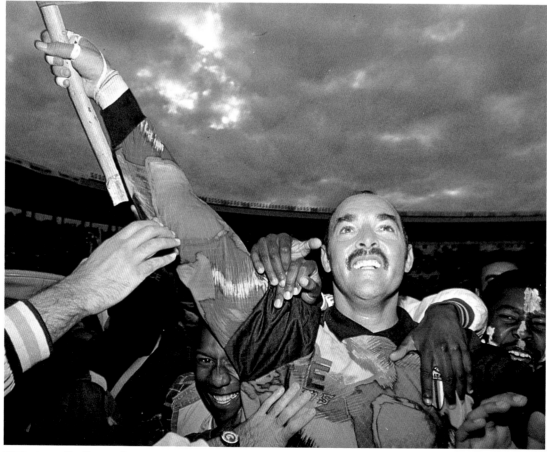

HARARE'S HERO *Goalkeeper Bruce Grobbelaar savours victory, but Zimbabwe just missed World Cup qualification*

ASIA

Sheer geography makes Asia the most awkward of FIFA's regional confederations. The varied time zones and climates between Lebanon in the west, the former Soviet republics in the north, Japan in the east and India in the south long hindered the development of credible international tournaments.

A signal that Asian football has come of age was evident when FIFA awarded Japan and South Korean rights to – uniquely – co-host the 2002 World Cup finals. It will be the first time the game's top event has been staged in Asia.

Although it is probably many years away, the time will come when an Asian nation – whether it is a current power such as South Korea or Saudi Arabia, or a new force such as Japan or China – wins the World Cup.

AFGHANISTAN

The Football Federation of the National Olympic Committee
Founded: 1922
FIFA: 1948

BAHRAIN

Bahrain Football Association
Founded: 1951
FIFA: 1966

BANGLADESH

Bangladesh Football Federation
Founded: 1972
FIFA: 1974

BHUTAN

Bhutan Football Federation
Founded: 1960
FIFA: Associate member

BRUNEI

Brunei Amateur Football Association
Founded: 1959
FIFA: 1969

CAMBODIA

Federation Khmere De Football Association
Founded: 1933
FIFA: 1953

CHINA

Football Association of the People's Republic of China
Founded: 1924
FIFA: 1931–58, 1979
China took part in the first international match played on Asian soil, when they met the Philippines, in Manila, in February 1913, in the Far Eastern Games. But progress was thwarted because of the Taiwan issue. A side containing only Hong Kong players took part in the 1954 Asian Games, calling themselves China. The Chinese Association protested that they were the controlling body and subsequently withdrew from FIFA in 1958.

Despite being the most populous country on earth, success has utterly eluded China. Their greatest achievement to date is a runners-up spot in the 1984 Asian Cup.

Efforts to improve the game are now being made, with the launch of a professional league backed by multi-national sponsorship, but China are still some way short of their Asian rivals – as a disappointing first-round exit in the 1994 World Cup qualifiers illustrates. FIFA's desire to spread the game globally may give the Chinese an advantage here, and staging the game's premier event would provide a massive boost.

GUAM

Guam Soccer Association
Founded: 1975
FIFA: Associate member

HONG KONG

Hong Kong Football Association
Founded: 1914
FIFA: 1954
Football has been played in Hong Kong since the 1880s. The Hong Kong Shield – an early knock-out competition – was launched in 1896, a football association was founded in 1913 and affiliated to the Football Association in London a year later.

The sport reached its peak in the colony in the 1970s. The league's top clubs became fully professional and imported a string of veteran players from England and continental Europe. South China were one of the last clubs to turn pro, by which time sponsorship had arrived with powerful teams organized by the Seiko and Bulova corporations.

The national team competed regularly in international events over the past 20 years – having first entered the World Cup in vain in 1974 – but football independence had to disappear when the colony was handed back to China in 1997.

INDIA

All India Football Federation
Founded: 1937
FIFA: 1948
India's only successes at international level have come in the Asian Games, which they won in 1951 and 1962. They finished third at the 1956 Olympics, but since then the national side's record has been poor, despite massive enthusiasm for football in this huge heavily-populated country.

The annual Nehru Cup tournament, featuring guest European and South American national sides or selections, is a popular event, though India have never won it. The Calcutta League – the best in the country – is dominated by India's most famous clubs, Mohammedan Sporting, East Bengal and Mohun Bagan. Originally brought to India by the British in the late 1800s (the Gloucestershire Regiment were the first Calcutta champions), football is now rapidly gaining popularity in a country where cricket has always been the top sport.

INDONESIA

All Indonesia Football Federation
Founded: 1930
FIFA: 1952

IRAN

Football Federation of the Islamic Republic of Iran
Founded: 1920
FIFA: 1948
Asian Championship: 1968, 1972, 1976
Iran emerged as a major Asian power in the 1960s, and in the 1970s they were the continent's most successful side. They took a hat-trick of Asian Championships, in 1968, 1972 and 1976, won the gold medal at the 1974 Asian Games and then qualified for the 1978 World Cup finals in Argentina. There, they shocked Scotland, holding them to a 1–1 draw, and the Scots' goal was an own goal!

The Asian Championship hat-trick was remarkable because Iran won every game they played in the tournament between 1968 and 1976. Since then, they have reached the semi-finals in each of the three subsequent tournaments that have been played, and almost qualified for the 1994 World Cup finals in the United States. In 1997 they set a new World Cup record beating Maldives 17–0 in

COMPETITIVE NEIGHBOURS *Iran (red shirts) and Iraq in World Cup action*

a qualifying match in June 1997.

Iranian teams have twice won the Asian Champions Cup – Taj Club in 1970 and Esteghlal SC in 1990.

IRAQ

Iraqi Football Association
Founded: 1948
FIFA: 1951

The 1970s witnessed a shift in the balance of power in Asian football towards the Arab states, and Iraq have been at the forefront of this movement. They won the Asian Games gold medal in 1982 and four years later qualified for the World Cup finals in Mexico, where they put up creditable performances.

Iraq have huge resources at their disposal, and this should ensure that the national side will remain strong for many years to come. Iraq were thrown out of FIFA and suspended from international football in 1991 because of the invasion of Kuwait, but have since been re-admitted to the international fold. They almost qualified for the 1994 World Cup finals. Iraq's most noted player was striker Ahmed Radhi.

JAPAN

The Football Association of Japan
Founded: 1921
FIFA: 1929–45, 1950

Japan have never won a major tournament, but that could soon change – their football authorities have begun an ambitious programme to put the country firmly on the international football map.

In 1993 a professional league, the J. League, was introduced, and the corporate-backed teams have used their wealth to attract numerous star veterans including England's Gary Lineker, Brazil's Zico, Italy's Daniele Massaro and Germany's Pierre Littbarski. The league has proved to be very successful with many teams drawing huge and fanatical crowds on a regular basis.

Simultaneously, the Japanese put together an impressive bid for the hosting rights to the 2002 World Cup. Japan undoubtedly had the stadiums, communications and facilities to stage the event alone but, ulti-

JAPANESE EXPORT *Kazu Miura starred in both the J. League and Serie A*

mately, political considerations within FIFA meant they were assigned to share host rights with South Korea.

Japan almost qualified for the 1994 World Cup finals. Going into the final game of the qualifiying tournament they needed a victory to qualify, but they missed out when in the last minute of the match against Iraq, they conceded a soft equaliser.

Several Japanese players have made an impact alongside the imported stars in the J. League, notably national team striker Kazuyoshi Miura, known as "Kazu", who had a brief spell with Genoa of Italy's Serie A in 1994.

JORDAN

Jordan Football Association
Founded: 1949
FIFA: 1958

KAZAKHSTAN

Football Association of the Republic of Kazakhstan
Founded: 1914
FIFA: 1994

KUWAIT

Kuwait Football Association
Founded: 1952
FIFA: 1962
Asian Championship: 1980

KYRGYZSTAN

Football Association of Kyrgyzstan
Founded: 1992
FIFA: 1994

LAOS

Fédération de Foot-Ball Lao
Founded: 1951
FIFA: 1952

LEBANON

Fédération Libanaise de Football
Founded: 1933
FIFA: 1935

MACAO

Associacao de Futebol de Macau
Founded: 1939
FIFA: 1976

MALAYSIA

Persuatuan Bolasepak Malaysia
Founded: 1933
FIFA: 1956

MALDIVES

Football Association of Maldives
Founded: 1983
FIFA: 1986

MYANMAR

Myanmar Football Federation
Founded: 1947
FIFA: 1947

NEPAL

All Nepal Football Association
Founded: 1951
FIFA: 1970

NORTH KOREA

Football Association of the Democratic People's Republic of Korea
Founded: 1945
FIFA: 1958

North Korea's national side has consistently lived in the shadow of more successful neighbours from the South, but in 1966 the North made headlines around the world. At the 1966 World Cup finals in England, the North Koreans stunned Italy in the first round, winning 1–0. Pak Do Ik will be remembered for ever as the man who scored the most famous goal in North Korean football history.

Then, in an incredible quarter-final against Portugal, the Koreans went 3–0 ahead after 22 minutes. But the dream faded almost as dramatically, as Portugal won 5–3.

North Korea has failed to qualify for the World Cup since then.

OMAN

Oman Football Association
Founded: 1978
FIFA: 1980

PAKISTAN

Pakistan Football Federation
Founded: 1948
FIFA: 1948

PALESTINE

Palestinian Football Federation
Founded: 1994
FIFA: 1995 (provisional member)

PHILIPPINES

Philippine Football Federation
Founded: 1907
FIFA: 1928

QATAR

Qatar Football Association
Founded: 1960
FIFA: 1970

SAUDI ARABIA

Saudi Arabian Football Federation
Founded: 1959
FIFA: 1959
Asian Championship: 1984, 1988
Saudi Arabia are one of the emergent nations of Asian football, and with untold oil-based wealth at their disposal, they could come to dominate the region's football as the Koreans and the Iranians have. Saudi's first honours came in the 1980s, when they won the 1984 and 1988 Asian Championships. The work continued with progress to the second round of the 1994 World Cup finals.

The Saudi Arabians are also developing their infrastructure and organization. Many foreign coaches have been employed and the magnificent King Fahd stadium in Riyadh is one of the best in the world.

They were the first hosts of the Intercontinental Cup in 1993 (a competition for the five continental champions), and the event is to become a regular feature of the FIFA calendar. Playing against the best nations in the world will further strengthen Saudi Arabia's already impressive hand.

SINGAPORE

Football Association of Singapore
Founded: 1892
FIFA: 1952

SOUTH KOREA

Korea Football Association
Founded: 1928
FIFA: 1948
Asian Championship: 1956, 1960
South Korea has always been the strongest nation in Asian football, and they won the first two Asian Championship tournaments, in 1956 and 1960. Their World Cup record is also the best in Asia, with qualification comingt first in 1954 and then for the three most recent tournaments: 1986, 1990 and 1994.

In the qualifying tournament for the 1994 World Cup they were undefeated in the first round, but were less impressive in the next stage and only scraped through from the second round group. Once in America, however, they scored two late goals to snatch a draw with Spain in Dallas, then held Bolivia to a goalless draw and almost embarrassed the defending champions Germany before going down by the odd goal in five.

Cha Bum Kun is probably South Korea's best-known player, having enjoyed a lengthy career in Germany's Bundesliga. In 1988 he helped Bayer Leverkusen win the UEFA Cup, scoring the crucial aggregate-levelling goal in the second leg of the final against Spain's Español.

In 1993, South Korea, decided to challenge front-runners Japan for the honour of becoming the first Asian hosts for the World Cup. Their competitive pedigree, plus positive memories of Seoul's staging of the 1988 Olympic Games, duly earned the Koreans joint hosting rights, with Japan in 2002.

SRI LANKA

Football Federation of Sri Lanka
Founded: 1939
FIFA: 1950

SYRIA

Association Arabe Syrienne de Football
Founded: 1936
FIFA: 1937

TAIWAN

Chinese Taipei Football Association
Founded: 1936
FIFA: 1954

TAJIKISTAN

Football Federation of Tajikistan
Founded: 1991
FIFA: 1994

ASIAN POWER *South Korea's 1986 World Cup finals team*

THAILAND

Football Association of Thailand
Founded: 1916
FIFA: 1925

TURKMENISTAN

Football Federation of Turkmenistan
Founded: 1992
FIFA: 1994

UNITED ARAB EMIRATES

United Arab Emirates Football Association
Founded: 1971
FIFA: 1972
With only 25 registered clubs and 3,400 players, the United Arab Emirates caused a big surprise when they qualified for the 1990 World Cup finals. Brazilian coach Mario Zagalo led them in qualifying, but he was surprisingly sacked just prior to the tournament, and a Pole, Bernard Blaut, took over in Italy. The UAE were somewhat out of their depth in Italy and were beaten in all three of their first-round matches.

UZBEKISTAN

Football Federation of Uzbekistan
Founded: 1946
FIFA: 1994
Uzbekistan gained independence after the collapse of the Soviet Union. The federation gained immediate admittance into the Asian confederation which they stey stunned by winning the Asian Games title on their debut.

VIETNAM

Association de Football de la République du Vietnam
Founded: 1962
FIFA: 1964

YEMEN

Republic of Yemen Football Association
Founded: 1962
FIFA: 1980

THE GREAT CLUBS

Professionalism swept through Britain in the 1880s and western Europe in the late 1920s. The big clubs of Spain, Italy, France and Portugal were importing star foreigners by the turn of the 1930s, but it was not until the mid-1950s that Belgium, Holland and then Germany caught up with full-time professionalism. When they did, the balance of the European game changed yet again.

The great traditions of football are kept alive, week in, week out, by the clubs. From Ajax in Holland to Vasco da Gama in Brazil, from Barcelona in Spain to Liverpool in England, they provide the first call of loyalty on the public. People who may never have attended a match in years still look out for the result of "their" club each week. Evidence of the depths of loyalty which certain clubs can inspire is widely available – from the way Real Madrid's fans came up with the money to fund the building of the Estadio Bernabeu in the 1940s to the proud boast from Portugal's Benfica of 122,000 members. Every club has its tales of the great days and great players, great managers and great victories. Some, like Manchester United, have been touched by tragedy, others, like Marseille, with controversy. The greatest, clearly, are those who have repeatedly proved their power and strength by lifting the continental club competitions in Europe and South America. Some of them are described here.

AJAX AMSTERDAM
HOLLAND

Founded: 1900
Stadium: Arena (50,000)
Colours: Red and white broad stripes/white
League: 26
Cup: 12
World Club Cup: 1972, 1995
European Cup: 1971, 1972, 1973, 1995
European Cup-winners' Cup: 1987
UEFA Cup: 1992
Supercup: 1972, 1973, 1995

Ajax, on beating Torino in the 1992 UEFA Cup Final, became only the second team after Italy's Juventus to have won all three European trophies and a full house of all seven titles on offer to clubs. The achievement was a popular one, bearing in mind the entertainment and style the Amsterdam club had consistently provided. The first hints of glory to come were in evidence in 1966–67, when, under former Dutch international Rinus Michels, Ajax thrashed Liverpool 5–1 in a European Cup tie. Two

years later Ajax became the first Dutch side to reach the European Cup Final, though they lost 4–1 to Milan. In 1971 Ajax were back as winners, beating Panathinaikos 2–0 at Wembley. In the next two Finals, they beat Internazionale 2–0, then Juventus 1–0. Johan Cruyff was their inspiration.

Ajax's trademark was the "total football" system, which involved taking full advantage of a generation of skilled all-rounders whose versatility and football intelligence allowed bewildering changes of position. It was "The Whirl", as envisaged early in the 1950s by that football prophet, Willi Meisl. After the sale of Cruyff to Barcelona in 1973, Ajax fell away and it took his return, a decade later, as technical director, to propel them back to the peaks of the European game. Under Cruyff, the new Ajax generation won the

FINNISHED ARTICLE *Ajax's Jari Litmanen*

Great Managers
Marinus "Rinus" Michels

Coach of Ajax Amsterdam (Holland), Barcelona (Spain), Los Angeles Aztecs (US), Bayer Leverkusen (Germany); also Holland national team (born February 9, 1928)

Michels, a Dutch international centre-forward in the early 1950s, led a revolution in the late 1960s when he developed the "total football" philosophy at Ajax. Much of Michels's coaching career with Ajax was linked with the presence, as leader on the pitch, of Johan Cruyff. Michels went to Barcelona after winning the European Cup with Ajax in 1971, went back to Ajax to sign Cruyff and the pair were partners again when Holland finished runners-up at the 1974 World Cup. "Iron Rinus" was never afraid to take tactical risks, such as when he guided Holland to European Championship success in 1988 by using Ruud Gullit as a static, right-side attacker. Nor was Michels ever afraid of stating his opinions, however blunt.

Cup-winners' Cup in 1987 – his friend and pupil Marco Van Basten scoring the goal which beat Lokomotive Leipzig in the Final in Athens. Cruyff's successor Louis Van Gaal then secured the UEFA Cup five years later. Despite continuing to sell many of their best players, Ajax's 1994–95 squad was statistically their best ever; the team won the League championship without losing a game, and the European Cup for the fourth time. Injury problems foiled their bid for a fifth Cup the following season when Ajax lost on penalties to Juventus after a 1–1 draw in Rome.

ANDERLECHT
BRUSSELS, BELGIUM

Founded: 1908
Stadium: Constant Vanden Stock/Parc Astrid (28,063)
Colours: White with mauve/white
League: 23
Cup: 7
European Cup-winners' Cup: 1976, 1978
UEFA Cup: 1983
Supercup: 1976, 1978

Anderlecht's international debut was not a happy one: they crashed 10–0 and 12–0 on aggregate to Manchester United in an early European Cup. Since then, however, the Royal Sporting Club have earned respect far and wide for their domestic domination and an international outlook which has brought success in both the European Cup-winners' Cup and the UEFA Cup. Much credit reflects on the coaching work of Englishman Bill Gormlie, a former Blackburn goalkeeper, who helped lay the foundations for success in the late 1940s and early 1950s. Equally important was the financial power of the millionaire brewer, Constant Vanden Stock. Before his take-over Anderlecht relied mainly on homegrown talent like Paul Van Himst, the greatest Belgian footballer of all time. As Anderlecht's prestige grew, particularly thanks to the European Cup competitions, they were able to compete in the international transfer market. A significant coaching influence, in the early 1960s, was Frenchman Pierre Sinibaldi, who perfected a tactical formation which relied on a flat back four, the offside trap, and possession football in midfield. It worked well against almost all opposition except British clubs, whose more direct style constantly caught the defenders on the turn. Thus, the first time Anderlecht reached a European final – in the Fairs Cup in 1970 – they were beaten by Arsenal. European success, in the Cup-winners' Cup in 1976 and 1978, had to await the more pragmatic coaching approach of Dutchman Wiel Corver and Belgian Raymond Goethals. Later, with Van Himst having returned as coach, Anderlecht won the UEFA Cup and in Enzo Scifo produced the finest Belgian player since Van Himst himself.

ENZO SCIFO *Anderlecht discovery, and the finest Belgian player of recent years*

GLORY GOAL *Arsenal's 1989 title-clincher*

ARSENAL
LONDON, ENGLAND

Founded: 1886
Stadium: Highbury (38,500)
Colours: Red/white
League: 10
Cup: 6
European Cup-winners's Cup: 1994
Fairs Cup: 1970

Arsenal, today a North London club, had their origins south of the Thames, at the Woolwich Arsenal. The club turned professional in 1891 and entered the Football League a year later, reaching the First Division in 1904 and the FA Cup semi-finals in 1906. After the First World War they moved to Highbury, and appointed the legendary Herbert Chapman as manager in 1925.

Chapman had a flair for publicity, an innovative approach to tactics and a talent for motivation. He spent heavily but wisely on the likes of first Charlie Buchan and Alex James, introduced the stopper centre-half and created the all-conquering outfit which won the League five times in the 1930s and the FA Cup twice. Arsenal won the League twice more and the FA Cup once in the eight years after the war. A 17-year hiatus then followed before the Gunners ended their longest trophy drought by winning the Fairs Cup.

Suddenly, the jinx was broken. A year later manager Bertie Mee was celebrating a historic league and cup "double". His team mixed the volatile flair of Charlie George, determined leadership of Frank McLintock, rugged tackling of Peter Storey and creative class of George Graham. He later returned as manager, masterminding a string of successes in the League League Cup, FA Cup and Cup-winners' Cup, but his reign ended abruptly in 1995 amid controversy over transfer "bungs".

ATLETICO MADRID
SPAIN

Founded: 1903
Stadium: Vicente Calderon/Manzanares (62,000)
Colours: Red and white stripes/blue
League: 9
Cup: 9
World Club Cup: 1974
European Cup-winners' Cup: 1962

Atletico Madrid have always existed in the shadow of neighbours Real, but they still rank among the Big Three of Spanish football and boast a proud record at international level. Not that life has always been easy. In the late 1930s, after the Spanish Civil War, it took a merger with the Air Force club to keep Atletico in business; in 1959, they just failed to reach the European Cup Final when Real beat them in a semi-final play-off; in the early 1960s they had to share Real's Estadio Bernabeu, because Atletico's Metropolitano had been sold to developers before the club's new stadium could be completed. European glory did come to Atletico in the shape of the Cup-winners' Cup in 1962 and was a well-deserved prize for players such as inside-left Joaquin Peiro and his wing partner Enrique Collar. But it was not until the early 1970s that Atletico put together a comparable team, thanks to the purchases of Argentines Ruben Hugo Ayala and Ramon Heredia. In 1974, Atletico secured that elusive place in the European Cup Final. But, after taking the lead against Bayern Munich in extra time, Atletico conceded a last-kick equalizer.

Consolation for their 4–0 defeat in the replay came with the opportunity to substitute for reluctant Bayern in the World Club Cup against Independiente of Argentina. By the time the tie came around Atletico had appointed as coach Luis Aragones, the midfielder who had scored their goal in the European Cup Final against Bayern. Atletico duly beat Independiente 1–0 and were, for a year at least, on top of the world. In the late 1980s the club was taken over by the extrovert builder Jesus Gil. He pumped millions of pounds into the club but generated more bad publicity than good, hiring and

KINGMAKER *Atletico Madrid's president Jesus Gil finally enjoyed success in 1996*

firing coaches at a breathtaking rate. It all came together in dramatic fashion when Atletico won the league and cup "double" in the spring of 1996.

ATLETICO NACIONAL
MEDELLIN, COLOMBIA

Founded: 1938
Stadium: Atanasio Giradot (35,000)
Colours: Green and white stripes/white
League: 5
South American Club Cup: 1989
Inter-American Cup: 1989

Atletico Nacional of Medellin are not the most famous club to come out of Colombia. That honour will always belong to Millonarios, who led the professional, pirate revolution in the early 1950s. But Nacional earned a

place in history by becoming the first club to take the Copa Libertadores, the South American Club Cup, across the Andes to the western side of the continent. Nacional, who provided the base of the Colombian World Cup team in 1990, were in 1954 the first champions of Colombia after the rapprochement with FIFA. Yet it was not until 1971 that they made their debut in the South American Club Cup under Argentine coach Osvaldo Zubeldia. He had earned a fearsome reputation as boss of the rugged Estudiantes de La Plata team which had dominated Argentine and South American club football in the late 1960s. However, without resorting to the cynicism which made Estudiantes hated, he turned Nacional into Colombian champions three times in the mid-1970s and early 1980s. Zubeldia was followed by Luis Cubilla, at

whose suggestion, in 1986, Nacional appointed a former stalwart central defender, Francisco Maturana, as boss. In 1987 and 1988 they finished championship runners-up and then, in 1989, seized the South American club crown. Unfortunately, their preparations for the world club showdown with Milan were wrecked when the government halted the league season because of the increasing violence being engendered on the fringes of the game by the drug and betting cartels. Nacional did not emerge with their reputation unscathed. It was not only that Medellin was the centre of the drugs trade; several Nacional players were friends of the notorious drugs baron Pablo Escobar. Indeed, when Escobar was eventually killed in 1993 by security forces, at his funeral the coffin was draped in a Nacional flag.

BARCELONA
SPAIN

Founded: 1899
Stadium: Nou Camp (115,000)
Colours: Blue and red stripes/blue
League: 14
Cup: 23
European Cup: 1992
European Cup-winners' Cup: 1979, 1982, 1989, 1997
Fairs Cup: 1958, 1960, 1966
Supercup: 1992

Barcelona finally ended a duel with destiny when, in 1992, they beat Sampdoria 1–0 at Wembley to win the European Cup. It was a case of third time lucky, for the greatest prize in the European club game had twice eluded them at the final hurdle. Barcelona had been the first winners of the Inter-Cities Fairs Cup and had won the Cup-winners' Cup three times. But their European Cup campaigns seemed to have been jinxed. First, in 1961, when Barcelona had apparently achieved the hard part by eliminating the title-holders and their bitter rivals Real Madrid, they lost to Benfica in the Final in Berne. Barcelona hit the woodwork three times, yet lost 3–2 against the run of play. Great players such as Luis Suarez, Ladislav Kubala, Sandor Kocsis and Zoltan Czibor had everything on their side except luck.

Great Managers

HELENIO HERRERA

Coach of Red Star Paris, Stade Francais (France), Atletico Madrid, Valladolid, Sevilla (Spain), Belenenses (Portugal), Barcelona (Spain), Internazionale and Roma (Italy); also Spanish and Italian national teams (born April 17, 1916)

One of the world's most innovative and single-minded coaches. Herrera, born in Argentina, brought up in Morocco and a player in France, experimented at Barcelona in the 1950s by using inside-forwards at wing-half to turn "easy" matches into goal sprees. His attacking tactics proved ineffective at Inter so Herrera developed, instead, the most ruthlessly disciplined catenaccio. Herrera demanded total obedience, insisting that his players place their hands on the ball and swear loyalty to each other before going out for a match. Stars who baulked at such rituals were sold, however popular or successful. Inter won the World and European Cups twice each before Herrera's career went into decline at Roma.

NO LOVE LOST *Jürgen Klinsmann (right) shoots for goal in Bayern Munich's UEFA Cup semi-final victory over Spain's Barcelona – one year earlier, the beaten defender, Gica Popescu, had been Klinsmann's team-mate at Tottenham*

IMPORT DUTY *Portugal's Luis Figo was one of the more recent of Barcelona's foreign acquisitions*

History repeated itself in even more galling circumstances in 1986. Barcelona, coached by Terry Venables and gambling on the fitness of long-time injured Steve Archibald, faced Steaua Bucharest in Seville. Barcelona lost in a penalty shoot-out after a goal-less draw.

It took the return of 1970s inspiration Johan Cruyff, this time as coach, to steer a new generation of international stars – including Ronald Koeman, Hristo Stoichkov and Michael Laudrup – to victory long overdue for one of the world's biggest clubs. Barcelona's 1994 league title was their fourth in a row, the last three of them achieved in the closing moments of the final day, twice at the expense of great rivals Real Madrid.

Failure to win a trophy in 1995 or 1996, however, resulted in Cruyff's dismissal after eight years in charge. He was replaced by Bobby Robson.

BAYERN MUNICH
GERMANY

Founded: 1900
Stadium: Olimpiastadion (69,261)
Colours: All red
League: 14
Cup: 8
World Club Cup: 1976
European Cup: 1974, 1975, 1976
European Cup-winners' Cup: 1967
UEFA Cup: 1996

Bayern are Germany's most glamorous club, even though high tax rates mean they have never been able to hold stars tempted by the rich pickings of Italy. In the 1980s Bayern became almost an Italian nursery as they lost Karl-Heinz Rummenigge, Andy Brehme and Lothar Matthäus to Internazionale and Stefan Reuter and Jurgen Kohler to Juventus. All this transfer activity underlined the fact that the Bayern success story is – with the exception of one championship in 1932 and one cup in 1957 – a relatively recent affair. The identities of the men who secured all the glittering titles read like a Who's Who of the world game: Franz Beckenbauer, Gerd Müller, Sepp Maier, Paul Breitner, Rummenigge and Matthäus. The German championship was originally organized in regional leagues, with the winners playing off at the end of each season for the title: only once in the pre-war years did Bayern win all the way through. That was in 1932, when they defeated Eintracht Frankfurt 2–0. Not until 1957, and a 1–0 win over Fortuna Düsseldorf in the cup final, did Bayern have anything more to celebrate. Indeed their record was so mediocre that they were not included in the inaugural Bundesliga in 1963–64. But, a year later, Bayern won promotion; in 1966 they won the cup, and in 1967 they secured the European Cup-winners' Cup, thanks to an extra-time victory over Rangers. That was the team led and inspired by Beckenbauer in the role of attacking sweeper, with Maier in goal and Müller up front. All three stars shone even more brightly as Bayern landed a European Cup hat-trick in the mid-1970s. In the 1980s Bayern were twice European Cup runners-up, but complacency set in and it was not until Beckenbauer returned – first as vice-president, then coach, then president – that Bayern regained their pre-eminence. Their 1996 UEFA Cup triumph made Bayern the fourth club to win all three European trophies.

BENFICA
LISBON, PORTUGAL

Founded: 1904
Stadium: Estadio do Benfica/Da Luz (92,385)
Colours: Red/white
League: 29
Cup: 26
European Cup: 1961, 1962

Benfica are a national institution with their huge stadium – rated as 130,000 before recent security constraints – and 122,000 membership. Living up to the standards of history is what Benfica believe they owe Cosme Damiao who, on February 28, 1904, organized the first recorded local game of futebol on a patch of Lisbon wasteland. The next day he formed his "team" into a club named Sport Lisboa and, two years later was instrumental in arranging a merger with neighbours Sport Clube de Benfica. In the early years it was cycling which brought the club its first prizes. From the launch of a unified Portuguese championship in the late 1920s, Benfica lorded it over Portuguese sport. In due course, Benfica set their sights on international glory and, in 1950, won the Latin Cup – a forerunner of the European Cup. English manager Ted Smith laid the foundations of a team which would dominate not only Portugal but then Europe.

In 1954 Benfica followed the example being set in Spain and built a vast new stadium. An exiled Hungarian named Bela Guttman became coach, and his team filled the new stadium as Benfica twice swept to success in the European Cup in 1961 and 1962. First they beat Barcelona, amid intense drama, by 3–2 in Berne, then Real Madrid 5–3 in Amsterdam. On both occasions Benfica were captained by their veteran centre-

forward, José Aguas. They also introduced one of the most famous Portuguese footballers of all time in Eusebio, greatest of the many fine players Benfica had discovered in the Portuguese colonies of Angola and Mozambique. Benfica's boast of only "Portuguese" (including colonial) players was scrapped in the mid-1970s, when the African colonies were cast adrift. Now they hunt Brazilians, Slavs and Danes with the rest.

BOCA JUNIORS
BUENOS AIRES, ARGENTINA

Founded: 1905
Stadium: Bombonera (58,740)
Colours: Blue with yellow hoop/blue
League: 19
World Club Cup: 1977
South American Club Cup: 1977, 1978
South American Supercup: 1989
Inter-American Cup: 1989

Boca are one of the two great clubs in the Argentine capital of Buenos Aires, along with old rivals River Plate. They were founded by an Irishman named Patrick MacCarthy and a group of newly-arrived Italian immigrants. They joined the league in 1913 and were immediately caught up in a domestic football "war" which saw two championships being organized for most of the 1920s and early 1930s. Boca bestrode the two eras. They won the last Argentine amateur championship in 1930 and the first unified professional one the following year. Two more titles followed in the next four years, thanks to some fine players, including the great Brazilian defender, Domingos da Guia. In the 1940s and 1950s Boca slipped into River Plate's shadow, re-emerging in 1963 when a team fired by the goals of José Sanfilippo reached the Final of the South American Club Cup.

Winning the title, however, would have to wait until the late 1970s. Then they reached the Final three years in a row – beating Brazil's Cruzeiro in 1977 and Deportivo Cali of Colombia in 1978 before losing to Olimpia of Paraguay in 1979. Boca's rugged style, under Juan Carlos Lorenzo, proved controversial. Not one Boca player figured in the squad

ITALIAN STYLE *Paolo di Canio brought Latin flair to Celtic Park*

which won the 1978 World Cup. But Boca had already secured their own world crown, beating West Germany's Borussia Mönchengladbach in the World Club Cup in 1977. Boca rebuilt their team around Diego Maradona in 1981, but had added few prizes to their trophy room when he rejoined them in 1995.

CELTIC
GLASGOW, SCOTLAND

Founded: 1888
Stadium: Celtic Park (51,709)
Colours: Green and white hoops/white
League: 35
Cup: 30
European Cup: 1967

Celtic and old rivals Rangers are Scottish football's greatest clubs, but it was Celtic who first extended that hunger for success into Europe when, in 1967, they became the first British club to win the European Cup. It was a measure of the way they swept all before them that season that they won every domestic competition as well: the League, the Cup and League Cup. No other team in Europe had, until then, ended the season with a 100 per cent record in four major competitions. In winning the European Cup Celtic refuted accusations – mostly from England – that their Scottish honours owed more to a lack of solid opposition than their own abilities. Celtic's 1967 team was shrewdly put together by manager Jock Stein, a former Celtic player. As well as new Scottish stars he included veterans such as goalkeeper Ronnie Simpson and scheming inside-left Bertie Auld. In the Lisbon Final they beat former holders Internazionale 2–1 with goals from full-back Gemmell and centre-forward Chalmers.

Sadly, Celtic's golden touch did not survive long. A few months later they were beaten by Kiev Dynamo right at the start of their European Cup defence, and were then dragged down to defeat and fisticuffs in the infamous World Club Cup battle with Racing of Argentina. In 1970 Celtic returned to the European Cup Final, only to lose to Feyenoord in Milan; and, two years later, they lost only on penalties after two goal-less draws in the semi-finals against Inter. More trouble lay ahead as Celtic proved unable to match Rangers' commercial and playing example in the late 1980s and slipped to the brink of bankruptcy before turning the corner after a boardroom revolution.

COLO COLO
SANTIAGO, CHILE

Founded: 1925
Stadium: Colo Colo (50,000)
Colours: White/black
League: 19
South American Recopa: 1991

Colo Colo, Chilean nickname for a wildcat, were founded by five angry members of the old Magallanes FC. Even though Chilean football is generally held to lag far behind that of traditional giants Brazil, Argentina and Uruguay, Colo Colo have an enviable reputation throughout the continent. The club's vision has always stretched beyond the Andes. Such a tradition was laid down by David Orellano. He was a founder member of Colo Colo and one of the five Magallanes rebels who disagreed over the choice of a new club captain. The choice of the five fell upon Orellano and, within two years of Colo Colo's foundation, they had sent a team off to tour Spain and Portugal. In 1933 Colo Colo were among the founders of a professional league; in 1941 they set another pioneering trend by introducing a for-

eign coach in the Hungarian, Ferenc Platko; and in 1948 they organized a South American club tournament which can now be seen as a forerunner of the Copa Libertadores, the official South American Club Cup launched in 1960. Record league winners in Chile and the supreme transfer destination for most domestic players, Colo Colo's greatest achievement was in reaching the 1973 South American Club Cup Final. The teams drew 1–1 in Avellaneda and 0–0 in Santiago, and thus went on to a play-off in Montevideo, which Independiente won 2–1 in extra time. Colo Colo's consolation goal was scored by their most famous and popular player of the modern era, Carlos Caszely.

EINTRACHT FRANKFURT
GERMANY

Founded: 1899
Stadium: Waldstadion (61,146)
Colours: Black and red stripes/black
League: 1
Cup: 4
UEFA Cup: 1980

Eintracht Frankfurt occupy a very special place in football legend as the team Real Madrid beat in the European Cup Final at Hampden back in 1960. The score was 7–3 to Madrid, but Frankfurt were far from crushed and had proved their class by putting six goals past Glasgow Rangers – both home and away – in the semi-finals. Frankfurt's team was built on the midfield strength of Dieter Stinka and Jurgen Lindner, plus the creative talents of veteran inside-left Alfred Pfaff and right-winger Richard Kress. It may sound odd to suggest that everything after a defeat was an anticlimax, but though Frankfurt were founder members of the West German Bundesliga in 1963, they have

achieved comparatively little.

Boardroom problems in the mid-1980s dogged the club until the businessman Matthias Ohms took over and appointed Bernd Holzenbein, a World Cup winner in 1974 and an old Frankfurt favourite, as his executive vice-president. Holzenbein put Frankfurt back on a sound financial footing and bought stars such as midfielder Andy Möller (later sold to Juventus) and the brilliant Ghanaian striker, Anthony Yeboah. In 1992–93 they were pipped for the league title after the controversial mid-season departure of charismatic Yugoslav coach, Dragoslav Stepanovic. His successor Jupp Heynckes did not last long either, after falling out with Yeboah who was allowed to depart for English club Leeds, leaving Frankfurt to sink towards a first-ever relegation.

Frankfurt's one European success over the years was in winning the UEFA Cup in 1980. Frankfurt beat their fellow Germans, Borussia Mönchengladbach, on the away goals rule in the Final, losing 3–2 away and then winning 1–0 back in the Waldstadion. Holzenbein had himself scored the all-important second away goal in the first leg.

FEYENOORD
ROTTERDAM, HOLLAND

Founded: 1908
Stadium: De Kuyp (52,000)
Colours: Red and white halves/black
League: 13
Cup: 10
World Club Cup: 1970
European Cup: 1970
UEFA Cup: 1974

Feyenoord were founded by mining entrepreneur C. R. J. Kieboom. Their star player in the successful pre-war years was left-half Puck Van Heel, who appeared in the final tournaments of both the 1934 and 1938 World Cups and set what was for many years a Dutch record of 64 international appearances. The post-war years were bleak until after the introduction of professionalism in the late 1950s. Then Feyenoord entered their most glorious domestic era, winning the league title six times in 13 years. Indeed, their 1965 and 1969 successes brought them league and cup "doubles". Stars included goalkeeper Eddie Pieters-Graafland, a then record £20,000 signing from Ajax, half-backs Reinier Kreyermaat, Hans Kraay and Jan Klaasens and, above all, outside-left Coen Moulijn. He was still a key figure when they won the European Cup in 1970, along with Swedish striker Ove Kindvall and burly midfield general Wim Van Hanegem. Feyenoord's coach, for their extra time victory over Celtic in Milan, was Ernst Happel, the former Austrian international. Feyenoord – and not Ajax – were thus the first Dutch club to break through to European success, and they went on to defeat Estudiantes de La Plata of Argentina in the World Club Cup Final.

In 1974, with Van Hanegem pulling the strings in midfield, Feyenoord added the UEFA Cup to their trophy room. But, as time went on, they lost their grip on the Dutch game. Star players had to be sold to balance the books, among them Ruud Gullit, whom Feyenoord had discovered with Haarlem. He was sold to PSV Eindhoven and, later, of course, moved on to Milan. Not until the arrival as general manager of

Wim Jansen, a former Feyenoord star who starred with Holland at the 1974 World Cup, did Feyenoord pull themselves back together and regain the league title in 1993.

FK AUSTRIA
VIENNA, AUSTRIA

Founded: 1911
Stadium: Horr (10,500) / Prater (62,270)
Colours: White with mauve/white
League: 21
Cup: 21

The history of the Fussball Klub Austria-Memphis began with a game of cricket. Just as the English exported their industrial know-how and educational skills around the world in the latter half of the nineteenth century, they also took with them their newly codified games and sports. Thus the Vienna Cricket and Football Club was founded by the expatriate community in the 1890s. Cricket did not gain universal acceptance, but football was another matter, and November 15, 1894 saw the first proper football match ever staged in Austria. The Vienna Cricket and Football Club beat 1st Vienna FC by 4–0 – and they have been winning matches and titles ever since.

Changing their name in 1925, FKA notched up many domestic honours in a list which includes runners-up spot in the European Cup-winners' Cup in 1978, when a team inspired by midfield general Herbert Prohaska became the first Austrian side to reach a modern-day European final. That was long overdue since, in the late 1920s, FK Austria were one of the pioneers of European international club soccer when the Mitropa Cup drew clubs from Austria, Czechoslovakia, Hungary, Yugoslavia, Switzerland and Italy. FK Austria were triumphant in 1933 and 1936, inspired by the legendary centre-forward Matthias Sindelar. Their delicate style of play, known as the "Vienna School", was modelled on the old Scottish close-passing game and had been taught them by Englishman Jimmy Hogan. His coaching genius contributed mightily to the development of the so-called "Wunderteam" which lost unluckily to England, by 4–3, at

GIVING CHASE *Gaston Taument (right, behind Vitesse Arnhem's Philip Cocu) is one of Feyenoord's rising young stars*

Stamford Bridge in 1932 and then reached the semi-finals of the 1934 World Cup. The backbone of the Wunderteam was provided by FK Austria. That tradition has been maintained ever since. Thus no fewer than six FKA stars travelled with the national squad to the 1990 World Cup Finals in Italy.

FLAMENGO
RIO DE JANEIRO, BRAZIL

Founded: 1895 as sailing club; 1911 as football club
Stadium: Gavea (20,000) and Maracana (130,000)
Colours: Black and red hoops/white
Rio state league: 22
Brazil championship (incl. Torneo Rio-São Paulo): 5
World Club Cup: 1981
South American Club Cup: 1981

Flamengo are the most popular club in Brazil, having been formed by dissident members of the Fluminense club but under the umbrella of the Flamengo sailing club – which now boasts more than 70,000 members. They first competed in the Rio league in 1912, winning the title two years later. In 1915 they regained the crown without having lost a game. A string of great names have graced the red-and-black hoops over the years, among them defenders Domingos Da Guia and the legendary centre-forward Leonidas da Silva. Known as the "Black Diamond", Leonidas played for Flamengo from 1936 to 1942, inspiring two state championship triumphs and earning a worldwide reputation through his brilliance in the 1938 World Cup finals in France.

Flamengo ran up a Rio state hat-trick in the mid-1950s with their team nicknamed the "Steamroller", but had to wait until 1981 for their greatest success. Then, riding high on the goals of a new hero, Zico – the so-called "White Pele" – they won both the South American and World Club Cups. The South American Club Cup campaign was one of the most hostile in memory. Flamengo won a first round play-off against Atletico Mineiro after their rival Brazilians had five players sent off, provoking referee José Roberto Wright to aban-

don the game. In the Final, Flamengo beat Cobreloa of Chile in a play-off in Montevideo which saw the expulsion of five players. Fears about the outcome of Flamengo's world showdown against Liverpool proved unfounded. Zico was in a class of his own. Liverpool could not touch him as he created all of Flamengo's goals in a 3–0 win. The players dedicated the success to the memory of Claudio Coutinho, a former coach who had died in a skin-diving accident. In the mid-1990s, Flamengo sought to revive the glory days by signing World Cup-winning striker Romario from Spain's Barcelona.

FLUMINENSE
RIO DE JANEIRO, BRAZIL

Founded: 1902
Stadium: Laranjeira (20,000) and Maracana (130,000)
Colours: Red, green and white stripes/white
Rio state league: 27
Brazil championship (incl. Torneo Rio-São Paulo): 4

Fluminense have yet to win an international trophy, but that does not alter their status as one of South America's great clubs. "Flu" were founded in 1902 by an Englishman named Arthur Cox, and many of their first players were British residents. The club's wealth and upper-class clientele resulted in the nickname "Po de Arroz" ("Face Powder", after the fashion of the time at the turn of the century). Today the club's fans wear white powder on their faces as a sign of loyalty. In 1905 Flu were founder members of the Rio de Janeiro league and of the Brazilian confederation; they won the first four Rio (Carioca) championships in 1906–09; and, in 1932, Flu became the first Brazilian club to go professional.

By this time the "Flu-Fla" derby (against Flamengo) had been flourishing for 20 years, the first meeting between the clubs having taken place in 1912. In 1963 their clash drew an official crowd of 177,656 to the Maracana stadium in Rio, which remains a world record for a club game. By 1930 Flu's stadium was the home of the national team and the club had launched a weekly newspaper, among other schemes. A few years later and Flu were ruling the roost with five Rio titles between 1936 and 1941. Star players were forwards Romeu, Carreiro and Tim – who coached Peru at the 1978 World Cup finals. In the early 1950s Fluminense's star was the World Cup winning midfield general Didi.

In the late 1960s and early 1970s the key player was another World Cup winner, Brazil's 1970 captain and right-back, Carlos Alberto Torres. In the 1980s the mantle of inspiration-in-chief passed to the Paraguayan Romerito (Julio César Romero). Fluminense won a hat-trick of Rio titles in 1983, 1984 and 1985 with Romero their guiding light. He was rewarded by being nominated as South American Footballer of the Year in 1985 and later starred at the 1986 World Cup finals.

HAMBURG
GERMANY

Founded: 1887
Stadium: Volksparkstadion (61,234)
Colours: White/red
League: 6
Cup: 3
European Cup: 1983
European Cup-winners' Cup: 1977

Hamburg can be considered by many to be the oldest league club in Germany, if one takes as their foundation date that of SC Germania, the oldest of three clubs which later amalgamated. The other two were Hamburger FC (1888) and FC Falke (1905). Hamburg's tradition, from that day to this, has been one of attacking football. The first major trophy

ROMERITO *Fluminense's midfield general scoring for Paraguay against Chile in a World Cup qualifying tie in Santiago*

KEVIN KEEGAN *European Footballer of the Year with Hamburg in 1978 and 1979*

could have been theirs in 1922. But when the championship play-off was abandoned because injury-hit Nürnberg had only seven men left on the pitch, Hamburg sportingly declined to accept the title. A year later Hamburg did win the championship, and again in 1928.

They did not win it again until 1960, by which time they were being led by the greatest footballer in the club's history. Centre-forward Uwe Seeler, son of a former Hamburg player, was four times Hamburg's top scorer in the old regional league system, and after the creation of the Bundesliga was on one occasion the country's leading marksman. He also spearheaded Hamburg's thrilling 1960–61 European Cup campaign, in which they lost to Barcelona only in a play-off in the semi-finals. Seeler went on to captain West Germany in their brave World Cup efforts of 1966 and 1970, but he had retired by the time Hamburg achieved a European breakthrough and won the Cup-winners' Cup in 1977. Hamburg beat defending cup-holders Anderlecht of Belgium 2–0 in a final which was the big-occasion debuts of two long-serving internationals, defender Manni Kaltz and midfield general Felix Magath.

Both were stalwarts of the side beaten by Nottingham Forest in the 1980 European Cup Final, when Englishman Kevin Keegan tried in vain to stimulate the Hamburg attack. Keegan had returned to England by the time Hamburg beat Juventus in Athens three years later.

After a decade in the doldrums Uwe Seeler returned as president

and Hamburg ended the 1995–96 German season in fifth position, their best placing for six years.

INDEPENDIENTE
AVELLANEDA, ARGENTINA

Founded: 1904
Stadium: Cordero (55,000)
Colours: Red/blue
League: 11
World Club Cup: 1973, 1984
South American Club Cup: 1964, 1965, 1972, 1973, 1974, 1975, 1984
Inter-American Cup: 1973, 1974, 1976

Independiente are perhaps the least familiar of international club football's great achievers, outside Argentina at least. This is because, despite two lengthy periods of command in South American club football, they won the world title only twice in five attempts, and that at a time when the competition's image was tarnished.

Also, Independiente have always relied on team football rather than superstar inspiration. One outstanding player who made his name with the club, however, was Raimundo Orsi. He was the left-winger who played for Argentina in the 1928 Olympics, signed for Juventus, and then scored Italy's vital equalizer on their way to victory over Czechoslovakia in the 1934 World Cup Final. Later, the Independiente fans had the great Paraguayan centre-forward, Arsenio Erico, to idolize. Erico had been the boyhood hero of Alfredo Di Stefano and, in 1937, set an Argentine First Division goalscoring

record of 37 in a season.

Independiente did not regain prominence until the early 1960s, when coach Manuel Giudice imported an Italian-style catenaccio defence which secured the South American Club Cup in both 1964 and 1965. Independiente were the first Argentine team to win the continent's top club prize. But in the World Club Cup Final they fell both years to the high priests of catenaccio, Internazionale of Italy.

In the 1970s Independiente's Red Devils won the South American Club Cup four times in a row and collected the World Club Cup. It was an odd victory: European champions Hamburg declined to compete, so runners-up Juventus took their place – on condition that the Final was a one-off match in Italy. Independiente not only agreed, they won it with a single goal from midfield general Ricardo Bochini.

INTERNAZIONALE
MILAN, ITALY

Founded: 1908
Stadium: Meazza (85,443)
Colours: Blue and black stripes/black
League: 13
Cup: 3
World Club Cup: 1964, 1965
European Cup: 1964, 1965
UEFA Cup: 1991, 1994

Internazionale were founded out of an argument within the Milan club in the early years of the century. Some 45 members, led by committee man Giovanni Paramithiotti, broke away in protest at the authoritarian way the powerful Camperio brothers were running the club. That was not the end of the politics, however. In the 1930s, fascist laws forced Internazionale into a name change to rid the club of the foreign associations of their title. So they took the name of the city of Milan's patron saint and became Ambrosiana. Under this title they led the way in continental club competition – being one of the leading lights in the prewar Mitropa Cup.

After the war, the club reverted to the Internazionale name and pioneered a tactical revolution. First manager Alfredo Foni, who had been a World Cup-winning full-back before the war, won the league title twice by withdrawing outside-right Gino Armani into midfield; then Helenio Herrera conquered Italy, Europe and the world with catenaccio. Goalkeeper Giuliano Sarti, sweeper Armando Picchi and man-marking backs Tarcisio Burgnich, Aristide Guarneri and Giacinto Facchetti were as near watertight as possible. They were

MATTHÄUS
Internazionale's driving force and Germany's World Cup captain in 1990

the foundation on which Spanish general Luis Suarez constructed the counter-attacking raids carried forward by Brazil's Jair da Costa, Spain's Joaquim Peiro and Italy's own Sandro Mazzola. Inter won the European and World Club Cups in both 1964 and 1965 – beating Real Madrid and Benfica in Europe, and Argentina's Independiente twice for the world crown. But even they could not soak up pressure indefinitely. In 1966 Real Madrid toppled Inter in the European Cup semi-finals, Celtic repeated the trick a year later in a memorable Lisbon final, and Herrera was lured away to Roma. Not until the late 1980s could Inter recapture their international and domestic allure, when West German midfielder Lothar Matthäus drove them to the 1989 league title, following up with success in the 1991 UEFA Cup.

JUVENTUS
TURIN, ITALY

Founded: 1897
Stadium: Delle Alpi (71,012)
Colours: Black and white stripes/white
League: 24
Cup: 10
World Club Cup: 1985, 1996
European Cup: 1985, 1996
European Cup-winners' Cup: 1984
UEFA Cup: 1977, 1990, 1993
Supercup: 1984, 1996

Juventus were founded by a group of Italian students who decided to adopt red as the colour for their shirts. In 1903, however, when the club was six years old, one of the committee members was so impressed on a trip to England by Notts County's black-and-white stripes that he bought a set of shirts to take home to Turin. In the 1930s Juventus laid the foundations for their legend, winning the Italian league championship five times in a row. Simultaneously they also reached the semi-finals of the Mitropa Cup on four occasions and supplied Italy's World Cup-winning teams with five players in 1934 and three in 1938. Goalkeeper Gianpiero Combi, from Juventus, was Italy's victorious captain in 1934, just as another Juventus goal-

RISING STAR *Alessandro del Piero*

keeper, Dino Zoff, would be in 1982.

After the war, the Zebras (after the colours of their shirts) scoured the world for talent to match their imported rivals. First came the Danes, John and Karl Hansen, then the Argentine favourite Omar Sivori and the Gentle Giant from Wales, John Charles, followed by Spanish inside-forward Luis Del Sol and French inspiration Michel Platini. In 1971 they lost the Fairs Cup Final to Leeds on the away goals rule but in 1977 they beat Bilbao in the UEFA Cup Final on the same regulation.

In 1982 no fewer than six Juventus players featured in Italy's World Cup winning line-up, and Cabrini, Tardelli, Scirea, Gentile and Paolo Rossi helped Juve win the 1984 European Cup-winners' Cup and the 1985 European Cup. Seeking new magic in the 1990s, Juventus paid huge fees for Roberto Baggio and Gianluca Vialli. Both shared in the 1995 league and cup double triumph but Baggio then left for Milan on the even of a season which saw Vialli captain Juventus to victory in the European Champions Cup Final over Ajax in Rome.

IGOR BELANOV *Kiev's European Footballer of the Year in 1986*

KIEV DYNAMO
UKRAINE

Founded: 1927
Stadium: Republic (100,100)
Colours: White/blue
League: 4 Ukraine, 13 Soviet
Cup: 2 Ukraine, 9 Soviet
European Cup-winners' Cup: 1975, 1986
Supercup: 1975

Kiev were founder members of the Soviet top division, yet had to wait until 1961 before they became the first club outside Moscow to land the title. Soon they were dominating the Soviet scene. They achieved the league and cup "double" five years later and went on to a record-equalling hat-trick of league titles. Key players were midfielders Iosif Sabo and Viktor Serebryanikov and forwards Valeri Porkuyan and Anatoli Bishovets. Porkuyan starred at the 1966 World Cup finals in England, and Bishovets four years later in Mexico.

In 1975 Kiev became the first Soviet team to win a European trophy when they beat Ferencvaros of Hungary by 3–0 in the Cup-winners' Cup. Later that year they clinched the league title for the seventh time in 14 seasons. It was then that the Soviet federation grew too demanding, saddling the Ukraine club en bloc with all the national team fixtures and, when the Olympic qualifying team began to falter, with their schedule as well. It all proved too much. But that did not deter Kiev coach Valeri Lobanovsky from going back to square one and painstakingly developing another formidable team around record goal-scorer Oleg Blokhin. In 1985, the renewed Kiev stormed to another league and cup "double". A year later, Kiev charmed their way to the European Cup-winners' Cup as well, defeating Atletico Madrid 3–0 in the Final. Igor Belanov was named European Footballer of the Year. Kiev were the richest and most powerful club in the Ukraine upon the collapse of the Soviet Union, but they failed to translan fluence into European success and were expelled from the 1995–96 Champions League after club officials were accused of trying to bribe a referee. A three-year ban was quashed by UEFA on compassionate grounds.

LIVERPOOL
ENGLAND

Founded: 1892
Stadium: Anfield (41,000)
Colours: All red
League: 18
FA Cup: 5
League Cup: 4
European Cup: 1977, 1978, 1981, 1984
UEFA Cup: 1973, 1976
Supercup: 1977

Liverpool: a name which says so much, in pop music, in sport – specifically, in soccer. The Beatles may have moved on, split up, become part of the memorabilia of a major industrial centre in the north-west of England. But the football club goes on, purveyor of dreams not only for the thousands who fill the seats and the condemned terracing but for the millions on Merseyside who achieved international acclaim through their footballers.

For years the proud boast of English football's hierarchy had been that such was the depth of talent that no one club would ever dominate the championship in the manner of Juventus in Italy, Real Madrid in Spain or Benfica in Portugal. Then, along came Bill Shankly. He was appointed manager of shabby, run-down, half-forgotten Liverpool FC in December, 1959. In two-and-a-half years he won promotion; the purchases of left-half Billy Stevenson and outside-left Peter Thompson, for a combined total of just £60,000, secured the League Championship in 1964; and a year later they had won the FA Cup. Those years and the succeeding 20 brought success on the greatest scale at home and abroad.

The secret was continuity. Shankly was succeeded in the manager's tracksuit by two of his former assistant coaches, Bob Paisley and Joe Fagan. A new player would be bought young and cheap, consigned to the reserves for a year to learn "the Liverpool way", then slotted in to replace one of the fading heroes whose game had lost its edge. Thus the generation of Emlyn Hughes, Ian St John, Roger Hunt and Ron Yeats gave way to the likes of Kevin Keegan and John Toshack, who were followed in turn by Alan Hansen, Kenny Dalglish and Graeme Souness, the last two of whom also later succeeded to Anfield managership. Under Dalglish Liverpool became in 1986 only the third English club to achieve the League and Cup "double" this century – a wonderful achievement on the pitch which was tarnished by the disasters off it, first at the Heysel stadium in 1985 and then at Hillsborough in 1989.

MANCHESTER UNITED
ENGLAND

Founded: 1878
Stadium: Old Trafford (55,000)
Colours: Red/white
League: 11
FA Cup: 9
League Cup: 1
European Cup: 1968
European Cup-winners' Cup: 1991
Supercup: 1991

Manchester United were appropriate leaders of English re-entry into Europe in 1990, after the five-year Heysel disaster ban, since United had been the first English club to play in Europe in the mid-1950s when they reached the semi-finals of the European Cup in both 1957 (losing to eventual winners Real Madrid) and in 1958. On the latter occasion they lost to Milan with a somewhat makeshift side which had been hastily pulled together in the wake of the Munich air disaster in which eight players, including skipper Roger Byrne and the inspirational young Duncan Edwards, had been killed.

It took United ten years to recover, in international terms. Thus it was in May 1968 that Busby's European quest was rewarded as United defeated Benfica 4–1 in extra time at Wembley. Bobby Charlton, a Munich survivor along with defender Bill Foulkes and manager Busby, scored twice to secure the club's most emotional triumph. Busby had been a Scotland international wing-half with Manchester City in the 1930s and took over United when war damage to Old Trafford meant playing home games at Maine Road. Yet within three years Busby had constructed a side who scored a superb FA Cup Final victory over Blackpool and created the entertaining, attacking style which has been mandatory for the club ever since. In the 1960s United boasted not only Charlton but great crowd-pullers such as Scotland's Denis Law and Northern Ireland's George Best. Later came England's long-serving skipper Bryan Robson, who was still in harness in 1993 when United, under Alex Ferguson, regained the English League title for the first time in 26 years.

Robson left in 1994, but not before United became the fourth team this century to complete the "double" of League and FA Cup. United achieved unique status in 1996 when they became the first club to repeat the feat, thanks to French genius Eric Cantona, wing wizard Ryan Giggs and Danish goalkeeper Peter Schmeichel.

Great Managers

Bill Shankly

Manager of Carlisle, Grimsby, Workington, Huddersfield and Liverpool (born September 2, 1913; died September 29, 1981)

Shankly played for Carlisle, Preston and Scotland in the 1930s and returned to Carlisle to begin his managerial career. He took over a faded Liverpool in the Second Division in December, 1959, and there was no stopping either him or the club once promotion had been achieved in 1962. Shankly's dry humour struck a chord with Anfield fans. He brought them League, FA Cup and League successes in consecutive seasons, signed some of the club's greatest servants and laid foundations for further success both on and off the pitch. Shankly had an eye for youthful talent — which he squirrelled away in the reserves until they were ready — and for managerial expertise. Later managers Bob Paisley, Joe Fagan and Roy Evans came out of Shankly's fabled "boot room".

Matt Busby

Manager of Manchester United (born May 26, 1909; died January 20, 1994)

Busby was a Scottish international wing-half who played before the Second World War for Liverpool and Manchester City and took over as manager at Manchester United in 1945 when air raid damage had reduced Old Trafford to near-rubble. Such was his gift for management that, within three years, he had created the first of three memorable teams. His 1948 side won the FA Cup, his Busby Babes of the mid-1950s went twice to the European Cup semi-finals before being wrecked by the Munich air disaster, and his third team completed the European quest with victory over Benfica in 1968's European Cup Final. Busby's love of entertaining football inspired some of British football's greatest talents —from Johnny Carey and Duncan Edwards to Bobby Charlton, Denis Law and George Best.

DOOMED *Marseille's Basile Boli, scorer of the only goal, robs Milan's Marco Van Basten in the French club's ill-fated 1993 European Cup Final triumph*

MARSEILLE
FRANCE

Founded: 1898
Stadium: Vélodrome (46,000)
Colours: All white
League: 9 (1993 title revoked)
Cup: 10
European Cup: 1993

No French club had ever won the European Cup before Marseille; and no one will ever forget what happened when they did. Millionaire entrepreneur Bernard Tapie, the club's high-profile president, had invested millions of pounds in pursuit of European glory. Unfortunately, some of the money had been used to try to fix matches along the road – if not in Europe then in the French championship. Barely had Marseille finished celebrating their Cup-winning 1–0 victory over Milan in Munich in May, 1993, than it emerged that midfielder Jean-Jacques Eydelie had passed cash to

three players from Valenciennes to "go easy" on Marseille in a league fixture a week earlier. Marseille were duly banned from their European defence in 1993–94, the French federation revoked their league championship title and they were subsequently further penalised with enforced relegation. Bankruptcy, inevitably, followed

Marseille's first championship had been celebrated back in 1929. Personalities in those days included Emmanuel Aznar (scorer of eight goals in a 20–2 league win over Avignon) and three English managers in Peter Farmer, Victor Gibson and Charlie Bell. After the war Marseille soon won the championship in 1948, but heavy expenditure on big-name foreigners such as Yugoslavia's Josip Skoblar, Sweden's Roger Magnusson and Brazil's Jairzinho and Paulo César drew only sporadic rewards, and Marseille had slipped into the Second Division by the time

ambitious businessman-turned-politician Tapie took over the helm in 1985. Marseille immediately gained promotion and then, thanks to the attacking genius of Jean-Pierre Papin and Chris Waddle, swept to four league titles in a row. They also suffered a penalty shoot-out defeat by Red Star Belgrade in the 1991 European Cup Final.

MILAN
ITALY

Founded: 1899
Stadium: Meazza (85,443)
Colours: Red and black stripes/white
League: 15
Cup: 4
World Club Cup: 1969, 1989, 1990
European Cup: 1963, 1969, 1989, 1990, 1994
European Cup-winners' Cup: 1968, 1973
Supercup: 1989, 1990

Milan's domination of the European club game in the late 1980s and the early 1990s was achieved on a unique stage

which would appear to represent the pattern of the future for a sport increasingly controlled by the intertwined commercial interests and demands of big business and television. In Milan's case, all these strands were in the hands of a puppet-master supreme in media magnate and then Prime Minister of Italy, Silvio Berlusconi. He had come to the rescue in 1986, investing £20 million to save Milan from bankruptcy and turn the club into a key player in his commercial empire. Milan had been one of the founders of the Italian championship back in 1898, but until the Second World War they tended to be in the shadow of neighbours Inter. After the war Milan achieved spectacular success, largely thanks to the Swedish inside-forward trio of Gunnar Gren, Gunnar Nordahl and Nils Liedholm. They also paid a then world record fee of £72,000 for Uruguay's Juan Schiaffino. They were dangerous rivals to Real Madrid in the new European Cup – losing narrowly to the Spanish

SAFETY FIRST *Milan's Alessandro Costacurta (right) clears his lines in the 1993 European Cup Final*

club in the semi-finals in 1956 and then only in extra time in the Final of 1958. That was the year Milan's scouts first saw the teenage "Golden Boy" Gianni Rivera, whose cultured inside-forward play and partnership with José Altafini inspired Milan to a European Cup victory in 1963 over Benfica. Rivera was Milan's figurehead as they won the European Cup again in 1969 and the European Cup-winners' Cup in 1968 and 1973. But even his charisma could not save the club from the scandals and financial disasters inflicted by a string of disastrous presidents. That was where Berlusconi came in, providing the money and the men – among them Holland's Ruud Gullit and Marco Van Basten, Liberia's George Weah and Yugoslavia's Dejan Savicevic – who turned Milan into a millionaires' club.

MILLONARIOS
BOGOTA, COLOMBIA

Founded: 1938
Stadium: El Campin – Estadio Distrital Nemesio Camacho (57,000)
Colours: Blue/white
League: 13

Millonarios remain a legendary name, if only because of the manner in which they led Colombia's fledgeling professional clubs into the El Dorado rebellion which lured star players from all over the world in the late 1940s and the early 1950s. Many famous names in the game made their reputations there. The then club president, Alfonso Senior, later became president of the Colombian federation and a highly-respected FIFA delegate. Star player Alfredo Di Stefano used Millonarios as a springboard to greatness with Real Madrid.

Taking massive advantage of an Argentine players' strike, Millonarios led the flight from FIFA and the chase for great players – not only Di Stefano but the acrobatic goalkeeper Julio Cozzi, attacking centre-half Nestor Rossi and attacking general Adolfo Pedernera. Nicknamed the "Blue Ballet", they dominated the pirate league and, when an amnesty was negotiated with FIFA, made lucrative "farewell" tours in Europe. Credit for the club's name goes to a journalist, Camacho Montayo. The club had been founded as an amateur side, Deportivo Municipal, in 1938. But as they pushed for a professional league, so Montayo wrote: "The Municipalistas have become the Millonarios." The name stuck. Millonarios remain a leading club but, despite appearing frequently in the South American Club Cup, the glory days have never been repeated.

MOSCOW DYNAMO
RUSSIA

Founded: 1923
Stadium: Dynamo (51,000)
Colours: White/blue
League: 11 Soviet
Cup: 6 Soviet

Dynamo are probably the most famous of all Russian clubs, having been the first Soviet side to venture out beyond the Iron Curtain in the 1940s and 1950s. Also, they were fortunate enough to possess, in goalkeeper Lev Yashin, one of the greatest personalities in the modern game – a show-stopper wherever he went.

Dynamo's origins go back to the start of soccer in Russia, introduced by the Charnock brothers at their cotton mills towards the end of the last century. The team won successive Moscow championships under the name Morozovsti and, after the

Russian Revolution, were taken over first by the electrical trades union and then by the police. Thus the 1923 date marks the formal setting-up of Moscow Dynamo rather than the foundation of the original club. Immediately after the end of the Second World War, Dynamo became a legend as a result of a four-match British tour in the winter of 1945. They drew 3–3 with Chelsea and 2–2 with Rangers, thrashed Cardiff 10–1 and beat a reinforced Arsenal 4–3 in thick fog. Inside-forward Constantin Beskov later became national manager, but it was goalkeeper Alexei "Tiger" Khomich whose reputation lasted long after he had retired to become a sports press photographer. He was succeeded in the team by an even greater goalkeeper in Yashin, who was to become the first Soviet player to be nominated as European Footballer of the Year. Given Dynamo's leadership, it was appropriate that, in 1972, they became the first Soviet side to reach a European final. But their 3–2 defeat by Rangers in Barcelona also stands as the high point of their modern achievement. Back home, Dynamo were pushed back down the ranks by neighbours Moscow Spartak.

MOSCOW SPARTAK
RUSSIA

Founded: 1922
Stadium: Olympic-Lenin/Luzhniki (102,000)
Colours: Red and white/white
League: 4 Russia; 12 Soviet
Cup: 10 Soviet

Moscow Spartak, champions of Russia for both the first two seasons after the collapse of the Soviet Union, face an enormous challenge in the years ahead. Spartak were a power in the land under the old system, but those were the days when players were not allowed to move abroad. Now Spartak must maintain their domestic command and compete effectively in Europe in an "open" transfer society. This is all the more challenging because Spartak had, for years, represented the Party line. They play their home matches in what was known as the Lenin stadium in the Luzhniki suburb, and their past heroes included such officially-approved characters as 1950s' top scorer Nikita Simonian (a club record-holder with 133 goals) and left-half Igor Netto (another club record-holder with 367 appearances). Spartak's best season in European competitions was 1990–91, when they beat both Napoli and Real Madrid to reach the semi-finals of the European Cup, before falling 5–1 on aggregate to Marseille.

For years the club had been ruled by the most respected members of the managerial old guard in veteran administrator Nikolai Starostin and former national coach Constantin Beskov. Starostin, a Spartak player in the club's early days, stayed on after the political upheaval, but Beskov handed over the coaching mantle to his former pupil and international full-back, Oleg Romantsev. Despite the loss of sweeper Vasili Kulkov and midfielders Igor Shalimov and Alexander Mostovoi, Romantsev kept Spartak on top of the table. New heroes were left-back and skipper Viktor Onopko, versatile Igor Lediakhov and the young forward Mikhail Beschastnikh. Not only did Spartak win the 1992, 1993, 1994 and 1996 Russian league titles; they also won – in both 1993 and 1994 – the pre-season CIS Cup, contested by the champions of all the former Soviet states.

NACIONAL
MONTEVIDEO, URUGUAY

Founded: 1899
Stadium: Parque Central (20,000) and Centenario (73,609)
Colours: White/blue
League: 36
World Club Cup: 1971, 1980, 1988
South American Club Cup: 1971, 1980, 1988
South American Recopa: 1988
Inter-American Cup: 1971

Nacional and Penarol are the two great clubs of Uruguay and bitter rivals on both the domestic and international stages. Nacional were formed from a merger of the Montevideo Football Club and the Uruguay Athletic Club, and in 1903 were chosen to line up as Uruguay's

VICTOR ONOPKO *New hero of Moscow Spartak in the post-Communist era*

national team against Argentina in Buenos Aires. Nacional won 3–2 and have enjoyed the international limelight ever since.

Penarol won the first South American Club Cup in 1960, but Nacional soon set about catching up: runners-up three times in the 1960s, they first won the cup by defeating Estudiantes de La Plata in 1971. That led Nacional on to the World Club Cup, where they beat Panathinaikos of Greece (European title-holders Ajax having refused to compete). The two decisive goals in Montevideo were scored by Nacional's former Argentine World Cup spearhead, Luis Artime. It was nine years before Nacional regained those crowds. This time they had a new centre-for-

ward in Waldemar Victorino, who scored the only goal in the 1980 South American Club Cup triumph over Internacional of Brazil, and then the lone strike which decided the world final against Nottingham Forest in Tokyo. By the time Nacional regained the crown in 1988 Victorino had left for Italy, just as so many Uruguayan stars before and since.

Back in the 1930s Nacional sold centre-half Michele Andreolo to Italy, with whom he won the 1938 World Cup. But Nacional quickly replaced him and, from 1939 to 1943, achieved what is nostalgically recalled as their Quinquenio de Oro: their golden five years. Nacional won the league in each of those seasons with a legendary forward line built around the prolific Argentine marksman Atilio Garcia. He was Uruguay's top scorer eight times and ended his career with a record of 464 goals in 435 games. Under Scottish manager William Reasdale, Nacional also celebrated an 8–0 thrashing of the old enemy from Penarol.

PENAROL
MONTEVIDEO, URUGUAY

Founded: 1891
Stadium: Las Acacias (15,000) and Centenario (73,609)
Colours: Black and yellow stripes/black
League: 43
World Club Cup: 1961, 1966, 1982
South American Club Cup: 1960, 1961, 1966, 1982, 1987
Inter-American Cup: 1969

Penarol were the first club to win the World Club Cup three times, but their success is no modern phenomenon. Penarol have been the pre-eminent power in Uruguayan football since its earliest days, providing a host of outstanding players for Uruguay's 1930 and 1950 World Cup-winning teams. Their own international awakening came in 1960, when Penarol won the inaugural South American Club Cup (the Copa Libertadores). They were thrashed by Real Madrid in the World Club Cup, but made amends the next year with victory over Benfica. It was no less than the talents of players such as William Martinez, centre-half Nestor Goncalves and striker Alberto Spencer deserved.

Penarol regained the world club crown in 1966, at the expense of Real Madrid, and then again in 1982 when they beat Aston Villa in Tokyo. By now Penarol had unearthed another superstar in centre-forward Fernando Morena. He was the latest in a long line of great players, which included the nucleus of the Uruguayan national team who shocked Brazil by winning the 1950 World Cup. Goalkeeper Roque Maspoli – later World Club Cup-winning coach in 1966 – captain and centre-half Obdulio Varela, right-winger Alcide Ghiggia, centre-forward Oscar Miguez, right-half Rodriguez Andrade and inside-right Juan Schiaffino all came from Penarol. Schiaffino was the greatest of all.

Penarol had been founded as the Central Uruguayan Railway Cricket Club in 1891, and changed their name in 1913 as the British influence waned. The railways sidings and offices were near the Italian Pignarolo district – named after the landowner Pedro Pignarolo – and so the Spanish style of the name was adopted for the club.

FC PORTO
OPORTO, PORTUGAL

Founded: 1893
Stadium: Das Antas (76,000)
Colours: Blue and white stripes/white
League: 16
Cup: 11
World Club Cup: 1987
European Cup: 1987
Supercup: 1987

Porto were always considered to be No. 3 in the Portuguese football hierarchy until their thrilling European Cup victory over Bayern Munich in Vienna in 1987. Events then and since have ensured that, while their trophy count may not yet match those of Benfica and Sporting, Porto are clearly seen as an alternative centre of power in the domestic game. Porto beat

EX COACH *Porto's Bobby Robson*

Bayern with the Polish goalkeeper Mlynarczyk, Brazilians Celso and Juary, and Algerian winger Rabah Madjer supporting Portugal's own wonderboy, Paulo Futre. But that was entirely appropriate since, in the early 1930s, Porto had been pioneers in the international transfer market.

They began by bringing in two Yugoslavs, and that ambition was reflected in Porto's initial championship successes in 1938 and 1939. In those days Porto's home was the old, rundown Campo da Constituciao. Now, as befits a club with European Cup-winning pedigree, home is the impressive, 76,000-capacity Estadio das Antas.

Not only have Porto won the Champions' Cup; they also finished runners-up to Juventus in the European Cup-winners' Cup in 1984. The creative force behind the club's progress in the 1980s was the late José Maria Pedroto. He led Porto to the cup in 1977 and league title in 1978 and 1979.

His work would be carried on by his pupil, former national team centre-forward Artur Jorge, who coached Porto to their 1987 European title and later took over the national side. Later, under Brazilian Carlos Alberto da Silva, duly succeeded by Bobby Robson, Porto enhanced their standing as members of the European establishment when they reached the semi-finals of the Champions League in 1994 and the quarter-finals in 1997. Robson left Porto in 1996 after building a team which won a hat-trick of league titles.

PHILIPS SV
EINDHOVEN, HOLLAND

Founded: 1913
Stadium: Philips (30,000)
Colours: Red and white stripes/white
League: 14
Cup: 7
European Cup: 1988
UEFA Cup: 1978

PSV equalled the achievements of Celtic (in 1967) and Ajax Amsterdam (in 1972) when they defeated Benfica in a penalty shoot-out to win the 1988 European Cup. Only those other two clubs had previously secured the treble of European Cup and domestic league and cup all in the same season. Remarkably, PSV achieved all they did despite having sold their finest player, Ruud Gullit, to Milan at the start of the season for a world record £5.7 million. The money was, however, invested wisely to secure the best players from Holland, Denmark and Belgium.

Such success was the reward for a long wait since PSV had been one of the invited entrants in the inaugural European Cup in 1955–56, when they crashed 1–0, 1–6 to Rapid Vienna in the first round. Surprisingly, considering PSV's position as the sports club of the giant Philips electrics corporation, they were long outshone by Ajax and Feyenoord. For years the Philips company took comparatively little interest in PSV, even though an estimated 40,000 of the 200,000 urban population of Eindhoven work directly or indirectly for Philips. Only in the past decade have Philips become seriously involved with club policy and finance.

PSV had won the 1976 UEFA Cup without much fanfare. But ten years later, realising the potential to be reaped from soccer sponsorship, the company came up with the funds, and were duly rewarded two years later with the European Cup. In 1992, taking the process a stage further, the club changed its name in order to promote itself outside Holland as Philips SV (while domestic sponsorship regulations required it to stick with the PSV abbreviation in Holland).

RANGERS
GLASGOW, SCOTLAND

Founded: 1873
Stadium: Ibrox Park (50,471)
Colours: Blue/white
League: 47
Cup: 27
League cup: 19
European Cup-winners' Cup: 1972

Rangers are one half of the "Old Firm" – their rivalry with Celtic having dominated Scottish football for a century. Yet Rangers have never extended that power into Europe, their only prize from virtual non-stop international competition being the 1972 Cup-winners' Cup Final win over Moscow Dynamo. Not that Rangers' history is short on proud moments. One particularly glorious era was the 1920s, when Rangers' heroes included the legendary "Wee Blue Devil", Alan Morton.

In the 1960s, Rangers endured heavy European defeats at the hands of Eintracht Frankfurt, Tottenham and Real Madrid. The start of the 1970s was a time of mixed emotions: 1971 saw the Ibrox disaster, when 66 fans died in a stairway crush at the end of a game against Celtic. Then, a year later, Rangers' European Cup-winners' Cup triumph was immediately followed by a European ban because of the way their celebrating fans ran amok in Barcelona. The upturn began in November, 1985, when Lawrence Marlboro bought control of the club. He brought in Graeme Souness as player-manager. In 1988 David Murray bought Rangers, and Souness revolutionized their image by buying 18 English players and smashing the club's traditional Protestants-only ethic with his £1.5 million capture of Catholic Mo Johnston. Subsequent big-name signings such as Brian Laudrup and Paul Gascoigne enabled Rangers to maintain their league title dominance for a remarkable eight years in a row. Striker Ally McCoist capitalized by smashing the club record of 233 goals set 60 years earlier by legendary Bob McPhail.

BRIAN LAUDRUP *The Dane is a double Scottish Footballer of the Year*

CROWN PRINCE *Raul Gonzalez is the latest sensation to grace the Bernabeu Stadium at "royal" Real Madrid*

RAPID VIENNA
AUSTRIA

Founded: 1899
Stadium: Hanappi (19,600)
Colours: Green and white/green
League: 29
Cup: 13

Rapid were founded as the 1st Arbeiter-Fussballklub (First Workers Football Club) but, on changing their name, also set about refining the short-passing style of the "Vienna School" to such good effect that they won the championship eight times between 1912 and 1923. The success story did not end there. In 1930 Rapid became the first Austrian club to win the Mitropa Cup, defeating powerful Sparta Prague 2–0, 2–3 in the Final. Several of Rapid's key players were members of the "Wunderteam", the national side who finished fourth in the 1934 World Cup under the captaincy of Rapid centre-half Pepe Smistik.

Four years later Austria was swallowed up into Greater Germany, and the Austrian league was incorporated into the Greater German championship. To the mischievous delight of their fans, Rapid not only won the German Cup in 1938 (3–2 against FSV Frankfurt in the Final) but also the German championship in 1941. On a day which has entered football legend Rapid hit back from 3–0 down to defeat an outstanding Schalke side 4–3 before a 90,000 crowd in the Olympic stadium in Berlin. Their hero was centre-forward Franz "Bimbo" Binder, whose hat-trick was crowned by the winning goal when he hammered a free-kick through the defensive wall. Binder ended a great career with 1,006 goals and later became club coach.

Many of Rapid's old heroes returned as coaches, among them Karl Rappan (who developed the Swiss Bolt system), Edi Fruhwirth and Karl Decker. Great players in the post-war years included wing-half Gerhard Hanappi – an architect by profession, who laid out the designs for the club stadium – tough-tackling defender Ernst Happel and another prolific goal-scoring centre-forward in Hans Krankl. He led Rapid's attack in 1985 in the first of their two defeats in the European Cup-winners' Cup Final, but had long retired when they fell to Paris Saint-Germain in 1996.

REAL MADRID
SPAIN

Founded: 1902
Stadium: Santiago Bernabeu (105,000)
Colours: All white
League: 28
Cup: 17
World Club Cup: 1966
European Cup: 1956, 1957, 1958, 1959, 1960, 1966
UEFA Cup: 1985, 1986

What else is there left to say about Real Madrid? Six times champions of Europe, 27 times champions of Spain – both record achievements. They have also won the World Club Cup, two UEFA Cups and 16 Spanish cups, which add up to a football honours degree for the club founded by students as Madrid FC. (The Real prefix, meaning Royal, was a title bestowed on the club later by King Alfonso XIII.) Madrid were not only among the founders of the Spanish cup and league competitions: it was also the Madrid president, Carlos Padros, who attended on Spain's behalf the inaugural meeting of FIFA in Paris in 1904. In the late 1920s Madrid launched a policy of buying big. They paid a then Spanish record fee of £2,000 for Ricardo Zamora, still revered as the greatest Spanish goalkeeper of all time.

The Spanish Civil War left Madrid's Chamartin stadium in ruins. At the time the club had no money, but boasted one of the greatest visionaries in European football history. He was Santiago Bernabeu, a lawyer who had been, in turn, player, team manager and secretary, and was now club president. Bernabeu launched an audacious public appeal which raised the cash to build the wonderful stadium which now bears his name. The huge crowds which flocked in provided the cash to build the team who dominated the first five years of the European Cup. Argentine-born centre-forward Alfredo Di Stefano was the star of stars, though Bernabeu surrounded him with illustrious team-mates such as Hungary's Ferenc Puskas, France's Ramond Kopa, Uruguay's José Santamaria and Brazil's Didi. They set impossibly high standards for all the players and teams who followed. Madrid won the European Cup again in 1966 and the UEFA Cup twice in the 1980s, but even later superstars such as Pirri, Santillana, Juanito, Hugo Sanchez and Emilio Butragueño would occasionally complain that nothing they achieved would ever be quite enough. The 1960 team had been, if anything, too good.

RED STAR BELGRADE
YUGOSLAVIA

Founded: 1945
Stadium: Crvena Zvezda (Red Star) (97,422)
Colours: Red and white stripes/white
League: 20
Cup: 15
World Club Cup: 1991
European Cup: 1991

This may be the most schizophrenic club in the world. In Germany they are known as Roter Stern; in France as Etoile Rouge; in Spain as Estrella Roja; in Italy as Stella Rossa; in Serbo-Croat it's Fudbalski Klub Crvena Zvezda; in English, of course, Red Star Belgrade. Under whichever name, the 1991 European and world club champions stood revered as one of the pillars of the worldwide establishment until civil strife in the former Yugoslavia led to international suspension for both country and clubs. The consequences for Red Star were almost disastrous, since millions of pounds paid in

transfer fees for their star players were suddenly frozen in banks around Europe.

But Red Star are no strangers to disaster, having been the last team to play Manchester United's "Busby Babes" before the Munich air disaster. Red Star fought back from 3–0 down to draw 3–3, but lost on aggregate despite all the efforts of balletic goalkeeper Vladimir Beara, gypsy midfielder Dragoslav Sekularac and dynamic striker Bora Kostic (scorer of a club record 157 goals in 256 league games). All three men later moved abroad, members of an ongoing exodus of more than 40 players including stars like Dragan Dzajic (to Bastia), Dragan Stojkovic (to

Marseille), Robert Prosinecki (to Real Madrid) and Darko Pancev (to Internazionale). This explains, perhaps, why Red Star, for all their talent, boast only one victory in the European Cup (the 1991 penalty shoot-out victory over Marseille in Bari) and one runners-up spot in the UEFA Cup (beaten on away goals by Borussia Mönchengladbach in 1979).

Red Star were formally set up by students of Belgrade University after the war. They play their home matches in the so-called "Marakana", which was the first stadium in eastern Europe to host a mainstream European final, when Ajax beat Juventus in the 1973 European Cup.

ROBERT PROSINECKI *Outstanding graduate of the Red Star football "university"*

RIVER PLATE
BUENOS AIRES, ARGENTINA

Founded: 1901
Stadium: Antonio Liberti/Monumental (76,000)
Colours: White with red sash/black
League: 24
World Club Cup: 1986
South American Club Cup: 1986, 1996
Inter-American Cup: 1986

River Plate are one of the two giants of Argentine football, Boca Juniors being the other. Traditionally the club from the rich side of Buenos Aires, River were founder members of the first division in 1908, then took a leading role in the "war" which accompanied the introduction of professional football in the 1920s. Over the years River have fielded some wonderful teams. In the 1930s they boasted Bernabe Ferreyra, a legendary figure in Argentine football; in the late 1940s their high-scoring forward line was so feared and admired they were nicknamed "La Maquina" (The Machine). The names of Muñoz, Moreno, Pedernera, Labruna and Loustau mean little outside Argentina today, but there they inspire awe like Real Madrid in Europe.

Later River produced more great players: Alfredo Di Stefano, who would one day turn Real Madrid into possibly the greatest team of all time; Omar Sivori, who would form a wonderful partnership with John Charles after joining Juventus; and then 1978 World Cup winners Ubaldo Fillol, Daniel Passarella, Leopoldo Luque and Mario Kempes. In 1986 they were joined in River's Hall of Fame by the likes of goalkeeper Nery Pumpido, centre-back Oscar Ruggeri and schemer Norberto Alonso, after victory in the South American Club Cup provided River with formal confirmation of their lofty status. River really should have succeeded to the crown years earlier, but were unlucky runners-up in 1966 to Penarol of Uruguay and in 1976 to Cruzeiro of Brazil. In 1986 they made no mistake, beating America of Colombia, then adding the World Club Cup by defeating Steaua of Romania 1–0 in Tokyo.

SANTOS
SÃO PAULO, BRAZIL

Founded: 1912
Stadium: Vila Belmiro (20,000)
Colours: All white
São Paulo state league: 15
Brazil championship (incl. Torneo Rio-São Paulo): 5
World Club Cup: 1962, 1963
South American Club Cup: 1962, 1963

The name of Santos will always be synonymous with that of Pele, who played all his mainstream career with the club and returned as a director at the end of 1993 to try to help lift his old club out of the depths of a severe financial and administrative crisis.

Santos had been founded by three members of the Americano club, who stayed home in the port of Santos when their club moved to São Paulo. Santos joined the São Paulo state championship in 1916, became only the second Brazilian club to embrace professionalism in 1933, but did not hit the headlines until the mid-1950s. Then, to organize a host of talented youngsters, they signed the 1950 World Cup veteran, Jair da Rosa Pinto, and discovered the 15-year-old Pele.

To say that Santos were a one-man team, as it often appeared from the publicity, would be unfair. Santos harvested millions of pounds from whistle-stop friendly match tours around the world and reinvested heavily in surrounding Pele with fine players: World Cup winners in goalkeeper Gilmar, centre-back Mauro and wing-half Zito; an outside-left with a ferocious shot in Pepe; and the precocious young talents of right-winger Dorval, schemer Mengalvio and centre-forward Coutinho, Pele's so-called "twin" with whom he established an almost telepathic relationship on the pitch. Santos were more than a football team; they were a touring circus.

Sadly, the constant touring and playing burned out many young players before they had a chance to establish their talent. But not before Santos had scaled the competitive heights as

PELE *The man who "made" Santos*

Pele inspired their victories in the South American Club Cup and the World Club Cup in both 1962 and 1963.

One more year and it was all over. Independiente beat Santos in the 1964 South American Club Cup semi-finals, and the spell had been broken. Santos went on touring and raking in cash, capitalizing on Pele's name, for as long as they could. Pele returned, briefly, as a director in the 1990s, but without inspiring the sort of success Santos had achieved when he was a player.

SÃO PAULO
BRAZIL

Founded: 1935
Stadium: Morumbi (150,000)
Colours: White with a red and black hoop/white
São Paulo state league: 17
Brazil championship (incl. Torneo Rio-São Paulo): 4
World Club Cup: 1992, 1993
South American Club Cup: 1992, 1993

São Paulo's victories over Barcelona and Milan in the 1992 and 1993 World Club Cups in Tokyo left no doubt about which was the finest club side in the world – for all the European hype which had surrounded the Italian champions. Those victories also underlined the depth of talent available to São Paulo, since their key midfielder, Rai (younger brother of 1986 World Cup star Socrates), had been sold to French club Paris Saint-Germain in the summer of 1993. Dual success also enhanced the reputation of coach Tele Santana, Brazil's World Cup manager in 1982 and 1986 and one of the most eloquent

and down-to-earth of football coaches and analysts.

São Paulo are, even so, comparative newcomers – having been founded in 1935, at a time when the likes of River Plate, Penarol and the rest were already well-established powers in their own lands. The club was formed from a merger between CA Paulistano and AA Palmeiras. A leading light was Paulo Machado de Carvalho, who would later, as a senior administrator, contribute behind the scenes to Brazil's World Cup hat-trick.

Within a decade of being founded, São Paulo developed into the strongest team in the country, winning the state title five times in the 1940s. They imported Argentine inside-forward Antonio Sastre, and the continuing pressure of success led to the construction of the 150,000-capacity Morumbi stadium – the world's largest club-owned sports arena.

In the 1960s São Paulo had to take a back seat to Santos. In 1974 they reached their first South American Club Cup Final (losing to Argentina's Independiente), but it was not until the arrival of Santana, in the late 1980s, that São Paulo emerged from the doldrums. Despite the continuing sale of star players – key defender Ricardo Rocha went to Real Madrid – São Paulo secured three state league titles in four years, used the cash to strengthen their squad and were duly rewarded at the highest level.

São Paulo's World Club Cup victory over the highly rated European giants Milan in Tokyo in 1993 was very impressive, with Cafu and Massaro the outstanding players. São Paulo became the first side to register consecutive wins in the Tokyo final.

JAN STEJSKAL *Maintaining Sparta's great traditions*

SPARTA PRAGUE
CZECH REPUBLIC

Founded: 1893
Stadium: Letna (36,000)
Colours: All red
League: 22
Cup: 9

Sparta are the most popular club in what is now the Czech Republic, as well as one of the oldest. They were founded as King's Vineyard in 1893, and took the name of Sparta, from one of the states of Ancient Greece, a year later. They were one Europe's great sides preceding the Second World War, winning the Mitropa Cup in the inaugural final in 1927 against Rapid Vienna. Victory over Ferencvaros of Hungary followed in 1935, and they were runners-up in 1936. Sparta's team then included the great inside-left, Oldrich Nejedly.

He was a star in the 1934 World Cup, when Czechoslovakia finished runners-up. Again in 1962, when the Czechs next reached the World Cup Final, there were key places in the team for Sparta men such as right-winger Tomas Pospichal and schemer Andrzej Kvasnak.

Sparta suffered after the last war, and were forced to alter their name to Sparta Bratrstvi and then Spartak Sokolovo. But their loyal fans never called them anything but Sparta, and reality was recognized when the club's present title was adopted in 1965. That same year they celebrated their first league title in more than a decade. Memories of the glory days of the Mitropa Cup were revived by the club's run to the European Cup-winners' Cup semi-finals in 1973 and by the impressive 1983–84 UEFA Cup campaign, during which they

---

Great Managers
TELE SANTANA

Coach of Atletico Mineiro, Gremio, Flamengo, Fluminense, Palmeiras (Brazil), Al Ahly (Saudi Arabia), São Paulo FC (Brazil); also Brazil national team (born July 26, 1933)

Santana was an outside-right with Fluminense in the early 1950s but never good enough to challenge Julinho or Garrincha in Brazil's World Cup teams. Instead, he reached the World Cup finals in both 1982 and 1986 as manager of Brazil. Santana's insistence on attacking football was criticized as naive after Brazil's failures in, respectively, the second round and quarter-finals. But Santana had the last laugh when he won the World Club Cup twice as boss of São Paulo in 1992 and 1993. Simultaneously, Santana was not afraid to pin-point high levels of corruption in the Brazilian game as well as poor refereeing for the failure to regain World Cup primacy in the 1980s and early 1990s.

scored notable victories over Real Madrid and Widzew Lodz. Sparta's continuing domination of the domestic game in the early 1990s was remarkable because, immediately after the World Cup finals, they lost a string of senior internationals, such as goalkeeper Jan Stejskal, defenders Julius Bielik and Michal Bilek, midfield general Ivan Hasek and striker Tomas Skuhravy, the second-top scorer at Italia '90 with five goals.

SPORTING CLUBE
LISBON, PORTUGAL

Founded: 1906
Stadium: José Alvalade (70,000)
Colours: Green and white hoops/white
League: 16
Cup: 16
European Cup-winners' Cup: 1964

Sporting Clube do Portugal last reached a European final back in 1964, when they won the Cup-winners' Cup. Now Benfica's deadly rivals – the grounds are barely a mile apart – dream of the day when they can bring those old heroes out of retirement obscurity to celebrate a European revival. The late 1980s and early 1990s brought Sporting the worst era in their history, an empty decade following the heady 1981–82 season in which they won the league and cup "double" under Englishman Malcolm Allison.

In 1992 the new president, José Sousa Cintra, brought in ex-England manager Bobby Robson to try to recapture the Allison magic. Robson was given only 18 months, however, before former Portugal national coach Carlos Queiros, instead, was given the task of reviving the glories of the 1950s, when Sporting rivalled Benfica as the country's top club and took the championship seven times in eight years.

En route to Sporting's sole European trophy, they beat APOEL Nicosia in the second round first leg by a European record 16–1. In the Final against MTK Budapest, an entertaining match saw Sporting go 1–0 down, recover to lead 2–1 then go 3–2 behind before securing a 3–3 draw and a replay. In Antwerp a single 20th-minute goal from winger Morais, direct from a corner, was enough to win the cup. Their back four

of Morais, Batista, José Carlos and Hilario starred in the Portugal team which finished third in the 1966 World Cup finals in England.

The nearest Sporting have since gone to European success was in 1990–91, when they reached the UEFA Cup semi-final before falling 0–0, 0–2 to eventual winners Internazionale.

STEAUA
BUCHAREST, ROMANIA

Founded: 1947
Stadium: Steaua (30,000)
Colours: Red/blue
League: 18
Cup: 17
European Cup: 1986

Steaua – the word means 'Star' – were one of the army clubs created in eastern Europe after the Communist takeovers of political power. Originally Steaua were known as CCA Bucharest, under which title they won the championship three times in a row in the early 1950s. Later, renamed Steaua, they won the cup five times in six seasons in the late 1960s and early 1970s.

In 1986 Steaua became the first eastern European team to win the European Cup when the beat Barcelona on penalties in Seville. Their penalty stopping hero in the climactic minutes was Helmut Ducadam, whose career ended prematurely by illness soon after. Steaua's power – including the right to sign any player they liked from

any other Romanian club – was significantly reduced after the overthrow of the Communist dicatorship of the Ceausescu family.

VASCO DA GAMA
RIO DE JANEIRO, BRAZIL

Founded: 1898 as sailing club, 1915 as football club
Stadium: São Januario (50,000) and Maracana (130,000)
Colours: All white with black sash
Rio state league: 17
Brazil championship (incl. Torneo Rio-São Paulo): 4

Like Flamengo, one of their long-time Rio de Janeiro rivals, Vasco grew from a sailing club – the impetus for football coming from former members of a club called Luzitania FC, who had been refused entry to the early Rio de Janeiro state championship because of their "Portuguese-only" policy. Transformed into Vasco da Gama, however, they were elected to the championship in 1915 and had progressed to the top flight by 1923. Support, both vocal and financial, has come to the club over the years from the city's Portuguese community. In spite of their original policies, Vasco quickly became noted for their inclusion of mixed-race players at a time, early in Brazilian football's development, when the game was riven by race and class divisions. Vasco led the way, too, by creating the São Januario stadium, which was the first national stadium in Brazil and hosted all major club and national team matches before the building of the Maracana in 1950.

In 1958 Vasco supplied Brazil's World Cup-winning team with centre-back Luiz Bellini, the captain, and centre-forward Vava. They earned a long-awaited consolation for events eight years earlier when no fewer than eight Vasco players had figured in the Brazilian squad which was pipped to the World Cup by Uruguay. In the 1960s and 1970s Vasco figured, as ever, among the most powerful of challengers to Fluminense and Flamengo – from whom they controversially signed the popular striker, Bebeto.

LEGENDS

In football, as in other sports, the word "great" is over-used and devalued, having been applied to almost any and every fleeting moment of drama or high skill. Thousands of players have been described in terms of ultimate praise. But at the highest echelon of the game there is a small elite group acknowledged by millions of fans as the truly great.

BECKENBAUER
WEST GERMANY

"Kaiser Franz" can boast that he has lifted the World Cup as both captain, in 1974, and manager, in 1990. But his achievements are not the only measure of his true greatness. Beckenbauer's innovative strength was through the revolutionary role of attacking sweeper which, with majestic calm and precision, he introduced in the late 1960s.

CHARLTON
ENGLAND

Bobby Charlton, throughout the world, is probably the most famous English footballer who has ever thrilled a crowd. He won 106 caps, and his name is synonymous with some of the greatest moments of the modern English game, but also with the highest traditions of sportsmanship, modesty and integrity.

CRUYFF
HOLLAND

Johan Cruyff stands out as not merely the greatest Dutch footballer but one of the greatest players of all time. He made his first-team debut at 17, his goal-scoring international debut at 19 and went on to inspire Ajax and Holland through most of their golden 1970s.

DI STEFANO
SPAIN

Alfredo Di Stefano is reckoned by many to be the greatest footballer of all. Although Pele's admirers may consider that sacrilege, the millions who wondered at Di Stefano's awesome majesty as he dominated European football in the 1950s and early 1960s will happily concur.

EUSEBIO
PORTUGAL

Eusebio, the greatest Portuguese footballer in history, did not come from Portugal at all. Born and brought up in Mozambique, then still one of Portugal's African colonies, Eusebio was the first African footballer to earn a worldwide reputation. Fans around the world took Eusebio to their hearts not only for his ability but for the sportsmanlike way he played.

MARADONA
ARGENTINA

Diego Maradona was not only the world's greatest footballer throughout the 1980s and early 1990s. He was also the most controversial and the most enigmatic player, unable to appear in public or on a football pitch without arousing the most contrasting of emotions.

MATTHEWS
ENGLAND

Stanley Matthews was the first great footballer of the modern era. There will be cases made for Billy Wright, Bobby Charlton, Bobby Moore and others but none dominated his particular era as long as the barber's son from Hanley in the Potteries area of the English Midlands.

PELE
BRAZIL

Pele remains one of those great examples and inspirations of world sport: a poor boy taking the world stage at 17, whose talent lifted him to the peaks of achievement, fame and fortune ... yet who, amidst all that, retained his innate sense of sportsmanship, his love of his calling, the desire to entertain fans and the respect of fellow players.

PUSKAS
HUNGARY

Ferenc Puskas remains one of the greatest players of all time – a symbol of the legendary "Magical Magyars" who dominated European football in the early 1950s and stand as perhaps the greatest team never to have won the World Cup. He very rarely used his right foot (except to stand on, as they say) but his left was so lethal that he hardly ever needed it.

YASHIN
USSR

In South America they called Lev Yashin the "Black Spider"; in Europe the "Black Panther". Eusebio described him as "the peerless goalkeeper of the century". Yashin's fame spread throughout the world, not merely for his ability as a goalkeeper to stop shots that no one else could reach, but as a great sportsman and ambassador for the game.

BECKENBAUER

"KAISER FRANZ" AND A UNIQUE DOUBLE

Career facts

1945 *Born on September 11 in Munich*

1955 *Began playing for the schoolboy team, FC 1906 Munich*

1959 *Joined Bayern Munich youth section*

1962 *Gave up a job as a trainee insurance salesman to sign full-time with Bayern*

1964 *Made his Bayern debut in a 4–0 win away to St Pauli in Hamburg*

1965 *Made his national team debut in a 2–1 World Cup qualifying win in Sweden*

1966 *Starred in midfield, on the losing side, for West Germany in the 4–2 World Cup Final defeat by England at Wembley*

1967 *Captained Bayern Munich, from sweeper, to victory over Rangers in the European Cup-winners' Cup Final*

1972 *Captained West Germany to European Championship victory over the Soviet Union in Brussels*

1974 *Captained Bayern Munich to victory in the European Cup Final and then West Germany to victory in the World Cup Final against Holland*

1976 *Completed a record 103 appearances for West Germany before transferring to the New York Cosmos in the North American Soccer League*

1984 *Appointed national manager of West Germany in succession to Jupp Derwall*

1986 *Guided an average side to the World Cup Final, where they lost 3–2 to Argentina*

1990 *Became the first man to captain and then manage a World Cup-winning team when West Germany beat Argentina 1–0 in Rome*

1993 *After a short spell as coach of Olympique Marseille, Beckenbauer returned to Bayern as executive vice-president*

1994 *Took over as coach, guiding Bayern to the league title first as team manager then as club president*

Franz Beckenbauer has always been accompanied by the sort of luck which only a player of his genius deserves.

The smile of fate was on him through an illustrious playing career and on into management when – in his first appointment at any level – he took West Germany to the Final of the World Cup in Mexico in 1986 and four years later went one better with victory in Italy.

Thus only "Kaiser Franz" can boast that he has lifted the World Cup as both captain, in 1974, and manager, in 1990.

No other footballer has ever had a career which reached such tangible heights. He was the first German to reach a century of international appearances before leaving Bayern Munich for spells with New York Cosmos and then with Hamburg, where he wound down his playing career.

His honours include the World Cup in 1974 (runner-up in 1966), the European Championship in 1972 (runner-up 1976), the World Club Cup (1976), the European Cup (1974, 1975, 1976), the European Cup-winners' Cup (1967), as well as the West German league and cup. He was also a runner-up in the UEFA Cup with Hamburg and a runner-up in the SuperCup with Bayern. With New York Cosmos, Beckenbauer also won the NASL Soccer Bowl in 1977, 1978 and 1980.

But achievement is not the only measure of true greatness. Beckenbauer's innovative strength was through the revolutionary role of attacking sweeper which, with the encouragement of Bayern Munich coach Tschik Cajkovski, he introduced in the late 1960s.

The boy Beckenbauer took his first steps on the football ladder with local club Munich 1906, before

BECKENBAUER *Attacking sweeper*

he switched to Bayern and was first recognized by West Germany at youth level. Within a year of making his league debut with Bayern, as an outside-left, Beckenbauer was promoted into the senior national team.

The occasion was one to test the nerve of the most experienced player, never mind a fledgeling newcomer: West Germany were away to Sweden in a decisive qualifier for the 1966 World Cup. The odds were against them. Yet they won 2–1. West Germany's place in the World Cup finals was all but secured as was Beckenbauer's place in the national team for almost a decade.

In due course he was voted German Footballer of the Year and European Footballer of the Year. Out on the pitch he was grace and elegance personified, combining an athlete's physique with a computer-like brain for the game which saw

> ## ❝He's converted football into an art form.❞
>
> *Willi Schulz, 1966 World Cup team-mate*

gaps before they had opened and goal opportunities – for himself and his team-mates – for which the opposing defence had not prepared.

The Elegant Manipulator

Beckenbauer spent almost all his senior career with Bayern Munich as attacking sweeper. Many critics said he was wasting his talent. But Beckenbauer, in an increasingly crowded modern game, found that the sweeper role provided him with time and space in which to work his magical influence on a match. He was the puppet master, standing back and pulling the strings which earned West Germany and Bayern Munich every major prize.

Not that Beckenbauer shied away from the attacking opportunity when it presented itself. He scored the goal which inspired West Germany's revival against England in the 1970 World Cup quarter-final.

During his four years with Cosmos Beckenbauer made many friends and admirers in the United States and was expected to take a central role in their 1994 World Cup build-up before other interests distracted him.

On retiring, Beckenbauer was much in demand as a newspaper and television columnist. Then he was invited to put his words into deeds when offered the post of national manager in succession to Jupp Derwall after the disappointing 1984 European Championship.

The Germans had always promoted managers from within their system. Beckenbauer was an outsider with no coaching experience: his appointment represented a huge gamble. It paid off. Such was Beckenbauer's Midas touch that "his" West Germany were crowned world champions in Rome and he earned his unique place in history.

CHARLTON

ENGLAND'S AMBASSADOR

THUNDERBOLT SHOOTING *Charlton on target against West Ham*

Bobby Charlton, throughout the world, is probably the most famous English footballer who has ever thrilled a crowd. His name is synonymous with some of the greatest moments of the English game, but also with the highest traditions of sportsmanship and integrity.

Long after he had finished playing Charlton's reputation worked wonders in breaking down the tightest security at World Cups and European Championships. It only needed a player or manager to glance out and see Charlton arriving for barred doors and gates to be flung open. Today's heroes may possess a string

of fan clubs and millions in Swiss banks, but they still recognize magic.

The delight which much of the English public took in Manchester United's success in the inaugural Premier League in 1992–93 may be partly explained by the respect in which Bobby Charlton is held for reasons which transcend "mere" football.

Football was always in the blood. The Charltons – Bobby and World Cup-winning brother Jackie – were nephews of that great Newcastle United hero of the 1950s, Jackie Milburn. They began in the back streets of Ash-

ington in the north-east of England, and Charlton fulfilled every schoolboy's dream when, at 17, he was signed by Manchester United.

Busby Babe and United Captain

Matt Busby had invested more time and determination than any other manager in seeking out the finest young talents in the country. Not only Charlton, but Duncan Edwards, Eddie Colman, David Pegg and many more had been singled out for the Old Trafford treatment: turned from boys into young footballing men under the tutelage of assistant Jimmy Murphy, and then released to explode into the League.

This was the philosophy behind the Busby Babes, the team of youngsters who took the League by storm in the mid-1950s and brought a breath of optimistic fresh air into an austere post-war England. The sense of that spirit of a new generation being lost added to the nation's grief when United's plane crashed in the snow and ice at the end of a runway in Munich on their way home from a European Cup quarter-final in Belgrade in February 1958.

Charlton had established

> ## "It's difficult enough replacing him as a monument in the team without having to replace him as a person as well."
> *Tommy Docherty, then Manchester United manager, after Charlton's retirement*

Career facts

1937 Born on October 11 in Ashington, County Durham

1957 Played in the FA Cup Final at 19

1958 Survived the Munich air crash to play in another FA Cup Final

1963 Played in his third FA Cup Final, and was at last on the winning side as United beat Leicester City 3–1

1966 Starred for England in the World Cup victory, scoring goals against Mexico and Portugal along the way to help earn him the European Footballer of the Year award

1968 Scored two of the goals as Manchester United finally won the European Cup, defeating Benfica 4–1 after extra time at Wembley

1970 Played his record 106th and last international for England in the 3–2 defeat by West Germany at the World Cup finals in Mexico

1973 Moved to Preston for two years as player-manager before becoming a director back at Old Trafford

1994 Received a knighthood

his first-team potential the previous season. He was initially an inside-right, later switched to outside-left with England, and finally settled as a deep-lying centre-forward, using his pace out of midfield and thunderous shot to score some of the most spectacular goals English football has ever seen. One such goal marked his England debut against Scotland, another broke the deadlock against Mexico in the 1966 World Cup finals, and dozens of them inspired Manchester United's post-Munich revival.

The European Cup victory at Wembley in 1968, when he captained United and scored twice, was a highly emotional moment.

Then, as now, the newly-ennobled Sir Bobby has been a perfect ambassador for the game.

CRUYFF

CLOSE CONTROL *Cruyff tantalizes Argentine defender Pedro Sa at the 1974 World Cup*

THE TOTAL FOOTBALLER

Johan Cruyff stands out as not merely the greatest Dutch footballer but one of the greatest players of all time, a status which owes much to the persistence of his mother.

She worked as a cleaner in the offices of the Ajax club and persuaded the club coaching staff to take Johan into their youth sections when he was still only 12 years old. The rest is history and a virtually unbroken 25-year succession of trophies and awards on the highest plane as first player and then coach.

Cruyff made his first-team debut at 17, his goal-scoring international debut at 19 and went on to inspire Ajax and Holland through most of their golden 1970s. This was the era of "total football", a concept of the game first described as "The Whirl" in the early 1950s by the Austrian expert Willy Meisl. He saw the day when every player in a team would possess comparable technical and physical ability and would be able to interchange roles at will.

Cruyff was The Whirl in action. Nominally he played centre-forward. But Cruyff's perception of centre-forward was as orthodox as the squad No. 14 he wore on his back for most of his career with Ajax.

> **❝ Johan's secret is that he loves football, seeking out new ways of trying to achieve perfection. ❞**
>
> *Stefan Kovacs, former Ajax coach*

FINAL SHOWDOWN *Cruyff's face-to-face with Berti Vogts*

Cruyff did turn up at the apex of the attack: but he was also to be found meandering through midfield and out on the wings, using his nimble, coltish pace to unhinge defences from a variety of angles and positions.

Single-handed he not only pulled Internazionale of Italy apart in the 1972 European Cup final but scored both goals in Ajax's 2–0 win. The next year, in Belgrade, he inspired one of the greatest 20-minute spells of football ever seen as Ajax overcame another strong Italian outfit, Juventus.

Already the vultures were gathering. Spain had reopened their borders to foreign players and Cruyff was an obvious target. Eventually Barcelona won the transfer race – but after the close of the Spanish federation's autumn deadline. However, such was the magnitude of the transfer that the federation bent their own regulations so that Cruyff could play immediately.

When Cruyff arrived in Barcelona, the Catalans were struggling down the table. By the season's end they were champions, Cruyff's triumphant progress having included a spectacular 5–0 victory away to deadly rivals Real Madrid. Surprisingly, apart from that league title, Barcelona won little else, though Cruyff himself completed the first ever hat-trick of European Footballer of the Year awards.

RED ALERT *Cruyff created panic when he had the ball.*

It was at the end of his first season with Barcelona that Cruyff's career reached its international zenith. At the 1974 World Cup finals Holland took their total football through round after round. No one could withstand them. Above all, no one could handle the mercurial Cruyff, who inspired victories over Uruguay and Bulgaria in the first round, then provided two goals to lead the way against Argentina in the second. The last group match – in effect the semi-final – was against Brazil: the old masters against the new. Cruyff scored Holland's decisive second goal in a 2–0 victory which signalled a new era.

The Final, of course, ended in defeat at the hands of West Germany and, though Holland reached the Final again in 1978, Cruyff, by then, had retired from the national team and was about to head west.

First he joined the Los Angeles Aztecs in the NASL. He won the Most Valuable Player award that year, moved to the Washington Diplomats in 1980 and, late in 1981, returned to Holland to win the Championship twice more with Ajax and once, mischievously, with old rivals Feyenoord.

Retracing his steps as a Manager

Cruyff's move into management, typically, aroused new controversy as he had never obtained the necessary examination qualifications. Not that it mattered. He guided Ajax to the European Cup-winners' Cup in 1987, and repeated the trick in 1989 after retracing his steps to Barcelona. His innovations now cause as much fuss as the total football of his playing days.

Thus Cruyff ranks not only among the game's greatest players and personalities but among its greatest innovators as well.

Career facts

1947 Born on April 25 in Amsterdam

1959 Enrolled by his mother in the Ajax youth section

1963 Signed his first Ajax contract at 16 on the recommendation of English coach Vic Buckingham, then marked his debut with a goal

1966 Made his debut for Holland in a 2–2 draw against Hungary and scored a last-minute equalizer in the first of his 48 internationals

1969 Made his first European Cup final appearance with Ajax, but Milan won 4–1 in Madrid

1971 Won the first of three successive European Cups, helping Ajax defeat Panathinaikos of Greece at Wembley. He was also voted European Footballer of the Year, the first of three such accolades

1973 Sold by Ajax to Barcelona for a world record transfer fee of £922,000

1974 Captained and inspired Holland to reach the 1974 World Cup Final in Munich, where they lost 2–1 to hosts West Germany

1978 Retired from the national team before the World Cup finals in Argentina, and left Barcelona to play in America with Los Angeles Aztecs and Washington Diplomats

1981 Returned to Europe to play for minor club Levante in Spain, then to Holland with Ajax and, finally, Feyenoord

1984 Went back to Ajax, this time as technical director

1987 Guided Ajax to victory in the European Cup-winners' Cup as a parting gift before being appointed coach to Barcelona

1992 Managed Barcelona to their long awaited victory in the European Cup Final, where they beat Sampdoria 1–0 at Wembley

1996 Left Barcelona after a record seven years in charge including four consecutive league championships

DI STEFANO

FIFA'S AMBASSADOR *Di Stefano leads the rest of the world by example against England at Wembley in 1963*

WORLD-CLASS ALL-ROUNDER

Alfredo Di Stefano is reckoned by many to be the greatest footballer of all. While Pele's admirers consider it sacrilege, the millions who wondered at Di Stefano's majestic domination of European football in the 1950s and early 1960s may concur.

Di Stefano's greatness lay not only in his achievement in leading Madrid to victory in the first five consecutive European Cup Finals – and inspiring a great breakthrough in international football – but also because no other footballer so effectively combined individual expertise with an all-embracing ability to organize a team to play to his command.

Today he is a wealthy elder statesman of soccer. Yet he was born in Barracas, a poor suburb of the Argentine capital of Buenos Aires, and learned his football first in the tough streets of the city, then out on the family farm. This was where he built up the stamina which would become legendary across the world in later years.

Di Stefano's grandfather had emigrated to Argentina from Capri. His father had played for the leading Buenos Aires club, River Plate, but abruptly ended his career when professionalism was introduced. To Di Stefano senior football was a recreation, not a means to earn a living. Thus he was not particularly pleased when his sons Alfredo and Tulio launched their own teenage careers with local teams.

THE BLOND ARROW
of Real Madrid and Spain

Eventually, he relented and young Alfredo – nicknamed "El Aleman" (the German), because of his blond hair – made his River Plate debut on August 18, 1944, at outside-right.

Plate left on Shelf

Di Stefano's hero had been Independiente's free-scoring Paraguayan centre-forward, Arsenio Erico. Di Stefano wanted to be a centre-forward himself. He learned his trade while on loan to Huracan, then returned to River Plate to replace the great Adolfo Pedernera.

River's forward line was nicknamed *La Maquina* (the Machine), for the remorseless consistency with which they took opposing defences apart. Di Stefano transferred his attacking prowess into the Argentine national team with equal success when they won the 1947 South American Championship.

In 1949 Argentine players went on strike. The clubs locked them out and completed their fixtures with amateur players. Meanwhile, the star professionals were lured away to play in the pirate league which had been set up, outside FIFA's jurisdiction, in Colombia.

Di Stefano was the star of stars there, playing for Millonarios of Bogota, the so-called "Blue Ballet". When Colombia was reintegrated in FIFA, Millonarios went on one last world tour . . . where Di Stefano was spotted by Real Madrid after starring in the Spanish club's fiftieth anniversary tournament.

Madrid agreed a fee with Millonarios and thus nearly outflanked rivals Barcelona, who had sealed a deal with Di Stefano's old club, River Plate. A Spanish soccer court ruled that Di Stefano should play one season for Madrid, one season for Barcelona. But after he made a quiet start to the season, Barcelona, unimpressed, sold out their share in Di Stefano to Madrid.

Four days later he scored a hat-trick in a 5–0 win against . . . Barcelona. A legend had been born.

"Two Players in every Position"

Madrid were Spanish champions in Di Stefano's first two seasons and European Cup winners in his next five. He scored in each of Madrid's European Cup Finals, including a hat-trick against Frankfurt in 1960 in a 90-minute spectacular which has become one of the most-admired football matches of all time.

Di Stefano was "total football" personified before the term had been invented. One moment he was defending in his own penalty area, the next organizing his midfield, the next scoring from the edge of the opponents' six-yard box. As Miguel Muñoz, long-time Madrid colleague as player and then coach, once said: "The greatness of Di Stefano was that, with him in your side, you had two players in every position."

> **❝ Di Stefano is the greatest player I have ever seen. The things he does in a match will never be equalled. ❞**
>
> *Luis Del Sol, 1960 European Cup-winning team-mate*

EUSEBIO

FRIENDLY INTENT *Eusebio outpaces Arsenal's admiring George Graham at Highbury*

HIS MAJESTY KING SOCCER

Eusebio, the greatest Portuguese footballer in history, did not, in fact, come from Portugal at all. Born and brought up in Mozambique, then still one of Portugal's African colonies, Eusebio was the first African footballer to earn a world-wide reputation.

The big Portuguese clubs such as Benfica, Sporting and Porto financed nursery teams in Mozambique and Angola and unearthed a wealth of talent which they then transported into not only Portuguese football but the Portuguese national team.

The young Eusebio, ironically, was a nursery product not of Benfica but of their great Lisbon rivals, Sporting. But when Sporting summoned him to Lisbon for a trial in 1961, he was virtually kidnapped off the aeroplane by Benfica officials and hidden away until the fuss had died down and Sporting, having all but forgotten about him, lost interest.

Hijacked by Benfica

Bela Guttmann, a veteran Hungarian, was coach of Benfica at the time. He had a high regard for the potential offered by Mozambique and Angola. The nucleus of the Benfica team which Guttmann had guided to European Cup victory over Barcelona that year came from Africa: goalkeeper Costa Pereira, centre-forward and captain Jose Aguas, and the two inside-forwards

112

terdam. In 13 seasons he helped Benfica win the League seven times and the Cup twice; he was European Footballer of the Year in 1965; top scorer with nine goals in the 1966 World Cup finals; scorer of 38 goals in 46 internationals and the league's leading scorer seven times before knee trouble forced a halt at 32.

But football was Eusebio's life. When the fledgeling North American Soccer League offered him the chance of a lucrative extension to his career, he flew west to play for the Boston Minutemen (alongside old Benfica team-mate Antonio Simoes), then for the Toronto Metros-Croatia, and then for the Las Vegas Quicksilver.

Benfica's faithful had mixed feelings about his self-imposed exile in North America. But controversy was soon forgotten when he returned to Lisbon to take up various appointments as television analyst, as assistant coach and as the most honoured public face of Benfica.

A Majestic Sportsman

Fans around the world took Eusebio to their hearts not only because of his ability but because of the sportsmanlike way he played the people's game. At Wembley in 1968 Eusebio very nearly won the European Cup Final for Benfica against Manchester United in the closing minutes of normal time, being foiled only by the intuition of Alex Stepney. Eusebio's reaction? He patted Step-

UNSTOPPABLE *against Milan*

ney on the back, applauding a worthy opponent.

Wembley Stadium played a major role in Eusebio's career. It was at Wembley, in a 2–0 World Cup qualifying defeat by England in 1961, that his youthful power first made the international game sit up; it was at Wembley, in 1963, that he scored one of his finest individual goals as consolation in a 2–1 European Cup Final defeat by Milan; and it was at Wembley again, in 1966, that Eusebio led Portugal to their best-ever third place in the World Cup. The semi-final, in which Portugal lost 2–1 to England, will long be remembered as as exemplary exhibition of sportsmanship under pressure.

Appropriately, a statue of Eusebio in action now dominates the entrance to the Estadio da Luz. Appropriately, also, a film made about his life was subtitled *Sua Majestade o Rei ... His Majesty the King.*

Joaquim Santana and Mario Coluna. But Eusebio would prove the greatest of all.

Guttmann introduced him to the first team at the end of the 1960–61 season. He was a reserve when Benfica went to France to face Santos of Brazil – inspired by Pele – in the famous Paris Tournament. At half-time Benfica were losing 3–0. Guttmann, with nothing to lose, sent on Eusebio. Benfica still lost, but Eusebio scored a spectacular hat-trick and outshone even Pele. He was still only 19.

A year later Eusebio scored two cannonball goals in the 5–3 victory Benfica ran up against Real Madrid in the European Cup Final in Ams-

> ❝ **Everywhere I go, Eusebio is the name people mention.** ❞
>
> *Mario Soares, President of Portugal*

HOLD-UP *Yashin foils Eusebio in the 1966 World Cup third place game*

MARADONA

IDOL OF TWO CONTINENTS

CROWD-PULLER, CROWD-PLEASER *Maradona, the inspiration of Napoli*

Diego Maradona was not only the world's greatest footballer throughout the 1980s and early 1990s. He was also the most controversial and the most enigmatic.

His admirers in Argentina, where he knew the early glory days with Argentinos Juniors and Boca Juniors, considered him little less than a god, and the *tifosi* in Italy, where he triumphed with Napoli, worshipped his bootlaces. So did all of Argentina after Maradona reached the zenith of his career, captaining his country to victory in the 1986 World Cup finals in Mexico.

English fans still rage over his "Hand of God" goal in the quarter-final in Mexico City. But Argentine fans remember most clearly his other goal in that game when he collected the ball inside his own half and out-witted five defenders and goalkeeper Peter Shilton before gliding home one of the greatest goals in the history of the World Cup. Maradona provided a repeat against Belgium in the semi-finals: another brilliant slalom through the defence but from the left, not the right. Then, in the Final against West Germany, his slide-rule pass sent Jorge Burruchaga away to score the dramatic winner.

Maradona's great ability made his subsequent fall all the greater. His love affair with Italian football went sour after the 1990 World Cup, when Maradona's Argentina defeated their hosts on penalties in the semi-final in Maradona's adopted home of Naples. The following spring a dope test showed cocaine traces. He was banned from Italian and then world football for 15 months, returned to Argentina and was arrested there for cocaine possession.

Released on probation, he sought to revive his playing career in Spain, but half a season at Sevilla proved a

> **"Pele was the supreme player of his era; Maradona is the pre-eminent player of his time. You cannot compare them. Such greatness does not submit to comparison. "**
> *Cesar Luis Menotti, former manager of Argentina*

disaster. Even his 1994 World Cup comeback ended in the shameful ignominy of dope-test failure and a new 15-month international playing ban. He turned briefly to coaching with Deportivo Mandiyu, then with Racing Avellaneda before undertaking yet another playing comeback with his old love, Boca Juniors.

A Roller-Coaster Career

It all began in the working-class Fiorito suburb of Lanus in the province of Buenos Aires where Maradona began playing for a kids' team named Estrella Roja (Red Star) at the age of nine. Later he and his friends founded a team known as Los Cebollitas (The Little Onions) who were so promising that the team was signed up en bloc by Argentinos Juniors as one of the club's youth sides.

On October 20, 1976, Maradona (wearing No. 16) made his league debut as a 15-year-old substitute against Talleres of Cordoba, and a week later he played his first full match against Newells Old Boys from Rosario. In February 1977 he made his international debut. It appeared odds-on that Maradona would be a member of the squad with which manager Cesar Luis Menotti planned to win the World Cup for Argentina for the first time in front of their own fanatical fans in 1978, but he was one of the three players dropped on the eve of the finals. It was months before he would speak to Menotti again, but their eventual peace talk paved the way for the first international success of Maradona's career at the 1979 World Youth Cup in Japan.

Boca Juniors bought him for a world record £1 million and resold him two years later to Barcelona for £3 million, another record. Before joining the Catalans he succumbed to the pressures of the World Cup, in Spain in 1982, where he was sent off for an awful lunge at Batista of Brazil. It was the recurring theme of his career: a unique talent for football shadowed by a similarly unique aptitude for arousing controversy.

It says much for the magical technique of his left foot that, despite all the negative vibes, Maradona continued to entrance the game. In 1984 Napoli paid another world record, this time

Career facts

1960 *Born on October 30 in Lanus, Buenos Aires*
1976 *Made his league debut at 15 for Argentinos Juniors*
1977 *Made his international debut at 16 for Argentina in a friendly against Hungary*
1980 *Sold to Boca Juniors for £1 million, a record for a teenager*
1982 *Sold to Barcelona for another world record £3 million, then out of the game for four months after a reckless tackle by Bilbao's notorious defender Andoni Goicochea*
1984 *Sold to Napoli for a third world record, now £5 million*
1986 *Inspired Argentina to victory at the World Cup finals in Mexico: was unanimous choice as Player of the Tournament*
1987 *Led Napoli to their first-ever Italian league title plus victory in the Italian cup*
1988 *Won his only European prize as Napoli beat Stuttgart in the UEFA Cup Final*
1990 *Despite a collection of injuries, Maradona led Argentina back to the World Cup Final, where they were defeated 1–0 by West Germany*
1991 *Failed a dope test and was banned for 15 months*
1992 *Made a disappointing comeback with Sevilla in Spain*
1993 *Sacked by Sevilla, Maradona began a second comeback in Argentina with Newells Old Boys*
1994 *Banned again, for 15 months, after a positive drugs test during the World Cup*
1995 *Returns to playing with Boca Juniors after coaching stints with Deportivo Mandiyu and Racing Avellaneda*

£5 million, to end Maradona's injury-battered two-year stay with Barcelona. Within weeks Napoli sold a staggering 70,000 season tickets. Two Italian League championships and one UEFA Cup success were the reward for the fans.

Seven glorious, roller-coaster years went by before the partnership was dissolved. Football in Naples will never be the same again.

PUSKAS

THE MAGICAL LEFT FOOT

Ferenc Puskas remains one of the greatest players of all time – a symbol of the legendary "Magic Magyars" who dominated European football in the early 1950s and stand as perhaps the greatest team never to have won the World Cup.

Puskas's father was a player and later coach with the local club, Kispest. At 16 Ferenc was a regular at inside-left, terrorizing opposing goalkeepers with the power of his shooting. He rarely used his right foot but then his left was so lethal that he seldom needed it.

At 18 he was in the national team, too. His brilliance had much to do with the decision to convert Kispest into a new army sports club named Honved, that formed the basis of the national side.

For four years Hungary, built around goalkeeper Gyula Grosics, right-half Jozsef Bozsik and the inside-forward trio of Sandor Kocsis, Nandor Hidegkuti and Puskas, crushed all opposition. They also introduced a new tactical concept. The inside-forwards, Kocsis and Puskas, formed the spearhead of the attack, with Hidegkuti a revolutionary deep-lying centre-forward. Hungary won the 1952 Olympic title before ending England's record of invincibility against continental opposition with a stunning 6–3 triumph at Wembley.

Early the following year, Hun-

gary thrashed England again, 7–1 in Budapest. No wonder they were overwhelming favourites to win the 1954 World Cup in Switzerland. But Puskas presented a problem. He had been injured in an early round game against West Germany and was a hobbling spectator at training before the Final, against these same West Germans, in Berne. Could his great left foot withstand the strain? Puskas thought so and decided to play, thus taking one of the most controversial gambles in the game's history. After only 12 minutes the gamble appeared to be paying off when Hungary led 2–0. However, they lost 3–2, their dominance finally ended in the one match which mattered most.

The Toast of Spain

It was eight long years before Puskas would return to the World Cup finals. Then, in Chile in 1962, his trusty left foot was doing duty for Spain, because Puskas had, in the meantime, defected to the West, joining

Real Madrid. Honved had been abroad when the Hungarian Revolution of 1956 erupted. Puskas and several team-mates decided to stay in the West. He made an attempt to sign for several Italian clubs, but they thought him too old. How wrong they were was underlined when Puskas developed, at Madrid, a new career to emulate his first in brilliance.

Four times Puskas was the Spanish league's top scorer and his partnership with the Argentine centre-forward, Alfredo Di Stefano, was one of the greatest of all time. They hit perfection together on the famous night when Madrid thrashed Eintracht Frankfurt 7–3 in the European Cup Final before a record 135,000 crowd at Hampden.

Di Stefano scored three goals, Puskas four. The Spanish fans loved him. In his Hungarian army club days at Honved, Puskas had been known as the Galloping Major. Now they called him *Cañoncito* – the little cannon.

In 1966 he finally retired. His future was secure, thanks to business investments which included a sausage factory near Madrid. He tried his hand at coaching without a great deal of success – save for the remarkable 1970–71 season when he took Panathinaikos of Athens to the European Cup Final.

In the course of time he was able to visit his native Hungary, where he was celebrated once more as a national hero. Hardly surprising. After all, how many can boast 83 goals in 84 games for their country?

> **" His was a name fit for any sporting hall of fame, worthy of any and every superlative. "**
> *Billy Wright,*
> *England captain against*
> *Hungary in 1953*

Career facts

1927 *Born on April 2 in Budapest*

1943 *Made his debut for his father's old club, Kispest*

1945 *Played his first international for Hungary against Austria*

1948 *Transferred with the entire Kispest playing staff to the new army club, Honved, and top-scored with 50 goals in the League championship*

1952 *Captained Hungary to victory over Yugoslavia in the final of the Olympic Games soccer tournament in Helsinki*

1953 *Earned a place in history by inspiring Hungary's historic 6–3 victory over England at Wembley*

1954 *Played despite injury, amid controversy, in the World Cup Final which Hungary lost 3–2 to West Germany in Berne – their first defeat for four years*

1956 *Stayed in western Europe when the Hungarian Revolution broke out while Honved were abroad to play a European Cup tie against Bilbao*

1958 *Signed for Real Madrid by his old manager at Honved, Emil Oestreicher*

1960 *Scored four goals for Madrid in their famous 7–3 demolition of Eintracht Frankfurt in the European Cup Final at Hampden Park, Glasgow*

1962 *Played in the World Cup finals in Chile, this time for his adopted country of Spain*

1966 *Retired and turned to coaching*

1971 *Achieved his greatest success as a trainer, guiding outsiders Panathinaikos of Athens to the European Cup Final (they lost 2–0 to Ajax at Wembley)*

1993 *Appointed, briefly, as caretaker-manager of Hungary during the 1994 World Cup qualifiers*

José Leandro Andrade

Born: November 20, 1898, Uruguay.
Clubs: Bella Vista, Nacional.

Andrade was an old-fashioned wing-half in the 2–3–5 tactical system which served much of the world for the first half of the century. He was a stalwart of the great Uruguayan teams of the 1920s and 1930s, winning gold medals at the Olympic Games soccer tournaments of both 1924 and 1928. Injury then threatened to end his career but Andrade was recalled, because of his vast experience, for the inaugural World Cup finals which Uruguay won on home ground in 1930. He played 41 times for his country before retiring in 1933. Andrade's nephew, Victor Rodriguez Andrade, won the World Cup in 1950 and was never once booked or sent off.

Giancarlo Antognoni

Born: April 1, 1954, Italy.
Club: Fiorentina.

In the 1970s and early 1980s Antognoni was considered by Italian fans to be the successor to Milan's Gianni Rivera as their Golden Boy of Italian football. A graceful, wonderfully intuitive midfield general, Antognoni cost Fiorentina £750,000 as a teenager from Fourth Division Astimacombi in 1972. He went straight into the Fiorentina team and made the first of his 73 appearances for Italy in the autumn of 1974. Antognoni was a regular transfer target for Italy's richest clubs but remained faithful to Fiorentina until he eventually wound down his career in Switzerland. Sadly, Antognoni missed Italy's victory over West Germany in the 1982 World Cup Final after suffering a gashed ankle in the semi-final defeat of Poland.

Osvaldo Ardiles

Born: August 3, 1952, Argentina.
Clubs: Huracan (Arg), Tottenham (Eng), Paris S-G (Fr), Tottenham, Queen's Park Rangers (Eng).

Ardiles combined legal and soccer studies in the mid-1970s when he earned his initial reputation as midfield general of Argentina under manager Cesar Luis Menotti. Hardly had Ardiles collected his winners'

ANTOGNONI *Italian football's golden boy of the 1970s*

medal at the 1978 World Cup when he and national team-mate Ricardo Villa were together subjects of a remarkable transfer to Tottenham Hotspur. Ardiles cost Spurs £300,000, which made him one of the greatest bargains of modern soccer history. He completed his outstanding playing career which included Tottenham's FA Cup success of 1981 and their UEFA Cup triumph of 1984. He returned to White Hart Lane as manager in the summer of 1993, but lasted little more than a year.

ARDILES *success on two continents*

Luis Artime

Born: 1939, Argentina.
Clubs: Atlanta, River Plate, Independiente (Arg), Palmeiras (Br), Nacional (Uru), Fluminense (Br).

Artime was a centre-forward in the traditional Argentine mould: powerful, aggressive and prolific. He scored 47 goals in two teenage seasons with minor Buenos Aires club Atlanta to earn a move in 1961 to River Plate, with whom he will always be most closely linked. He climaxed

a three-year spell, including 66 league goals, by leading Argentina's attack at the 1966 World Cup finals. Artime then joined Independiente, scoring 44 goals in 18 months before moving on to Palmeiras and then to Nacional of Montevideo, with whom he was top Uruguayan league marksman three years in a row. He also scored 24 goals for Argentina.

Georgi Asparoukhov

Born: May 4, 1943, Bulgaria.
Clubs: Botev Plovdiv, Spartak Sofia, Levski Sofia.

"Gundi" Asparoukhov remains one of the most outstanding yet tragic players in Bulgaria's history. A tall, direct centre-forward, he had scored 19 goals in 49 internationals when he died in a car crash, aged 28, in 1971. Asparoukhov led Bulgaria's attack in the World Cup finals of 1962, 1966 and 1970 and scored 150 goals in 245 league games for his only senior club, Levski Sofia. Portuguese club Benfica tried to sign him in 1966 after he impressed in a European Cup tie. But Asparoukhov did not want to move because he had all he wanted in Bulgaria...including his favourite Alfa Romeo sports car which, ultimately, proved the death of him.

José Augusto

Born: April 13, 1937, Portugal.
Clubs: Barreirense, Benfica.

Augusto was originally a centre-forward, and had already made his debut for Portugal in this position when Benfica bought him from local

club Barreirense in 1959 on coach Bela Guttmann's recommendation. He then succesfully converted him into an outside-right. Augusto was considered, after Frenchman Raymond Kopa, as the best "thinking" player in Europe and appeared in five European Cup finals. He was a winner in 1961 and 1962 and a loser in 1963, 1965 and finally in 1968 against Manchester United, by which time he had been transformed again into an attacking midfield player. Augusto was a key member of the Portugal side which finished third at the 1966 World Cup, and later coached both Benfica and Portugal.

Roberto Baggio

Born: February 18, 1967, Italy.
Clubs: Fiorentina, Juventus, Milan.

Roberto Baggio became the world's most expensive footballer when Juventus bought him from Fiorentina on the eve of the 1990 World Cup finals. In those finals he showed why he was worth £8 million by scoring a marvellous solo goal against Czechoslovakia. His transfer provoked three days of riots by angry fans in the streets of Florence. Juventus saw Baggio as the successor to Michel Platini as the inspiration of their attack and, in 1993, he led Juventus to victory in the UEFA Cup. The following season he topped a century of league goals, was voted World and European Footballer of the Year and inspired Italy's run to the World Cup Final. Baggio helped Juventus to win the league in 1995 before leaving to join Milan – with whom he immediately won it again.

Gordon Banks

Born: December 20, 1937, England.
Clubs: Leicester, Stoke.

A product of the prolific Chesterfield "goalkeeper academy", Banks went on to undying fame with England. He

ROBERTO BAGGIO *An inspiration to Italy in the 1994 World Cup finals*

BANKS *Saving England in the 1966 World Cup Final*

set all kinds of keeping records, including 73 caps, 23 consecutive internationals, and seven consecutive clean sheets, a run eventually ended by Eusebio's penalty in the 1966 World Cup semi-final. His late withdrawal from the 1970 quarter-final probably cost England the match from 2–0 up; he was a loser in two FA Cup finals with Leicester (at fault with two goals in the second); and, unluckiest of all, he lost an eye in a car crash when he still had years left to play. Only Shilton, perhaps, has equalled him as a goalkeeper for England.

Franceschino "Franco" Baresi

Born: May 8, 1960, Italy.
Club: Milan.

Baresi has been the latest in a long line of outstanding Italian sweepers. He began as an attacking midfielder with Milan in the late 1970s and was kept waiting for an international opportunity because of the dominance of Juventus's Gaetano Scirea. Finally, in 1987, Baresi secured a place in the national team, simultaneously providing the defensive foundation on which coach Arrigo Sacchi built Milan's all-conquering club team. While Dutchmen Ruud Gullit and Marco Van Basten were granted much of the glory, discerning observers recognized the enor-

mous influence of Baresi. In the 1994 World Cup Final, Baresi shone like a beacon, despite having undergone knee surgery only two weeks earlier.

Bebeto (full name: Jose Roberto Gama de Oliveira)

Born: February 16, 1964, Brazil.
Clubs: Flamengo, Vasco da Gama (Br), Deportivo de La Coruña (Sp).

Bebeto could have made an international impact earlier in his career, but for weak temperament and bad luck with injuries. He came to prominence with Flamengo in 1982, was outstanding when they won the Rio championship in 1986 and was the club's top scorer four years in a row. He was

BARESI *Key to Milan's revival*

controversially transferred to Rio rivals Vasco da Gama in 1989 but quietened doubters in Brazil's 1989 South American Championship triumph by scoring six goals. Bebeto moved to Europe with Spain's La Coruña in 1993 then scored three goals in Brazil's World Cup triumph a year later.

Franz Beckenbauer

see Legends (pages 104–05).

Ferenc Bene

Born: December 17, 1944, Hungary
Clubs: Kaposzvar, Ujpest Dozsa.

Bene was a versatile attacker who played centre-forward for Ujpest Dozsa but usually outside-right for Hungary because of the presence of Florian Albert. Bene was first capped in 1962 but did not make much impact on the international scene until two years later when he top-scored with 12 goals in Hungary's victory at the Tokyo Olympics. Three times Bene was the Hungarian league's leading scorer and he won the championship four times with Ujpest. In the 1966 World Cup Bene was an outstanding member of the Hungarian team which scored a 3–1 victory over Brazil at Goodison Park, Liverpool. Hungary fell to the more organised Soviet Union side in the quarter-finals, but Bene's consolation was having scored in each of their four matches.

Dennis Bergkamp

Born: May 10, 1969, Holland.
Clubs: Ajax Amsterdam (Hol), Internazionale (It), Arsenal (Eng).

Bergkamp was a youth product of Ajax, promoted to the first team at 17 and quickly hailed as either a "new Cruyff" or a "new Van Basten". His talent was so obvious that he made his European club debut for Ajax in a match against Malmö for which he had to fly out on the day of the game after sitting school examinations the previous afternoon. Bergkamp starred for Holland at the 1992 European Championship finals, and Inter beat Barcelona, Juventus and Milan to his £8 million signature the following spring. Bergkamp never settled in Italy, and in 1995 he was transferred to Arsenal for £7.5 million – a record fee for the London club.

Orvar Bergmark

Born: November 16, 1930, Sweden.
Clubs: Örebro, AIK Solna (Swe), Roma (It).

Bergmark's record of 94 international appearances stood for years as a Swedish record and established him as one of the great European fullbacks of the 1950s and early 1960s. He began with Örebro in 1949 as a centre-forward but quickly switched to full-back and made his debut there for Sweden in 1951. He was voted best right-back at the 1958 World Cup finals, in which his steady play helped the hosts reach the Final against Brazil. Bergmark also had a spell in Italy with Roma before retiring. He was appointed manager of Sweden in 1966 and guided them to the 1970 World Cup finals. One of his players then was Tommy Svensson, who would emulate him as World Cup boss in 1994.

George Best

Born: May 22, 1946, Northern Ireland.
Clubs: Manchester United, Fulham (Eng), Hibernian (Scot), Tampa Bay Rowdies (US).

George Best was perhaps the outstanding British player of all time, despite a career much shorter than it could and should have been. "Wayward genius" is a cliché that cannot be bettered as a description of a player with so many incredible gifts packed into a slight frame: balance, two twinkling feet, a surprisingly high leap, a cold eye for the finishing chance … everything. Best was twice a league championship winner with United, and won both the European Cup and the European Footballer of the Year award in 1968. Then fame and fortune and the temptations of the world beyond football all combined to force a sad finale scattered with retirements and comebacks.

Franz "Bimbo" Binder

Born: December 1, 1911, Austria.
Clubs: St Polten, Rapid Vienna (Aus).

Binder was a prolific marksman, either from centre-forward or inside-forward, and is popularly considered to have been the first European player to have topped 1,000 goals in his first-class career. When he retired in 1950 to become manager of his old club, Rapid, Binder claimed career

DIFFERENT CLASS *Arsenal's Dennis Bergkamp leaves Leeds' Lucas Radebe behind*

figures of 1,006 in 756 games. Binder was Rapid's greatest player in the 1930s, playing 20 times for Austria before being selected nine times for Greater Germany after the Anschluss of 1938. Binder's greatest achievement for Rapid was in the 1941 Greater German championship play-off, when he scored a hat-trick against Schalke

BEST *So appropriately named*

in Rapid's 4–3 victory. Later he coached not only Rapid but also the Austrian national team.

Danny Blanchflower

Born: February 10, 1926, Northern Ireland.
Clubs: Barnsley, Aston Villa, Tottenham (Eng).

A tactically astute play-maker, Danny Blanchflower was one of the major forces in Ireland's valiant 1958 World Cup side and Tottenham's excellent team of the early 1960s. The League and Cup "double" was followed by another Cup and the European Cup-winners' Cup, with Blanchflower's cerebral approach blending perfectly with the more robust forays of the other wing-half,

Dave Mackay. In the days when few sportsmen appeared on TV, the loquacious Blanchflower was a media darling, always entertaining and forthright in speech or in print. As so often with gifted players, his foray into management, with Chelsea, was an anti-climax. He died in 1993.

Oleg Blokhin

Born: November 5, 1952, Soviet Union.
Clubs: Kiev Dynamo (USSR), Vorwärts Steyr (Austria).

Blokhin was originally an outside-left, but, according to his friend, Olympic sprint champion Valeri Borzov, he could have been a star sprinter. Certainly he used his pace to electric effect, his key role in Kiev's European Cup-winners' Cup triumph of 1975 earning him the accolade of European Footballer of the Year. Blokhin played in the World Cup finals of 1982 and 1986, having by then become the first Soviet player to top a century of international appearances. By the time Blokhin, now a central striker, was "freed" to move west with Vorwärts Steyr of Austria, he had totalled a Soviet record 39 goals in a further record 109 internationals. After retiring he turned to coaching with the Greek champions, Olympiakos of Piraeus.

Steve Bloomer

Born: January 20, 1874, England.
Clubs: Derby, Middlesbrough, Derby.

England's most famous player before the First World War, Bloomer established long-lasting records: his 352 league goals were not exceeded until the 1930s; his 28 goals for his country, in only 23 games, were not surpassed until the 1950s. Bloomer was of medium height and slightly built, often the target for unscrupulous defenders with heavy boots and desperate intent. But he survived, thanks to agility and a sharp brain, through 22 years until the start of the First World War, when he was in his 41st year. Born at Cradley Heath in the West Midlands' "Black Country", he was, nevertheless, a Derby player throughout his career apart from a four-year spell with Middlesbrough. In later years he coached Derby players and did odd jobs at the ground.

Zvonimir Boban

Born: October 8, 1968
Clubs: Dinamo Zagreb (Yug/Cro), Bari, Milan (It)

Boban first made a name as a member of the former Yugoslavia team which won the 1987 World Youth Cup. He became Dinamo Zagreb's

BLOKHIN *Electrifying pace*

youngest-ever captain at 18 and was hailed a local hero after he came to the defence of Croat fans being man-handled by police at a high-tension match against Red Star Belgrade, for which he was given a six-month suspension. It cost him a place with Yugoslavia at the 1990 World Cup finals. His brilliant ball control, astute passing and explosive free kicks were noticed in Italy, however. A year later Boban became Croatia's most expensive player, costing a reported £8 million when he left Zagreb for Milan. Boban has won four Italian championships with Milan and was a key part of Milan's 4–0 European Champions Cup Final victory over Barcelona in 1994.

Zbigniew Boniek

Born: March 3, 1956, Poland.
Clubs: Zawisza Bydgoszcz, Widzew Lodz (Pol) Juventus (It) Roma (It)

Boniek must be considered the greatest Polish footballer of all time. He was the product of the next soccer generation after the outstanding side of the mid-1970s but his talents shone in World Cups and in European club competition with Juventus. Boniek made his name with Widzew Lodz and his hat-trick against Belgium in the 1982 World Cup finals persuaded Juventus to pay £1.1 million for him – then a record for a Polish player. Boniek scored Juve's winner in the 1984 European Cup-winners' Cup Final defeat of FC Porto and was a member of the side which won the

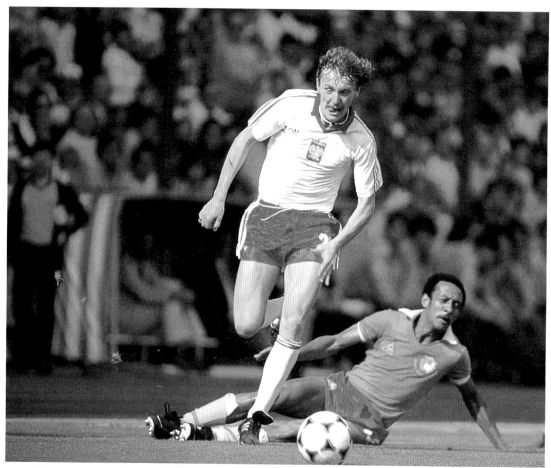

BONIEK *The greatest Polish player of all time thanks to his feats with Juventus*

European Cup a year later, playing the Final against Liverpool in the shadow of the Heysel disaster. Boniek scored 24 goals in 80 internationals.

Giampiero Boniperti

Born: July 4, 1928, Italy.
Club: Juventus.

Boniperti was the original Golden Boy of Italian football. He enjoyed a meteoric rise: within a few months of being signed by Juventus from minor club Momo, in July 1946, he was promoted to the Italian national team and made his debut in a 5–1 defeat by Austria in Vienna. Originally a centre-forward, Boniperti later switched to inside-forward and played on the right wing for FIFA's World XI against England in 1953 (scoring twice in a 4–4 draw). Boniperti won five Italian league titles with Juventus, for whom he played a record 444 league games. He was a "father figure" in the Charles/Sivori team of the late 1950s and scored eight goals in 38 internationals. On retiring from

the game he took up a business career which eventually turned full circle when he became a hugely successful president of Juventus in the 1970s and early 1980s under the Agnelli family patronage.

Jozsef Bozsik

Born: September 28, 1929, Hungary.
Clubs: Kispest, Honved.

Bozsik will always be remembered as right-half of the wonderful Hungarian national team of the early 1950s. A team-mate of Ferenc Puskas with Kispest and then Honved, Bozsik was the midfield brains but could also score spectacular goals, including one from 30 yards in the historic 6–3 win over England at Wembley in 1953. Bozsik made his debut for Hungary against Bulgaria in 1947, returned home – unlike team-mates Puskas, Kocsis and Czibor – after the 1956 Revolution and combined a career as a footballer with that of an MP. In 1962 he scored a goal against Uruguay in a friendly to mark

his 100th and last game for his country. Bozsik had been a member of Hungary's victorious side at the 1952 Helsinki Olympics.

Raymond Braine

Born: April 28, 1907, Belgium.
Clubs: Beerschot (Bel), Sparta Prague (Cz), Beerschot (Bel).

Braine was considered the greatest Belgian footballer until the advent of Paul Van Himst in the 1960s. In 1922 he made his league debut for Beerschot at the age of 15 and was chosen, that same year, for a Belgian XI against Holland. Clapton Orient of London tried to sign Braine in 1928 but could not obtain a work permit for him to come to England, so instead he turned professional in Czechoslovakia with the great Sparta Prague club. The Czechs wanted him to take citizenship and play for them in the 1934 World Cup, but Braine preferred to represent Belgium – and did so at the 1938 World Cup after returning home to Beerschot. Braine's centre-forward talents

earned him selection for Western Europe against Central Europe in 1938, and then for Europe against England that same year. He won 54 caps for Belgium.

Paul Breitner

Born: September 5, 1951, West Germany.
Clubs: Bayern Munich (W Ger), Real Madrid (Sp), Eintracht Braunschweig, Bayern Munich (W Ger).

Breitner was a flamboyant virtuoso of a left-back when Helmut Schön brought him into the West German national team in 1971–72. He was a key member of a the new, Bayern-dominated side which also featured Franz Beckenbauer, Sepp Maier, Uli Hoeness and Gerd Müller. Breitner demonstrated his big-match temperament by nervelessly converting the penalty which brought West Germany level in the 1974 World Cup Final against Holland. A footballing intellectual, he considered he was being stifled at Bayern and moved forward to midfield on transferring to Real Madrid. A falling-out with the German football authorities caused him to miss the 1978 World Cup, but he returned in 1982 and again scored in the Final — this time only the Germans' consolation goal in their defeat by Italy on his old home ground in Madrid. Only four players have scored in two World Cup Finals.

BREITNER *Football intellectual*

Billy Bremner

Born: December 9, 1942, Scotland.
Clubs: Leeds United, Hull, Doncaster (Eng).

Bremner made his debut for Leeds at 17, as a winger partnered by Don Revie, a man nearly twice his age. Later midfielder Bremner and manager Revie were outstanding figures as Leeds emerged from decades of mediocrity to be a force feared throughout the game. Bremner's fierce tackling, competitive spirit and selflessness made him a winner of various medals, though the list of second places was much longer. He was not a prolific scorer, but a useful one, providing the winner in each of three FA Cup semi-finals. He also won 55 caps, including three at the 1974 World Cup finals, when Scotland were eliminated, unbeaten, after three matches.

Tomas Brolin

Born: November 29, 1969, Sweden.
Clubs: GIF Sundsvall (Swe), Parma (It), Leeds United (Eng), Parma (It).

Brolin had long been considered one of Sweden's outstanding attacking prospects before proving the point by scoring twice on his debut for the senior team in the 4–2 win over Wales in the spring of 1990. Brolin followed up with two more against Finland to earn a late call into Sweden's World Cup team. At Italia '90, although Sweden were quickly eliminated, Brolin's outstanding displays alerted Italian clubs and Parma immediately bought him. He starred for Sweden at the 1992 European Championship – scoring a marvellous solo goal against England – and then helped Parma to success in the 1993 European Cup-winners' Cup. Brolin was one of the real giants on view at USA '94, but a bad injury put him out for most of the 1994–95 season. In late 1995, Brolin moved to English club Leeds United, but he could not adjust to life and football in England.

Emilio Butragueño

Born: July 22, 1963, Spain
Clubs: Castilla, Real Madrid (Sp), Celaya (Mex).

Butragueño, nicknamed "the Vulture", was once considered not good enough by Real Madrid's youth coaches. Real's nursery club, Castilla, had second thoughts and Butragueño became "leader" of Madrid throughout the 1980s. His close control and talent as a marksman helped Madrid win the UEFA Cup in 1985 and 1986, and in both years Butragueño won the Prix Bravo as Europe's best young player. He made a scoring debut for Spain in 1984, and in 1986 became a World Cup sensation when he scored four times for Spain in a five-goal thrashing of the well-fancied Denmark in the second round of the finals in Mexico.

TOMAS BROLIN *Rocketed from nowhere to world star in six months in 1990*

Rodion Camataru

Born: June 22, 1958, Romania.
Clubs: Universitatea Craiova, Dinamo Bucharest (Rom), Charleroi (Bel).

Camataru was a bluff, determined centre-forward who scored more than 300 goals in Romanian league football before transferring to Belgium towards the end of his career. In 1986–87 he won the Golden Boot awarded to Europe's top league marksman, albeit in controversial circumstances. Camataru totalled 44 goals but many of them were scored in a string of "easy" matches towards the end of the season and revelations after the collapse of the Communist regime cast doubt on the integrity of the matches. Not that this detracted from Camataru's abilities which were rewarded, even in the twilight of his career, with selection for the 1990 World Cup finals.

Claudio Paul Caniggia

Born: January 9, 1967, Argentina.
Clubs: River Plate (Arg), Verona, Atalanta, Roma (It), Benfica (Por), Boca Juniors (Arg).

Caniggia was one of the most intriguing stars of the 1994 World Cup, having only just completed a 13-month drugs suspension in Italy. He scored on his return to international duty in a 3–0 win over Israel, but was injured when Argentina lost to Romania in USA '94. Caniggia began with River Plate, moving to Italy in 1988. His play was one of Argentina's few redeeming features

CAMATARU *Golden Boot-winner*

at the 1990 World Cup, when he scored the quarter-final winner against Brazil and semi-final equalizer against Italy. Caniggia missed the Final through suspension and, without him, Argentina had nothing to offer in attack.

Eric Cantona

Born: May 24, 1966, France.
Clubs: Martigues, Auxerre, Marseille, Bordeaux, Montpellier (Fr), Leeds, Manchester United (Eng).

Eric Cantona's career has been a mixture of glorious success and disciplinary muddle. Cantona, born in Marseille, was discovered by Auxerre and sold to Marseille for £2 million in 1988. Two months later he scored on his international debut against West Germany. Later he was banned for a year from the national team for insulting manager Henri Michel, then bounced controversially to Bordeaux, Montpellier and Nimes before quitting the game after a shouting match with a disciplinary panel. Cantona relaunched his career in England – winning the championship in 1992 with Leeds and times in four years with Manchester United. A skirmish with a hooligan fan at Crystal Palace cost him a seven-month ban from football and a community service sentence from the courts, but he returned to the field all the more hungry for success. He was voted as Footballer of the Year and then, as captain, sealed United's 1996 "double" by scoring the winning goal in the FA Cup Final against Liverpool.

Antonio Carbajal

Born: June 7, 1929, Mexico.
Clubs: España, Leon.

Carbajal set a record, at the 1966 World Cup in England, as the only man to appear in five finals tournaments. A tall, agile goalkeeper, he played for Mexico in Brazil in 1950, in Switzerland in 1954, in Sweden in 1958 and in Chile in 1962. The 1966 finals provided an appropriate retirement point, since Carbajal had made his international debut at the 1948 London Olympic Games. On his return to Mexico that year he turned professional with Leon and played for them until his retirement in 1966. Later he was presented with FIFA's gold award for services to the world game.

Careca

Born: October 5, 1960, Brazil.
Clubs: Guarani, São Paulo (Br), Napoli (It), Hitachi (Jap), Santos (Br).

Careca was one of the outstanding spearheads in the world game throughout the 1980s and early 1990s. Born in Brazil's Campinas state, he helped unrated Guarani win the 1987–88 national championship and was later sold to São Paulo. Careca missed the 1982 World Cup after being injured in training on the eve of the finals. He made superb amends with five goals in Mexico in 1986, was voted Brazil's Sportsman of the Year and was subsequently transferred to Italy's Napoli. His attacking partnership with Diego Maradona lifted Napoli to the 1989 UEFA Cup and 1990 Italian league titles.

Johnny Carey

Born: February 23, 1919, Rep. of Ireland.
Club: Manchester United (Eng).

Johnny Carey was one of the early all-purpose players, at home as full-back, wing-half, inside-forward, even as deputy goalkeeper. He was a calming influence, short on pace but long on perception. At £200 to a Dublin junior club he was one of the transfer bargains of all time. He captained Manchester United in the early post-war years, winning League and Cup once each and narrowly missing several more, earned 37 caps, and led the Rest of Europe selection against Great Britain in 1946. Carey later managed Black-

CAREY *One of the great captains*

burn (twice), Everton – until he was sacked in the back of a taxi when they were lying fifth in the table – Orient and Nottingham Forest.

Amadeo Carrizo

Born: June 12, 1926, Argentina.
Clubs: River Plate (Arg), Alianza (Peru), Millonarios (Col).

Carrizo set a string of longevity records in a goalkeeping career which lasted from the mid-1940s to the mid-1960s. A dominant character with great personality, Carrizo played 520 Argentine league matches over 21 seasons until he was 44. He won five league championships with River Plate in the early 1950s and played in the 1958 World Cup finals in Sweden. Carrizo was blamed for Argentina's

6–1 defeat by Czechoslovakia but was recalled two years later with great success when Argentina beat England and Brazil to win the 1960 "Little World Cup" in Brazil. After parting company with River Plate he played on in Peru and Colombia before returning home to coach youth teams.

Carlos Caszely

Born: July 5, 1950, Chile.
Clubs: Colo Colo (Chile), Levante (Sp), Colo Colo (Chile).

Caszely was outstanding as a goal-scoring inside-forward in the early 1970s when Colo Colo became the first Chilean club to reach a final of the South American club cup (Copa Libertadores). However, his loudly-proclaimed left-wing political beliefs placed him at risk after the revolution which overthrew President Allende in 1973, and he moved to Spain with Levante. Caszely played for Chile in the 1974 World Cup finals in West Germany and then again eight years later in Spain. By this time, the political situation had eased back home and he had returned to Colo Colo to end his playing days there.

Jan Ceulemans

Born: February 28, 1957, Belgium.
Clubs: Lierse, Club Brugge.

Ceulemans was the central pillar of Belgium's national team throughout the 1980s, first as a striker and then as a midfield general. He began with Lierse and cost Brugge a then record

JAN CEULEMANS *The pillar of Belgium's recent World Cup success*

STÉPHANE CHAPUISAT *Even more famous son of a famous father*

Stéphane Chapuisat

Born: June 28, 1969, Switzerland.
Clubs: FC Malley, Red Star Zurich, Lausanne (Swz), Bayer Uerdingen, Borussia Dortmund (Ger).

Chapuisat, the finest current Swiss striker, is son of a former international, Pierre-Albert Chapuisat, who earned notoriety in his day as a sharp-tempered defender. Son Stéphane, by contrast, not only plays his football at the other end of the pitch but has the most even temperament, which has helped him lead Dortmund's revival in goal-scoring partnership with Denmark's Flemming Povlsen. Chapuisat moved to Germany in 1991 with Uerdingen and transferred to Dortmund a year later. His starring role at the 1994 World Cup finals led to a Footballer of the Year accolade.

John Charles

Born: December 27, 1931, Wales.
Clubs: Leeds (Eng), Juventus (It), Leeds (Eng), Roma (It), Cardiff (Wales).

Known as the Gentle Giant, John Charles allied great skill to an awesome physique, and was good enough to set a Leeds record of 42 goals in one season as a centre forward, while also playing as a dominant central defender for his country. He was one of the first British exports to Italy, in 1957, and probably the best. The £67,000 fee, a record for a British player, bought Juventus a man who became a legend and helped to win the Serie A title three times in five years, scoring 93 times in 155 games. After some unhappy final seasons he became a non-league manager, publican and shopkeeper.

Bobby Charlton

see Legends (pages 106–07)

Igor Chislenko

Born: January 4, 1939, Soviet Union.
Clubs: Moscow Torpedo, Moscow Dynamo.

Chislenko was one of Europe's most incisive outside- or inside-rights in the 1960s, despite standing only 5ft 7in. He began with the Moscow Torpedo youth section but transferred to Dynamo at 17 and played 300 league games, winning two league titles, with the club. Chislenko, also a good ice hockey player, appeared at the World Cups of 1962 and 1966 as well as in the European Nations Championship in between. He was the best Soviet forward in the 1966 World Cup, and their prospects of reaching the Final disappeared when he was sent off during the semi-final against West Germany.

Hector Chumpitaz

Born: April 12, 1944, Peru.
Club: Sporting Cristal.

Chumpitaz, a powerful, inspirational centre-back, starred for Peru in the World Cup finals of both 1970 and 1978. On the first occasion he was a promising youngster, on the second an experienced, resilient organizer of an otherwise fragile defence. Chumpitaz played all his senior career with Sporting Cristal of Lima and appeared around 100 times for his country between his debut in 1966 and the six-goal thrashing by Argentina which controversially ended Peru's 1978 World Cup campaign. Earlier claims that he played 147 full internationals have been discounted, Peru having played "only" 110 matches in that time.

Mario Esteves Coluna

Born: August 6, 1935, Mozambique.
Clubs: Deportivo Lourenço Marques (Mozambique), Benfica (Port).

Coluna was midfield general of Benfica's outstanding club side on the 1960s as well as commander of the Portuguese national team which reached the World Cup semi-finals in 1966. Born in Mozambique, Coluna was the local long-jump record-holder when he was lured away by Benfica to play football in 1954. Originally a centre-forward, he was converted to inside-left and then midfield by Benfica and won 73 caps for Portugal. In both of Benfica's European Cup Final victories of 1961 and 1962, he scored with typically spectacular long-range efforts. Coluna later turned to coaching and became Sports Minister in Mozambique.

Gianpiero Combi

Born: December 18, 1902, Italy.
Club: Juventus.

Combi was goalkeeper and captain of the Italian team which won the 1934 World Cup, thus pre-dating Dino

---

domestic fee of £250,000 in the summer of 1978. In 1980 he scored 29 of their 76 goals in a league title win and was voted Footballer of the Year for the first time. A year later Ceulemans was poised to join Milan but his mother persuaded him to stay in Belgium, a decision which he never regretted. Ceulemans played with distinction in the Belgian team which finished fourth at the 1986 World Cup finals in Mexico. In 96 internationals a Belgian record he scored 26 goals.

Cha Bum Kun

Born: May 21, 1953, South Korea.
Clubs: Darmstadt, Eintracht Frankfurt, Bayer Leverkusen (W Ger).

Thanks to his record at the peak of the European game in West Germany's Bundesliga, Cha ranks as South Korea's finest player. He was a popular fixture from 1978, when he arrived at Darmstadt, until his retirement in 1986 after appearing at his first and only World Cup finals. Cha, who won the UEFA Cup with Eintracht Frankfurt in 1980, was ignored by his country after moving to Germany, and recalling him for those World Cup finals in 1986 demanded a major diplomatic exercise. Original South Korean records claimed an astonishing 141 international appearances for Cha, but on further scrutiny this was later reduced to the more probable total of 41.

Zoff in that dual role by nearly 50 years. Combi was considered Italy's best goalkeeper until Zoff came along. He started unpromisingly, beaten seven times by Hungary in Budapest in his first international in 1924, and did not gain a regular place in Italy's team until the Paris Olympics of 1928. He was goalkeeper in Juventus's four consecutive league title successes of 1931 to 1934, the year when he retired – immediately after captaining Italy to victory over Czechoslovakia in the World Cup Final in Rome. That was Combi's 47th international.

Bruno Conti

Born: March 13, 1955, Italy.
Clubs: Roma, Genoa, Roma.

Wingers made a comeback on the tactical scene thanks to the displays of Bruno Conti at the 1982 World Cup. Italy's right-winger proved a crucial influence in increasing the momentum of their campaign, which took them past Argentina and Brazil and on via Poland to victory over West Germany in the Final. Conti had struggled to make an impression in the early years of his career but was rescued by Swedish coach Nils Liedholm, who brought Conti back from a loan spell with Genoa and turned him into one of the most consistently effective creative players in *Calcio*. Conti scored five goals in 47 internationals between his debut against Luxembourg in 1980 and the second round defeat by France at the 1986 World Cup.

Henri "Rik" Coppens

Born: April 29, 1930, Belgium.
Clubs: Beerschot, Charleroi, Crossing Molenbeek, Berchem, Tubantia.

Coppens was the *enfant terrible* of Belgian football in the 1950s: a centre-forward or occasional outside-left of great goal-scoring talent, but one who carried his aggression over into his dealings with team-mates, clubs and other officials. Coppens began with Beerschot as a 10-year-old, and on his debut at 16 in a crucial relegation match he scored twice and made Beerschot's two other goals. Three times he was the league's leading scorer and ended his career with a then

CONTI *Outwits West Germany's Uli Stielike in the 1982 World Cup Final*

record total of 217 goals. He once scored six goals in a game against Tilleur. Coppens altogether played 47 times for Belgium.

Alberto da Costa Pereira

Born: 1929, Portuguese East Africa.
Club: Benfica.

Costa Pereira was another of Portugal's great discoveries in the African colonies. He was born in Nacala, Portuguese East Africa, and joined Benfica in 1954. He was a tower of strength in their biggest triumphs, though prone to the odd unpredictable error when the pressure was off. Costa Pereira won seven league titles with Benfica and played in four European Cup finals – the victories of 1961 and 1962 and the defeats of 1963 and 1965. In the latter game, against Internazionale on a quagmire of a pitch in Milan, Costa Pereira was injured early in the game and had to leave the pitch. He retired soon after to take up coaching. Costa Pereira played 24 times for Portugal, but is not to be confused with the José Pereira who kept goal at the 1966 World Cup.

Johan Cruyff

see Legends (pages 108–09)

Teofilo Cubillas

Born: March 8, 1949, Peru.
Clubs: Alianza (Peru), Basel (Swz), FC Porto (Port), Alianza (Peru), Fort Lauderdale Strikers (US).

Cubillas was a key figure in Peru's greatest international successes, their appearances at the 1970 and 1978 World Cup finals, in which he scored a total of 10 goals. A powerfully-built inside left, he forged an ideal partnership with the more nimble Hugo Sotil in 1970 then, in 1978, emerged as an attacking director. Cubillas also packed a powerful shot, scoring

CUBILLAS *Attacking director*

a memorable goal against Scotland in the 1978 finals. He was not particularly successful in Europe, where he grew homesick. But in Peru he remained a legend after 38 goals in 88 internationals and an appearance for the World XI in a 1978 UNICEF charity match.

Zoltan Czibor

Born: 1929, Hungary.
Clubs: Ferencvaros, Csepel, Honved (Hun), Barcelona, Español (Sp).

Czibor was outside-left in the great Hungarian team of the early 1950s. He had pace and a powerful shot, which he used to great effect in 43 internationals before he moved to Spain following the Hungarian Revolution of 1956. Czibor and team-mate Sandor Kocsis were persuaded to sign for Barcelona by Ladislav Kubala and enjoyed five more years in the international spotlight, reaching a climax when Barcelona, most unluckily, lost to Benfica in the 1961 European Cup Final. Czibor had a short spell with neighbours Español before he retired and eventually returned home to live in Hungary.

Kenny Dalglish

Born: March 4, 1951, Scotland.
Clubs: Celtic (Scot), Liverpool (Eng).

Kenny Dalglish is the most "decorated" man in senior British soccer, having won 26 major trophies as player and manager, in addition to 102 caps (a record for Scotland) and 30 goals (another record, held jointly with Denis Law). Dalglish's signing for Celtic was their other coup – aside from their European Cup triumph – in 1967. He went on to inspire the club to more great deeds before joining Liverpool for £400,000 in 1977, to replace Kevin Keegan. Already a very good player, he became legendary at Anfield, thanks to initial pace, excellent control and an eye for a chance. He won many new friends for his dignified bearing after the two disasters of Heysel and Hillsborough. Those pressures contributed to Dalglish's surprise departure from Liverpool. He returned to manage Blackburn Rovers to the 1995 Premier League title then replaced Keegan – again – as manager of Newcastle United.

Bill "Dixie" Dean

Born: January 22, 1907, England.
Clubs: Tranmere, Everton, Notts Co.

Anybody who begins his international career by scoring 2, 3, 2, 2, 3 – even in days of lax defence and five forwards – deserves a place in the Hall of Fame. Curly-topped Bill Dean was 20 at the time, and still only 21

DALGLISH *A winner as player and manager*

when he scored his record 60 League goals in one season for Everton, finishing 2, 4, 3 to overhaul George Camsell's 59 for Middlesbrough. Overall, he scored 18 goals in 16 England appearances, 47 in 18 of the other representative matches which were so popular in pre-television days, 28 in 33 Cup ties (one in the 1933 Wembley win), and 379 in 438 League games. All this despite, as a teenager, fracturing his skull.

Luis Del Sol Miramontes

Born: 1938, Spain.
Clubs: Betis Seville, Real Madrid (Sp), Juventus (It).

Del Sol was inside-right in the legendary Real Madrid forward line which won the 1960 European Cup against Eintracht Frankfurt at Hampden. A neat, aggressive midfielder, he had been a wing-half at his hometown club, Betis of Seville, when the Madrid management decided that the great Brazilian, Didi, was not fitting in well enough alongside Alfredo Di Stefano. Del Sol was hurriedly bought in the middle of the 1959–60 season and ran his legs off in support of veterans Di Stefano and Puskas. In 1962 Madrid sold Del Sol to Juventus to raise the cash for a vain attempt to buy Pele from Santos. Del Sol was a pillar of the Italian league, consistently reliable and inspirational through eight seasons with Juventus and two with Roma, before his retirement and return to Spain in 1972.

Kazimierz Deyna

Born: October 23, 1947, Poland. *Clubs:* Starogard, Sportowy Lodz, Legia Warsaw (Pol), Manchester City (Eng), San Diego (US).

Poland's emergence as a world power in the early 1970s owed a huge debt to the skilled grace of Deyna, their midfield fulcrum. Deyna played centre midfield, supported by workers such as Maszczyk and Kasperczak, and was constantly creating openings for strikers Lato and Gadocha. He earned a domestic reputation in helping army club Legia win the league in 1969 and was promoted into the national squads when the Legia coach, Kazimierz Gorski, was appointed manager of Poland. Deyna won an Olympic gold medal with Poland in

DIDI *Making the ball "talk" in the 1958 World Cup finals*

Munich in 1972 then returned to the Olympiastadion two years later to celebrate Poland's best-ever third-place finish at the World Cup. He was never quite the same player after moving abroad, first to England and then to the United States, where he died in a car crash. Deyna scored 38 goals in 102 internationals.

Didi (full name: Waldyr Pereira)

Born: October 8, 1928, Brazil.
Clubs: FC Rio Branco, FC Lencoes, Madureiro, Fluminense, Botafogo (Br), Real Madrid, Valencia (Sp), Botafogo (Br).

The success of Brazil's 4–2–4 system, revealed in all its glory internationally at the 1958 World Cup, rested heavily on the creative talent of Didi, one of the greatest of midfield generals. Didi's technique was extraordinary. Team-mates said he could "make the ball talk", and drop it on a coin from any distance, any angle. Didi was the first to perfect the "dead leaf" free kick, with which he scored a dozen of his 31 goals in 85 appearances for Brazil. He won the World Cup in 1958 and 1962 and counted as the only failure of his career a spell in between with Real Madrid, where he failed to settle in alongside Di Stefano and Puskas.

Alfredo Di Stefano

see Legends (pages 110–11)

Domingos Antonio da Guia

Born: November 19, 1912, Brazil.
Clubs: Bangu, Vasco da Gama (Br), Nacional (Uru), Boca Juniors (Arg), Flamengo, Corinthians, Bangu (Br).

Domingos was a full-back of the old school, as much a pivoting central defender as a marker in the old-fashioned 2–3–5 formation. His talents earned him transfers all round South America, and he remains less of a legend in Uruguay and Argentina than he is in Brazil. The Uruguayans nicknamed him the Divine Master. Domingos made his debut for Brazil in 1931, was a key member of the team which reached the 1938 World Cup semi-finals, and did not retire until 1948. By this time he had returned to his original club, Bangu. His contemporary, centre-forward Leonidas da Silva, once said no defender ever "read a game" better than Domingos.

Dunga (full name: Carlos Bledorn Verri)

Born: October 31, 1963, Brazil.
Clubs: Vasco da Gama (Br), Pisa, Fiorentina, Pescara (It), Stuttgart (Ger), Jubilo Iwata (Jpn).

Dunga, one of the most controversial of modern Brazilian players, obtained the ultimate revenge over his critics when he lifted the World Cup after the victory over Italy in the 1994 Final Dunga was criticized because, as a defensive midfield player, he was strong and keen in the tackle but slightly slow and relatively clumsy on the ball when comparised with his compatriots. But he possessed a strong shot in both feet and 1994 World Cup boss Carlos Alberto Parreira considered Dunga's tactical

discipline vital to his strategy. Not surprisingly, Dunga proved a success in Germany with Stuttgart and, after deciding not to extend his contract, attracted a string of offers from many of his former detractors back in Brazil.

Dragan Dzajic

Born: May 30, 1956, Yugoslavia.
Clubs: Red Star Belgrade (Yug), Bastia (Fr), Red Star (Yug).

The British press baptized Dzajic the "magic Dragan" after his left-wing skills helped take England apart in the semi-finals of the 1968 European Nations Championship. Dzajic had pace, skill and intelligence and was perhaps the greatest football hero to have emerged in post-war Yugoslavia. He was five times a national champion, four times a cup-winner and earned selection for a variety of World and European XIs on five occasions. Dzajic remained an outside-left throughout a career which brought him 23 goals in 85 internationals, never needing to fade back into midfield like so many wingers who lose the edge of their talent. He retired in 1978 and became general manager of his original club, Red Star.

Duncan Edwards

Born: October 1, 1936, England.
Club: Manchester United.

Duncan Edwards was a giant who is still revered by generations who never saw him play. Comparatively few did, for his career was brief, but his awesome power and genuine all-round skill, as creator as well as destroyer, made him a man apart. His death in the 1958 Munich air disaster robbed England of possibly its most-capped player of all time, after 18 appearances in under three years. He remains England's youngest international this century. At club level, Edwards was the outstanding discovery among Manchester United's many fine Busby Babes. Sometimes he seemed to be a team in himself, as at Wembley in 1958, when ten men fought so bravely in a vain effort against an Aston Villa side set on depriving United of a merited cup and league "double".

Arsenio Erico

Born: 1915, Paraguay.
Clubs: FC Asuncion (Par), Independiente, Huracan (Arg).

The quality of Erico as a centre-forward can best be illustrated by the fact that he was the boyhood hero of none other than Alfredo Di Stefano. Born in Paraguay, Erico went to Buenos Aires at 17 to play for a fund-raising team organized by the Paraguay Red Cross during the war with Bolivia. Directors of Independiente

EDWARDS *Epitome of the Busby Babes*

in the crowd were so impressed that immediately after the match they obtained his signature – in exchange for a donation to the Red Cross. Erico started badly, twice breaking an arm, but once he was fully fit he scored goals at a prolific rate and set a record with 47 goals in the 1936–37 league season. Several times he scored five goals in a game before going home to Paraguay in 1941 after squabbling over terms with Independiente. The club persuaded him to return, but knee cartilage trouble forced his premature retirement in 1944.

Eusebio

see Legends (pages 112–13)

Giacinto Facchetti

Born: July 18, 1942, Italy.
Clubs: Trevigliese, Internazionale.

Full-back was never a romantic role until the revolutionary emergence of Facchetti in the early 1960s. He had been a big, strapping centre-forward with his local club in Treviso when he was signed by Inter and converted into a left-back by master coach Helenio Herrera. The rigid man-to-man marking system perfected by Herrera permitted Facchetti the freedom, when Inter attacked, to stride upfield in support of his own forwards. Facchetti scored 60 league goals, a record for a full-back in Italy, including 10 in the 1965–66 season. But his most

FACCHETTI *Great attacking full-back*

important goal was reserved for the 1965 European Cup semi-finals when he burst through in the inside-right position to score a decisive winning goal against Liverpool. Later Facchetti switched to sweeper, from which position he captained Italy against Brazil in the 1970 World Cup Final. He would surely have taken his total of 94 caps to 100 but for an injury before the 1978 World Cup finals.

Giovanni Ferrari

Born: December 6, 1907, Italy.
Clubs: Alessandria, Juventus, Internazionale, Bologna.

"Gioanin" Ferrari was inside-left of the Italian team who won the 1934 World Cup and was one of only two team members – the other was Giuseppe Meazza – retained for the 1938 triumph in France. Appropriately, both men made their international debut in the same game against Switzerland in Rome in 1930. Ferrari played then for Alessandria but soon moved to Juventus, with whom he won a record five consecutive league titles. He won further championship honours with Ambrosiana-Inter in 1940 and with Bologna in 1941. He scored 14 goals in 44 internationals and managed Italy at the 1962 World Cup finals in Chile.

Bernabe Ferreyra

Born: 1909, Argentina.
Clubs: Tigre, River Plate.

Nicknamed "the Mortar" for his ferocious shooting, Ferreyra was the first great hero of Argentine football. He scored more than 200 goals for Tigre and then River Plate in the 1930s, having joined River for 45,000 pesos in one of the first formal transfers in Argentina after the establishment of professionalism. In his first season with River, 1932–33, Ferreyra scored a league record 43 goals and was such a regular feature of the weekly scoresheets that one Buenos Aires newspaper offered a gold medal to any goalkeeper who could defy him. Ferreyra played only four internationals before retiring in 1939 and going back to his home town of Rufino. In 1943 he returned to River's front office and in 1956 was honoured with a testimonial match in recognition of his loyalty and service to one of Argentina's great club institutions.

Tom Finney

Born: April 5, 1922, England.
Club: Preston.

Moderate in height, thin and fair, Finney was nondescript in appearance, but a player whose versatility was matched by his skill. "Grizzly strong" was the description applied to him by Bill Shankly, who played wing-half behind winger Finney at Preston – "Grizzly" in the sense of bear-like power rather than miserable attitude, for he always had a generous word for opponents as well as a rock-like solidity that belied his frame. Finney was genuinely two-footed, brave as they come, and in his later

TOM FINNEY *Preston plumber equally skilled at dismantling defences*

years a deep-lying centre-forward on Hidegkuti lines. Lack of support left him bereft of honours at club level, but a 12-year England career, with 76 caps and a then-record 30 goals, established him at the highest peak.

Just Fontaine

Born: August 18, 1933, France.
Clubs: AC Marrakesh, USM Casablanca (Mor), Nice, Reims (Fr).

Fontaine secured a place in the history books when he scored a record 13 goals in the 1958 World Cup finals. Yet he was a surprising hero. Born in Morocco, he was a quick, direct centre-forward who had played only twice for France before 1958. He had been discovered by Nice, then bought by Reims as replacement for Raymond Kopa, who had joined Real Madrid in 1956. He expected to be reserve to Reims team-mate René

FONTAINE *World Cup record*

Bliard at the 1958 World Cup, but Bliard was injured on the eve of the finals and Fontaine took his opportunity in record-breaking style. He owed most of his goals to Kopa's creative work alongside him and the partnership was renewed when Kopa returned to Reims in 1959. Sadly Fontaine had to retire in 1961 owing to two double fractures of a leg. He was twice top league scorer and totalled 27 goals in 20 internationals. Later he was president of the French players' union and, briefly, national manager.

ENZO FRANCESCOLI *Sends Melgar of Bolivia (No. 7) the wrong way in a World Cup qualifier*

Enzo Francescoli

Born: November 12, 1961, Uruguay.
Clubs: Wanderers (Uru), River Plate (Arg), Matra Racing, Marseille (Fr), Cagliari, Torino (It), River Plate (Arg).

Francescoli followed in a long line of Uruguayan superstars, starting with the heroes of the 1920s and 1930s and continuing through Schiaffino, Goncalves and Rocha. He began with a small club, Wanderers, and then both Uruguayan giants, Penarol and Nacional, were outbid by River Plate of Argentina. Francescoli was top scorer in the Argentine league and voted South American Footballer of the Year before transferring to France with Racing in 1986. Even Francescoli's 32 goals in three seasons were not enough to save Racing from financial collapse. He scored 11 goals in Marseille's championship season of 1989–90 before moving, first, to Italy, then back to River Plate to wind down his career.

Arthur Friedenreich

Born: 1892, Brazil.
Clubs: Germania, Ipiranga, Americao, Paulistano, São Paulo FC, Flamengo.

Friedenreich was the first great Brazilian footballer and the first player officially credited with more than 1,000 goals. His overall total was 1,329. The son of a German father and a Brazilian mother, Friedenreich was also significant as the first black player to break through the early racial/cultural barriers in Brazilian soccer. Nicknamed "the Tiger", Friedenreich began playing senior football at 17 and did not retire until 1935, when he was 43. He scored eight goals in 17 internationals for Brazil between 1914 and 1930. His first representative appearance for Brazil was in a 2–0 win against the English club Exeter City on July 21, 1914, when he lost two teeth in a collision with a defender.

Paulo Futre

Born: February 28, 1966, Portugal.
Clubs: Sporting, FC Porto (Port), Atletico Madrid (Sp), Benfica (Port), Marseille (France), Reggiana, Milan (It), West Ham United (Eng).

Futre was only 17 when he made his international debut and his star continued to shine brightly after FC Porto snatched him away from Sporting to inspire their European Cup victory of 1987. A few weeks later Futre was signed by Atletico Madrid as the first major coup in the controversial presidency of Jesus Gil. Futre survived all the tempests at Atletico until the start of 1993, when he forced his sale home to Benfica. However, financing the deal proved beyond even Benfica. They sold him to Marseille, who also had to sell him after only a few months to resolve their own cash crisis. Reggiana of Italy paid £8 million to become Futre's fourth club in a year – but he was never the same player after tearing knee ligaments.

G

Garrincha (full name: Manoel Francisco dos Santos)

Born: October 28, 1933, Brazil.
Clubs: Pau Grande, Botafogo, Corinthians (Br), AJ Barranquilla (Col), Flamengo (Br), Red Star Paris (Fr).

Garrincha was up there alongside Pele in Brazilian football in the 1960s. Born in poverty, childhood illness left his legs badly twisted and the surgeons who carried out corrective surgery thought he would do well merely to walk, let along turn out to be one of the quickest and most dangerous right-wingers of all time. Garrincha was a great practical joker, a trait which nearly cost him his place in Brazil's team. It took a players' deputation to persuade manager Vicente Feola to include him in the 1958 World Cup side in Sweden. Once in, Garrincha was there to stay and was the dominant personality at the 1962 finals after the early injury to Pele. Sadly, his private life was chaotic and he died prematurely of alcoholic poisoning.

Paul Gascoigne

Born: May 27, 1967, England.
Clubs: Newcastle, Tottenham (Eng), Lazio (It), Rangers (Scot).

Gascoigne's career has been blighted by his own indiscipline and misfortune with injuries. A powerful midfielder, with a deft touch, he was England's star of the 1990 World Cup. He was memorably inconsolable when his second yellow card ruled him out of the third place game. Gascoigne left Newcastle for Spurs and led them to the 1991 FA Cup Final, where he suf-

PAULO FUTRE *skipping over a tackle from Switzerland's Bregy*

GARRINCHA *Team-mates' favourite*

fered a bad knee injury making a rash tackle. After missing over a year through injury he signed with Lazio but played only 42 games in three seasons and broke a leg in a training incident. Gascoigne wore out his welcome at Lazio in 1995 and made a sensational start with Scottish champions Rangers. He won the league title in both his first two seasons and was voted Scotland's Footballer of the Year in 1996.

Tommy Gemmell

Born: October 16, 1943, Scotland.
Clubs: Celtic (Scot), Nottingham Forest (Eng).

A big and sometimes clumsy fullback who became a folk hero because

of his goals. He scored eight in European matches for his club, a remarkable record for a defender, and two of them were in European Cup Finals. Gemmell crashed one past Internazionale to equalize when Celtic won in 1967, and also against Feyenoord when they lost in 1970. His extroverted style of play was well suited to upsetting foreign defences during Celtic's greatest years, but he also collected a large haul of domestic honours before a final fling at Forest.

Francisco Gento

Born: October 22, 1933, Spain.
Clubs: Santander, Real Madrid.

Real Madrid's great team of the 1950s and 1960s was more than "only" Di Stefano and Puskas. Tearing great holes in opposing defences was outside-left Gento, whose pace earned him the nickname of "El Supersonico". Gento began with Santander and was considered a player with pace but little else when Madrid signed him in 1953. Fortunately, he found a marvellous inside-left partner in José Hector Rial, who tutored Gento in the arts of the game. Gento is the only man to have won six European Cup medals. He scored 256 goals in 800 games for Madrid, with whom he won Spanish championship medals on 12 occasions. He played 43 times for Spain despite the challenging rivalry of Enrique Collar, an outstanding left-winger with Atletico Madrid.

Sergio Javier Goycochea

Born: October 17, 1963, Argentina.
Clubs: River Plate (Arg), Millonarios (Col), Racing (Arg), Brest (Fr), Cerro Porteno (Par), River Plate, Deportivo Mandiyu (Arg).

Goycochea earned fame at the 1990 World Cup finals when he stepped into the action during Argentina's match against the Soviet Union after Nery Pumpido had broken a leg. Goycochea's heroics in the penalty shootout victories over Yugoslavia and Italy subsequently took Argentina to the Final. Yet he had not played a competitive game over the previous six

GOYCOCHEA *Magic touch in World Cup penalty shoot-outs*

months because of the domestic unrest in Colombia, where he had been contracted to Millonarios of Bogota. After the 1990 World Cup finals Goycochea signed for the ambitious French provincial club, Brest. They soon went bankrupt, however, and he returned to Argentina.

Jimmy Greaves

Born: February 20, 1940, England.
Clubs: Chelsea (Eng), Milan (It), Tottenham, West Ham (Eng).

Greaves was an instinctive goalscorer, whose speed in thought and deed made up for lack of size and power. His 44 goals in 57 full internationals included two hauls of four goals and four threes, and his 357 in League games (all First Division) included three fives. An unhappy interlude in Italy did little to mar his scoring ability, and he gave wonderful value for

money until his closing chapter with West Ham. By then drink had taken a grip, and his overcoming that blight to become a popular television pundit set an inspiring example to others in the same position.

Harry Gregg

Born: October 25, 1932, Northern Ireland.
Clubs: Dundalk (Rep. of Ire.), Doncaster, Manchester United, Stoke (Eng).

Genial, popular Gregg won his first cap after only nine Football League games for Second Division Doncaster, and had established himself as Ireland's first choice before the fateful 1957–58 season. Hardly had he left Yorkshire for Manchester United when, as a survivor of the Munich air crash, he became a hero by helping to rescue some of the injured. Later that year he performed well in helping his club to the FA Cup Final, where they lost 2–0 to Bolton, and the Irish to the quarter-final of the World Cup in Sweden. Injury kept him out of United's FA Cup-winning side in 1963.

John Greig

Born: September 11, 1942, Scotland.
Club: Rangers.

A 16-year spell of hard labour in defence and midfield brought Greig a record 496 League appearances for Rangers and a considerable number of honours, although Celtic were the dominant team in Scotland for a large

TOMMY GEMMELL *Historic goal in the 1967 European Cup Final*

part of that time. He was Footballer of the Year in 1966, the season in which he scored a spectacular goal against Italy in a World Cup qualifier, and won 44 caps, often as skipper. Greig also played in two European Cup-winners' Cup finals, losing in 1967 and winning in 1972. Later, he had a spell as manager at Ibrox.

Gunnar Gren

Born: October 31, 1920, Sweden.
Clubs: IFK Gothenburg (Swe), Milan, Fiorentina (It), Orgryte, GAIS Gothenburg (Sw).

Gren, nicknamed "the Professor", claimed Italian attention when in the Olympic Games winning team in London in 1948. His nickname stemmed both from his premature baldness and his astute inside-forward play. Milan won the transfer race and Gren forged, with fellow Swedes Nordahl and Liedholm, the legendary "Grenoli" trio which took Italian football by storm. In 1955, after a spell with Fiorentina, he returned home to Sweden and, at 37, helped the hosts to the Final of the 1958 World Cup. That was the last of Gren's 57 internationals. Later he returned to IFK Gothenburg – with whom he had won the Swedish championship in 1942 – as manager of the souvenir shop.

Ruud Gullit

Born: September 1, 1962, Holland.
Clubs: Haarlem, Feyenoord, PSV Eindhoven (Hol), Milan, Sampdoria, Milan, Sampdoria (It), Chelsea (Eng).

It was not merely his distinctive dreadlocks hairstyle which made Gullit stand out from European football in the late 1980s and early 1990s: he was the outstanding player. He began his career as a sweeper, but at PSV Eindhoven he moved forward and after his world record £6.5 million sale to Milan in 1987 he became an out-and-out attacker. A year later he led Holland to victory in the European Championship and won the European Cup with Milan. The early 1990s were marred by serious knee injuries but moving to England with Chelsea in 1995 led him on, a year later, to an FA Cup-winning appointment as the club's player-manager.

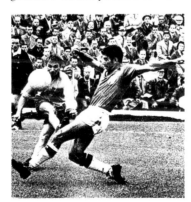

RUUD GULLIT *Showing off the 1988 European Championship trophy*

Gheorghe Hagi

Born: February 5, 1965, Romania.
Clubs: FC Constanta, Sportul Studentesc, Steaua Bucharest (Rom), Real Madrid (Sp), Brescia (It), Barcelona (Sp), Galatasaray (Tur).

Hagi was always destined for stardom. He played for Romania's youth team at 15, was a top-flight league player at 17, an international at 18, and a year later, in 1984, was taking part in the finals of the European Championship. One year more and Hagi was 20-goal top league marksman, as he was again in 1986 when he totalled 31 goals after scoring six in one match. Steaua Bucharest virtually kidnapped Hagi from neighbours Sportul without a transfer fee – an escapade approved by the ruling Ceaucescu family, who were Steaua supporters and directors. After the 1990 World Cup Hagi wandered to Spain and Italy – returning, briefly, to Spain with Barcelona after inspiring Romania to reach the quarter-finals of the 1994 World Cup.

Helmut Haller

Born: July 21, 1939, Germany.
Clubs: BC Augsburg (W Ger), Bologna, Juventus (It), Augsburg (W Ger).

Haller earned a teenage reputation as an inside-forward in West Germany in the late 1950s, before the advent of full-time professionalism and the Bundesliga. Italian club Bologna gambled on his youth and were

HAGI *Accelerates away from Irish defender Paul McGrath*

superbly rewarded: in 1963 Haller's partnership with the Dane Harald Nielsen brought Bologna their first league title in more than 20 years. Later Haller played with success for Juventus before returning to Augsburg. He will be remembered above all for his outstanding contribution to West Germany's 1966 World Cup campaign.

Kurt Hamrin

Born: November 19, 1934, Sweden.
Clubs: AIK Sola (Swe), Juventus, Padova, Fiorentina, Milan, Napoli, Caserta (It).

Hamrin ranks close behind Matthews and Garrincha among the great outside-rights of the modern game. He was a quick, darting attacker who was not only nimble and clever but one of the most successful goal-grabbers in Italian league history. Hamrin disappointed Juventus and they sold him off after only one year. Once he had adjusted, however, Hamrin proved an irresistible one-man strike force with Fiorentina, with whom he scored 150 goals in nine seasons and won the European Cup-winners' Cup in 1961. At 34, while with Milan, he added a European Cup winners' medal to his collection.

Gerhard Hanappi

Born: July 9, 1929, Austria.
Clubs: Wacker, Rapid Vienna.

Hanappi was one of the most versatile footballers to be found anywhere in the world in the 1950s. He played mainly wing-half or occasionally inside-forward for his long-time club, Rapid, but also lined up at centre-forward and at full-back in the course of winning 93 caps for Austria. He would have topped a century had it not been for a row with officialdom. Hanappi, an architect by profession, designed a new stadium for Rapid which was, after his premature death, named in honour of his memory. Hanappi was Austrian champion and a cup-winner once each with Wacker then national champion six times and cup-winner once again with Rapid. He played for FIFA's World XI against England at Wembley in 1953.

Eddie Hapgood

Born: September 27, 1908, England.
Club: Arsenal.

Hapgood was small for a left-back, but as tough as teak. He was an inspiring captain who led England in 21 of his 30 games during the 1930s, with 13 more during the war. In his teens he was an amateur with Bristol Rovers, but was allowed to leave and was with non-league Kettering when Arsenal recruited him. He went on to earn five championship medals and played in three FA Cup finals, winning two. His first international was against Italy in Rome; his first as captain was also against Italy but on his club ground in the infamous "Battle of Highbury" – when he returned to play on after an opponent's elbow had smashed his nose.

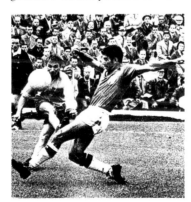

HAMRIN (LEFT) *Goes for goal*

After retirement he managed Black-burn and Watford, but with little success.

Ernst Happel

Born: June 29, 1925, Austria.
Clubs: Rapid Vienna, 1st FC Vienna (Aus), Racing Club Paris (Fr).

Happel was a redoubtable centre-back with Rapid and Austria in the 1950s, his 51-cap playing career reaching a climax at the 1958 World Cup finals. He possessed a powerful shot and once scored a hat-trick, with free-kicks and a penalty, in an early European Cup tie against Real Madrid. After retiring, Happel became one of Europe's most successful coaches, taking Feyenoord to the World Club Cup and European Cup in 1970. In Argentina in 1978, he was manager of Holland when they reached the World Cup Final, and he had further success in the 1983 European Cup with Hamburg.

HURST *World Cup legend*

Johnny Haynes

Born: October 17, 1934, England.
Clubs: Fulham (Eng), Durban City (SA).

Like Tom Finney, Haynes won precisely nothing in nearly two decades with one club. However, he was the hub of many an England team in a 56-cap career, hitting long passes through a needle's eye and scoring a surprising number of goals with an incredibly powerful shot that belied his comparatively slight frame. As England's first £100-a-week player he often was unjustly criticized, but he earned every penny in the service of Fulham (generally struggling) and England (frequently rampant).

He was England captain from 1960 till a serious car accident in 1962, in a period when, in successive games, England won 5–2, 9–0, 4–2, 5–1, 9–3 and 8–0. The 9–3 result was a slaughter of Scotland, perhaps the best performance of his era. His career might have added up differently if Milan had persisted in their bid for him, or if, after his accident, a record-breaking bid from Tottenham Hotspur had succeeded. He ended his playing career in South Africa, winning a championship medal with Durban City.

Willie Henderson

Born: January 24, 1944, Scotland.
Clubs: Rangers (Scot), Sheffield Wednesday (Eng).

If "Wee Willie" had performed throughout his career as he did in his first few years, he would have been perhaps the best Scottish player ever. Despite persistent foot trouble and far from perfect eyesight, he had won all four domestic honours – league, cup, League Cup and cap – before his 20th birthday. By then Rangers had sold international winger Alex Scott to Everton in order to make room for the kid. Henderson went on to play in 29 internationals and captivate fans with his wizardry, but his career was marred by discontent, and gradually petered out in disappointment.

Geoff Hurst

Born: December 8, 1941, England.
Club: West Ham, Stoke.

A big man who was made for the big occasion, Hurst, strong and deceptively fast, was frequently mundane in West Ham's toils through their League programmes. But when needed in the big events, he was out of the traps like a greyhound. He scored the remarkable total of 46 goals in the League Cup, 23 in the FA Cup (including a fluke in the 1964 Final) and three in the 1966 World Cup Final, when he appeared virtually from nowhere to put the trophy on the nation's sideboard with his hat-trick against West Germany. Like so many big-name players, he became a mundane manager, at Chelsea. Memories of him as a player will last much longer.

Jairzinho (full name: Jair Ventura Filho)

Born: December 25, 1944, Brazil.
Clubs: Botafogo (Br), Marseilles (Fr), Cruzeiro (Br), Portuguesa (Ven).

Jairzinho was the heir to Garrincha's glory, both with Botafogo and with Brazil. He moved from his home town of Caxias to sign professional with Botafogo at 15, and played in the same Brazil squad as his hero at the 1966 World Cup. Four years later Jairzinho made history by scoring in every game in every round of the World Cup on the way to victory. He scored seven goals, including two in Brazil's opening win over Czechoslovakia and one in the defeat of Italy in the Final. He tried his luck in Europe with Marseille but returned home after disciplinary problems to win yet another trophy, the South American club cup, with Cruzeiro at the age of 32.

Alex James

Born: September 14, 1901, Scotland.
Clubs: Raith (Scot), Preston, Arsenal (Eng).

Eight caps were meagre reward for the outstanding inside-forward of the 1930s. James began as a fiery attacking player (sent off twice in successive matches at Raith) but

JAIRZINHO *Unique World Cup feat*

changed his style to fit Arsenal manager Herbert Chapman's "W" formation. He scored only 26 League goals in eight years at Highbury, but made countless others with his astute passing from deep to the flying wingers or through the middle. Despite his superb display in the 5–1 rout of England by the "Wembley Wizards", James was often thought too clever by the selectors, though not by fans: at club level he won six major medals and undying fame.

Pat Jennings

Born: June 12, 1945, Northern Ireland.
Clubs: Newry Town (NI), Watford, Tottenham, Arsenal (Eng).

A goalkeeper with character and charm to match his size, Jennings even bowed out of football in a big way by winning his 119th cap on his 41st birthday – and in a World Cup, too. Only defeat, by Brazil, marred the occasion. By then Jennings had played well over 1,000 senior matches in a 24-year career, four of them in FA Cup finals. He won with Spurs

PAT JENNINGS *Veteran of more than 1,000 first-class matches*

in 1967 and Arsenal in 1979, lost with Arsenal in 1978 and 1980. Jennings also scored a goal with a clearance from hand during the 1967 Charity Shield against Manchester United. He remains one of the finest British goalkeepers ever seen.

Jimmy Johnstone

Born: September 30, 1944, Scotland.
Clubs: Celtic (Scot), San José (US), Sheffield United (Eng), Dundee (Scot), Shelbourne (Ire).

Johnstone was a remarkably talented winger, but infuriatingly inconsistent, as shown by the fact that his 23 caps were spread over 12 years. Small and nippy, he was an old-style "tanner-ball dribbler" and nicknamed The Flea. He won 16 medals with his club – one European Cup, eight league, three Scottish cup, four League Cup. Johnstone also earned a reputation for occasional wayward behaviour, on the field and off, but his courage was never in doubt, as many a far bigger opponent found to his cost. He was particularly effective in the 1966–67 season, when Celtic won every competition they entered, culminating in the European Cup Final defeat of Internazionale in Lisbon.

Kevin Keegan

Born: February 14, 1951, England.
Clubs: Scunthorpe, Liverpool (Eng), Hamburg (Ger), Southampton, Newcastle (Eng).

Keegan, the only British player to have won the European Footballer of the Year twice, cost Liverpool a bargain £35,000 when he signed from Scunthorpe United in 1971. He was an overnight success, first in his original position of outside-right, then as a free-ranging attacking raider. Keegan won two league titles with Liverpool, leaving for Hamburg after the European Cup victory of 1977. Keegan was a European Cup Final loser with Hamburg against Nottingham Forest in 1980 before breathing new life into first Southampton then Newcastle. His rapport with the Geordie fans later persuaded him to enter management back at St James' Park with remarkable success until his shock departure in January 1997.

Jack Kelsey

Born: November 19, 1929, Wales.
Club: Arsenal (Eng).

Big Jack was beaten five times on his debut for Arsenal in 1951, but he went on to be first-choice keeper for 11 years until a spinal injury, sustained in a collision with Vava of Brazil, forced him to retire. He remained a familiar figure at Highbury as manager of the club shop. He was powerful enough to withstand the challenges of an age when keepers were not well protected, and agile enough to make many remarkable stops, helped by rubbing chewing gum into his palms. Kelsey won 43 caps for Wales and played for Britain against the Rest of Europe in 1955.

Mario Alberto Kempes

Born: July 15, 1952, Argentina.
Clubs: Instituto Cordoba, Rosario Central (Arg), Valencia (Sp), River Plate (Arg), Hercules (Sp), Vienna, Austria Salzburg (Austria).

Kempes, an aggressive young striker with legs like tree trunks, had a first taste of World Cup football in West Germany in 1974. He swiftly earned a transfer to Spain with Valencia, where he developed into such a devastating hammer of opposing defences that he was the only foreign-based player recalled to join the hosts' World Cup squad under Cesar Luis Menotti in 1978. His addition proved decisive: Kempes was the event's top scorer with six goals, including two in the 3–1 defeat of Holland in the Final. Strangely, he was never able to scale those heights again, despite playing once more for Argentina in the 1982 finals in Spain, where he should have felt at home.

Jürgen Klinsmann

Born: July 30, 1964, Germany.
Clubs: Stuttgart Kickers, VfB Stuttgart (Ger), Internazionale (It), Monaco (Fr), Tottenham (Eng), Bayern Munich (Ger), Sampdoria (It).

Jürgen Klinsmann needed little time before breaking through as the German league's top scorer and the country's Footballer of the Year during his first Bundesliga spell with VfB Stuttgart, whom he also led to the UEFA Cup Final in 1989. Stuttgart lost to Napoli and, shortly afterwards, Klinsmann moved south himself to join Internazionale. Three successful years included the 1990 World Cup Final victory over Argentina in Rome. When Inter decided to replace their German foundation with Dutchmen, Klinsmann moved to France with Monaco and then, with enormous success, for a season to England at Tottenham before returning to Germany and Bayern Munich in July 1995. A year later Bayern won the UEFA Cup with Klinsmann contributing a European club competition single-season record of 15 goals.

Ronald Koeman

Born: March 21, 1963, Holland.
Clubs: Groningen, PSV Eindhoven (Hol), Barcelona (Sp), Feyenoord (Hol).

Despite lacking pace, Koeman turned himself into one of the world's best sweepers as well as becoming a free-kick expert. It was from a free kick that Koeman thundered the winner for Barcelona in the 1992 European Cup Final, a trophy he also won with PSV Eindhoven in 1988. Ronald and brother Erwin began with their father's old club, Groningen and were later members together of the Holland side which won the 1988 European Championship in Germany. Ronald won the treble of European Cup, Dutch league and cup in 1988 then moved to Barcelona in 1989, before returning to Holland and Feyenoord in 1995.

Ivan Kolev

Born: November 1, 1930, Bulgaria.
Club: CDNA/CSKA Sofia.

Kolev was the first great Bulgarian footballer, often compared for control and vision with Hungarian contemporary Ferenc Puskas. Kolev, who could play outside- or inside-left, spent all his career with the Bulgarian army club, variously known as CDNA and then CSKA Sofia. He scored 25 goals in 75 internationals and led Bulgaria on their first appearance at a major soccer tournament in

NICE WHILE IT LASTED *Jürgen Klinsmann was a hero in his season at Spurs*

the 1952 Helsinki Olympic Games. With CDNA/CSKA he was champion of Bulgaria on 11 occasions and won the cup four times.

Sandor Kocsis

Born: September 30, 1929, Hungary.
Clubs: Ferencvaros, Honved (Hun), Young Fellows (Swz), Barcelona (Sp).

Kocsis was an attacking inside-right for Honved and Hungary in the early 1950s. He and fellow inside-forward Puskas pushed forward while the nominal centre-forward withdrew towards midfield, creating gaps for the others to exploit. Kocsis did so to the extent of 75 goals in 68 internationals. He was three times the Hungarian league's top scorer, as well as the leading marksman, with 11 goals, at the 1954 World Cup finals. After the Hungarian Revolution of 1956 Kocsis decided to stay abroad and joined Barcelona with further success,

winning the Fairs Cup in 1960. A year later Kocsis was on the losing side with Barcelona at the European Cup Final against Benfica in Bern.

Raymond Kopa

Born: October 13, 1931, France.
Clubs: Angers, Reims (Fr), Real Madrid (Sp), Reims (Fr).

Born Kopaszewski, the son of an emigrant Polish miner, Kopa gained an added incentive to escape from a mining future when he damaged a hand in a pit accident as a teenager. He was spotted by Angers and then sold on to Reims in 1950. Originally a right-winger, Kopa soon switched to a creative centre- or inside-forward role. He led Reims to the first European Cup Final in 1956, being transferred afterwards to their conquerors on the day, Real Madrid. Kopa starred in midfield for third-placed France at the 1958 World Cup, and

returned to Reims a year later as European Footballer of the Year. He played 45 times for France but his playing career ended amid controversy over his outspoken espousal of the cause of freedom of contract.

Johannes "Hans" Krankl

Born: February 14, 1953, Austria.
Clubs: Rapid Vienna (Austria), Barcelona (Sp), 1st FC Vienna (Austria), Barcelona (Sp), Rapid, Wiener Sportclub (Austria).

For Krankl everything happened in 1978. He scored 41 goals for Rapid Vienna, to win the Golden Boot as Euorpe's leading league marksman, and starred for Austria at the World Cup finals in Argentina. He joined Barcelona and inspired their victory in the 1979 European Cup-winners' Cup. Serious injury in a car crash interrupted Krankl's career in Spain and he went home to Austria briefly. Later he returned to Rapid, with whom he became general manager after retiring. Krankl scored 34 goals in 69 internationals and was top league scorer four times in Austria and once in Spain.

Ladislav Kubala

Born: June 10, 1927, Hungary.
Clubs: Ferencvaros (Hun), Bratislava (Cz), Vasas Budapest (Hun), Barcelona, Español (Sp), FC Zurich (Swz), Toronto Falcons (Can).

One of the ironies of 1950s football was that Hungary created a great team without one of their very greatest players. Centre- or inside-forward Kubala had escaped to the West after having played international football for both Czechoslovakia and Hungary in the late 1940s. In exile in Italy, Kubala formed a refugees' team called Pro Patria which played exhibition tours and provided him with the springboard to join Spain's Barcelona. There Kubala was Spanish champion five times and twice won the Fairs Cup. He also gained international recognition with a third country, winning 19 caps for Spain to add to his seven for Czechoslovakia and three for Hungary. He left Barcelona after the 1961 European Cup Final defeat by Benfica, but later returned to coach both Barcelona and the Spanish national team.

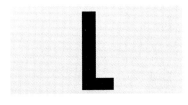

L

Angel Amadeo Labruna

Born: September 26, 1918, Argentina.
Clubs: River Plate, Platense (Arg), Green Cross (Chile), Rampla Juniors (Uru).

Labruna remains one of the greatest Argentine football personalities of all time. Not only was he a great inside-left, but he earned longevity records by playing with River Plate for 29 years and won a reputation as a South American Stanley Matthews by playing on until he was 41. At the 1958 World Cup finals in Sweden, Labruna was recalled at the age of 40 to complete an international career which brought him 17 goals in 36

games for Argentina. Labruna began with River Plate when he was 12 and won nine league championships. In the late 1940s he was a member of the legendary "Maquina", or "Machine", forward line. In 1986 Labruna was coach when River at last won the South American club cup.

Marius Lacatus

Born: April 5, 1964, Romania.
Clubs: Steaua Bucharest (Rom), Fiorentina (It), Oviedo (Sp), Steaua.

Tall, slim and sharp in front of goal, Lacatus was a key figure in the Romanian upsurge of the 1980s. Playing nominally as outside-right, he used his pace to great effect to help shoot his country to the 1990 World Cup finals. After the finals, he stayed on in Italy with Fiorentina, and the Romanian federation allocated much of the fee to the redevelopment of

LAUDRUP *Brilliant elder brother*

sports facilities in the country. Lacatus found it hard to adjust to Italian football and later moved on to Spain before returning home in the autumn of 1993.

Grzegorz Lato

Born: April 8, 1950, Poland.
Clubs: Stal Mielec (Pol), Lokeren (Bel), Atlante (Mex).

Lato was a Polish phenomenon, an outstanding striker who later proved equally influential when he moved back into midfield. At the 1974 World Cup finals, Lato was top scorer with seven goals. He had made his debut for Poland against Spain in 1971 and was a member of the squad which won the Olympic gold medal in Munich a year later. Lato became a fixture in the senior national team in 1973, after impressing manager Kazimierz Gorski on a tour of the United States and Canada, and he went on to score 46 goals in 104 internationals, a Polish record. After leading Poland's attack at the 1978 World Cup finals in Argentina, Lato was permitted the "reward" of a transfer to Lokeren in Belgium, and he ended his career in Mexico with Atlante.

Michael Laudrup

Born: June 15, 1964, Denmark.
Clubs: Brondbyernes (Den), Lazio, Juventus (It), Barcelona, Real Madrid (Sp), Vissel Kobe (Jap).

Michael and younger brother Brian are sons of a former Danish international, Finn Laudrup, who closely

guided their early careers. Michael, as a teenager, attracted scouts from all Europe's top clubs but finally chose Juventus, who loaned him to Lazio before recalling him to replace Poland's Zbigniew Boniek. With Juventus Laudrup won the World Club Cup before becoming disillusioned with *Calcio* and moving on to win the European Cup with Barcelona. He starred at the 1986 World Cup finals before falling out with Denmark's national manager Richard Moller Nielsen and thus missing the 1992 European Championship triumph – where younger brother Brian stepped into his boots as their nation's attacking inspiration.

Denis Law

Born: February 22, 1940, Scotland.
Clubs: Huddersfield, Manchester City (Eng), Torino (It), Manchester United, Manchester City (Eng).

Denis Law and Jimmy Greaves were born within four days of each other, and spent several years as rival scorers and supreme entertainers. Law, of only medium height and slim in build, had a lion's heart and a salmon's leap, scoring many spectacular goals with headers and acrobatic shots. He was also an incisive passer of the ball, and a fierce competitor. Suspensions and injury cost him many more goals. He was European Footballer of the Year in 1964, won two league titles and the 1963 FA Cup, and scored 30 goals in 55 internationals, but missed United's European Cup victory in 1968 through knee trouble.

Tommy Lawton

Born: October 6, 1919, England.
Clubs: Burnley, Everton, Chelsea, Notts County, Brentford, Arsenal.

One of the first footballers to realize what his market value was, and to work at getting it. Lawton made frequent moves, at a time when there rarely was any percentage for a transferred player. Lawton was a star from his dubbin-smothered toe-caps to his glistening centre parting. He got a hat-trick on his senior debut aged 16, was the First Division top scorer two years in a row, won a title medal aged 19, scored 23 goals in 22 full internationals, and goals by the dozen

DENIS LAW *The promising youngster in Huddersfield days*

during the Second World War. Lawton was still frightening foes deep into his 30s and pulling in fans everywhere he went.

Leonidas da Silva

Born: November 11, 1910, Brazil.
Clubs: Havanesa, Barroso, Sul Americano, Sirio Libanes, Bomsucesso (Br), Nacional (Uru), Vasco da Gama, Botafogo, Flamengo, São Paulo (Br).

Leonidas was Brazil's 1930s superstar although he played only 23 times for his country. He was the inventor of the overhead bicycle kick, which was unveiled to the international game when he scored twice on his international debut against Uruguay in 1932. The Uruguayans were so impressed he was immediately signed by the top club, Nacional. Later he returned home with Vasco da Gama and was top scorer at the 1938 World Cup with eight goals, including four in a 6–5 victory over Poland. Unfortunately, an overconfident management rested Leonidas from the semi-final against Italy, wanting to keep him fresh for the Final . . . and they lost.

Billy Liddell

Born January 10, 1922, Scotland.
Club: Liverpool (Eng).

An accountant, Justice of the Peace and youth worker, Liddell allied all these activities to football. He is still revered as one of the greatest players in Liverpool's history, which is saying a great deal. Liddell missed six years on war service and spent all his career with one club. Apart from the championship in 1947 and a Cup Final defeat three years later, Liverpool achieved little during his 15 years, but he set club records with 492 league appearances and 216 goals, as well as representing Scotland 28 times and Great Britain in two games against the Rest of Europe.

Nils Liedholm

Born: October 8, 1922, Sweden.
Clubs: Norrköping (Swe), Milan (It).

Liedholm played originally at inside-forward, later moved back to wing-half and finally became one of the best of sweepers in his veteran years. He began with Norrköping, winning two championship medals and playing

LITTBARSKI *Testing the resolve of Italian defender Claudio Gentile*

18 times for his country. After helping Sweden win, from outside-left, the 1948 Olympic title, he moved to Italy. There Liedholm formed Milan's celebrated trio with Gunnar Gren and Gunnar Nordahl and he scored 60 goals in 367 league games. At the end of his career Liedholm captained hosts Sweden to runners-up spot at the 1958 World Cup finals. After retiring as a player, he stayed with Milan as a youth coach and later took charge of

the senior team in 1964. He also managed Fiorentina and Roma.

Gary Lineker

Born: November 30, 1960, England.
Clubs: Leicester, Everton (Eng), Barcelona (Sp), Tottenham (Eng), Nagoya Grampus 8 (Jap).

All sorts of records fell to this unassuming son of a market trader, who accepted good and bad with the smiling sincerity that, allied to his skill,

GARY LINEKER *Scoring, against the Irish Republic in the 1990 World Cup, one of his 48 international goals*

made him such a popular figure. This was never more evident than in the desperate days when serious illness struck his first-born son. He went within one goal of England's 49-goal scoring record, ten coming in World Cup final stages, led the First Division marksmen with three different clubs, scored a hat-trick for Barcelona against Real Madrid, and won the FA Cup despite missing a penalty. Lineker retired after two injury-plagued seasons in Japan, and immediately became a broadcaster.

Pierre Littbarski

Born: April 16, 1960, Germany.
Clubs: Hertha Zehlendorf, Köln (Ger), Racing Paris (Fr), Köln (Ger), JEF United (Japan).

Littbarski, an outside-right who later took his dribbling skills back into midfield, shot to prominence by hitting two goals on his debut for West Germany in a World Cup qualifier against Austria in 1981. He joined Köln, the club with which he is most associated, in 1978, played in the 1982 and 1986 World Cup Finals and finally achieved victory in Italy in 1990. Before heading out to Japan to wind down his career, Littbarski described his career ambition as "scoring a goal after beating all 10 outfield players, dribbling round the goalkeeper and putting the ball in the net with a back-heel".

Wlodzimierz Lubanski

Born: February 28, 1947, Poland.
Clubs: GKS Gliwice, Gornik Zabrze (Pol), Lokeren (Bel), Valenciennes, Quimper (Fr), Lokeren (Bel).

Lubanski ranks among Poland's finest players even though injuries were not kind to him. He emerged with the miners' club, Gornik, in the mid-1960s taking over the mantle of inspiration with both club and country from Ernest Pol. Lubanski was four times top league marksman in Poland and captained his country to the 1972 Olympic Games victory in Munich. The following year he suffered a serious thigh injury in a World Cup qualifier against England and missed the finals in which Poland finished third. He returned to national team duty at the 1978 finals in Argentina, before winding down his career in Belgium and France.

Ally McCoist

Born: September 24, 1962, Scotland.
Clubs: St. Johnstone (Scot), Sunderland (Eng), Rangers (Scot).

A powerful striker who survived a disastrous spell in England to become a hugely successful and popular player back in his homeland. McCoist was born in Bellshill, home town of Alex James and Matt Busby, and St Johnstone earned a club record £400,000 when selling him to Sunderland in 1981. After two unsettled seasons, 56 games and a mere eight goals, he was sold to Rangers, and began a decade of almost constant medal-collecting as the club dominated the Scottish game. He won the Golden Boot as Europe's leading league marksman and recovered from a broken leg to smash the legendary Bob McPhail's record of 233 league goals for Rangers.

McCOIST *Crowned his goal-grabbing career with the Golden Boot*

Paul McGrath

Born: December 4, 1959, England.
Clubs: Manchester United, Aston Villa.

McGrath is a fine player whose career has been dogged by ill-luck and – on occasions – lack of self-discipline. Born in Middlesex of Irish parentage, McGrath had a troubled progress through Manchester United's junior ranks and on into the senior squad, with injuries and authority combining to hinder him. But manager Ron Atkinson kept faith, and took McGrath with him when he moved to Villa. As a club player, one FA Cup win in 1985 – he performed heroically for ten-man United – was poor reward. As an international for the Republic of Ireland, his not inconsiderable skill and total commitment made him a folk hero among the Irish fans during European Championship and World Cup campaigns.

Jimmy McIlroy

Born: October 25, 1931, Northern Ireland.
Clubs: Glentoran (NI), Burnley, Stoke, Oldham (Eng).

If Blanchflower was the key man of

McGRATH *Defied knee injuries*

the Irish World Cup campaign in 1958, Jimmy McIlroy was only a little way behind him. His unhurried, elegant work at inside-forward proved ideal for the tactics devised by team manager Peter Doherty. Altogether McIlroy played 55 games for his country, to go with more than 600 at club level, earning a Championship medal with the attractive young Burnley squad in 1960, and a runners-up medal in the FA Cup two years later – against Blanchflower's Spurs. He later enjoyed a brief but brilliant combination with Stanley Matthews at Stoke.

Sammy McIlroy

Born: August 1, 1954, Northern Ireland.
Clubs: Manchester United, Stoke, Manchester City (Eng).

Another valuable midfielder, like his namesake, but of a totally different type. Sammy McIlroy's all-action style was in complete contrast to Jimmy's deliberate method, but was ideally suited to the hurly-burly of the modern game. It earned him 88 games for his country, spread over 15 years, but only five goals. He also played in three FA Cup Finals with United, losing to Southampton in 1976 and Arsenal in 1979, beating Liverpool in 1977. McIlroy's late equalizer in the 1979 Final seemed sure to take the game to extra time, but Arsenal went downfield to snatch the winner straight from the restart.

MICHEL *Grounds Northern Ireland's Kingsley Black with his skill*

Michel (full name: José Miguel Gonzalez Maria del Campo)

Born: March 23, 1963, Spain.
Clubs: Castilla, Real Madrid (Sp), Celaya (Mex).

Michel was one of European football's classic midfield operators throughout the 1980s and early 1990s. He made his debut with Castilla, the nursery team of Real Madrid, and was promoted to the senior outfit in 1984. A year later he starred in the UEFA Cup Final defeat of Videoton, scoring Madrid's first goal and making the other two in their 3–0 win in the first leg in Hungary. Michel made his Spain debut in 1985. He was unlucky to be denied a goal at the 1986 World Cup finals when his shot was cleared from behind the line against Brazil, but in 1990 in Italy he claimed a hat-trick against South Korea.

Roger Milla

Born: May 20, 1952, Cameroon.
Clubs: Leopard Douala, Tonnerre Yaounde (Cam), Valenciennes, Monaco, Bastia, Saint-Etienne, Montpellier (Fr).

Centre-forward Milla – real name Miller – delighted crowds at the 1990 World Cup with his celebratory dances around the corner flags. His goals, especially the winner against Colombia, made him the first player to become African Footballer of the Year for a second time. Milla played most of his club football in France, winning the cup there in 1980 with Monaco and in 1981 with Bastia. He was first voted African Footballer of the Year in 1976. He became, at the age of 42, the oldest player ever to appear in the World Cup finals at USA '94.

Milos Milutinovic

Born: February 5, 1933, Yugoslavia.
Clubs: FK Bor, Partizan, OFK Belgrade (Yug), Bayern Munich (Ger), Racing Paris, Stade Français (Fr).

Milutinovic, a powerful, aggressive centre-forward, was head of a famous dynasty of footballers which has included Bora Milutinovic, coach to the United States' 1994 World Cup side. Milos began with FK Bor, made his debut for Yugoslavia in 1951 and, the same year, transferred to Belgrade with army club Partizan. He scored 183 goals in 192 games before moving controversially to neighbours OFK, then to Germany with Bayern Munich and finally settling in France. Milutinovic proved a huge success with Racing Paris before injury forced his retirement in 1965. He scored 16 goals in 33 internationals between 1953 and 1958.

Severino Minelli

Born: September 6, 1909, Switzerland.
Clubs: Kussnacht, Servette, Grasshoppers.

Minelli was a steady, reliable right-back with great positional sense who played a then record 79 times for Switzerland during the inter-war years. In 1930 he made his national team debut while simultaneously winning his first league championship medal with Servette of Geneva. In the next 13 years he won another five league medals as well as eight cup finals with Grasshoppers of Zurich. Minelli was a key figure in the " *errou*" or "bolt" defence introduced by fellow-countryman Karl Rappan, and played to great effect for Switzerland in the World Cups of both 1934 and 1938. One of his finest games was Switzerland's 2–1 defeat of England in Zurich in May 1938.

Luisito Monti

Born: January 15, 1901, Argentina.
Clubs: Boca Juniors (Arg), Juventus (It).

Monti was an old-style attacking centre-half in the late 1920s and early 1930s. He was notable for a rugged, ruthless style but was also one of the great achievers of the inter-war years. Monti won an Olympic Games silver medal in 1928 when Argentina lost to Uruguay in Amsterdam and was again on the losing side against the same opponents at the first World Cup Final two years later. In 1931 Juventus brought Monti to Italy. At first he looked slow and vastly overweight, but a month's lone training brought him back to fitness and, little more than a year later, he made his debut for Italy in a 4–2 win over Hungary in Milan. Monti was not only a key figure in the Juventus side which won four successive league titles in the 1930s but he also played for Italy when they first won the World Cup, defeating Czechoslovakia in Rome in 1934.

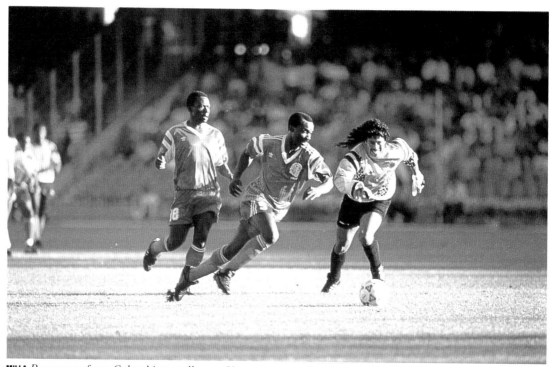

MILLA *Runs away from Colombian goalkeeper Higuita to score the winner in the 1990 World Cup second round*

MOORE *Leadership by example*

Bobby Moore

Born: April 17, 1941, England.
Clubs: West Ham United, Fulham (Eng), San Antonio Thunder, Seattle Sounders (US).

Bobby Moore was the inspirational, ice-cool captain of England's victorious 1966 World Cup side. Yet an FA Cup, one European Cup-winners' Cup, the 1966 World Cup and 108 England caps (100 of them under Sir Alf Ramsey) represent only part of his value to West Ham and England. Even at 34 he went back to Wembley, for Fulham against his old club, but by then fate was no longer smiling on him. He is likely to remain the only English captain to receive the World Cup trophy. Cruelly he developed cancer, from which he died in 1993, but which he defied with the utmost bravery to the end.

Juan Manuel Moreno

Born: August 3, 1916, Argentina.
Clubs: River Plate (Arg), España (Mex), River Plate (Arg), Universidad Catolia (Chile), Boca Juniors (Arg), Defensor (Uru), FC Oeste (Arg), Medellin (Col).

Many Argentines consider Moreno to have been the greatest footballer of all time. An inside-right for most of his career, Moreno began with River Plate's youth teams and was a league championship winner in 1936. He won four league titles with River

and was a member of the legendary forward line of the late 1940s, together with Muñoz, Pedernera, Labruna and Loustau. Moreno played for España in Mexico between 1944 and 1946, returned to River for two more years, then wandered off again to Chile, Uruguay and Colombia. He scored an impressive 20 goals in 33 internationals.

Stan Mortensen

Born: May 26, 1921, England.
Clubs: Blackpool, Hull, Southport.

As fast over ten yards as any English forward, with finishing skill to round off the openings his pace created, Mortensen scored four times in a 10–0 win over Portugal (away!) in his first international, and his goal in his last England game was his 23rd in 25 appearances. That was against the 1953 Hungarians, a few months after he had become the first man to score a hat-trick in a Wembley Cup Final: his third, after two defeats. Morty loved the FA Cup, scoring in each of Blackpool's first 12 post-war rounds in the tournament and finishing with 28 Cup goals as well as 225 in the league.

Alan Morton

Born: April 24, 1893, Scotland.
Clubs: Queen's Park, Rangers.

"The Wee Blue Devil" was a left-winger with elusive dribbling skill and a waspish shot who had a 20-year career and gained nine championship medals and three for the Scottish Cup. He was a mining engineer who spent several seasons with the amateurs at Queen's Park, before becoming the first signing for new Rangers manager, William Struth, who remained in charge for 34 years. Morton played well over 500 games for Rangers and is reputed never to have appeared in the reserves. He was always very much the gentleman, often appearing for matches in a bowler hat and carrying an umbrella.

Coen Moulijn

Born: February 15, 1937, Holland.
Clubs: Xerxes, Feyenoord.

Moulijn was perhaps Holland's first post-war superstar. A brilliant outside-left, he played 38 times for Holland between his debut in a 1–0 defeat

by Belgium in Antwerp in 1956 and his last game, a 1–1 World Cup draw against Bulgaria, in October 1969. That may have been Moulijn's last international, but his final and greatest achievement came the following May when Feyenoord beat Celtic in the European Cup Final in 1970. Moulijn helped Feyenoord go on to beat Estudiantes de La Plata in the World Club Cup and retired in 1972 with five league championships to his name. At the insistence of the Dutch federation, Feyenoord had inserted a clause in Moulijn's contract that he should never be sold abroad.

Gerd Müller

Born: November 3, 1945, Germany.
Clubs: TSV Nordlingen, Bayern Munich, Fort Lauderdale (US).

Coach Tschik Cajkovski was not impressed when Bayern bought a stocky new centre-forward in 1964. "I can't put that little elephant in among my string of thoroughbreds," said Cajkovski. But once he had done so, Bayern never looked back. Müller not only had the opportunist's eye for goal, but he was a powerful header of the ball. His goals shot Bayern out of the regional league to victory in the European Cup-winners' Cup in little more than three years. He went on to score well over 600 goals, including a record 365 in the Bundesliga and an astonishing 68 in 62 internationals for West Germany. Müller once scored four goals in a victory over Switzerland, but his most famous goal was his last, the one with which the Germans beat Holland in the 1974 World Cup Final. Müller won the European Cup three times and was also a European Championship winner in 1972.

MÜLLER *Volleys the dramatic winner against England in 1970 in Leon*

Frank Rijkaard

Born: September 30, 1962, Holland.
Clubs: Ajax (Hol), Sporting (Port), Zaragoza (Sp), Milan (It), Ajax (Hol).

Rijkaard has been one of the most universally-admired and versatile players over the past decade at both club and international level. He turned professional under Johan Cruyff at Ajax in 1979 and made his Holland debut at 19 despite Ajax protests that he was "too young". In 1987 Rijkaard fell out with Cruyff and had brief spells in Portugal and Spain before committing the key years of his career to Milan

with whom he won the World Club Cup and the European Cup twice apiece. Rijkaard played in midfield for Milan, but usually in central defence for Holland, with whom he won the 1988 European Championship. Following Milan's defeat by Marseille in the 1993 European Cup Final he returned to Ajax, and was a vital member of their victorious 1995 European Cup and Dutch title-winning teams, after which he retired.

Luigi "Gigi" Riva

Born: November 7, 1944, Italy.
Club: Cagliari.

Riva is remembered as one of the finest strikers in Italian football history. Orphaned in early childhood, he made a teenage reputation with Third Division Legnano as a left-winger

RAVELLI *Sweden's calming influence*

and was signed by Second Division Sardinian club Cagliari in 1963. Riva's formidable left foot and nose for goal sent Cagliari rocketing out of the shadows to league championship success in 1970. Riva was top league marksman three times, including the 1969–70 season when he scored 21 goals in 28 games. His 35 goals in 42 internationals meant Riva bore much of the responsibility for Italy's World Cup challenge in 1970. He scored three times in the quarter- and semifinal defeats of Mexico and West Germany before Italy's defeat in

the Final. Complications stemming from two broken legs ultimately enforced a premature retirement.

Roberto Rivelino

Born: January 1, 1946, Brazil.
Clubs: Corinthians, Fluminense.

Rivelino was originally the deeply-lying left-winger who filled the Zagalo role in Brazil's 1970 World Cup-winning side. He was not particularly quick, but was possessed of a superb technique which made him a perpetual danger with his banana-bending of free-kicks and corners. Riv-

RIJKAARD *Great all-rounder*

elino later moved into centre midfield and was influential in the third-place finish of 1978. Rivelino is credited unofficially with the fastest goal in football history: scored in three seconds with a shot from the starting pass after he noticed the opposing goalkeeper still concentrating on his pre-match prayers.

Gianni Rivera

Born: August 18, 1943, Italy.
Clubs: Alessandria, Milan.

The "Bambino d'Oro", the Golden Boy: that was Rivera in the early 1960s. As a creative inside-forward, he had the lot: skill, pace and a deft shot, plus the rare natural gift of grace. Rivera in full flight was football poetry in motion. Milan paid Alessandria £65,000 for a half-share in the 15-year-old Rivera and signed him "for real" in 1960. In 16 years with the "Rossoneri" he was twice a winner of the World Club Cup, the European Cup and the Italian league, as well as three times an Italian cup-winner and once European Footballer of the Year, in 1969. Rivera became a controversial figure, however, as successive national managers struggled to build teams around him. Thus he played only the last six minutes of the 1970 World Cup Final – although his Italy career produced 14 goals in 60 games. On retiring Rivera turned to politics and became a member of the Italian parliament.

Bryan Robson

Born: January 11, 1957, England.

Clubs: West Bromwich, Manchester United, Middlesbrough.

A considerable part of English football in the 1980s was played to the accompaniment of breaking bones, many of them Bryan Robson's. Despite his season ticket to the surgery he won an impressive list of honours, with 90 caps (often as captain), three FA Cup medals, European Cup-winners' Cup in 1991, and inaugural Premier League championship in 1992–93. Robson was an inspiring, driving force in midfield and a believer in the value of an early strike: three of his England goals were in the first minute. He broke a leg twice as a teenager with West Bromwich, and then broke the transfer fee record when Manchester United bought him for £1.5 million. He moved into management in 1994, immediately leading Middlesbrough into the Premier League.

Pedro Rocha

Born: December 3, 1942, Uruguay.
Clubs: Penarol (Uru), São Paulo (Br).

Rocha was far removed from the typical image of angry, temperamental Uruguayans. A statuesque inside-left of great skill to match his height, he was surprisingly quick and soon became a local hero after joining mighty Penarol of Montevideo at 17. Seven times in the next nine seasons Rocha was a champion of Uruguay, and he inspired Penarol to victory both home and away over Real Madrid in the 1966 World Club Cup final. He captained Uruguay into the 1970 World Cup finals but was injured in the first match. Fit again, he moved to Brazil and led São Paulo to victory in the Paulista state championship in his debut season. Rocha won 62 caps for Uruguay.

Romario da Souza Faria

Born: 29 January, 1966, Brazil.
Clubs: Vasco da Gama (Br), PSV Eindhoven (Hol), Barcelona (Sp), Flamengo (Bra).

Romario has been arguably the finest attacker in the world game in the 1990s. Discovered by Vasco da Gama, he was still a teenager when he began to establish a reputation for controversy after being banished from Brazil's World Youth Cup

BRYAN ROBSON *Manchester United and England's oft-injured captain*

squad for flouting a hotel curfew. After starring at the 1988 Seoul Olympics, he transferred to PSV Eindhoven. There he clashed with coaches and team-mates, yet still totalled 98 league goals in five seasons to earn a £3 million sale to Barcelona in the summer of 1993. Simultaneously, he was recalled for USA '94 by Brazil after almost a year in the wilderness. Romario scored five crucial goals and followed Brazil's World Cup triumph by returning home to play for Flamengo.

Ronaldo (full name: Ronaldo Luiz Nazario da Lima)

Born: September 22, 1976, Brazil.
Clubs: Sao Cristovao, Cruzeiro (Br), PSV Eindhoven (Hol), Barcelona (Sp).

Ronaldo has been the most talked about footballer in Europe in the mid-1990s – a status underlined by his award as the 1996 FIFA Player of the Year, pipping George Weah and Alan Shearer. He was compared favourably with Pele at his age by the likes of past Brazilian heroes as Zico and Tostao. Ronaldo grew up in the working class district of Bento Ribeiro, on Rio's west side. He failed a trial with Flamengo but was signed by minor club Sao Cristovao where his potential was discovered by 1970 World Cup star Jairzinho – who then sold Ronaldo on to Cruzeiro of Belo Horizonte. In his first year he scored 54 goals in 54 games. Ronaldo then moved to Europe with PSV Eindhoven and joined Barcelona in the summer of 1996 for £12.9 million. He ended his first season in

Spain as the league's top scorer with 34 goals. Ronaldo was a member of Brazil's 1994 World Cup-winning squad, but never played. Coach Car-

PAOLO ROSSI *Stranger than fiction*

los Alberto Parreira insisted he was taken along, "just for experience".

Paolo Rossi

Born: September 23, 1956, Italy.
Clubs: Prato, Juventus, Como, Lanerossi Vicenza, Perugia, Juventus, Milan.

Paolo Rossi's story is more fantastic than fiction. As a teenager Juventus gave him away because of knee trouble. Later, when they tried to buy him back, they were outbid by provincial Perugia, who paid a world record £3.5 million. Rossi, a star already at the 1978 World Cup, was then banned for two years for alleged involvement in a betting-and-bribes scandal. Juventus finally got him back, but he was only three matches out of his ban when Italy took him to the 1982 World Cup finals, where he top-scored with six goals and collected a winner's medal from the Final victory over West Germany. Rossi was only 29 when he retired into legend.

Karl-Heinz Rummenigge

Born: September 25, 1955, West Germany.
Clubs: Lippstadt, Bayern Munich (W Ger), Internazionale (It), Servette (Swz).

Rummenigge was one of the great bargains of German football. Bayern Munich paid Lippstadt just £4,500 for their young, blond right-winger in 1974 and sold him to Italy a decade later for more than £2 million. In between Rummenigge had

RUMMENIGGE *Twice best in Europe*

won the World Club championship and the European Cup and had twice been hailed as European Footballer of the Year. The former bank clerk, who first impressed Internazionale officials with a World Cup hat-trick against Mexico in 1978, developed

into a central striker, as his career progressed. Injuries reduced his effectiveness in the early 1980s, and controversy lingered over whether national manager Jupp Derwall was right to play his injured captain from the start in the 1982 World Cup Final defeat by Italy.

Ian Rush

Born October 20, 1961, Wales.
Clubs: Chester, Liverpool (Eng), Juventus (It), Liverpool, Leeds Utd (Eng).

Rush was the goal-scorer supreme in modern British football, but he would have been a great player even if he had never hit a net. His off-the-ball running and excellent passing were bonuses to go with his acutely developed finishing ability. Rush was only 18 when Liverpool had to pay £300,000 to get him, but the fee was repaid many times over. In two spells at Anfield, interrupted by a none-too-happy Italian adventure, he broke scoring records for club, country and FA Cup Finals (five goals in three winning appearances), with medals for five league titles and four League Cups as well. Released on a free transfer in 1996, he was snapped up immediately by Leeds United.

Hugo Sanchez

Born: June 11, 1958, Mexico.
Clubs: UNAM (Mex), Atletico Madrid, Real Madrid (Sp), America (Mex), Rayo Vallecano (Sp).

Hugo Sanchez was top league goalscorer in Spain five seasons in a row in the late 1980s and early 1990s. His 230-plus goals in Spain left him second overall behind Bilbao's Telmo Zarra and underlined his claim to be considered one of the great strikers of the modern game. Each one of Sanchez's goals was followed by a celebratory somersault, taught him originally by a sister who was a gymnast in Mexico's team for the 1976 Olympics in Montreal – at which Hugo made his football debut on the international stage. Despite a World Cup finals debut as far back as 1978, Sanchez totalled only around 50 games for Mexico – his many absences caused either by club commitments in Spain or by disputes with Mexican soccer bureaucracy.

Leonel Sanchez

Born: April 25, 1936, Chile.
Club: Universidad de Chile.

Leonel Sanchez was the outstanding left-winger in South America in the late 1950s and early 1960s – perhaps not as fast as Pepe of Brazil or as intelligent a player as Zagalo of Brazil, but far more forceful when it came to making his presence felt in the penalty box. Sanchez was a star of the Chilean side which finished third as hosts in the 1962 World Cup, but he also featured in controversy: earlier in the tournament he somehow escaped punishment from the match referee for a punch which flattened Humberto Maschio in the so-called Battle of Santiago against Italy. Sanchez played 106 times for Chile, though only 62 of those appearances may be counted as full internationals. He was seven times national champion with "U", his only club.

José Emilio Santamaria

Born: July 31, 1929, Uruguay
Clubs: Nacional (Uru), Real Madrid (Sp).

Santamaria was a ruthless centre-back whose finest years were spent at Real Madrid in the 1950s and early 1960s, closing down the defensive gaps left by great attacking colleagues such as Di Stefano, Puskas and Gento. Santamaria was first called up at 20 by Uruguay but missed the 1950 World Cup finals because his club, Nacional, refused to let him accept the inside-forward spot allocated to him in the squad bound for Brazil. Four years later Santamaria was one of the stars of the 1954 World Cup, this time in his traditional place in the centre of defence. Madrid brought him to Europe in 1957 and, having played 35 times for Uruguay, he collected another 17 caps in the service of Spain, including the 1962 World Cup. He was a World Club championship and triple European Cup winner with Real Madrid and later managed hosts Spain at the 1982 World Cup finals.

Djalma Santos

Born: February 27, 1929, Brazil.
Clubs: Portuguesa, Palmeiras, Atletico Curitiba.

Djalma Santos is considered a cornerstone of the Brazil side which won the World Cup in 1958 and 1962 and lost it in 1966. Yet, in Sweden in 1958, he was brought in only for the

DJALMA SANTOS *A great survivor*

IAN RUSH *One of the great bargains, at £300,000 from Chester*

PETER SCHMEICHEL *In winning command of defence for Denmark*

THE STADIUMS

The role of the stadium is simple: to organize spectators so that as many as possible can watch the action. Many grounds enjoy a fame which equals that of the clubs and individuals: permanent witnesses to the game's twin impostors of triumph and disaster.

NOU CAMP
BARCELONA, SPAIN

Capacity: 115,000
Opened: 1957
Club: FC Barcelona
Hosted: 1982 World Cup Opening Match (Belgium 1, Argentina 0); 1992 Olympic Final (Spain 3, Poland 2); 1989 European Cup Final (Milan 4, Steaua Bucharest 0); 1982 European Cup-winners' Cup Final (Barcelona 2, Standard Liège 1)

PRIDE OF CATALONIA *Barcelona's 130,000 capacity Nou Camp stadium*

Higher and higher, bigger and better could be the motto of Barcelona's towering and breathtaking Nou Camp, "the new ground", which opened its doors on September 24, 1957 and was financed to the tune of 66 million pesetas by club members. In Europe today only Benfica's Estadio da Luz can claim to be larger. Sport, it has been said, is the acceptable substitute for war, and Barcelona has always been a vehicle for the fervent nationalism of Catalonia. The rivalry with Madrid is intense, and the Nou Camp's con-

tinual improvements and expansion have much to do with the desire to outdo Real's Bernabeu stadium.

Barcelona, formed in 1899, outgrew their old Les Corts ground in the 1940s and moved to the new stadium, built in an area of gardens and allotments to the west, in 1957. When Nou Camp was inaugurated with a match against Legia Warsaw, plans had already been laid to

extend facilities and increase capacity to 150,000.

An indoor sports hall, connected to Nou Camp by a concourse, was opened in 1971 and houses the club's basketball, handball and volleyball teams. Ice hockey is held in the adjacent Ice Palace. Even more remarkably, there is a walkway over a road leading to another football stadium, the 16,500 capacity Mini-

Estad, opened in 1982 and used by Barcelona's nursery team in the Spanish Second Division as well as by the club's top amateur side.

The first major redevelopment of the main stadium was in the early 1980s, when the addition of a third tier increased capacity to 120,000 in time for Nou Camp to host the opening ceremony of the 1982 World Cup, after which a crowd of 85,000 saw Belgium upset the holders Argentina 1–0.

When the old Les Corts ground was opened in 1922, "Barca" had a membership of 5,000. When Pope John Paul II visited the Nou Camp in World Cup year he was enrolled as member No. 108,000. Since then membership has passed 110,000, making Barcelona the largest club in the world.

The work never stops. For the 1992 Olympic Games in Barcelona, two more tiers holding 10,000 seats were installed above the previous roof line, with a suspended cantilevered roof soaring overhead.

OLYMPIASTADION
BERLIN, GERMANY

Capacity: 76,006
Opened: 1936
Clubs: Hertha BSC, Blau-Weiss 90
Hosted: 1936 Olympic Final (Italy 2, Austria 1); 1974 World Cup group matches

Berlin's historic – or notorious – stadium may be considered not so much a theatre of dreams, more a monument to the nightmarish world of Adolf Hitler and his national socialism. It was here that Hitler opened the 1936 Olympics, a giant propaganda exercise, to Wagnerian strains before an ecstatic 100,000 crowd. It was here, much to his chagrin, that the black American athlete Jesse Owens won four gold medals to challenge the myth of Aryan superiority. It was here two years later that the England team played Germany and avenged the politically-engineered demand that they give the Nazi salute by winning 6–3.

The Olympiapark, of which the Olympiastadion is the neo-classical cen-

LEGACY OF THE GREAT DICTATOR *Berlin's Olympiastadion was originally a stage for Adolf Hitler and his Nazis*

tre-piece, had its origins before the First World War since Germany had been chosen to stage the Games in 1916. The unused facilities, adjacent to the Grunewald racecourse, were taken over when Hitler came to power in 1933. His grand plan involved the 86,000 capacity stadium on a 131-hectare sports field which also included hockey, riding and swimming stadia plus an open-air amphitheatre. These were all linked to the vast Maifeld, used by the Nazis for mass rallies.

The stadium suffered from Allied bombing but was repaired by the mid-1960s, when Hertha Berlin drew 70,000 crowds in the early years of the Bundesliga, the new national championship of West Germany. The stadium was renovated for the 1974 World Cup when it staged three group matches. The use of the Olympiastadion in the first place had caused political tension between East and West, and its incorporation in the World Cup programme at all

was a triumph for German football chief Hermann Neuberger.

The unique political problems of Berlin meant that the stadium was underused for years. It was the home of both Hertha and Blau-Weiss Berlin but that meant mainly Second Division football. Now, since reunification, the Olympiastadion has regained its status as a focal point for German football and it is once again the permanent home of the German Cup Final.

HAMPDEN PARK
GLASGOW, SCOTLAND

Capacity: 50,000
Club: Queen's Park
Hosted: 1960 European Cup Final (Real Madrid 7, Eintracht Frankfurt 3), 1976 (Bayern Munich 1, Saint-Etienne 0); 1961 European Cup-winners' Cup (Fiorentina 2, Rangers 0), 1962 (Atletico Madrid 1, Fiorentina 1, replay in Stuttgart), 1966 (Borussia Dortmund 2, Liverpool 1); 1989 World Under-17 Championship Final (Saudi Arabia 1, Scotland 1 aet: Saudi Arabia 5–4 on pens).

As early as 1908, Glasgow had three of the largest grounds in the world:

GIANT OF THE PAST *In its heyday Hampden Park attracted record crowds*

Ibrox, home of protestant Rangers, Celtic Park, home of Catholic Celtic, and Hampden, owned by amateurs Queen's Park. Hampden was already the national stadium, never more vibrant than when hosting games against the old enemy England, whom Scotland had met in the first-ever international in 1872. It was the largest stadium in the world until the Maracana opened in 1950 and still holds several attendance records. In 1937, 149,415 paid to see the Scots beat England, a record for a match in Europe. A week later, 147,365 saw Celtic beat Aberdeen for the Scottish Cup, a European club record. In 1960, 135,000 watched Real Madrid trounce Eintracht Frankfurt 7–3 in the European Cup Final. That record was bettered five years later, when 136,505 saw Celtic's semi-final with Leeds. Since then there has been major redevelopment. First came a £3 million refurbishment in 1975 then a £12 million remodelling in the early 1990s. Hampden was shut again after the 1996 Scottish Cup Final for the construction of an 18,000-capacity new South Stand.

ESTADIO DA LUZ
LISBON, PORTUGAL

Capacity: 130,000
Opened: 1954
Club: Benfica
Hosted: 1991 World Youth Cup Final (Portugal 0, Brazil 0: Portugal 4–2 on pens); 1967 European Cup Final (Celtic 2, Internazionale 1); 1992 European Cup-winners' Cup Final (Werder Bremen 2, Monaco 0)

Although the "Stadium of Light" is one of the most evocatively named arenas in the world, it takes its name not from the power of its floodlighting but from the nearby Lisbon district of Luz. Yet one of the most dazzling players in history, the "Black Pearl" Eusebio, led Benfica to unparalleled heights here during the 1960s and 1970s when 14 league titles, two European Cup wins (1960 and 1961) and three more final appearances established Benfica among the aristocracy of European football. In 1992, a statue of their greatest son was unveiled to celebrate his fiftieth birthday, before a match with old rivals Manchester United, and this now greets visitors as they arrive at the entrance.

Benfica, or Sport Lisboa e Benfica as they are officially named, were formed in 1908, and by the 1950s had long outgrown their fifth ground at Campo Grande. Plans for the 60,000 capacity Estadio da Luz were drawn up by a former Benfica athlete in 1951 and the two-tiered stadium was opened in 1954. Porto won the first game 3–0, and Portugal's first floodlit game, again won by Porto, took place four years later. By 1960 a third tier increased capacity to 75,000, and by the late 1970s the Estadio Da Luz, all white and bright, seated 130,000, and was a legend in Europe.

SANTIAGO BERNABEU
MADRID, SPAIN

Capacity: 105,000
Opened: 1947
Club: Real Madrid
Hosted: 1982 World Cup Final (Italy 3, West Germany 2); 1964 European Championship Final (Spain 2, Soviet Union 1); 1957 European Cup Final (Real Madrid 2, Fiorentina 0), 1969 (Milan 4, Ajax 1), 1980 (Nottingham Forest 1, Hamburg 0).

It is thanks to the visionary foresight of long-time president Santiago Bernabeu that Real Madrid boast an imposing edifice on Madrid's most prestigious street, the Castellana, housing one of the world's foremost clubs and a trophy room bulging with silverware and displaying more than 5,000 items. The ground, which began life as the Nuevo Chamartin Stadium in 1944 on five hectares of prime land, was

Bernabeu's brainchild. He was a lawyer who had been, in turn, player, captain, club secretary, coach and then, from 1942, president. The old stadium had been ravaged during the Spanish Civil War and Bernabeu decided that a super new stadium was needed if the club were to raise the funds needed to build a super new team. Real, who now include the King and Queen of Spain and President of the International Olympic Committee Juan Antonio Samaranch among their members, raised an astonishing 41 million pesetas by public subscription to finance the land purchase and first stage of building. The stadium was opened, with a 75,000 capacity, for a testimonial match for veteran player Jesus

MONUMENT TO A VISIONARY *The Bernabeu stadium is a most exclusive venue*

Alonso against Belenenses of Lisbon in December, 1947.

In the 1950s the finance raised by Real's dominance of the fledgling European Cup enabled capacity within the distinctive white towers to be extended to 125,000. The name Estadio Santiago Bernabeu was adopted in 1955 and the floodlights were switched on in 1957 for the European Cup Final.

Bernabeu, who died in 1978, had plans for a new stadium north of the city but for once did not get his way and, instead, Spain's hosting of the 1982 World Cup led to more improvements. A total of 345,000 people watched three group matches and an outstanding Final in a stadium offering 30,200 seats and standing room for 60,000. Ten years on, the improvements continue. A third tier has been completed and further remodelling has increased the seating to 65,000 within a total capacity of 105,000.

STADIO GIUSEPPE MEAZZA
MILAN, ITALY

Capacity: 83,107
Opened: 1926
Clubs: Milan, Internazionale
Hosted: 1965 European Cup Final (Internazionale 1, Benfica 0), 1970 (Feyenoord 2, Celtic 1 aet); 1990 World Cup opening and group matches.

Fantastic is a much misused word but it seems appropriate to describe the home of two of Europe's leading clubs in the city which can claim to be the continent's premier soccer centre. The cylindrical towers which

allowed builders to construct a third tier and roof in advance of the 1992 World Cup have become just as much a trademark as the ramp system which gave access to the original two tiers of what used to be known as the San Siro. The cost of the remodelling came close to £50 million – even before the extra expense of sorting out problems with the pitch caused by shutting out both light and breeze.

San Siro, named after the suburb, was originally the home of Milan, formed in 1899 by the Englishman Alfred Edwards. They outgrew their original ground in the mid-1920s, and the site of their new stadium was bought by their wealthy president,

MAGNIFICO *Inter and Milan's home*

Piero Pirelli of tyre fame. It was Inter of all teams who ruined the opening party at the 35,000 capacity Stadio Calcistico San Siro by winning 6–3 in September 1926. The stadium was bought from Milan by the local council and was gradually enlarged until a 65,000 crowd were able to watch

Italy play their Axis partners Germany in 1940. Inter had outgrown their own Stadio Arena by 1947; but the proposed groundshare needed an even larger stadium. The San Siro reopened in 1955 with an increased capacity of 82,000 as the home ground for two teams who have been bettered in domestic football by Juventus and Torino but are second to none in European success. The San Siro was renamed Stadio Giuseppe Meazza in 1979 to honour the memory of one of the only two players to appear in both Italy's 1934 and 1938 World Cup-winning sides. The inside-forward had been hero-worshipped while playing for both Milan clubs.

LUZHNIKI STADIUM
MOSCOW, RUSSIA

Capacity: 100,000
Opened: 1956
Club: Spartak Moscow
Hosted: 1980 Olympic Final (Czechoslovakia 1, East Germany 0)

A statue of Vladimir Ilyich Lenin, the now discredited father of the Russian Revolution, for years welcomed the visitor to the Centralny Stadion

Lenina on the banks of the Moscow River, which is the site of possibly the largest and most popular sports complex in the world. There are 140 separate sports centres, including a Palace of Sports, an open-air swimming centre, a multi-purpose hall, 22 smaller halls, 11 football pitches, four athletics tracks, three skating rinks and 55 tennis courts. Many countries cannot offer as much! The all-seater football stadium plays host to the capital's most popular club,

Spartak, and internationals. It is built on the site of the old Red Stadium where Spartak, then Moscow Sports Club, were founded in 1922. They adopted the present name in 1935 after affiliating to the trade unions for producers' co-operatives. The new stadium opened in 1956 with the first All Union Spartakia, which brought together 34,000 athletes to celebrate Communist sport. But the history of the Luzhinski is darkened by one of soccer's major disasters:

in 1982, Spartak were playing Haarlem of Holland in a UEFA Cup tie. Most of the crowd were leaving just before the end when Spartak scored a late goal. As fans tried to get back up the icy steps a fatal crush occurred. The Soviet people only learned of the tragedy seven years later, and then the official death toll was way below the 300 estimated at the time. The stadium was shut in the spring of 1996 for major redevelopment and refurbishment.

OLYMPIASTADION
MUNICH, GERMANY

Capacity: 74,000
Opened: 1972
Club: Bayern Munich
Hosted: 1972 Olympic Final (Poland 2, Hungary 1); 1974 World Cup Final (West Germany 2, Holland 1); 1988 European Championship Final (Holland 2, Soviet Union 0); 1979 European Cup Final (Nottingham Forest 1, Malmo 0), 1993 (Marseille 1, Milan 0), 1997 (Borussia Dortmund 3, Juventus 1)

NOTHING QUITE LIKE IT *Munich's futuristic Olympiastadion*

Descriptions of the individualistic Olympiastadion vary from a futuristic Bedouin tent to a steel and glass spider's web – although the desert analogy can feel rather tenuous in the depths of a Bavarian winter on the site of the airfield to which Neville Chamberlain flew in 1938 for his infamous ("Peace in our time") meeting

with Hitler. The tragic shadow of history fell across the stadium again at the end of the 1972 Olympics for which it had been built, when Arab terrorists took hostage and murdered Israeli athletes competing at the Games.

The bill for Behnisch and Otto's

staggering creation at the centre of the green and pleasant Olympiapark came to 137 million marks. It was money well spent. The Park has become Germany's leading tourist attraction and a stunning venue for major events.

Bayern Munich, about to establish themselves as European giants with players such as Franz Beckenbauer, Paul Breitner and Gerd Müller, moved into the new stadium in 1972, two seasons before they lifted the first of their three successive European Champions Cups. Müller had helped to celebrate the opening by scoring all four goals in West Germany's 4–1 win over the Soviet Union in 1972. Two years later the stocky striker's place in soccer's hall of fame was assured by his winning goal against Holland in the 1974 World Cup Final in front of his home fans.

The Dutch took happier memories away from the 1988 European Championship Final when they overcame the Soviets 2–0. Most recently Marseille became the first French club to win a European trophy by defeating Milan 1–0 there ... only to become embroiled in a major bribery scandal at home.

SAN PAOLO
NAPLES, ITALY

Capacity: 85,102
Opened: 1960
Club: Napoli
Hosted: 1968 European Championship semi-final (Italy 2, Soviet Union 1); 1980 European Championship finals venue; 1990 World Cup semi-final (Italy 1, Argentina 1: Argentina 4–3 on pens)

Regarded purely as a stadium, the concrete bowl of San Paolo, complete with roof since the 1992 World Cup, is unremarkable. But on match days it is transformed into a vibrant, uninhibited place by the local *tifosi*, some of the most colourful, eccentric and volatile fans (hence the moat and fences) in the world.

San Paolo represents the third home for Napoli, a club formed in 1904 with the help of English sailors and looked upon with some disdain by the more sophisticated clubs of Turin and Milan, though one of them, Juventus, deigned to come south to play the first match in the new stadium in the Olympic year of 1960.

Napoli, despite the largesse of millionaire president and shipping

UNRIVALLED ATMOSPHERE *Napoli's colourful fans turn a match in the San Paolo into an unforgettable experience*

owner Achille Lauro, had little success until the arrival of the Argentine superstar Diego Maradona in the mid-1980s. He filled San Paolo as it had never been filled before. The size of the stadium enabled Napoli to sell 70,000 season tickets, an Ital-

ian record, and thus not only pay Barcelona the then world record transfer fee of £5 million for Maradona but afford his wages and bring in other superstars, such as Brazil's Careca, into the bargain.

Sadly, the club has recently been

embroiled in controversy, first over links with the Camorra (the local version of the Mafia) and then over the misuse and misappropriation of funds set aside for development work in and around the stadium for the 1990 World Cup.

A THING OF BEAUTY *France's national stadium, but soon to be superseded*

PARC DES PRINCES
PARIS, FRANCE

Capacity: 49,700
Opened: 1897 (rebuilt 1932, 1972)
Clubs: Paris Saint-Germain, Racing Club
Hosted: 1984 European Championship Final (France 2, Spain 0); 1956 European Cup Final (Real Madrid 4, Reims 3), 1975 (Bayern Munich 2, Leeds 0), 1981 (Liverpool 1, Real Madrid 0); 1978 European Cup-winners' Cup Final (Anderlecht 4, FK Austria 0);

1994 European Cup-winners' Cup Final (Zaragoza 2, Arsenal 1)

The award of the 1998 World Cup to France has spelled the beginning of the end of the chequered career of the Parc des Princes as a major soccer venue. The all-concrete near-50,000 capacity stadium designed by Roger Taillibert for soccer and rugby union in the early 1970s fails to meet FIFA's minimum capacity of 80,000 for a Final, and the French government announced in October 1993 that £300 million is to be spent on a new

stadium in the northern suburb of St Denis.

The Parc des Princes lies in the south-west and, as the name suggests, before the Revolution it was a pleasure ground for royalty. The stadium began life as a velodrome at the end of the last century and, until 1967, was the finish for the Tour de France.

When professional football was introduced in 1932 it became home to Racing Club de France, but they enjoyed only limited success and the Stade Colombes remained the favourite ground for internationals and the 1938 World Cup. Until the current stadium was built, one of the biggest soccer matches staged was the first European Cup Final in 1956, when a sell-out 38,000 crowd saw Real Madrid beat Stade Reims 4–3. Paris, sad to say, is the great capital underachiever in soccer terms.

The creation of the Périphérique, the Paris ring road, led to the new

two-tiered state-of-the-art stadium being built. It was the first in Europe with integral floodlighting and closed-circuit television. Problems with the pitch dogged its early years, but these ills were cured by the time the Parc was needed to host three group matches and the Final of the 1984 European Championship, won in style by France's finest ever team, led by Michel Platini.

Racing Club went out of professional soccer business in 1964, and Paris Saint-Germain, an amalgamation of Paris FC and Saint-Germain, moved into the new stadium in 1973. They drew 20,000 crowds, became only the second Paris club to win the Championship and dominated the domestic game in the mid-1990s. In 1982, a new club Racing de Paris – unconnected with the old one – began to share the Parc des Princes. They may have exclusive use from 1998.

OLIMPICO
ROME, ITALY

Capacity: 80,000
Opened: 1953
Clubs: Roma, Lazio
Hosted: 1960 Olympic Final (Yugoslavia 3, Denmark 1); 1990 World Cup Final (West Germany 1, Argentina 0); 1968 European Championship Final (Italy 1, Yugoslavia 1; replay, Italy 2, Yugoslavia 0), 1980 (West Germany 2, Belgium 1); 1977 European Cup Final (Liverpool 3, Borussia Mönchengladbach 1), 1984 (Liverpool 1, Roma 1: Liverpool 4–2 on pens) 1996 (Juventus 1, Ajax 1: Juventus 4–2 on pens)

Benito Mussolini was bad news for Italy. But allegedly he did make the trains run on time, and he also left the beautiful Foro Italico sports complex at the foot of Monte Mario as a legacy. His original plan was to stage the 1944 Olympics there, much as Hitler used Berlin for propaganda purposes in 1936. Then the Second World War intervened. The stadium was originally called Stadio dei Cipressi, but was inaugurated in 1953 as the Olimpico by the legendary Hungarian team who beat Italy 3–0 in front of an 80,000 crowd. The stadium became the focal point of the 1960 Olympic Games, a home to both Roma and Lazio, and the scene of a home triumph in the 1968 Euro-

pean Championship when Italy overcame Yugoslavia in a replay.

All roads led to Rome for Liverpool in 1977, when they turned the stadium into a sea of red celebrating the first of their four European Cup triumphs. They returned for the 1984 Final to beat Roma, playing on their own ground but unable to take

BELLA *Rome's Olympic Stadium*

advantage. Liverpool eventually won on penalties.

To allow the stadium to stage the 1990 World Cup, individual seating had to be increased to 80,000 and a roof added to give two-thirds cover. Only in Italy could the wrangling and talking have gone on until May 1988. A year later the roof design was ditched, costs had risen to £75 million, and the odds shifted against the stadium being ready.

FIFA's threat to move the final to Milan eventually saw to it that this beautiful venue was ready for West Germany's revenge over Argentina: a gracious setting for what proved to be an uninspiring contest.

ERNST-HAPPEL
VIENNA, AUSTRIA

Capacity: 62,958
Opened: 1931
Club: None as permanent
Hosted: 1964 European Cup Final (Internazionale 3, Real Madrid 1), 1987 (Porto 2, Bayern Munich 1), 1990 (Milan 1, Benfica 0), 1995 (Ajax 1, Milan 0); 1970 European Cup-winners' Cup Final (Manchester City 2, Gornik Zarbrze 1)

Long known as the Prater, the Ernst-Happel stadion gained its new name in memory of the late Austrian international defender and coach. It overlooks the pleasure grounds forever associated with Orson Welles and *The Third Man*, but Austrian fans associate it more with the Hugo Meisl "Wunderteam" of the 1930s, who counted England among their victims in 1936. The Stadium has been transformed in recent years into one of Europe's leading venues, the original open two-tiered amphitheatre topped by a remarkable roof

which was erected in 10 months during 1985 at a cost of £17.5 million. The original 60,000-capacity stadium, a legacy of the socialist-controlled city administration, opened in July 1931 with a match appropriately between two workers' teams, and hosted athletics championships and the long-forgotten Workers Olympiad.

After the *Anschluss*, the stadium became an army barracks and, staged wartime internationals while serving as a staging post for Austrian Jews on their way to concentration

camps. Though badly damaged by Allied troops, the stadium was quickly restored after the war. Rapid played Real Madrid under floodlights in 1955 and a record 90,593 watched Austria play Spain in 1960. In the 1970s, the insertion of an all-weather track cut capacity to 72,000.

No club has used it permanently for league matches since FK Austria moved out in 1982. But Rapid, FK Austria and even Casino Salzburg have all used it intermittently for important European cup-ties.

WEMBLEY
LONDON, ENGLAND

Capacity: 80,000
Opened: 1923
Club: None
Hosted: 1948 Olympic Final (Sweden 3, Yugoslavia 1); 1966 World Cup Final (England 4, West Germany 2 aet); 1996 European Championship; 1963 European Cup Final (Milan 2, Benfica 1), 1968 (Manchester United 4, Benfica 1 aet), 1971 (Ajax 2, Panathinaikos 0), 1978 (Liverpool 1, Brugge 0), 1992 (Barcelona 1, Sampdoria 0 aet); 1965 Cup-Winners Cup Final (West Ham 2, Munich 1860 0), 1993 (Parma 3, Antwerp 1)

Wembley may be the ageing *grande dame* of stadia but, steeped in history and with its distinctive twin towers, it remains the Mecca of English football and is revered by players and fans throughout the world. Wembley is synonymous with England internationals, the FA Cup Final and the

WEMBLEY *England's football home*

epic World Cup Final of 1966.

Unusually for a major stadium, Wembley is privately owned and financed by its staging of major soccer, greyhound racing, rugby league, showpiece American football games, and ancillary sporting activities at the nearby 9,000-seater Arena. In the 1920s the green fields of Wembley Park were chosen as the site for the 1923 Empire Exhibition. The then Empire Stadium was built between January 22 and April 23. It was hailed as the largest monumental building of reinforced concrete in the world, and a

troop of soldiers marched up and down the terracing in a unique safety check.

Since a crowd of "only" 53,000 had turned up for the 1922 FA Cup Final at Stamford Bridge, the authorities were concerned that Bolton and West Ham might not fill the new 126,000 capacity ground the following year. But on April 28 more than 200,000 people besieged Wembley, and that Bolton were eventually able to defeat West Ham 2–0 was due in no small part to the good nature of the crowd in the presence of King George V and a celebrated policeman on his white horse. The Wembley legend was born.

The watersheds of English football followed: the Cup was taken out of England for the only time by Cardiff in 1927; a year later Scotland destroyed England 5–1 with their famous forward line, dubbed the Wembley Wizards; Stanley Matthews

had the 1953 Final "named" after him, when he inspired Blackpool to beat Bolton 4–3 from 3–1 down. Later that year, Hungary changed world football by crushing England 6–3 there.

England held their heads high again in 1966, and when Manchester United became the first club to win the European Cup on a memorable June night two years later they could not have triumphed on more appropriate turf.

Wembley has moved with the times. The surrounding exhibition centre was redeveloped while the stadium was remodelled in the 1980s at a cost of £60 million. Adapting to all-seater demands meant a capacity reduction from the historic 100,000. The addition of an Olympic Gallery beneath the roof edge kept an 80,000 level at which Wembley could take a pivotal role in England's hosting of the 1996 European Championship.

ROSE BOWL
PASADENA, CALIFORNIA, USA

Capacity: 102,083
Opened: 1922
Hosted: 1984 Olympic Final (France 2, Brazil 0); 1994 World Cup Final (Brazil 0, Italy 0 – Brazil win 3–2 on penalties).

The Rose Bowl, synonymous with American football, came into its own as a soccer venue at the 1994 World Cup when it served as a home from home for the United States, then hosted second round matches, a semi-final, the third place match and the Final itself.

The rose-covered stadium, based in the leafy city of Pasadena seven miles north-west of downtown Los Angeles, cut its teeth on soccer in the 1984 Olympics, when the tournament drew massive crowds. Yugoslavia versus Italy drew 100,374, France's semi-final against Yugoslavia 97,451, and 101,799 watched France defeat Brazil in the Final. That topped the record attendance for gridiron football's Superbowl XVII in 1983, when 101,063 watched the Washington Redskins defeat the Miami Dolphins.

The Rose Bowl has hosted five Super Bowls but is best known as the home of UCLA and the annual Rose Bowl game on New Year's Day.

CALIFORNIA ROSE *The Rose Bowl rarely hosts professional sports events, but will forever be remembered as the venue for the 1994 World Cup Final*

NATIONAL OLYMPIC STADIUM
TOKYO, JAPAN

Capacity: 62,000
Opened: 1972
Club: None
Hosted: 1979 World Youth Cup Final (Argentina 3, Soviet Union 1); World Club Cup finals (every year since 1980)

Soccer is the 1990s growth sport in Japan, and it was natural that the stadium built to host the 1964 Olympics should serve as the home of the national team and launch the successful professional J-League in 1993. Japan's appetite for big-time soccer was whetted in 1980 when Tokyo became the permanent home of the World Club Cup Final sponsored by Toyota. This previously two-leg affair between the European and South American Club Champions had become progressively discredited since its inception in 1960, often degenerating into violence. But the decision to change the format to a one-off game in front of an excitable but well-behaved Japanese crowd, beginning with Nacional of Uruguay's 1–0 defeat of Nottingham Forest in 1980, has transformed it into a popular fixture in the international calendar on the second Sunday each December. There is currently doubt about the stadium as a major venue following the Japanese bid to stage the 2002 World Cup. The capacity is well below the 80,000 required by FIFA, and the city of Tokyo and the Japanese government have yet to agree how a replacement venue should be funded. There is no room to expand the current stadium, and officials may decide to project the exciting new stadium in the port of Yokohama as a replacement to play prospective host to a Japanese World Cup Final in 2002.

GROWING PAINS *Surging crowds may make the Olympic stadium obsolete*

AZTECA
MEXICO CITY, MEXICO

Capacity: 110,000
Opened: 1960
Club: America (but others for big matches)
Hosted: 1968 Olympic Final (Hungary 4, Bulgaria 1); 1970 World Cup Final (Brazil 4, Italy 1); 1986 World Cup Final (Argentina 3, West Germany 2)

The Azteca, pride and joy of Mexican football, has been the venue for some of the most memorable World Cup matches in history. It is also one of the most enjoyable, passionate and colourful stadiums in which to watch a game since its lower tier is only thirty feet from the pitch, thus providing fans there with a sense of immediacy while those in the upper tier benefit from the steep, cliff-like design. The Azteca was the first stadium to have staged two World Cup Final matches and the 1970 tournament also produced an incredible semi-final between West Germany and Italy. The drama was won 4–3 by the talented Italians who were, in turn, swept aside 4–1 in the Final

PRIDE AND JOY *Azteca stadium, home of two World Cup Finals, and an amazing experience for spectators*

by a Brazilian side, rated as the finest to take the field in the history of the competition.

Some 16 years later Mexico stepped in at short notice to beat the United States and Canada to the right to host the finals after Colombia pulled out. Argentina, led by Diego Maradona at the height of his powers, lifted the crown for a second time against West Germany. The stadium, built on scrubland to the southwest of the sprawling mass which is Mexico City, required 100,000 tons of concrete, four times more than was used to build Wembley. It was planned for the 1968 Olympics and opened in June 1966 with a match betweeen Mexico and Turin, but the first major internationals came during the 1968 Games. Since then, America, Atlante, Necaxa and Cruz Azul have all used the the three-tiered Azteca for important games.

MARIO FILHO/MARACANA
RIO DE JANEIRO, BRAZIL

Capacity: 120,000
Opened: 1950
Clubs: Botofago, Vasco da Gama, Flamengo, Fluminense
Hosted: 1950 World Cup Final (Uruguay 2, Brazil 1); 1989 South American Championship

What Wembley is to the old world, the Maracana is to the new. This architectural marvel is the largest stadium in the world and the spiritual home to Brazil's second religion, football. However, it has spent much of the last few years out of commission while work has been carried out to renovate a bowl which had started, literally, to fall apart.

The Maracana, which quite simply takes its name from the little river that runs close by, was begun outside the city in 1948 in preparation for the 1950 World Cup, but was not completed until 1965. What has become Brazil's national stadium was originally intended to replace Vasco da Gama's club ground and was built and is still owned by the city, being formally named after the mayor, Mario Filho, who carried the project through. It was officially opened in June 1950 with a game beween Rio and São Paulo, the first goal being scored by Didi.

The first great matches were staged in the fourth World Cup, which culminated in the hosts losing to old rivals Uruguay before a world record crowd of 199,850. Like Hampden Park in Glasgow, the Maracana sets and holds attendance records. In 1963, 177,656 watched a league match between Flamengo and and Fluminense, a world club record attendance. Internationals have drawn crowds of 180,000, and league matches in the

1980s were watched regularly by 130,000. Santos even flew north to use Maracana for their World Club Cup Final ties against Benfica and Milan in 1962 and 1963.

The stadium is oval in shape and topped by a breathtaking cantilevered roof while a moat separates the fans from the pitch. Like Wembley and the Olympiastadion in Munich, the Maracana has become a major tourist attraction and is held in such esteem that several smaller versions have been built throughout Brazil. Next to the stadium is the Maracanazinho, a scaled down indoor version which stages boxing, tennis, festivals and concerts.

A FADING GIANT *The Maracana still conjures up magic visions*

MONUMENTAL
BUENOS AIRES, ARGENTINA

Capacity: 76,000
Opened: 1938
Club: River Plate
Hosted: 1978 World Cup Final (Argentina 3, Holland 1 aet); 1946, 1959 and 1987 South American Championships

There were many misgivings about holding the 1978 World Cup in Argentina, not the least of which concerned the political climate. Ultimately, the ruling military junta invested huge sums in the renovation of the Monumental, which had been the home of the national side and of one of the world's great clubs, River Plate.

A MONUMENTAL VICTORY *Home advantage told for Argentina in 1978*

Several of River's own players – skipper Daniel Passarella, goalkeeper Ubaldo Fillol and forwards Leopoldo Luque and Oscar Ortiz – featured in the side which defeated The Netherlands 3–1 in the Final amid a paper snowstorm which tumbled down their "own" Monumental. Work had begun on the Monumental on September 27, 1936 and it was ready for River to move in by May 1938. The dressing-rooms and offices were of a standard then unique in South America, while

the three-sided horseshoe boasted an original capacity of 100,000, with the potential of a third tier which would lift it to 150,000. Needless to say, it was never needed.

The opening game, a 3–1 win over the Uruguayan champions Penarol, was watched by a crowd of 70,000. But the stadium itself was not completed, even in its initial phase, until 1957, when River invested much of the world record fee of £97,000 they had received from Italy's Juventus for inside-forward Omar Sivori.

Apart from the 1978 World Cup, the Monumental has played host to many internationals and South American club ties, as well as key games when Argentina have taken their turn to host the Copa America (the South American Championship).

CENTENARIO
MONTEVIDEO, URUGUAY

Capacity: 76,609)
Opened: 1930
Clubs: Penarol, Nacional
Hosted: 1930 World Cup Final (Uruguay 4, Argentina 2); 1942, 1956, 1967, 1983 and 1995 South American Championships

The Centenario holds a special place in football history, having been the stage for the first World Cup Final in 1930 when Uruguay, then Olympic champions and enjoying their golden age in international football, defeated Argentina, their old rivals from across the River Plate, by 4–2 after being 2–1 down at half-time. But it was a close call for Montevideo's magnificent new stadium, which was being built especially for the fledgeling world championship and to celebrate one hundred

HISTORY MAKER *The Centenario staged the first World Cup Final*

years of the country's independence. Work continued throughout the first days of the tournament to have it ready for the Final.

It has since become the regular venue for internationals, the South American Championship (the world's longest running international competition since the demise of the British Home Championship in 1984), the World Club Championship, the South American club championship (Copa Libertadores), Supercopa and Recopa. Uruguay's most recent international

success came in the 1995 South American Championship, when Brazil were beaten on penalties in the Centenario after a 1–1 draw.

Football in Uruguay is really all about football in Montevideo and the Centenario is home to two of the leading clubs, Penarol and Nacional, who dominated the Copa Libertadores, in its early years. From 1960, when Penarol defeated Olimpia of Paraguay 1–0 in the Centenario and 2–1 on aggregate, they and Nacional were involved in 10 of the first 11 finals, and in 1968 the stadium was full to see Estudiantes beat Palmeiras 2–0 in a final play-off. Penarol entertained Real Madrid in the first World Club Championship in 1960, but were held to a goalless draw and lost 5–0 away. They took their revenge by beating Benfica the next season in a play-off, and Real, by 2–0 both home and away, in 1966.

MORUMBI
SÃO PAULO, BRAZIL

Capacity: 150,000
Opened: 1978
Clubs: São Paulo FC, Corinthians
Hosted: 1992 Copa Libertadores (South American club championship)

Final 2nd leg (São Paulo 1, Newells Old Boys 0: agg 2–1)

The rivalry between Rio de Janeiro and São Paulo provides much of the dynamic which fires domestic football within Brazil. Fans from the respective cities consider "their" state championships – the Carioca and the Paulista – as the best and most important, and fail to understand why

players from the other city should ever be preferred to any of their favourites for the national team.

They are equally partisan about their stadia. Just as Rio de Janeiro boasts the Maracana, so São Paulo football centres on the magnificent Morumbi. The name, in fact, is that of the local suburb of São Paulo, and the stadium is formally entitled the

Estadio Cicero Pompeu de Toledo – explaining, perhaps, why it is generally known by the much shorter name "barrio".

São Paulo FC and Corinthians both play all their big games in the Morumbi, though Corinthians did have to move out briefly for a South American club tie in 1993 when the date clashed with a pop concert.

THE BUSINESS OF FOOTBALL

Professional football is a multi-million pound business in which 22 highly-trained, highly-paid, highly-valued athletes chase a ball around a potentially priceless development site. But it wasn't always so. . .

England are European champions when it comes to developing soccer's commercial opportunities. The financial and promotion innovations of the early 1990s drew observers from almost all the top clubs in Europe – including the giants of Italy, Spain and Germany.

This was all the more remarkable considering the fact, in many ways, British football's administration at national and club level remained steeped in an amateur tradition which owed more to the 19th century than the rapidly-approaching 21st.

Since organized football began in Britain in the middle of the nineteenth-century, the main source of income has come from gate receipts. From the 1970s on, however, other sources of revenue opened up. Advertising, sponsorship, and money paid by television companies to televise football grew in importance.

Gate money, although providing an ever-reducing percentage of overall income, remained the foundation of the average professional football club's balance sheet even after the advent of the Premier League.

BOOM TIME *Arsenal vs. Sunderland in 1937 attracted a massive crowd*

THE CLUBS

In 1991 Manchester United – one of the most famous clubs in world football – were floated on the London Stock Exchange. Net assets were estimated at £39.9 million, with each share offered at £3.85 with a guaranteed first dividend of 17.4 pence per share in the first year. All this is a far cry from the way United, in common with the rest of British football, used to be run. By 1991 gate receipts accounted for less than half United's income, with television, sponsorship, advertising and cater-

ing tipping the balance. This is a situation which is now becoming more and more common in world football.

One of the main sources of new revenue is sponsorship. Between 1976 and 1990 the sponsorship money spent in Britain rocketed from £2 million to £230 million. The High Street bank, Barclays, paid £11.5 million for the right to sponsor the Football League for six years from 1987; and brewers Bass took up sponsorship of the FA Premier League in 1993 – through its Carling brand – at a cost of £12 million over four years, to add to its patronage of the Scottish League and the Charity Shield. The attractions for the sponsors are obvious. Football is a huge market-place attracting all socio-economic groups. TV coverage provides nation-wide exposure, encourages brand loyalty and is a form of covert advertising.

Licensing the logos of clubs, national teams and competitions is another moneyspinner. The Football Association estimates that licens-

KITTED UP *England's strip 1993-style*

ON THE FRINGE *Perimeter advertising seen here at a ground during the 1993–94 European Champions League has become a lucrative business*

ing the logos of the England national team and the FA Cup alone could generate £25 million for the game. To this end, Littlewoods (the football pools company) became the first – discreet – FA Cup sponsors in 1994.

Merchandising is also an area of expansion – and controversy. Clubs have, for years, sold replica kits, but in recent times there has been an explosion of "official" club memorabilia. Tottenham Hotspur produce a lavish catalogue containing hundreds of items ranging from pens to pillow cases. But kit sales have attracted the most controversy. Many clubs have been accused of ripping off younger fans by constantly changing the design of their kit, knowing that fans will always want to wear the latest style. With junior kits costing anything up to £60, and with many clubs now having three kits – Manchester United in 1993–94 had four – there was a growing feeling that clubs were taking financial advantage of the loyalty of their supporters.

In the spring of 1994 Manchester United signed what was then the most lucrative kit deal in British football. The four-year deal negotiated with manufacturers Umbro guaranteed United £25 million, eclipsing the previous record – Umbro's £16 million four-year package with the England team.

Britain's pools companies also provide valuable income for the game, but without having any direct influence on it. It is thanks to the monies generated from pools revenue and channelled through the Football Trust that clubs have been able to meet the capital costs incurred by redeveloping their grounds in the wake of the Taylor Report into the Hillsborough disaster.

More than 30 years earlier, the advent of floodlighting in the early 1950s had opened up another, perhaps less obvious, route to riches. The ability to play matches under lights in the evenings brought in mid-

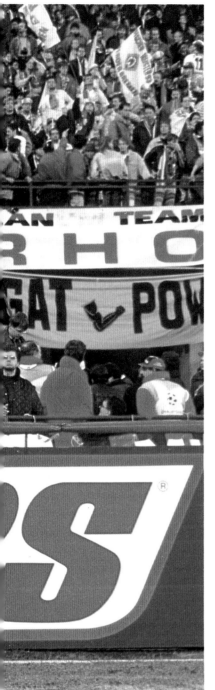

week European competitive football and the switching of Football League Cup and even international matches from the weekend to midweek. Thus clubs – and national teams – were able to lure the paying public to more matches . . . and bind them still further and deeper into the commercial fabric of the game.

Closely allied to the development of sponsorship is advertising. Important income for many clubs comes from advertising on stadium perimeter boards around their pitches.

CHAMPIONS LEAGUE

The importance of and correlation between sponsorship, advertising and television is clearly displayed in the thinking behind the UEFA Champions League. By binding all three together to create a high-prestige "product", UEFA has effectively driven the cost of sponsorship up.

Originally, the Champions League had four sponsors who were guaranteed sole category rights covering all advertising within the stadia. Clubs taking part were not even allowed to display the name of their own domestic sponsors on their shirts – but that lasted two seasons. Nevertheless UEFA's thinking, it seems, is that exclusivity equals maximum returns.

The 1995–96 Champions League involved an entry of 24 clubs with the overspill of league title-winners being diverted into the UEFA Cup preliminaries. Further amendments were made for 1997–98 with the controversial decision to admit the eight runners-up from the domestic championship of Europe's top eight nations. That meant expanding the mini-league section to six groups of four teams with the group winners and two "best" runners-up entering the traditional knock-out quarter-finals.

Clubs reaching the closing stages can earn £10million-plus from UEFA's appearance money and performance bonuses plus their own gate and catering revenues. No wonder Europe's big clubs all want a slice of the action and have pushed the creation of a European super league close to the top of UEFA's agenda.

Average European Top Division League Attendances (to 1 January 1994)

Country	Average attendance
Belgium	8,147
England	21,125
France	14,062
Germany	27,041
Holland	9,698
Italy	31,118
Portugal	16,884
Spain	24,331

THE PLAYERS

December 15, 1995, will go down in football history as the day the sky fell in on more than a century of financial and contractual tradition. That was the day when the European Court of Justice in Luxembourg ruled in favour of a restraint of trade complaint brought against the football authorities by Jean-Marc Bosman.

An ordinary, lower-division professional, Bosman had battled through the national and international courts after being denied the right to transfer from Belgian club FC Liege to French club Dunkerque.

The European Court ruled, after an exhausting five-year fight which cost Bosman not only his career, but his savings and his marriage too, that football's traditional transfer system and foreign player restrictions were illegal. It decreed that players whose contracts have expired are free to move to a club in another country without a transfer fee being due. It also ruled that no European Union country could restrict the number of EU citizens in any one team, on the grounds that this was a restraint of trade prohibited by the Treaty of Rome.

The judgement affected specifically only the 15 countries of the European Union. But since that means almost all western Europe (excluding Switzerland) it also meant the financial heart of the international game and thus football throughout the world. UEFA was virtually paralysed by shock and it was the national associations of western Europe, rather than their governing body, which initiated steps to resolve the immediate crisis.

Most quickly scrapped all restrictions on foreign players, or at least, those from other EU countries. Several – such as Holland, Germany and Italy – went further and extended the 'free transfer' concept for out-of-contract players into their domestic systems. Until then, players had been little more than personified banknotes in the game's financial structure.

A football club's most versatile and liquid assets are the players. For clubs everywhere, particularly those in the lower divisions, selling their best players to clubs further up the League is often the key to survival. One big sale can bring in more money than a season's gate receipts and help keep a struggling club afloat for another season.

The Bosman Judgement caused international consternation because it threatened the "trickle-down" financial value to minnow clubs of the transfer market, it wiped millions of pounds of playing assets off clubs' balance sheets, it opened up the prospect of the richest clubs buying perpetual control of competitive success ... and it handed the top players the prospect of becoming multimillionaires, comparable to the superstars of American team sports, gridiron football, baseball and basketball.

But one basic value the Bosman Judgement could not undermine was the very existence of the transfer market.

For the clubs at the top end of the league, the need – some would say pressure – to buy players is twofold. First, clubs must have the best players available if they are to compete for survival in the FA Premiership – the top priority – and then for the prizes. Secondly, many clubs feel obliged to make big-name, big-money purchases during the summer months to help boost season ticket sales and

191

maintain interest in the team. There are, after all, only three domestic trophies to be won, and with 20 teams in the Premiership, 17 are bound to go empty-handed each season – 18 if two trophies are won by the same club, as happened in 1993 when Arsenal won the FA Cup and the Coca-Cola-sponsored League Cup, and 1994, when Manchester United won the Premiership and the FA Cup. There are other, less obvious reasons for buying players. For example, if a club is coming to the end of its financial year and has too much cash sitting in the bank, the directors may well buy to reduce the tax liabilities.

Given that players are the most valuable asset, it follows that they are likely to be highly rewarded for agreeing to sign for a new club. A new player can add thousands to attendances and, with so many clubs competing for relatively few top-class players, transfer fees, signing-on fees and wages have spiralled much faster than the rate of inflation.

In Britain in the mid-1990s, the average weekly wage for a player in the Premiership was £3,000. In the First Division, the figure falls to £910; in the Second Division it is £456; in the Third Division £330. For those players at the top of their profession, the rewards are immense.

When Eric Cantona was on his best behaviour at Manchester United he was reputed to earn more than £10,000 a week. Even this seemingly unjustifiable wage is paltry compared with what players may earn in Italy. England's Paul Gascoigne was signed by Lazio in 1992 to a contract worth £18,000 a week; David Platt earned even more on transferring to Sampdoria in the summer of 1993; and Des Walker's season with Sampdoria in 1992–93 earned him a staggering £28,000 a week.

Even these vast figures pale into insignificance, however, when compared with the monumental sums lavished on top sportsmen in America. At his peak, Michael Jordan, of the Chicago Bulls basketball team, earned an estimated £24 million ... £461,000 a week!

The wage gap between the Premiership and the First Division is widening – partly owing to Sky TV's

	Amount £	Player	Clubs involved	Year
WORLD RECORD TRANSFERS	1,000	Alf Common	Sunderland to Middlesbrough	1905
	10,890	David Jack	Bolton to Arsenal	1929
	23,000	Bernabe Ferreyra	Tigre BA to River Plate	1932
	52,000	Hans Jeppson	(amateur) to Napoli	1952
	72,000	Juan Alberto Schiaffino	Penarol to Milan	1954
	93,000	Enrique Omar Sivori	River Plate to Juventus	1957
	142,000	Luis Suarez	Barcelona to Internazionale	1961
	250,000	Angelo Sormani	Mantova to Roma	1963
	500,000	Pietro Anastasi	Varese to Juventus	1968
	922,000	Johan Cruyff	Ajax Amsterdam to Barcelona	1973
	1.20m	Giuseppe Savoldi	Bologna to Napoli	1975
	1.75m	Paolo Rossi	Juventus to L R Vicenza	1978
	3.00m	Diego Maradona	Boca Juniors to Barcelona	1982
	5.00m	Diego Maradona	Barcelona to Napoli	1984
	6.00m	Ruud Gullit	PSV Eindhoven to Milan	1987
	8.00m	Roberto Baggio	Fiorentina to Juventus	1990
	10.00m	Jean-Pierre Papin	Marseille to Milan	1992
	12.00m	Gianluca Vialli	Sampdoria to Juventus	1992
	13.00m	Gianluigi Lentini	Torino to Milan	1992
	15.00m	Alan Shearer	Blackburn Rovers to Newcastle United	1996
	20.00m*	Ronaldo	Barcelona to Internazionale	1997

* Transfer fee subject to ratification by FIFA Players' Committee

£304 million, five-year deal with the Premiership – and this in itself causes problems. Some reserves would rather be highly paid in the Premiership than move down to the First Division, where regular football would be accompanied by a wage cut. This denies other clubs and their supporters a "dead" pool of talent.

Another reason for the increase in players' wages, particularly in the top two divisions, is the activity of agents playing clubs in search of the most lucrative deals.

Arguments for and against agents raged for many years. Yet even the Football Association employed agents such as Harry Swales and then Jon Smith to try to ensure that the rulers of the domestic game were not trapped in a commercial minefield. In 1995 FIFA finally launched a system by which agents could be licensed for work in the transfer market and in match arrangement. Until Bosman, the English transfer market of the 1990s had turned over players to a value per season of up to £100 million. It was remarkably good business in a time of recession.

During the 1992–93 season in England £80 million changed hands in transfer fees, all during a time of

SIGNING ON *Roy Keane puts pen to Manchester United paper*

recession. The "Big Five" clubs, Manchester United, Liverpool, Everton, Tottenham and Arsenal, are traditionally the "buying" clubs of English football. They have, however, been joined in recent seasons by clubs with wealthy benefactors, such as Blackburn Rovers, Newcastle United, Wolverhampton Wanderers and Derby County.

Blackburn's involvement in the transfer market has been expensive, effective and dramatic. With the backing of steel multi-millionaire Jack Walker, then manager Kenny Dalglish spent more than £20 million in taking the side from the First Division to the Premiership and then European football.But Blackburn had broken the British record for a transfer in July 1994 when they paid £3.6 million to Norwich City for striker Chris Sutton.

A similar path was followed by Newcastle who, financially underpinned by entrepreneur Sir John Hall, splashed ever more dizzy sums on the likes of England striker Alan Shearer and controversial Colombian, Faustino Asprilla.

With more and more clubs competing for the top players, and, crucially, more of them able to afford such huge transfer fees and wages, the price of a top player has continued to rise. In 1993 Rangers broke the British transfer record by paying £4 million to Dundee United for forward Duncan Ferguson, and Manchester United set another English record, in January 1995, with their £7 million signing of Newcastle United's Andy Cole.

Newcastle's world record £15 million signing of Shearer from Blackburn Rovers in the summer of 1996 may prove the high watermark of British transfer dealing now that the Bosman Judgement has significantly questioned the asset-value of each and every contracted player. The way ahead for the clubs is the introduction of long-term contracts – a trend set by Ajax Amsterdam when they signed Peter Hoekstra of PSV Eindhoven to an eight-year deal in the spring of 1996.

But the players – and their agents – will demand a very high price, indeed.

POLITICS

KING OF THE HILL *FIFA's Brazilian President Joao Havelenge*

From its humble beginnings at London's Freemasons Tavern in 1863, Association Football has developed into a truly global game. Almost every country on earth plays the game and its smooth running requires the authority of an international body. This has been provided since 1904 by the Fédération Internationale de Football Association, or FIFA for short.

In that year, representatives from France, Belgium, Holland, Denmark, Switzerland, Sweden and Spain met in Paris to discuss the possibility of founding an international governing body. An initial setback was the refusal of the four British associations to join, but by 1910 all four had entered the fold. In 1920, however, they withdrew, and, having rejoined four years later, they with-

drew again in 1928 over the broken-time (amateurism) dispute which arose during the 1928 Amsterdam

NO MORE MR MARSEILLE *Bernard Tapie*

Olympics. The British associations stayed out for nearly twenty years, thus denying themselves the chance to enter the World Cup until after the Second World War.

Membership of FIFA is restricted solely to national associations, one per country, and these associations must represent either a sovereign nation, a dominion or a protectorate. Each national association has one vote at the FIFA Congress held every two years. FIFA is responsible for reviewing the Laws of the Game, organizing and administering world competitions, regulating the international movement of players, administering standards for referees, co-ordinating developments in sports medicine, settling disputes over amateurism and professionalism, aiding in the development of soccer in underdeveloped countries, disciplining clubs or individuals in violation of the regulations and managing the game's finances.

Disputes between countries are supposed to be resolved internally and without bias. The essential aim of the organization is to promote the good of the game as a whole, rather than the interests of one member over another. Although FIFA may occasionally seem to lean in one ideological direction or another, it strives to maintain the integrity of its statutes, and succeeds, for the most part, in remaining politically neutral.

In 1953, to further assist the administration and organization of a growing sport, FIFA authorized the formation of continental confederations. Europe and Asia established confederations in 1954, Africa in 1956, North and Central America in 1961, and Oceania in 1966. The South American confederation, founded in 1916, also became an affiliate of FIFA. The six continental confederations – UEFA (Europe), AFC (Asia), CAF (Africa), CONCACAF (North/Central America and the Caribbean), OFC (Oceania) and CONMEBOL (South America) – are affiliated to FIFA, and each in turn controls its own geographic region. Meanwhile the national associations in each continent are affiliated to their respective confederations, and the various national and regional leagues are in turn affiliated

THE MEDIA

to the national associations. In this way, every football club in the world has access to FIFA through its league, national association and continental confederation.

From its modern headquarters overlooking Lake Zurich, FIFA controls everything in world soccer. Its statutes give it wide enforcement powers over 200 million players and more than one million teams worldwide. Recent crackdowns on doping and match-fixing serve to demonstrate the wide-ranging power within FIFA's mandate.

FIFA are not afraid to flex their muscles. After Marseilles's 1993 European Champions Cup was tainted by match fixing allegations, FIFA forced its European affiliate, UEFA, to take sanctions against the French club even before a trial had been held. And when the club's owner – Bernard Tapie – threatened his own legal action, FIFA threatened to ban France from all competitions, so he was forced to back down.

Above all, FIFA's control of participation in the game's golden egg, the World Cup, provides it with the ultimate weapon for bringing wayward parties to heel. Chile were expelled from the 1990 World Cup when their goalkeeper Roberto Rojas faked an injury, claiming it came from a fire-cracker thrown from the crowd, and the team, losing to Brazil in a qualifying match, walked off.

Joao Havelange of Brazil, who secured the FIFA presidency at the expense of England's incumbent Sir Stanley Rous in 1974, proved a pragmatic visionary, and has done much to spread the global commercialization of the game – not least by his politically-inspired expansions of the World Cup finals from 16 teams to 24 in 1982 and now to 32 in 1998.

Not that Havelange has been without critics. European football leaders became increasingly disturbed by what they considered Havelange's autocratic approach. In 1995, under the leadership of UEFA president Lennart Johansson, they began to agitate for changes in both FIFA's political structure and handling of World Cup finances.

MILAN MAN *Silvio Berlusconi*

The success of football around the world has generated massive interest in the professional game, a fact not lost on the world's media, which eagerly exploits the sport. The relationship, generally, is mutually beneficial, and in the case of television, particularly, the direct financial benefits are obvious. But while television could survive without soccer, it is becoming increasingly true that soccer in many countries could not survive without television and its huge investment in the game. The dangerous day ahead is the one on which TV moguls discover superior weapons in the ratings war.

To understand the relationship, it is necessary first to understand why television is so keen to show football. The entertainment value of football is not consistently high enough to merit its purchase alone, although televised football in Europe does attract large audiences. To the TV companies, the value of televised football comes not from the game itself, but from the access it provides advertisers to those who follow it. In televising football, they are not so much paying for the right to show the match, as they are buying the right to sell advertising space

during it. Football fans, and by logical extension, those who watch football on TV, are generally young males, with high disposable incomes. What better time, then, to advertise products such as cars, toiletries, hi-fi, alcohol and financial services than during a football match on TV?

Perhaps the best example of this intertwining of football and television comes from Italy. Silvio Berlusconi is owner of the Fininvest group which owns, among many other things, Milan football club, a string of local commercial TV stations including the flagship Canale 5, a supermarket chain and dozens of other non-related companies. Berlusconi has pumped millions of pounds into Milan to make them the best club side in Europe, if not the world. And, by showing football on his various TV channels, Berlusconi has a captive audience at which to aim his advertisements. It would seem to be the perfect relationship. Not only that, but Berlusconi hijacked Italy's football slogan – Forza Italia – for his political party when he won the General Election in March, 1994.

Press coverage of football varies. Italy, France, Portugal, Spain, Hungary, Poland, Slovakia, Romania and Bulgaria all sustain at least one daily sports newspaper. Yet Britain, such a sports-loving nation, is unable to do so. Or rather, it does not need to. In Britain the national press has always given far greater priority to football coverage than "general" daily newspapers on the continent – thus removing the need for a sports daily. Indeed the importance of football to the British newspaper industry can be gauged from the fact that the now-defunct *Today* newspaper sponsored the Football League during the 1986–87 season.

In Europe the situation is different, creating a need for daily newspapers such as the seven-day-a-week *Gazzetta dello Sport*, *Tuttosport* and *Corriere dello Sport/Stadio* (Italy), *A*

Bola (Portugal), *Marca* and *Mundo Deportivo* (Spain) and *L'Equipe* (France). These football papers devote wide coverage to the game and feature in-depth investigations, interviews and opinion as well as results and statistics. Britain does have many weekly and monthly football magazines, but a majority are aimed at the younger reader and are often little more than glorified posters. In Europe, football magazines tend to be aimed at older teenagers and adults, and there can be little doubt that *France Football*, *Kicker* (Germany), *Voetbal International* (Holland) and *Guerin Sportivo* (Italy) are "serious" football magazines.

Football is, it seems, an endless source of fascination to book publishers. Every year hundreds of football books are published worldwide, covering every conceivable angle. Many are straightforward statistical logs and yearbooks; others explore the wider influences of football on society. Britain has a tradition for the "kick and tell" book in which a famous player tells his life/career story in autobiographical terms with the help of a friendly journalist, who acts as "ghost" writer. Such books would not, generally, be commercially viable without a few controversial chapters which can be sold for serialization in one of the popular (usually Sunday) newspapers for a fee which helps to underwrite the book publisher's capital costs.

Radio has an important role to play too. In Britain, for example, BBC Radio 5 Live broadcasts live match commentaries as often as possible. The station also provides regular news bulletins and score checks – its output and style having been revolutionized in the 1990s to compete with the plethora of commercial local radio stations which have sprung up around the country.

Managers and players can be notoriously sensitive to bad publicity. But, in commercial terms, no general business, no single company could afford to buy the acres of print and technological space being filled hour by hour, day by day, by football. All free publicity. The media, as ever, will always have the last word.

EXCLUSIVELY LIVE *Sky Sports' slogan for their coverage of top-flight English soccer*

THE LAWS AND TACTICS

The first Laws of football were drawn up at Cambridge University in 1848, since when they have been considerably rewritten and amended. As the game changed, so tactics, too, have developed as teams try to outwit each other with bolts, liberos, 4–4–2 and the like.

THE LAWS OF FOOTBALL

The Laws (not the rules) of football have been honed down to 17 in number, with numerous sub-clauses. This evolutionary process began in the mid-nineteenth century and continued through to the 1930s, when Stanley Rous recodified the Laws. Recently the Laws were redrafted by FIFA. Law changes are made by the International Board, made up of eight members, four of them from the Home Countries of England, Scotland, Wales and Northern Ireland, and four from FIFA. It takes a three-quarter majority to alter a Law.

What follows is a summary of the Laws, as published by FIFA, simplified for general use.

THE OBJECT OF THE GAME

The game is played by two teams, each consisting of 11 players, one of whom must be a goalkeeper. The goalkeeper must wear clothing that distinguishes him from his team-mates and does not clash with the colours worn by his opponents or the referee. Substitutes are allowed to each team, but once a player has been replaced that player may not re-enter the game. Each competition has its own rules which dictate how many substitutes per side are permitted. In international soccer it is now usually three, selected from seven named before the match, but this does vary. Most domestic competitions allow either two or three, the third being a goalkeeper, all of whom have to be named beforehand.

On the pitch the game is regulated in senior football by a referee and two linesmen, whereas in junior football it is permitted simply to have a referee.

The object of the game is to propel a ball by foot or any part of the body other than the hands or arms into your opponents' goal. At each end of the field there is a goal consisting of two uprights placed eight yards (7.32m) apart (the inside measurement between the two posts), and joined at the top by a cross-bar eight feet in height (2.44m to the lower part of the bar) above the ground. The uprights and cross-bars should not exceed five inches (0.12m) in width and must be the same width. Normally these are made of wood or tubular steel. In senior football a net is is attached to the uprights and cross-bar or free-standing supports, to indicate clearly when a goal has been scored.

THE FIELD OF PLAY

The game is played on a pitch the surface of which is usually grass, although some competitions allow artificial surfaces of different types. The field of play is rectangular and measures between 100 to 130 yards (90–120m) in length and 50 to 100 yards (45–90m) in width. Under no circumstances can the pitch be square. The field of play is bounded by painted lines. Those down the longer side are known as the touch-lines, and those across the shorter side, on which the goals are positioned, as the goal-lines. All such boundary lines and other pitch markings, which should be no more than five inches (0.12m) wide, form part of the field of play.

Other pitch markings consist of a centre-line drawn across the pitch at a point midway between the two goal-lines. In the middle of this is

THE FIELD OF PLAY *The dimensions and appurtenances of a soccer field*

CORNER FLAG

CORNER FLAG

MAXIMUM 100 YDS   MINIMUM 50 YDS

6 YDS

8 YDS

20 YDS

44 YDS

TOUCH LINE

MINIMUM 100 YDS

MAXIMUM 130 YDS

10 YDS

HALFWAY LINE

OPTIONAL FLAGSTAFF

OPTIONAL FLAGSTAFF

CENTRE CIRCLE

TOUCH LINE

10 YDS

PENALTY AREA

PENALTY MARK

18 YDS

6 YDS

GOAL AREA

12 YDS

1 YD

GOAL LINE

CORNER FLAG

8 YDS   18 YDS

CORNER FLAG

placed a centre spot, from which play commences at the start of each half and after a goal is scored. A circle is drawn, with a ten-yard (9.15m) radius from the centre spot, within which no opponent is allowed to encroach until the ball is kicked into play. In each corner of the field, where the goal-line and touch-line meet, is a corner flag with a minimum height of five feet (1.5m). A quadrant with a one-yard (1m) radius is drawn at each corner of the field. As an optional extra, flags may be placed opposite the centre-line but must be at least one yard (1m) behind the touch-lines.

The goals are placed at the centre of each goal-line, and two lines are drawn at right angles to the goal-line six yards (5.5m) from the goal-posts. They extend into the field of play for a distance of six yards (5.5m) and are joined by a line of 20 yards (18.3m) parallel to the goal-line. This section defines the goal area. The goal area is enclosed within the larger penalty area, which is created by drawing two lines at right angles to the goal-line, 18 yards (16.5m) from each goal-post, which extend into the field of play a distance of 18 yards (16.5m) and are joined by a line of 44

yards (40.3m) parallel to the goal-line.

The penalty mark from where penalty kicks must be taken is marked twelve yards (11m) from the goal-line and facing the mid point of the goal. The Laws decree that there must be no encroachment when a penalty kick is taken. In order to ensure that all players apart from the kicker stand 10 yards (9.15m) from the ball until such a kick is taken, an arc with a radius of ten yards (9.15m), using the penalty spot as its centre, is drawn outside the penalty area, and the players must stand outisde the penalty area and outside this arc.

The game is played with a ball which must be round and made of leather or any other approved material, its circumference being between 27 and 28 inches (0.68–0.71m) and its weight between 14 and 16 ounces (396–453gm).

The object of the game is to score more goals than the opposition. In order to score a goal the whole of the ball must pass between the goal posts, under the cross-bar and across the goal-line. The whole of the ball must cross the whole of the line. If no goals are scored, or the teams have an equal number of goals, the match is termed a draw.

THE PENALTY KICK

This is for the serious offences mentioned. Taken from the penalty mark, it can be awarded irrespective of where the ball is at the time the offence is committed, provided that the ball is in play and the offence takes place in the penalty area. A goal may be scored directly from a penalty and the only players allowed in the penalty area until the ball has been kicked are the one taking the kick and the goalkeeper. If either team infringes these regulations, the kick will be retaken, except in the case of an infringement by the defending team where a goal has been scored. In that event the goal will normally be awarded, because to do otherwise would be to allow the offending team to gain an advantage from the infringement.

Examples of when a retake is ordered are: where the goalkeeper saves the ball or the kick is missed, but the goalkeeper moved forward from goal-line before the kick was taken or there is encroachment by the defending side; where a goal is scored and there is encroachment by the attacking side; and, finally, where the kick is taken, whether or not a goal is scored, and there is encroachment by both sides. A match shall be extended at half-time or full-time to allow the penalty kick to be taken or retaken, but the extension shall last only until the moment that the penalty kick has been completed, whether it results in a goal, a miss or a save. Different rules apply in cup competitions when the teams are level at full-time and the game is to be decided by the taking of an initial five penalties by each side.

THE DURATION OF PLAY

The match starts with a kick-off, with the ball placed on the centre spot and kicked forward by one of the attackers. Prior to that, the captains of the two teams meet the referee to spin a coin for choice of ends or kick-off. The winning captain generally makes the election for the first half, since the teams change ends to start the second half. The ball is in play once it has travelled its own circumference in the opponents' half of the pitch. The player taking the kick-off may not play the ball again until it has been touched by another player.

Play is divided into two equal halves, and in senior football a half lasts 45 minutes (although this can be reduced either by the rules of the competition or by agreement between the teams), and there is a half-time interval lasting a minimum of five minutes.

To decide cup matches which are drawn after 90 minutes, extra time, usually of 15 minutes each way, is played. Some competitions allow for a penalty kick decider to occur to ascertain the winner. A 'sudden death' system in extra-time, with the first goal deciding the outcome, will be used in the finals of the 1996 European Championship and 1998 World Cup.

EQUIPMENT

A player's equipment consists of a jersey or shirt, shorts, socks, shin-guards and footwear. The teams must wear colours that do not clash with each other or the referee. A player shall not wear anything that is dangerous to another player.

IN PLAY AND OUT OF PLAY

The ball is in play at all times from the start of the match to the finish, including where an infringement of the Laws occurs (until a decision is given and the game is stopped by the referee). It is still in play when it rebounds inside the boundaries of the field from a goal-post, cross-bar or cor-

ner flag. The ball only goes out of play when it wholly crosses the boundaries of the field, whether on the ground or in the air.

When the ball leaves the field of play over the touch-line it re-enters the field by means of a throw-in. The throw is taken by a member of the team opposing that of the player who put it out of play. The throw must be taken from as close as possible to the point at which the ball left the field. If not taken from there it is described as a foul throw and the throw-in given to the other team. The thrower takes the ball in both hands and throws it from behind and over his head. He must face the pitch with both feet on the ground on or behind the touchline at the moment he delivers the throw.

When the ball leaves the field of play over the goal-line it is returned into play either by means of a goal-kick, if last touched by an attacker, or a corner kick, if last touched by a defender. At a goal-kick the defending side (usually the goalkeeper) restarts the game by kicking the ball from either half of his goal area, and the ball is not deemed to be in play until it has passed out of the penalty area. Any infringement of this procedure results in the kick being retaken.

At a corner-kick the ball is played from the quadrant, which is a quarter circle with a radius of one yard (1m) situated in the corner of the field. The ball must be within the quadrant, and the kick must be taken at the end of the defending side's goal-line nearest to where the ball went out of play. Again the player taking the corner-kick may not play the ball a second time until it has been touched by another player, and defenders must remain at a distance of ten yards (9.15m) until the ball has been kicked.

Where there is no other method of restarting the game, following an injury, interference by spectators or for any other accidental reason, the restart is achieved by dropping the ball at the point where it was when play was suspended. The ball is deemed to be in play the moment it touches the ground, and no player may kick or attempt to kick the ball until that moment. In the event of a breach of this procedure the drop is retaken.

OFFSIDE

Arguably the most complex of the 17 Laws is Law 11, relating to "offside". Even the wording is difficult, which pronounces that "a player is offside if he is nearer his opponents' goal-line than the ball and interfering with play or an opponent at the moment the ball is last played unless . . ." Then follow four exceptions: (1) from restarts, namely goal-kicks, corner-kicks and throw-ins, but not free-kicks; (2) if a player is in his own half of the field; (3) if the ball was last played to him by an opponent; (4) if he is not nearer to the goal-line than at least two defenders, even if one is the goalkeeper.

In these cases he is not offside. The main problems come in deciding when the ball was last "played", and whether or not an attacker is "interfering". If the referee considers that an attacking player, albeit in an "offside position", is not interfering with play or with an opponent or seeking to gain an advantage by being in that offside position, he shall refrain from penalizing him and stopping play. A player who is level with the penultimate defender is not in an offside position. In such cases, the attacking player must be given the benefit of any doubt. A player cannot be offside if he is behind the ball when it is played, even if there are no defenders between him and the goal.

INFRINGEMENTS OF THE LAWS

As football is a physical contact sport, infringements of the Laws will inevitably occur, giving rise to punishment by the referee in the form of "free-kicks". These free-kicks may be either "direct" or "indirect". The difference is that a goal may be scored directly from a direct free-kick but not from an indirect free-kick. At an indirect free-kick a second player must play the ball after the kicker before a goal can be scored.

A direct free-kick is awarded for more serious offences, and if these occur in the penalty area a penalty is awarded. All free-kicks (except penalties) are taken from the place

SEEING RED *Jonas Thern is sent off during Sweden's 1994 World Cup semi-final defeat by Brazil*

EQUIPMENT

When football first took root in England during the 1870s, it was a game for the upper classes, played by gentlemen to a strict amateur code. Early photographs of teams such as Old Harrovians and Hampstead Heathens show players dressed more like Little Lord Fauntleroy than serious sportsmen. But with the advent of professionalism a decade or so later, working-

class teams from the north of England soon started to dominate the game, bringing with them a demand for cheap, basic clothing. Even in today's highly commercialized game, a complete football strip remains relatively inexpensive when compared to other sports, explaining the huge appeal and rapid growth of football in Third World countries.

Today, well over a hundred years after the beginning of professional football, many aspects of the football kit still look remarkably familiar in basic design. The materials may have changed, but the function remains the same — as the following pages will demonstrate.

1994

The shirt worn by modern Swedish internationals demonstrates the influence of commercialism on design. The three stripes have little to do with aesthetics, nothing to do with tradition and everything to do with the manufacturers' branding.

One of football's greatest appeals is its simplicity. Law IV of the Laws of the Game merely states: "the basic compulsory equipment of a player shall consist of a jersey or shirt, shorts, stockings, shinguards and footwear. A player shall not wear anything which is dangerous to another player. The goalkeeper shall wear colours which will distinguish him from the other players and the referee."

1909

The first football shirts were made of thick wool, but cotton soon proved to be cheaper and more practical. This shirt, worn by Manchester United right-back George Stacey in the FA Cup Final, shows the original lace-up collar design which briefly resurfaced in recent seasons.

1911

Two years on and buttons have replaced laces in this England trialist's shirt. The original England kit for the 1872 game against Scotland was white jerseys, dark blue caps and white knickerbockers.

1948

The shirt worn by Charlie Mitten for Manchester United against Blackpool in the FA Cup Final bears a remarkable resemblance to modern day rugby shirts, with thick cuffs and button-up collars.

1960

Thick woollen goalkeeper's jersey as worn by Dominguez of Real Madrid. It wasn't until 1913 that goalkeepers had to wear distinctive colours. Until then they wore the same shirt as their teammates and were distinguished by a cap.

1982

The development of synthetics from the 1960s signalled the end of cotton. This Brazilian shirt of light nylon is specially designed for maximum ventilation to cope with the heat and altitude of South American football.

1992

Multi-coloured, synthetic goalkeeper's shirt, worn by Denmark's Peter Schmeichel in the 1992 European Championship Final. Less than ten years previously the rules stated that goalkeepers could wear only green, yellow or white. How times change!

Equipment

1958

(Top right) *The arrival of the modern football boot. Superior quality leather was used in a design cut under the ankles in these boots belonging to Manchester United's David Pegg. The specially designed leather soles allowed for screw-in moulded nylon studs.*

1936

(Below) *Arsenal socks, made of thick wool and weighing a couple of pounds each when wet! During the Second World War, in Britain such items of football equipment were available only with clothing coupons allocated by the Board of Trade.*

1994

(Bottom right) *Millions are spent on the research and manufacture of boots, and the results are plain to see. Today's top quality boots are usually made of kangaroo leather with aluminium studs and moulded plastic soles.*

The changing face of football is demonstrated by the way boots have developed. Manufacturing is now a huge industry, generating millions of pounds on the back of improved scientific and technical developments.

1936
Leather shinpads with wool lining. Invented in the 1880s, they were originally worn over the socks.

1972
Stylo Matchmaker boots as worn by George Best. Possibly seeking to reflect the image of the wearer rather than provide solid protection, these look more like a pair of slippers than football boots.

1930
Ankle-length boot. Nineteenth century footballers nailed studs into their ordinary working boots for matches.

1936
Stud-making kit. Using the hand stamp, three circles were removed from a 5 mm thick strip of leather and nailed together to make one stud.

209

Even ordinary items like footballs and goalkeeper's gloves have changed over the years. Medals and caps change, too, though only the lucky few who win them would know...

1992
Modern day goalkeeper's gloves. Like so many other areas of football kit, these now represent a lucrative market for the manufacturers. Until the mid-1970s, keepers were more than happy with simple cotton gloves.

1968
Captain's armband, as worn by Manchester United's Bobby Charlton during his side's European Cup campaign. They were once worn only in European ties to help the referees identify captains.

1990
Official World Cup ball. Modern balls actually weigh an ounce more than pre-War footballs but seem lighter due to the plastic coating and superior manufacturing techniques that mean virtually no water retention.

1948
FA Cup Final ball with laces. During the previous two finals the ball had burst due to the inferior quality leather that was used shortly after the Second World War.

1961

This cap was won by Dennis Viollet, in a 4–1 victory.

1963

A pennant presented to Manchester United in a friendly played at Old Trafford. It is customary for teams to exchange favours before international matches.

1930

FA Cup winner's medal, won by Arsenal's Jack Lambert in the 2–0 defeat of Huddersfield Town.

1913

One of the seven England caps awarded to Manchester United's George Wall. This earlier cap is a different colour and lacks the embroidery and tassel.

1958

Although the white ball had come into official use in 1951, the brown ball continued to dominate for another 20 years. The lacing had now been replaced by stitched panels, saving dedicated headers of the ball too many headaches.

1931

Championship winners' medal awarded to Arsenal forward Jack Lambert. Players no longer have to appear in a specific number of games to win one.

SOCCER CULTURE

Football supporters are as much a part of football as the players themselves. Without them, there would be no professional game. It would cease to exist. Football needs its supporters in order to survive.

Soccer still looks for its largest single source of revenue to the fans who flood into the stadia – though how long this may continue is open to question in an age of multi-million TV contracts, sponsorship, corporate hospitality, merchandising and advertising.

But even those commercial undertakings depend on one common denominator: that ever since the second half of the 19th century, people have been prepared to pay to watch soccer. The devotion to soccer is universal. It is – by far – the biggest spectator sport in the world, uniting men, women and children from all walks of life, and from nations whose social and political ideologies may conflict most harshly.

This chapter examines the culture of football supporters and considers how the game has catered for them over the years. From the early days of standing on vast open terraces to the modern game, with executive boxes and satellite television, football has held a unique appeal.

Vast crowds now travel long distances to watch their teams in action and, belatedly, clubs are starting to appreciate their importance. In the United Kingdom, facilities are being improved, and watching is now becoming a more pleasant experience. This is because fans will no longer accept second-rate conditions while being asked to pay ever larger sums of money for the privilege of watching their side.

The authorities' slow awakening of the supporters' value is leading to a better relationship between the corridors of power and the stadium gangways. Only while that relationship improves can the game expect to continue to grow and prosper.

A WORKING-CLASS GAME

Football, for much of the century, was considered the game of the working classes. Once the game had been codified by the universities and public schools in the middle of the last century it was quickly popularized among the common man because it did not discriminate between the haves and have-nots. It was a recreational and spectator pursuit which was readily accessible to all, not merely the well-off. And it was that welcoming outlook which attracted so many people.

As the game grew in the early 1900s, men would spend all week working in blue-collar jobs, and then either play themselves or congregate on the terraces on a Saturday afternoon. The development of Wednesday half-day closing in the

SAMBA SOCCER *Brazilian fans celebrate a victory during the 1986 World Cup*

High Street led to the proliferation of many popular Wednesday league competitions for amateurs to contest and support at amateur levels up and down the country.

Soon Saturday on the terraces became the traditional meeting place where men could lose themselves for 90 minutes and escape the pressures of everyday life. Football was a man's game then, both on and off the pitch.

But what was it really like for the football supporter of those times? Not for those hardy souls the luxury of all-seater, covered stadiums with excellent toilet and refreshment facilities. Times were hard and the conditions reflected those times. Huge wide open terraces were the norm and biting winds and rain often made watching decidedly unpleasant. There was none of the protection that fans today take for granted, but the public still turned up in their thousands as the game developed into the biggest spectator sport in the world.

For a few old pence, a man could enjoy an afternoon's entertainment with his friends and they flocked into grounds all over the country.

It is estimated that 250,000 people crammed into Wembley to try to watch the 1923 FA Cup Final between Bolton and West Ham. Perhaps it was unfortunate for the FA, who had switched the game from Stamford Bridge when the construction of Wembley finished a year earlier than planned, that West Ham were one of the finalists. The authorities, used to the smaller crowds who had attended finals at Chelsea's home, clearly felt that Wembley's capacity would be sufficient. But the Hammers – as events would prove – were one of the biggest draws of those times and practically the whole of the East End wanted to see the game.

Huge attendances were not unusual in the years between the wars. On February 12, 1938, 75,031 people crammed into The Valley to watch Charlton take on Aston Villa in an FA Cup fifth-round tie. Never again will British football see a crowd like that at a domestic game, other than for cup finals at Wembley.

Indeed, when The Valley re-opened in December 1991 after being closed for nearly seven years, it was with a capacity of just 7,600 all-seated, which will eventually rise to around 16,000.

Not only were the grounds different, so were the people. It was common to see fathers entering grounds with their young sons, a feature that is now, thankfully, beginning to return. But it was easy, then. Football stadiums were considered safe places, far removed from the ugly violence which beset the British and European game in the 1970s and 1980s. Fans supported their local teams and that was all. Fighting for its own sake would not have occurred to them and the sights and sounds of the stadiums were far removed from those we know today.

Community singing, brass bands and rattles were once the norm where now crude chanting reflects a change in society which has left football the poorer. Clubs had their "wags" on the terraces – jokers who were the forerunners of today's fanzine wits. The humour was sharp but not malicious, and visiting teams were treated sportingly.

Perhaps the best time to be a football fan was in the 1960s. Certainly those who grew up in those times speak fondly of the era. Britain as a whole was on the up and the mood of the people reflected that. Nowhere was it more evident than on Merseyside. The area boasted The Beatles, the biggest thing ever to hit the music scene, and it also boasted Liverpool, about to be the biggest thing ever to hit domestic football. Liverpool Football Club, under the management of Bill Shankly, was set for a period of unprecedented success and there was no better place to watch football than on the Kop.

Television pictures of the day have captured forever the unique atmosphere that was generated by those fans on that particular block of concrete. Tens of thousands of fans singing as one was truly a sight and sound to behold . . . and which the arrival of all-seater stadiums denied the game's next generation.

THE KOP *A last glance at the Anfield terrace stronghold demolished in May 1994*

INVADERS *England fans earned a reputation for violence at home and abroad, but they were also a soft target for hooligans of other nations*

SOCCER TRIBES

Supporters may be the lifeblood of the game but their presence and involvement brings problems of their own. And those problems in recent years have threatened to tear the game apart.

As a competitive sport played between two teams, football will always generate rival opinions and loyalties. And rival opinions and loyalties can lead to trouble.

Football will always create that special kind of rivalry because it is a tribalistic game. Not in a malevolent or evil way, but by its very nature. Supporters of one particular team become their own tribe, with their own identity, and repel anyone who threatens it. When supporters travel away to watch their team, they are bonded together even more closely. It's as simple as that. There's no

malice intended – or at least, not usually, not among the real fans.

Most of the time the banter between rival fans is good-natured and limited to exchanging chants from opposing ends of the ground. Sadly though, particularly during the 1970s and 1980s, this rivalry occasionally spilled over into mindless violence. There was no excuse for some of the sickening behaviour witnessed at grounds around the world, but it took a long time for the authorities to bring the problem under control.

The disease has been seen worldwide but English fans developed the worst hooligan reputation for the manner in which they exported their terrace and street violence. Partly this was because the culture of the travelling fan is much more widely accepted in a comparatively small country

such as England than in, say, Spain, Italy or France.

When European football arrived with increasingly easy foreign travel facilities, so the disease travelled too and the problem has not been confined to English football followers alone. The 1988 European Championship finals in Germany, and those in Sweden in 1992, were marred by violent clashes between rival supporters. English fans were sometimes caught in the middle and there was a feeling that they had become victims of their own reputation. Certainly gangs among the Dutch and Germans took great delight in trying to prove that they had the "hardest fans in football".

Sadly the disease has sometimes led to tragedy. The 1985 European Cup Final in Brussels will always be

remembered as the Heysel Disaster, the night 39 Juventus fans lost their lives trying to escape a terrace charge by Liverpool supporters. No one who was present or saw those pictures will ever forget the terror that was wreaked on that fateful night in Belgium. No sporting event can be worth such a price and the scenes shocked and sickened the world.

As a result of that shameful night, English teams spent five years in European exile, first withdrawn and then banned from international club competition – as much to protect innocent citizens in continental towns and cities as punishment.

The situation provoked calls in Parliament for drastic measures of control. The Government threatened to ban the England national team and moves were made to introduce an ID card scheme which would make it easy to spot – and do something about – the hooligans. The proposal caused uproar among genuine fans who considered it an infringement of civil liberties.

The move eventually proved unworkable and was quietly forgotten though many clubs did undertake tighter control of membership and season ticket arrangements in an effort to combat hooliganism.

The result was the turning of a corner: the game is no longer blighted in such measure by the terrace thugs and, for the first time, football is beginning to think in terms of full-family entertainment – catering for female as well as male spectators. But the game never dare lapse into complacency. Tighter crowd security does not mean hooligan violence has been eradicated. A chilling reminder was witnessed in Dublin in 1995, when the Ireland v England "friendly" had to be abandoned after less than half an hour because of trouble fomented by England followers.

PROGRAMMES AND FANZINES

One of the biggest changes down the years has been in the development of club programmes. In dim and distant days gone by, they consisted of nothing more than a single sheet of paper containing the team line-ups and a few advertisements. At the turn of the century, they would sell at around one old penny. Now, they are glossy brochures which retail at £1.50 or more just for a normal League fixture. As for the "brochures" which accompany major internationals and Cup finals, the cost goes spiralling up to £6. That was how much supporters of Chelsea and Middlesbrough were asked to pay for the programme at the 1997 FA Cup Final.

As programmes became, more and more, vehicles for the football establishment's commercial, promotional face, so the arrival of the fanzine became inevitable. Fans had become increasingly disillusioned by the "everything in the garden is rosy" outlook of club programmes and their growing demand for their own voice within the game led to a nationwide movement to secure outlets for independent comment. Generally witty and irreverent, the fanzines became a vehicle in which the fans could express their honest – frequently caustic – opinions of the people running "their" clubs and "their" game. The days of supporters accepting everything their clubs told them are long gone and fanzines have played an important role in the mobilisation of terrace opinion on issues such as bond schemes and the redevelopment of stadia.

TERRACE SOUNDS

Viewing the old newsreel television pictures of supporters in the 1930s and 1940s, it is hard to associate them with today's modern game. Cloth caps and overcoats as far as the eye could see with wooden rattles providing the most distinguishable sounds of the games gone by. Wooden and heavy, they would be twirled around the air to make that distinctive, ratchet sound that was unique to football grounds. There are modern equivalents, such as the klaxon horn, but the daddy of all football instruments was that old wooden rattle.

Not that the boys and men who twirled them would recognize today's terrace sounds as a development of the same culture. The community singing, which now lives on only through the moving relic of "Abide With Me" before the FA Cup Final, has been replaced by repetitive chants with no more stirring lyrics than "Here we go! Here we go! Here we go!"

Some clubs' fans have kept their link with past traditions alive. Bristol Rovers fans sing "Goodnight, Irene," Birmingham City supporters still persist with "Keep right on to the end of the road", but the street culture of the 1960s and 1970s led to many clubs replacing their traditional songs with pop-led creations, few of which lasted more than a season or two.

Of course, "You'll never walk alone", has surged and inspired several generations of players at Liverpool and served the community anew in sad circumstances in 1989, when a new recording by the Merseyside singer, Gerry Marsden, raised thousands of pounds for the Hillsborough disaster fund.

Many of the other modern terrace sounds, however, have done the game a disservice. "Industrial language" echoed through the traditional shouts of encouragement and criticism and the increasing influence of black players met volleys of racial abuse, often quite illogically aimed by fans whose own teams included black players.

With Me" before the FA Cup Final, has been replaced by repetitive chants with no more stirring lyrics than "Here we go! Here we go! Here we go!"

In the 1990s, as part of English football's drive to clean up its act and raise the class profile of the game, stringent attempts were launched to police bad language and eject the louts whose foul-mouth abuse hindered the drive to attract a family audience.

The message for the 21st century is that attending a match should be an enjoyment and that the traditional humour can still flourish.

SCARVES AND COLOURS

Wearing your club colours is a trait which is, largely, unique to football. It's become a tradition to go to games wearing replica shirts, scarves and badges to let everyone know who you support.

A down side has been the criticism heaped upon sportswear manufacturers and clubs – Manchester United having been a prime target of consumer groups. Both sides of the industry have been accused of exploiting young fans (and their parents) with frequent changes of colours and styles. Nor has the Football Association, responsible for the England strip, been exempt from criticism.

ROLIGANS *Danish fans, so-called because of the derivation from a word meaning "peace"*

FACE IN THE CROWD *Courtesy of a giant screen, video technology brings the teams to the fans at Arsenal's Highbury stadium*

CHANGING FACE OF FOOTBALL

In the approach to the year 2000, professional football is changing radically. Money talks. Football is big business which needs to generate serious income and is targeting the "middle class" as a more lucrative audience.

That shift in emphasis has brought increasing demands on the game; people want better value for their money. Thus clubs are learning to listen to supporters' views and act on them – particularly now that many more leisure interests are competing for the public's support and cash.

For too long, football's rulers remained oblivious to the reasons why the public might prefer to spend its time and money watching other sports in a civilized atmosphere rather

than huddling together on a cold terrace in the pouring rain. Clubs now realize that their facilities must be improved if they expect to continue to attract the crowds their budgets demand.

Europe has led the way – proof is to be seen in the superb stadiums in Italy, Germany and Spain – but it took the pressure of disaster and legislation before English football finally got the message.

After the Hillsborough Disaster in 1989, in which 95 Liverpool fans died at an FA Cup semi-final against Nottingham Forest, the Taylor Report deemed that all higher-division clubs must make their grounds all-seater.

This was obviously going to take

time, as well as vast sums of money, but it was a development which was long overdue – despite many fans' initial opposition that the removal of terraces would take something away from the game and lead to a more muted atmosphere.

A significant by-product is that, with so many all-seater stadiums available, England could once more compete to host major international events – starting in 1996 with the European Championship finals whose successful staging was followed by an application to host the World Cup finals in 2006.

Indeed, after an pre-event inspection of the eight stadiums designated for use at the 1996 European Championship, UEFA's stadium chief,

Ernie Walker, said: "City for city, England now has the best football stadiums in the world."

EXECUTIVE BOXES

Despite initial terrace resistance, executive boxes generate huge revenue to help keep prices down elsewhere within grounds. Perhaps the image of supporters in pin-stripe suits smoking cigars behind glass panels is alien to the football tradition, but football today is a branch of the entertainment industry and needs its high-income supporters. Corporate entertainment is a thriving business and companies are prepared to pay substantial sums of money to wine and dine potential clients at top sporting events.

INDOOR STADIUMS

When England played Germany in the Pontiac Silverdome near Detroit in the US Cup in June 1992, it represented a revolutionary new move in world soccer. For the first time, a major international was being played on artificially-grown grass in an indoor stadium. With science and technology becoming more and more advanced in the cause of sport, the numbers of fully-covered stadiums will increase. If it is possible to recreate the same playing conditions as outdoors, then it must be a logical step forward. The indoor stadiums would mean no more games falling victim to extreme weather conditions, and no more tedious midfield battles played out on mud-bath pitches in the middle of winter. So-called "plastic pitches" were tried, without conspicuous success, but the fully-covered stadium is something the elements cannot touch.

VIDEO SCREENS

For years, clubs have been seeking ways to encourage supporters to arrive early for matches and one solution is the "entertainment package". Pre-match entertainment, in various guises, has been tried by just about everybody, with varying degrees of success. What better way to keep fans happy before kick-off than by showing action on giant video screens? Arsenal were the first club in Britain to get in on the act and such huge screens have proved popular with fans. Attitudes still vary from country to country, however, on the replaying of important match incidents.

FAMILY AUDIENCES

Clubs are now beginning to cater for the whole family on match-days. With ideas ranging from family stands to the introduction of crèches, the English game is doing its best to appeal to a brand new audience. Clubs have realized – not before time – that if a father can sit with his wife and son or daughter in an area just for them, then he is more likely to take them along.

Family stands boast a two-fold attraction: they offer reduced admission prices compared with other areas of the ground, and they are safe places from where to watch. The youngsters who now take their place in those stands are the fans of tomorrow. Clubs should do everything possible to keep them.

POMPOM PAGEANTRY *Brazilian fans were as colourful as the nation they followed at World Cup '94*

SAMBA SOCCER

Pele once described football as "the beautiful game". And that sums up Samba Soccer. The Brazilians are the best exponents of it, both on the pitch and off it. The fans who play their part in Samba Soccer certainly know how to enjoy themselves.

Whether their team is winning or losing, you can rely on the Brazilians to give you a show. The Samba beat of the lone drummer is always heard from the terraces, where the fans treat the event as a carnival. Brightly coloured clothing and frantic dance routines are all part of the culture of Samba Soccer.

That culture has been adapted by the rest of the world as fans seek to reap maximum enjoyment from sporting events. A world away from the snarling and intimidating attitude of the hooligans, it's a practice which should be encouraged. Thus Spain's national team was accompanied all over the world in the 1980s and 1990s by the familiar figure of the drummer known only as Manolo; thus Holland's total football was played out to the vibrant, strident tones of a brass band; and the medium of television allowed fans of different countries to swap their favourite tune chants.

The Danish fans added to the fun not only with their enthusiasm for their nation's cause but by introducing the practice of face-painting. Now the sight is commonplace at football grounds around the world, even in the exciting new J. League in Japan.

It seems that everyone, from the youngest fan to the oldest, has been caught up in the craze of decorating themselves in the colours of club and country. The World Cup and European Championship have now become a pageant of facial colour as thousands of fans take their places proudly coloured in their country's flag for the whole world to see. Some have even gone as far as to dye their hair in the appropriate colours in order to demonstrate their allegiance.

"Football watching" around the world can be very different to watching in Britain. Even the English love of the game pales in comparison with the demonstrations of passion to be seen in, say, Italy.

In Italy, football is a religion. Everyone it seems is a supporter, right across the social and financial divides, and that has helped establish the Italian league championship as the world's No 1. Supporters of the top Italian clubs have the best of everything. The stadiums are magnificent and so are the facilities. So, too, are the prices. That is why the Italian clubs compete regularly to sign the game's greatest players: they learned long ago that their passionate fans demand value for money. The fact that Italy, until recently, boasted the highest average top division attendances in the world – around 30,000-plus on average – proves that such a philosophy works.

SCANDALS & DISASTERS

Football has always had its seamy side and its tragic side. With so much money involved there was bound to be financial crookedness, and with such large and passionate crowds there were bound to be disasters.

SOCCER BABYLON

Ever since professionalism transformed an English public school pastime towards the end of the last century, the game's underworld has been hard at work refining its activities. For years, the little tax-free extras or inducements took the form of "boot money" – a few notes left surreptitiously in a player's boot – but in the era of the multi-million pound transfer, corruption, feeding on ambition and greed, has embroiled leading chairmen, players and referees, and the new breed of shadowy middlemen, the agents, have devised ever more sophisticated ways of keeping a cut for themselves and their clients, even to the extent of using off-shore tax havens.

In 1993–94 alone European champions Marseille, Italian giants Torino, and leading English clubs Tottenham Hotspur and Arsenal were tainted by the seamy side of

the game. At the same time, the growing curse of drug-taking reduced Diego Maradona, one of the greatest players the game has ever seen, to a pathetic figure in the twilight of his career.

Even in the Edwardian era, however, with the Football League in its infancy, the leading lights of the game were already being brought to book for bribery, illegal payments, and match-fixing, either to ensure league placings or to make profit from betting.

Billy Meredith, Manchester City captain and the Wales outside-right, a figure as famous in his day as Matthews, Best or Maradona, was at the heart of British football's first major scandal in 1905 when he was suspended for a season for attempting to bribe the Aston Villa captain with £10 to lose a game as City challenged for the title.

A year earlier, ambitious City had been found guilty of illegal payments to players, but the Meredith case eventually proved catastrophic for the club when he fell out with his employers and informed the FA of widespread financial corruption in the club's affairs. In 1906, seventeen current or former City players were fined, suspended for a year and forbidden to play for the club again because

BILLY MEREDITH *Brought to book for an attempted bribe*

220

MARADONA *His football was sublime but drugs were his downfall and he was arrested for possession in Argentina*

they had accepted illegal payments.

The whole issue of these payments stemmed from the attempt by the English football authorities to impose limits on wages and signing-on fees. In Meredith's day wages were £4, and the maximum wage, rising to £20, survived until 1961. Within months of its abolition, Fulham were paying England international Johnny Haynes £100 per week. Incredibly, the £10 signing-on fee was abolished in Britain only in 1958, a year after John Charles is reputed to have received £10,000 for joining Juventus.

The system was abused by the majority for years, involving even such famous names as Herbert Chapman, manager of Leeds City when they were thrown out of the League in 1919, and Stanley Matthews, manager of Port Vale when they were expelled, then re-elected in the 1960s.

Meredith exposed the hypocrisy which still survives when he said: "Clubs are not punished for breaking the laws. They are punished for being found out." But the end of the maximum wage did not bring an end to under-the-counter payments in England, which are still widespread and have become an integral part of the transfer system.

Today it is not just the football mandarins clubs and officials have to fear, but an increasingly vigilant taxman. The English can of worms was

opened when Swindon Town were raided in 1990 and manager Lou Macari, the former Scotland and Manchester United player, and chairman Brian Hillier were arrested. The inquiry uncovered illegal payments, petty cash being paid to club officials as perks, and the understating of gate receipts. Macari was acquitted, Hillier jailed for tax fraud.

In 1994 Tottenham were punished with a 12-point deduction, heavy fine and ban from the FA Cup for financial irregularities which had come to light during a power struggle between chairman Alan Sugar and dismissed manager Terry Venables. The punishments were later quashed in the law courts, but the image of the club and game had been seriously damaged.

But the tip of an English iceberg

pales into insignificance beside the bribery and match-fixing scandals affecting Italy and France, as the European club competitions have grown in stature since the 1950s and begun to attract television deals capable of financing some Third World countries. Italy, a country where corruption in public life is little short of endemic, has suffered post-war match-fixing and bribery scandals involving Lazio, Milan, Roma and now Torino, while France's league boom in the 1980s led to problems with the taxman over illegal payments. In 1993 French football was rocked to the core when their first European champions, Marseille, were found to have bought a match to ensure they retained the championship.

MADNESS *Eric Cantona's infamous kung-fu assault on a Crystal Palace fan*

CASH AND CORRUPTION

1891 Maximum £10 signing-on fee introduced.

1900 Maximum wage of £4 introduced in England, but not Scotland.

1900 Burnley goalkeeper Jack Hillman banned for one year for trying to bribe Nottingham Forest to lose. Forest won 4–0, Burnley were relegated.

1904 Second Division Glossop fined £250 for wholesale mismanagement and deception. Four directors suspended for three seasons, secretary censured, six players suspended for three months.

1904 Sunderland fined £250 and directors and secretary suspended for one to three seasons for illegal payments.

1904 Manchester City found to have broken transfer rules involving Glossop players Irvine Thornley and Frank Norgrove. Clubs fined £250, Hyde Road ground shut for two games, five directors suspended and Thornley banned for a season.

1905 Billy Meredith, Manchester City's captain and Welsh international outside-right, banned for a season after attempting to bribe Aston Villa captain Alec Leake towards end of 1904–05 season when City were making a challenge for the championship.

1905 Middlesbrough, who had just paid the first £1,000 transfer fee for Alf Common from Sunderland (three times the previous record), fined £250, 11 of 12 directors suspended until 1908 for illegal payments.

1906 Seventeen current and former Manchester City players fined a total of £900, suspended for six months and banned from playing for the club again after accepting illegal payments. Chairman W. Forrest and manager Tom Maley banned sine die, directors suspended. Players later auctioned by League for £2,600.

1909 George Parsonage of Fulham banned for life after requesting £50 signing-on fee from Chesterfield.

1911 Middlesbrough's respected manager Andy Walker and chairman Thomas Gibson Poole, a prospective MP, banned from football for trying to fix home game against local rivals Sunderland. Boro won 1–0.

1919 An example is made. Leeds City expelled from League for making illegal payments.

1924 John Browning, former Scotland player, and Archibald Kyle of Rangers, Blackburn and Airdrie, given 60 days' hard labour for offering Bo'Ness players £30 to fix Second Division match with Lochgelly.

1932 Former Montrose captain Gavin Hamilton given 60 days' jail for offering £40–£50 to Montrose player David Mooney to fix home match against Edinburgh City.

1957 Sunderland fined record £5,000 by Football League for illegal payments to players.

1958 Leyton Orient fined £2,000 for irregularities in accounts.

1965 Everton alleged to have been involved in match-fixing during their 1962–63 championship. No proof.

1965 England's most sensational match-fixing scandal. Ten League professionals found guilty at Nottingham Assizes of match-fixing. Jimmy Gauld, an inside-forward for Charlton, Everton, Plymouth, Swindon and Mansfield between 1955 and 1960, was jailed for four years, the others for terms between four and 15 months. After years of rumours, Gauld had told all for £7,000. Although Gauld was the ringleader, the three most celebrated players among the ten were England players Peter Swan (Sheffield Wednesday) and Tony Kay (Everton, but previously with Wednesday) and their Sheffield Wednesday colleague David Layne.

1965 Kay, Layne and Swan banned from football for life, although after many campaigns the bans were lifted in 1972.

1967 Peterborough United fined £500 and demoted from Third to Fourth Division for illegal payments.

1967 Millwall fined £1,000 for attack on referee by spectators at The Den.

1968 Port Vale fined £4,000 and expelled from League for illegal payments, but re-elected for following season.

1969 Manchester United fined £7,000 for administrative irregularities.

1970 Derby fined £10,000 and barred from Fairs Cup for a year for administrative irregularities.

CLOUD OVER TORINO *A bribery scandal erupted over Torino's (in white vs. Aberdeen) 1991–92 UEFA Cup campaign*

1971 Officials of Arminia Bielefeld found guilty of putting up £90,000 to fix four West German League games.

1973 Wolverhampton Wanderers player Bernard Shaw alleged he was approached to sell a championship deciding game against Leeds in 1972.

1974 The Solti-Lobo Case. Juventus accused of using a go-between, Deszo Solti, to try to bribe Portuguese referee Francisco Marques Lobo, the official for their European Cup semi-final against Derby in 1973.

1974 Italian players accused by Polish opponents of offering money to them on the field to lose a World Cup match in Stuttgart. Italy, needing a draw to stay in the finals, lose 2–1.

1978 Millwall fined £1,500 and have their ground closed for two weeks after crowd trouble during FA Cup tie against Ipswich. Millwall's notorious fans had also caused The Den to be closed in 1934, 1947 and 1950.

1978 Fulham fined £15,000 for illegal payments.

1978 Scotland's top referee John Gordon and linesmen Rollo Kyle and David McCartney suspended by Scottish FA after admitting they accepted presents worth £1,000 from Milan before a UEFA Cup match with Levski Spartak. Milan, fined £8,000 by UEFA, had drawn 1–1 in Bulgaria and won 3–0 at home.

1980 The world's highest paid player, Italian striker Paolo Rossi, is one of more than 30 banned for their part in widespread Italian match-fixing on behalf of an illegal betting ring. Milan and Lazio relegated. Rossi's ban ended just in time for him to lead Italy to their 1982 World Cup victory in Spain.

1983 Derby fined £10,000 by the Football League for poaching manager Roy McFarland from Bradford City.

1983 Tottenham fined £8,000 for illegal payments to Argentine World Cup stars Osvaldo Ardiles and Ricky Villa.

1985 Celtic fined £17,000 by UEFA for crowd trouble at a European Cup-winners' Cup replay against Rapid Vienna at Old Trafford.

1986 UEFA bar Roma from their competitions for a season and president Dino Viola from UEFA activities for four years after he tried to bribe a European Cup referee in a

FALLEN IDOLS *Peter Swan (left) and Tony Kay were gaoled for match-fixing*

semi-final game against Dundee United in 1982. Roma won 3–0, and 3–2 on aggregate, before losing to Liverpool in the Final.

1988 Peterborough fined £2,500 for transfer irregularity.

1988 Hungarian full-back Sandor Sallai and former national team manager Kalman Meszoly are among more than 40 players and officials arrested in match-fixing investigation.

1988 Chelsea fined record £75,000 by FA for serious crowd trouble in play-off against Middlesbrough.

1989 Nottingham Forest manager, Brian Clough, fined £5,000 by FA and banned from touchline for a season for striking a spectator at League Cup tie against QPR.

1989 Wimbledon fined £10,000 for making unauthorized loans to their players.

1989 Bradford City fined £10,000 for poaching manager Terry Yorath from Swansea.

1990 Swindon Town fined £7,500 by FA, former manager Lou Macari £1,000 and censured, chairman Brian Hillier suspended from football for three years after breaching rules by betting on Newcastle vs. Swindon FA Cup tie in January 1988.

1990 Swindon, having been promoted to Division One via play-offs, demoted to Division Three (Division Two on appeal), for irregular payments to players over four years.

1990 FA deduct two points from Arsenal, one from Manchester United and fine both clubs £50,000 after players involved in mass brawl.

1991 League fine Chelsea record £105,000 for illegal payments to three players. A company linked to Chelsea was found to have paid £100,000 over market price for the Scottish home of England defender Graham Roberts, who signed from Rangers.

1991 Diego Maradona arrested in Argentina for possession of drugs. He had just left Italy where he was banned from playing for 15 months after taking cocaine before a Napoli match. He is also given a 14-month suspended sentence by a Naples court for possessing cocaine.

1992 FA fines Vinnie Jones of Wimbledon £20,000 – a record for an individual – for bringing game into disrepute by narrating the Soccer

Hard Men video.

1993 League newcomers Barnet fined £25,000 for making irregular payments and warned that any further indiscretion could cost them their League status.

1993 Jean-Jacques Eydelie, Marseille midfielder, arrested and accused of trying to bribe three Valenciennes players to lose league match, six days before the French champions beat Milan to win the European Cup. General manager Jean-Pierre Bernes also charged. An envelope containing £30,000 is dug up in the garden of the mother-in-law of Valenciennes player Christophe Robert.

1993: In the High Court battle over Tottenham Hotspur between Terry Venables and Alan Sugar, evidence is offered suggesting that some managers accept cash "bungs" as part of transfer deals.

1993 UEFA bar Marseille from defending the European Cup over the Valenciennes bribery scandal.

1994 Four directors and five referees accused by federal police of fraud for their alleged involvement in Brazilian match-fixing. The directors included Eduardo Viana, president of the Rio de Janeiro federation, and Eurico Miranda, a director of leading club Vasco da Gama. Former referee Reginaldo Mathias claims match-fixing had been common since 1985.

1994 Bernard Tapie is charged with corruption and ordered to quit as president of Marseille. He is later sentenced to two years in jail, with one suspended, for match-fixing.

1994 Torino are placed under investigation by the Italian fraud squad after being accused of providing prostitutes for match officials in their attempt to win the 1992 UEFA Cup. The club are also alleged to have siphoned off under-the-counter cash from transfers, including £465,000 for the "phantom transfer" of Alessandro Palestro, son of a club secretary and not registered with the club but studying at university.

1995 Malaysian football embroiled in huge bribery scandal in 1994 league season. Dozens of players are arrested, some are sent into internal exile. Australian-born Singapore international Abbas Saad is first to be convicted and fined $36,000.

SEASON OF SLEAZE

The 1994–95 season has gone down in English football history as the "Season of Sleaze" when the game reeled from one unsavoury incident to another.

• *The Sun* newspaper alleged that Southampton and former Liverpool goalkeeper Bruce Grobbelaar took bribes to fix matches. The FA charged him with misconduct. Grobbelaar denied any wrongdoing – as did Wimbledon goalkeeper Hans Segers and Aston Villa forward John Fashanu, who were also questioned by police.

• Arsenal and England striker Paul Merson spent six weeks in a rehabilitation clinic after admitting to cocaine, alcohol and gambling addiction.

• Chelsea fans invaded the pitch after losing to London rivals Millwall in the FA Cup at Stamford Bridge. Mounted police separated brawling fans

• England's friendly international against the Republic of Ireland was abandoned after English hooligans tore up their seats and threw them at spectators below. Wimbledon's Vinnie Jones, a spectator at the match in Dublin, was dropped by his club for three matches after biting a reporter's nose in a city hotel bar.

• George Graham was dismissed as Arsenal manager after a Premier League inquiry alleged he received £425,000 in under-the-table transfer payments. He denied any wrongdoing and initiated legal proceedings for wrongful dismissal.

• Chelsea captain Dennis Wise was sentenced to three months in jail after a being found guilty of assaulting a taxi driver. He was released on bail pending an appeal, when the conviction was overturned.

CRYSTAL PALACE v MANCHESTER UNITED

Manchester United's French striker Eric Cantona launched a two-footed, kung-fu-style assault on a taunting Crystal Palace fan – after he had been sent off – at Selhurst Park. He was later suspended by the FA until the end of September 1995 and sentenced by a court to a 120 hours of community service. Upon leaving the court, he said, "When seagulls follow the trawler, it is because they think sardines will be thrown into the sea."

In the aftermath of Cantona's attack, team-mate Paul Ince was charged with common assault by police for attacking another Crystal Palace fan. He was found not guilty at a trial in May 1995.

A Crystal Palace fan died after an incident at a bar five miles from the ground which was hosting the FA Cup semi-final tie between the two teams.

In the FA Cup semi-final replay Darren Patterson (Palace) and Roy Keane (Man Utd) were sent off for fighting – despite public pleas from their managers before the game for the match to be an example of peace and sportsmanship.

SOCCER DISASTERS

Drama and excitement have attracted huge crowds to soccer stadiums around the world, just as ambition and the explosion of international competition have kept the world's airlines busy with teams criss-crossing the oceans and continents. Sadly, but inevitably, the game could not avoid the accompanying disasters which turned sporting events into national and international tragedies. From the Superga air disaster of 1949 to the Zambian air crash in 1993; from the first Ibrox Park disaster in 1902 to the Corsica tragedy more than 90 years later … sad shadows have been cast over the game.

STADIUM DISASTERS AND PLANE CRASHES

1902: Scotland play out a 1–1 draw with England, largely unaware that 25 fans have been killed and hundreds more injured after wooden planking, 40 feet above the ground, collapses in Ibrox Park's new 20,000-capacity West Stand.

1946: The Burnden Park gates are closed on 65,000 fans before Bolton meet Stoke in a sixth round FA Cup tie, but another 20,000 are milling around outside. Many force their way in and two crush barriers collapse under sheer weight of numbers. Thirty-three die from crush injuries and more than 500 are injured. The match is eventually completed, scoreless and without an interval, Bolton winning 2–0 over the two legs.

1949: The cream of Italian football is wiped out when the plane carrying the Torino team back from a match in Portugal crashes into a hillside at Superga just outside Turin. Eighteen players die, including the bulk of Italy's team led by captain Valentino Mazzola. Journalists, officials and English coach Leslie Lievesley raise the death toll to 31. Torino had won four successive League

BUSBY'S TRAGIC BABES *Manchester United's team in 1957; in February 1958 seven of this team perished at Munich*

titles and were four points clear at the top on the day of the crash. The Torino youth team complete the season and receive the championship trophy.

1958: Manchester United's plane crashes on take-off at snowy Munich airport, killing eight of the famous Busby Babes, three club officials and eight journalists. United are returning from a 3–3 draw with Red Star Belgrade which had earned them a place in the European Cup semi-finals.

1961: A plane crashes into the Las Lastimas mountain, killing 24 members of the Green Cross team on their way from Santiago to Osorno for the Chile Cup play-offs.

1962: In Libreville, Gabon, an international between Congo-Brazzaville and Gabon is halted when a landslide hits the stadium. Nine spectators die and 30 are injured.

1964: The world's worst soccer disaster. In Lima, Peru, 318 people die and another 500 are injured during rioting sparked by a last-minute

Peruvian goal being disallowed in an Olympic tie against Argentina. The goal would have sent Peru to the Tokyo Games. Martial law was in force for 30 days after the game.

1967: Another disallowed goal sparks rioting during a Turkish championship game, and 41 people die with a further 600 injured, many being trampled as they flee the stadium.

Jun 23, 1968: In Buenos Aires at the Monumental Stadium, venue ten years later for the World Cup Final, 74 people die and another 113 are injured

---

1931 JOHN THOMPSON

Tragedy struck in the Old Firm derby between Rangers and Celtic on September 5, 1931 when Celtic's 23-year-old goalkeeper John Thomson dived at the feet of Rangers' Sam English.

Thomson, who had joined Celtic as a 17-year-old and had already established himself in the Scotland team, was renowned for his dashes off the line to thwart opposing forwards. This time, Thomson did not get up, having fractured his skull. He died five hours later in the local hospital.

Such was his popularity that 30,000 mourners saw his coffin off at Glasgow's Queen Street Station, and 3,000 attended his funeral.

1934 HERBERT CHAPMAN

If ever a man died in harness, it was the great Arsenal manager Herbert Chapman. On New Year's Day, 1934, Arsenal were dominating English football and the envy of the world. They had won the League twice and the Cup once in the previous four seasons under the innovative and tactically astute Chapman, and were top of the League again.

Chapman caught a chill watching a game at Bury, but still decided to go and watch Arsenal's next opponents Sheffield Wednesday the following day. Against doctor's advice, he also travelled to Guildford to see Arsenal's reserves. When he eventually took to his bed it was too late, pneumonia had set in, and he died at 3 a.m. on Saturday, January 6.

Stunned Arsenal fans learned the news from newspaper billboards on their way to Highbury for the game against Wednesday.

when Boca Juniors supporters drop lighted torches on their arch rivals from River Plate and panic ensues.

1969: Nineteen players and officials of The Strongest, Bolivia's most popular team, die when their plane crashes in the Andes, 72 miles from their destination La Paz.

1969: El Salvador and Honduras go to war over a World Cup tie played in Mexico and won 3–2 by the Salvadorians. Hundreds of Hondurans launch attacks on Salvadorians living in their country, causing deaths, and the Salvadorian government retaliates with an armed attack lasting a week. The conflict is stopped eventually by the intervention of the Organization of American States.

1971: Sixty-six people die and 150 are injured when they tumble down a stairway while leaving a Rangers vs. Celtic match. A last-minute Rangers equalizer has led to departing fans attempting to get back in the ground, with horrific results.

1979: Seventeen players of Pakhtakor Tashkent of the Soviet Union are killed in a plane crash on their way to a league match.

1981: Eighteen fans die and a further 45 are injured when a wall collapses during a match between Deportes Tolima and Deportivo Cali in Ibague, Colombia.

1982: In Cali, Colombia, drunken youths urinate from the upper deck of the Pascual Geurrero stadium, causing a stampede in which 22 die and more than 100 are injured.

1982: More than 300 Soviet fans die at a UEFA Cup match between Spar-

STEPS TO DISASTER *66 died at Ibrox Park when fans tried to return to the terraces*

tak Moscow and Haarlem of Holland. As revealed seven years later by the authorities, a last-minute Spartak goal sent departing fans surging back into the Lenin Stadium, causing an horrific crush.

1985: A day of celebration turns to tragedy. Fifty-six people are burned to death and more than 200 taken to hospital when Bradford City's 77-year-old wooden main stand is engulfed by flames within five minutes just before half-time in the last match of the season against Lincoln City.

Before the game City had been presented with the Third Division championship.

1985: Thirty-nine people die and more than 400 are injured when a wall collapses during rioting started by English fans an hour before the European Cup Final between Liverpool and Juventus in the the Heysel Stadium, Brussels. Live TV pictures relay the tragedy around the world. The game is eventually played, Juventus winning 1–0, but as a result English club teams are banned from European competition.

1987: Forty-three players, officials' wives and supporters of Alianza Lima die while returning from a league game, their plane crashing into the sea six miles north of the Peruvian capital.

1988: A stand collapses just before half-time at an international between Libya and Malta in Tripoli, causing 30 deaths and many injuries. A man runs amok brandishing a gun among the 65,000 crowd, causing a stampede for the exits, and the weight of numbers breaks a retaining wall.

1988: Between 70 and 100 fans die in Katmandu when a violent hailstorm

causes a stampede among the 25,000 fans at a game between Janakpur of Nepal and Mukti Jodha of Bangladesh.

1989: In Britain's worst sports disaster, 95 Liverpool supporters are crushed to death and almost 200 injured at Hillsborough, Sheffield, before an FA Cup semi-final against Nottingham Forest. Crowds anxious to see the start surge into the Leppings Lane End and pin fans against the security fences designed to keep people off the pitch. The tragedy leads to the dismantling of security fences and to requirements for all-seater stadiums.

1989: Twelve people in Lagos, Nigeria, are trampled to death, and a player dies on the field during a World Cup qualifier between Nigeria and Angola. Nigerian winger Sam Okwaraji collapses with exhaustion in the 82nd minute and cannot be revived.

1991: Forty people are killed and more than 50 injured in South Africa's worst sports disaster at a match in the gold mining town of Orkney, 80 miles from Johannesburg. Most of the victims are trampled as they try to escape fighting between fans, following the referee's decision to allow Kaizer Chiefs a disputed goal against arch rivals Orlando Pirates.

1992: Disaster strikes before a French Cup semi-final in the Corsican town of Bastia, whose team are due to play Marseille. Fifteen spectators die and 1,300 are injured when a temporary metal stand collapses. The whole competition is cancelled by the authorities at the insistence of the clubs.

1993: Eighteen members of the Zambian national team are killed when their plane crashes into the sea off Gabon after a refuelling stop on their way to a World Cup qualifying tie against Senegal.

1995: A 21-year-old Genoa fan is stabbed to death when he is set upon by a group of Milan fans.

1996: Incompetent crowd control measures bring disaster in the national Mateo Flores stadium in Guatemala City when 82 fans are crushed to death and more than 150 are injured before a World Cup qualifying tie against Costa Rica.

1953 DEREK DOOLEY

Derek Dooley was 23 and on the brink of a great career as a prolific goalscorer with Sheffield Wednesday. The big centre-forward had earned a reputation for scoring from apparently impossible situations, with 46 goals in 30 games as Wednesday won promotion, and 16 in 29 First Division games up to St Valentine's Day, 1953.

On that day, he broke his right leg challenging the Preston goalkeeper for a 50–50 ball. A few days later, when he was about to be discharged from hospital, it was discovered that gangrene had set in and there was no alternative but to have it amputated.

Dooley stayed in football, eventually managing Wednesday and being sacked by them, and later joining rivals Sheffield United as commercial manager.

FOOTBALL IN GREAT BRITAIN AND IRELAND

Association football has flourished in the British Isles for well over 100 years. The game has distinct origins in the four "home countries" and has developed along separate lines at club and international level. The Republic of Ireland, too, has a long soccer-playing history, nurtured in the 1990s by World Cup success.

ENGLAND

Association football is a game of speed, strength, colour, excitement and passion. These may not all be qualities one instantly associates with the English, but football is also a structured recreation, dependent on formal rules and regulations and a spirit of sportsmanship which are particular to what might be termed "the English way".

Although football was probably played in its earliest forms in China and in medieval Italy, it was in the context of English society that the tradition of kicking a ball around was developed – right through to the days in the nineteenth century when the universities and public schools sought to codify the game.

The FA Makes the Rules

The most significant day is a matter of record: October 26, 1863, when captains and other representatives from metropolitan and suburban clubs met at the Freemasons Tavern in London to set up the Football Association, which was to become one of the world's greatest sporting institutions.

Agreement, however, was not easily reached. The 11 founders soon fell out over the question of "hacking", the unpleasant practice of kicking opponents on the shin. Supporters of the handling game wanted hacking to remain in the rules. When it came to the vote, which they lost 13–4 on December 1, they withdrew from the Football Association.

Significant advances were made when the Sheffield Association – the Sheffield club being the oldest on record – threw in their lot in with the FA; when C.W. Alcock was installed as secretary in 1870; and through the appointments of Major Marindin as president and the Hon. A.F. (later Lord) Kinnaird as treasurer.

Alcock's inspiration was the FA Cup, which was instituted in 1871–72, and international competition, which he introduced a year later. The first official England vs. Scotland clash was staged in Glasgow on November 30, 1872. Alcock was the driving force behind the FA for a quarter of a cen-

tury, holding the reins of administration during the game's rapid evolution.

The FA is the ultimate governing body in English football, its primacy expressed in its title as simply the Football Association without need of "English".

Football's administrative development has not been without conflict. In the formative world of the late nineteenth century the first crisis was produced by the encroachment of professionalism, which the FA did not legalize until 1885.

The other major body in England, only 25 years younger, is the Football League. The prime instigator was a Scot, William McGregor of Aston Villa, who became known as "the father of the League", and who had become frustrated by teams failing to arrive to fulfil fixtures or crying off at short notice. McGregor, together with the representatives of Bolton Wanderers, Derby County, Everton, Accrington Stanley, Preston North End, Burnley, Stoke City, Blackburn Rovers, Notts County, West Bromwich Albion and Wolverhampton Wanderers, formed a separate competition on April 17, 1888. It remained unchallenged as the major unifying competition in English football for more than a century, until the pressures of a changing commercial world led to the historic breakaway now formalized as the Premier League.

The Football League was launched on September 8, 1888, Preston North End becoming the first champions. Undefeated with 18 wins and four draws, they finished a clear 11 points above second-placed Aston Villa. Preston became known as the "Old Invincibles" as they completed the League and Cup "double" with a 3–0 win over Wolverhampton Wanderers in the FA Cup Final that year. They did not concede a single goal in the cup competition.

Preston retained their League title in 1890 and were close to winning it again in 1891. But it was Huddersfield Town who made history in 1926 by clinching their third successive League Championship. In 1924 they pipped Cardiff City on goal average; in 1925 they finished two points ahead of West Bromwich; and they completed their hat-trick of titles with a five-point margin over Arsenal.

Showing the Foreigners

Huddersfield's manager, Herbert Chapman, was later to take charge at Highbury, where he repeated the three-championship trick with Arsenal in 1933, 1934 and 1935. These were the founding years of an awesome tradition and reputation which saw Arsenal's fame spin around the world. Today clubs of the same name may be found as far afield as Chile, Uruguay and Argentina. The credit all belongs to that era in the 1930s during which, inspired by Chapman, the Gunners secured five championships in eight years.

Success in soccer always attracts its critics. In Chapman's case the carping was focused on his revolutionary tactic of the stopper centre-half. To many at the time this was a negative step which undermined the quality of domestic football. Not that 100-plus goals in three seasons out of five (as Arsenal managed in 1930–31, 1932–33 and 1934–35) would be considered negative by later standards. But the stopper centre-half was a step down a long road which did eventually lead to the *catenaccio* system of defence.

The years immediately after the Second World War saw a one-off resurgence in support, with many clubs setting attendance records which will never be beaten. England – and the other three home associations – had only rejoined FIFA in 1946, having left it in 1928 following what now appears a ludicrous row over broken-time payments for amateurs. Significantly, one clause of the agreement by which England, Scotland, Wales and Northern Ireland returned to FIFA was a guarantee within FIFA statutes that the separate, historical identity of the four home associations should remain inviolate within the international game.

A product of returning to FIFA was entry into the 1950 World Cup, where a 1–0 defeat by the United States in Belo Horizonte, Brazil, was shrugged off as the sort of embarrassment at international level to which the great clubs are occasionally subjected by the giant-killers of the FA Cup.

English football remained supremely confident of its superiority over the rest of the world right through into the early 1950s, when Stan Cullis's Wolves swept aside the likes of Hungary's Honved and Moscow Spartak with a long-ball style which was the epitome of the English game. Billy Wright, at wing-half and then centre-half, was their inspirational skipper; Johnny Hancocks and Jimmy Mullen provided the devastating wing-to-wing passes which left opponents breathless. Wolves blasted more than 100 goals in four successive First Division campaigns from 1957–58 to 1960–61.

But the days of English self-sufficiency and complacency were coming to an end. Continental superiority in tactics and technique was never better illustrated than at Wembley on Wednesday, November 25, 1953. On that grey afternoon England's best, including goalkeeper Gil Merrick, right back Alf Ramsey, Wright, fellow wing-half Jimmy Dickinson, Stan Mortensen and Stanley Matthews, were humiliated by Hungary 6–3. Apart from a 2–0 defeat by the Irish Republic at Goodison Park, Liverpool, in 1949, it was the first home defeat ever inflicted on England by a foreign side. On that day Hungary's captain, Ferenc Puskas, inscribed his name indelibly on the pages of English football history. The scoreline in the return match in Budapest the following year was an even more emphatic 7–1.

Wolves' success in those early floodlit friendlies prompted such trumpeted fuss in the English newspapers as to provoke the launch of the European Cup. Here, the true worth of the English club game was exposed as successive League champions were put to the test and, for a decade, found wanting. Only Manchester United's Busby Babes could hold their heads high alongside clubs such as Real Madrid, Milan and Reims. In 1957 Manchester United won the League Championship for a second successive year and just missed out on the "double" when they lost in controversial circumstances to Aston Villa in the FA Cup Final. Alas, they were cut down in their prime, eight players being killed when their plane crashed on the runway at Munich on February 6, 1958.

Ten years later United became the first English club to win the European Cup. Yet it was Liverpool who were to emerge as the most successful club side in English football.

Many greats teams had entranced and entertained over the years in their varied ways, including Arthur Rowe's "push and run" Tottenham Hotspur side of the early 1950s and Bill Nicholson's double-winning wonders of the early 1960s. Perhaps none have matched the precision and sheer artistry of that 1960–61 Tottenham side, yet none have matched the consistency and quality of Liverpool, who dominated the 1970s and 1980s in a manner which had always been considered impossible under the physical pressures of the English game.

The foundations laid by their own legendary Scottish manager, Bill Shankly, produced achievements which no English club can match: a record 18 League Championships; five FA Cup triumphs; plus successes in the League Cup, the European Champions Cup, the UEFA Cup and the European Supercup.

Increasingly, however, the advent of sponsorship and a realization of football's value as a weapon in the television ratings wars were changing the face of the game. The big clubs were slowly growing away from the traditional roots of what was now a 92-club, four-division Football League. In the autumn of 1991 the First Division, virtually en masse, signalled their joint intention to resign from the Football League and set up a new competitive structure, the Premier League, under the auspices of the Football Association.

In a strange way, this return to the FA fold had brought English football full circle. Manchester United won the first Premier League championship, their first league title for 26 years. Alex Ferguson's team not only retained the title in 1994 but secured the League and Cup "double" with a 4–0 win over Chelsea in the FA Cup Final. United thus emulated the achievements of Preston North End (1889), Aston Villa (1897), Tottenham Hotspur (1961), Arsenal (1971) and Liverpool (1986).

Even better, in 1996, United created history by becoming the first club to win the "double" twice. They followed up victory in an exciting league duel with a revived Newcastle United by beating Liverpool 1–0 in the FA Cup Final with controversial Frenchman Eric Cantona not only scoring the winning goal but collecting the Cup as captain on the day.

Not that domestic excitement was translated into European success. United in 1991 and Arsenal in 1994 both won the Cup-winners' Cup but this is now considered the most inferior of the three European club events. The real barometer of international club standards will continue to be the Champions League.

FOOTBALL LEAGUE

Season	Champions	Pts	Runners-up	Pts
1888–89	Preston NE	40	Aston Villa	29
1889–90	Preston NE	33	Everton	31
1890–91	Everton	29	Preston NE	27
1891–92	Sunderland	42	Preston NE	37

FIRST DIVISION

1892–93	Sunderland	48	Preston NE	37
1893–94	Aston Villa	44	Sunderland	38
1894–95	Sunderland	47	Everton	42
1895–96	Aston Villa	45	Derby County	41
1896–97	Aston Villa	47	Sheffield Utd	36
1897–98	Sheffield Utd	42	Sunderland	37
1898–99	Aston Villa	45	Liverpool	43
1899–1900	Aston Villa	50	Sheffield Utd	48
1900–01	Liverpool	45	Sunderland	43
1901–02	Sunderland	44	Everton	41
1902–03	Sheffield Wed	42	Aston Villa	41
1903–04	Sheffield Wed	47	Manchester C	44
1904–05	Newcastle Utd	48	Everton	47
1905–06	Liverpool	51	Preston NE	47
1906–07	Newcastle Utd	51	Bristol City	48
1907–08	Manchester Utd	52	Aston Villa*	43
1908–09	Newcastle Utd	53	Everton	46
1909–10	Aston Villa	53	Liverpool	48
1910–11	Manchester Utd	52	Aston Villa	51
1911–12	Blackburn R	49	Everton	46
1912–13	Sunderland	54	Aston Villa	50
1913–14	Blackburn R	51	Aston Villa	44
1914–15	Everton	46	Oldham Ath	45
1919–20	WBA	60	Burnley	51
1920–21	Burnley	59	Manchester C	54
1921–22	Liverpool	57	Tottenham H	51
1922–23	Liverpool	60	Sunderland	54
1923–24	Huddersfield T*	57	Cardiff C	57
1924–25	Huddersfield T	58	WBA	56
1925–26	Huddersfield T	57	Arsenal	52
1926–27	Newcastle Utd	56	Huddersfield T	51
1927–28	Everton	53	Huddersfield T	51
1928–29	Sheffield Wed	52	Leicester C	51
1929–30	Sheffield Wed	60	Derby County	50
1930–31	Arsenal	66	Aston Villa	59
1931–32	Everton	56	Arsenal	54
1932–33	Arsenal	58	Aston Villa	54
1933–34	Arsenal	59	Huddersfield T	56
1934–35	Arsenal	58	Sunderland	54
1935–36	Sunderland	56	Derby County	48
1936–37	Manchester C	57	Charlton Ath	54
1937–38	Arsenal	52	Wolves	51
1938–39	Everton	59	Wolves	55
1946–47	Liverpool	57	Manchester Utd*	56
1947–48	Arsenal	59	Manchester Utd*	52
1948–49	Portsmouth	58	Manchester Utd*	53
1949–50	Portsmouth*	53	Wolves	53
1950–51	Tottenham H	60	Manchester Utd	56
1951–52	Manchester Utd	57	Tottenham H	53
1952–53	Arsenal*	54	Preston NE	54
1953–54	Wolves	57	WBA	53
1954–55	Chelsea	52	Wolves	48
1955–56	Manchester Utd	60	Blackpool*	49
1956–57	Manchester Utd	64	Tottenham H*	56
1957–58	Wolves	64	Preston NE	59
1958–59	Wolves	61	Manchester Utd	55
1959–60	Burnley	55	Wolves	54
1960–61	Tottenham H	66	Sheffield Wed	58
1961–62	Ipswich T	56	Burnley	53
1962–63	Everton	61	Tottenham H	55
1963–64	Liverpool	57	Manchester Utd	53
1964–65	Manchester Utd*	61	Leeds Utd	61
1965–66	Liverpool	61	Leeds Utd*	55
1966–67	Manchester Utd	60	Nottm Forest*	56
1967–68	Manchester C	58	Manchester Utd	56
1968–69	Leeds Utd	67	Liverpool	61
1969–70	Everton	66	Leeds Utd	57
1970–71	Arsenal	65	Leeds Utd	64
1971–72	Derby County	58	Leeds Utd*	57
1972–73	Liverpool	60	Arsenal	57
1973–74	Leeds Utd	62	Liverpool	57
1974–75	Derby County	53	Liverpool*	51
1975–76	Liverpool	60	QPR	59
1976–77	Liverpool	57	Manchester C	56
1977–78	Nottm Forest	64	Liverpool	57
1978–79	Liverpool	68	Nottm Forest	60
1979–80	Liverpool	60	Manchester Utd	58
1980–81	Aston Villa	60	Ipswich T	56
1981–82	Liverpool	87	Ipswich T	83
1982–83	Liverpool	82	Watford	71
1983–84	Liverpool	80	Southampton	77
1984–85	Everton	90	Liverpool*	77
1985–86	Liverpool	88	Everton	86
1986–87	Everton	86	Liverpool	77
1987–88	Liverpool	90	Manchester Utd	81
1988–89	Arsenal*	76	Liverpool	76
1989–90	Liverpool	79	Aston Villa	70
1990–91	Arsenal+	83	Liverpool	76
1991–92	Leeds Ud	82	Manchester Utd	78

Notes: * Position decided by goal average or goal difference, + 2 points deducted

FA PREMIER LEAGUE

1992–93	Manchester Utd	84	Aston Villa	74
1993–94	Manchester Utd	92	Blackburn R	84
1994–95	Blackburn R	89	Manchester Utd	88
1995–96	Manchester Utd	82	Newcastle Utd	78
1996–97	Manchester Utd	75	Newcastle Utd	68

FOOTBALL LEAGUE CUP

Year	Winners	Runners-up	Result
1961	Aston Villa	Rotherham Utd	0–2,3–0*
1962	Norwich C	Rochdale	3–0, 1–0
1963	Birmingham C	Aston Villa	3–1, 0–0
1964	Leicester C	Stoke C	1–1, 3–2
1965	Chelsea	Leicester C	3–2, 0–0
1966	WBA	West Ham Utd	1–2, 4–1
1967+	QPR	WBA	3–2
1968	Leeds Utd	Arsenal	1–0
1969	Swindon T	Arsenal	3–1*
1970	Manchester C	WBA	2–1*
1971	Tottenham H	Aston Villa	2–0
1972	Stoke C	Chelsea	2–1
1973	Tottenham H	Norwich C	1–0
1974	Wolves	Manchester C	2–1
1975	Aston Villa	Norwich C	1–0
1976	Manchester C	Newcastle Utd	2–1
1977	Aston Villa	Everton	0–0*, 1–1*, 3–2*
1978	Nottm Forest	Liverpool	0–0*, 1–0
1979	Nottm Forest	Southampton	3–2
1980	Wolves	Nottm Forest	1–0
1981	Liverpool	West Ham Utd	1–1*, 2–1
1982	Liverpool	Tottenham H	3–1*
1983	Liverpool	Manchester Utd	2–1*
1984	Liverpool	Everton	0–0*, 1–0
1985	Norwich C	Sunderland	1–0
1986	Oxford Utd	QPR	3–0
1987	Arsenal	Liverpool	2–1
1988	Luton Town	Arsenal	3–2
1989	Nottm Forest	Luton Town	3–1
1990	Nottm Forest	Oldham Ath	1–0
1991	Sheffield Wed	Manchester Utd	1–0
1992	Manchester Utd	Nottm Forest	1–0
1993	Arsenal	Sheffield Wed	2–1
1994	Aston Villa	Manchester Utd	3–1
1995	Liverpool	Bolton Wanderers	2–1
1996	Aston Villa	Leeds Utd	3–0
1997	Leicester City	Middlesbrough	1–1*, 1–0*

Notes: * After extra time, + One-leg Final from this year

FA CUP

Year	Winners	Runners-up	Result
1872	Wanderers	Royal Engineers	1–0
1873	Wanderers	Oxford University	2–0
1874	Oxford University	Royal Engineers	2–0
1875	Royal Engineers	Old Etonians	1–1*, 2–0
1876	Wanderers	Old Etonians	0–0*, 3–0
1877	Wanderers	Oxford University	2–0*
1878	+Wanderers	Royal Engineers	3–1
1879	Old Etonians	Clapham Rovers	1–0
1880	Clapham Rovers	Oxford University	1–0
1881	Old Carthusians	Old Etonians	3–0
1882	Old Etonians	Blackburn R	1–0
1883	Blackburn Olympic	Old Etonians	2–1*
1884	Blackburn R	Queens Park Glasgow	2–1
1885	Blackburn R	Queens Park Glasgow	2–0
1886	Blackburn R	WBA	0–0*, 2–0
1887	Aston Villa	WBA	2–0
1888	WBA	Preston NE	2–1
1889	Preston NE	Wolves	3–0
1890	Blackburn R	Sheffield Wed	6–1
1891	Blackburn R	Notts County	3–1
1892	WBA	Aston Villa	3–0
1893	Wolves	Everton	1–0
1894	Notts County	Bolton W	4–1
1895	Aston Villa	WBA	1–0
1896	Sheffield Wed	Wolves	2–1
1897	Aston Villa	Everton	3–2
1898	Nottm Forest	Derby County	3–1
1899	Sheffield Utd	Derby County	4–1
1900	Bury	Southampton	4–0
1901	Tottenham H	Sheffield Utd	2–2*, 3–1
1902	Sheffield Utd	Southampton	1–1*, 2–1
1903	Bury	Derby County	6–0
1904	Manchester C	Bolton W	1–0
1905	Aston Villa	Newcastle Utd	2–0
1906	Everton	Newcastle Utd	1–0
1907	Sheffield Wed	Everton	2–1
1908	Wolves	Newcastle Utd	3–1
1909	Manchester Utd	Bristol C	1–0
1910	Newcastle Utd	Barnsley	1–1*, 2–0
1911	Bradford C	Newcastle Utd	0–0*, 1–0
1912	Barnsley	WBA	0–0*, 1–0
1913	Aston Villa	Sunderland	1–0
1914	Burnley	Liverpool	1–0
1915	Sheffield Utd	Chelsea	3–0
1920	Aston Villa	Huddersfield T	1–0*
1921	Tottenham H	Wolves	1–0
1922	Huddersfield T	Preston NE	1–0
1923	Bolton W	West Ham Utd	2–0
1924	Newcastle Utd	Aston Villa	2–0
1925	Sheffield Utd	Cardiff C	1–0
1926	Bolton W	Manchester C	1–0
1927	Cardiff C	Arsenal	1–0
1928	Blackburn R	Huddersfield T	3–1
1929	Bolton W	Portsmouth	2–0
1930	Arsenal	Huddersfield T	2–0
1931	WBA	Birmingham C	2–1
1932	Newcastle Utd	Arsenal	2–1
1933	Everton	Manchester C	3–0
1934	Manchester C	Portsmouth	2–1
1935	Sheffield Wed	WBA	4–2
1936	Arsenal	Sheffield Utd	1–0
1937	Sunderland	Preston NE	3–1
1938	Preston NE	Huddersfield T	1–0*
1939	Portsmouth	Wolves	4–1
1946	Derby County	Charlton Ath	4–1*
1947	Charlton Ath	Burnley	1–0*
1948	Manchester Utd	Blackpool	4–2
1949	Wolves	Leicester C	3–1
1950	Arsenal	Liverpool	2–0
1951	Newcastle Utd	Blackpool	2–0
1952	Newcastle Utd	Arsenal	1–0
1953	Blackpool	Bolton W	4–3
1954	WBA	Preston NE	3–2
1955	Newcastle Utd	Manchester C	3–1
1956	Manchester C	Birmingham C	3–1
1957	Aston Villa	Manchester Utd	2–1
1958	Bolton W	Manchester Utd	2–0
1959	Nottm Forest	Luton T	2–1
1960	Wolves	Blackburn R	3–0
1961	Tottenham H	Leicester C	2–0
1962	Tottenham H	Burnley	3–1
1963	Manchester Utd	Leicester C	3–1
1964	West Ham Utd	Preston NE	3–2
1965	Liverpool	Leeds Utd	2–1*
1966	Everton	Sheffield Wed	3–2
1967	Tottenham H	Chelsea	2–1
1968	WBA	Everton	1–0*
1969	Manchester C	Leicester C	1–0
1970	Chelsea	Leeds Utd	2–2*, 2–1*
1971	Arsenal	Liverpool	2–1*
1972	Leeds Utd	Arsenal	1–0
1973	Sunderland	Leeds Utd	1–0
1974	Liverpool	Newcastle Utd	3–0
1975	West Ham Utd	Fulham	2–0
1976	Southampton	Manchester Utd	1–0
1977	Manchester Utd	Liverpool	2–1
1978	Ipswich T	Arsenal	1–0
1979	Arsenal	Manchester Utd	3–2
1980	West Ham Utd	Arsenal	1–0
1981	Tottenham H	Manchester C	1–1*, 3–2
1982	Tottenham H	QPR	1–1*, 1–0
1983	Manchester Utd	Brighton & HA	2–2*, 4–0
1984	Everton	Watford	2–0
1985	Manchester Utd	Everton	1–0*
1986	Liverpool	Everton	3–1
1987	Coventry C	Tottenham H	3–2*
1988	Wimbledon	Liverpool	1–0
1989	Liverpool	Everton	3–2*
1990	Manchester Utd	Crystal Palace	3–3*, 1–0
1991	Tottenham H	Nottm Forest	2–1*
1992	Liverpool	Sunderland	2–0
1993	Arsenal	Sheffield Wed	1–1*, 2–1*
1994	Manchester Utd	Chelsea	4–0
1995	Everton	Manchester Utd	1–0
1996	Manchester Utd	Liverpool	1–0
1997	Chelsea	Middlesbrough	2–0

Notes: * After extra time; + Cup won outright but restored to the FA;

INTERNATIONAL RESULTS 1872–1899

Date	Opponents	Venue	Score
30/11/72	Scotland	Glasgow	0–0
8/3/73	Scotland	Kennington Oval	4–2
7/3/74	Scotland	Glasgow	1–2
6/3/75	Scotland	Kennington Oval	2–2
4/3/76	Scotland	Glasgow	0–3
3/3/77	Scotland	Kennington Oval	1–3
2/3/78	Scotland	Glasgow	2–7
18/1/79	Wales	Kennington Oval	2–1
5/4/79	Scotland	Kennington Oval	5–4
13/3/80	Scotland	Glasgow	4–5
15/3/80	Wales	Wrexham	3–2
26/2/81	Wales	Blackburn	0–1
12/3/81	Scotland	Kennington Oval	1–6
18/2/82	Ireland	Belfast	13–0
11/3/82	Scotland	Glasgow	1–5
13/3/82	Wales	Wrexham	3–5
3/2/83	Wales	Kennington Oval	5–0
24/2/83	Ireland	Liverpool	7–0
10/3/83	Scotland	Sheffield	2–3
25/2/84	Ireland	Belfast	8–1
15/3/84	Scotland	Glasgow	0–1
17/3/84	Wales	Wrexham	4–0
28/2/85	Ireland	Manchester	4–0
14/3/85	Wales	Blackburn	1–1
21/3/85	Scotland	Kennington Oval	1–1
13/3/86	Ireland	Belfast	6–1
29/3/86	Wales	Wrexham	3–1
31/3/86	Scotland	Glasgow	1–1
5/2/87	Ireland	Sheffield	7–0
26/2/87	Wales	Kennington Oval	4–0
19/3/87	Scotland	Blackburn	2–3
4/2/88	Wales	Crewe	5–1
17/3/88	Scotland	Glasgow	5–0
31/3/88	Ireland	Belfast	5–1
23/2/89	Wales	Stoke	4–1
2/3/89	Ireland	Everton	6–1
13/4/89	Scotland	Kennington Oval	2–3
15/3/90	Wales	Wrexham	3–1
15/3/90	Ireland	Belfast	9–1
5/4/90	Scotland	Glasgow	1–1
7/3/91	Wales	Sunderland	4–1
7/3/91	Ireland	Wolverhampton	6–1

Date	Opponent	Venue	Score
6/4/91	Scotland	Blackburn	2–1
5/3/92	Wales	Wrexham	2–0
5/3/92	Ireland	Belfast	2–0
2/4/92	Scotland	Glasgow	4–1
25/2/93	Ireland	Birmingham	6–1
13/3/93	Wales	Stoke	6–0
1/4/93	Scotland	Richmond	5–2
1/3/94	Ireland	Belfast	2–2
12/3/94	Wales	Wrexham	5–1
7/4/94	Scotland	Glasgow	2–2
9/3/95	Ireland	Derby	9–0
18/3/95	Wales	Queen's Club, London	1–1
6/4/95	Scotland	Goodison Park	3–0
7/3/96	Ireland	Belfast	2–0
16/3/96	Wales	Cardiff	9–1
4/4/96	Scotland	Glasgow	1–2
20/2/97	Ireland	Nottingham	6–0
29/3/97	Wales	Sheffield	4–0
3/4/97	Scotland	Crystal Palace	1–2
5/3/98	Ireland	Belfast	3–2
28/3/98	Wales	Wrexham	3–0
2/4/98	Scotland	Glasgow	3–1
18/2/99	Ireland	Sunderland	13–2
20/3/99	Wales	Bristol	4–0
8/4/99	Scotland	Birmingham	2–1

1900–1929

Date	Opponent	Venue	Score
17/3/00	Ireland	Dublin	2–0
26/3/00	Wales	Cardiff	1–1
7/4/00	Scotland	Glasgow	1–4
9/3/01	Ireland	Southampton	3–0
18/3/01	Wales	Newcastle	6–0
30/3/01	Scotland	Crystal Palace	2–2
3/3/02	Wales	Wrexham	0–0
22/3/02	Ireland	Belfast	1–0
3/5/02	Scotland	Birmingham	2–2
14/2/03	Ireland	Wolverhampton	4–0
2/3/03	Wales	Portsmouth	2–1
4/4/03	Scotland	Sheffield	1–2
29/2/04	Wales	Wrexham	2–2
12/3/04	Ireland	Belfast	3–1
9/4/04	Scotland	Glasgow	1–0
25/2/05	Ireland	Middlesbrough	1–1
27/3/05	Wales	Liverpool	3–1
1/4/05	Scotland	Crystal Palace	1–0
17/2/06	Ireland	Belfast	5–0
19/3/06	Wales	Cardiff	1–0
7/4/06	Scotland	Glasgow	1–2
16/2/07	Ireland	Goodison Park	1–0
18/3/07	Wales	Fulham	1–1
6/4/07	Scotland	Newcastle	1–1
15/2/08	Ireland	Belfast	3–1
16/3/08	Wales	Wrexham	7–1
4/4/08	Scotland	Glasgow	1–1
6/6/08	Austria	Vienna	6–1
8/6/08	Austria	Vienna	11–1
10/6/08	Hungary	Budapest	7–0
13/6/08	Bohemia	Prague	4–0
13/2/09	Ireland	Bradford	4–0
15/3/09	Wales	Nottingham	2–0
3/4/09	Scotland	Crystal Palace	2–0
29/5/09	Hungary	Budapest	4–2
31/5/09	Hungary	Budapest	8–2
1/6/09	Austria	Vienna	8–1
12/2/10	Ireland	Belfast	1–1
14/3/10	Wales	Cardiff	1–0
2/4/10	Scotland	Glasgow	0–2
11/2/11	Ireland	Derby	2–1
13/3/11	Wales	Millwall	3–0
1/4/11	Scotland	Goodison Park	1–1
10/2/12	Ireland	Dublin	6–1
11/3/12	Wales	Wrexham	2–0
23/3/12	Scotland	Glasgow	1–1
15/2/13	Ireland	Belfast	1–2
17/3/13	Wales	Bristol	4–3
5/4/13	Scotland	Stamford Bridge	1–0
14/2/14	Ireland	Middlesbrough	0–3
16/3/14	Wales	Cardiff	2–0
4/4/14	Scotland	Glasgow	1–3
25/10/19	Ireland	Belfast	1–1
15/3/20	Wales	Highbury	1–2
10/4/20	Scotland	Sheffield	5–4
23/10/20	Ireland	Sunderland	2–0
14/3/21	Wales	Cardiff	0–0
9/4/21	Scotland	Glasgow	0–3
21/5/21	Belgium	Brussels	2–0
22/10/21	Ireland	Belfast	1–1
13/3/22	Wales	Anfield	1–0
8/4/22	Scotland	Birmingham	0–1
21/10/22	Ireland	West Bromwich	2–0
5/3/23	Wales	Cardiff	2–2
19/3/23	Belgium	Highbury	6–1
14/4/23	Scotland	Glasgow	2–2
10/5/23	France	Paris	4–1
21/5/23	Sweden	Stockholm	4–2
24/5/23	Sweden	Stockholm	3–1
20/10/23	Ireland	Belfast	1–2
1/11/23	Belgium	Antwerp	2–2
3/3/24	Wales	Blackburn	1–2
12/4/24	Scotland	Wembley	1–1
17/5/24	France	Paris	3–1
22/10/24	Ireland	Anfield	3–1
8/12/24	Belgium	West Bromwich	4–0
28/2/25	Wales	Swansea	2–1
4/4/25	Scotland	Glasgow	0–2
21/5/25	France	Paris	3–2
24/10/25	Ireland	Belfast	0–0
1/3/26	Wales	Selhurst Park	1–3
17/4/26	Scotland	Manchester	0–1
24/4/26	Belgium	Antwerp	5–3
20/10/26	Ireland	Anfield	3–3
12/2/27	Wales	Wrexham	3–3
2/4/27	Scotland	Glasgow	2–1
11/5/27	Belgium	Brussels	9–1
21/5/27	Luxembourg	Luxembourg	5–2
26/5/27	France	Paris	6–0
22/10/27	Ireland	Belfast	0–2
28/11/27	Wales	Burnley	1–2
31/3/28	Scotland	Wembley	1–5
17/5/28	France	Paris	5–1
19/5/28	Belgium	Antwerp	3–1
22/10/28	Ireland	Anfield	2–1
17/11/28	Wales	Swansea	3–2
13/4/29	Scotland	Glasgow	0–1
9/5/29	France	Paris	4–1
11/5/29	Belgium	Brussels	5–1
15/5/29	Spain	Madrid	3–4
19/10/29	Ireland	Belfast	3–0
20/11/29	Wales	Stamford Bridge	6–0

1930–1939

Date	Opponent	Venue	Score
5/4/30	Scotland	Wembley	5–2
10/5/30	Germany	Berlin	3–3
14/5/30	Austria	Vienna	0–0
20/10/30	Ireland	Sheffield	5–1
22/11/30	Wales	Wrexham	4–0
28/3/31	Scotland	Glasgow	0–2
14/5/31	France	Paris	2–5
16/5/31	Belgium	Brussels	4–1
17/10/31	Ireland	Belfast	6–2
18/11/31	Wales	Anfield	3–1
9/12/31	Spain	Highbury	7–1
9/4/32	Scotland	Wembley	3–0
17/10/32	Ireland	Blackpool	1–0
16/11/32	Wales	Wrexham	0–0
7/12/32	Austria	Stamford Bridge	4–3
1/4/33	Scotland	Glasgow	1–2
13/5/33	Italy	Rome	1–1
20/5/33	Switzerland	Berne	4–0
14/10/33	Ireland	Belfast	3–0
15/11/33	Wales	Newcastle	1–2
6/12/33	France	White Hart Lane	4–1
14/4/34	Scotland	Wembley	3–0
10/5/34	Hungary	Budapest	1–2
16/5/34	Czechoslovakia	Prague	1–2
29/9/34	Wales	Cardiff	4–0
14/11/34	Italy	Highbury	3–2
6/2/35	Ireland	Goodison Park	2–1
6/4/35	Scotland	Glasgow	0–2
18/5/35	Holland	Amsterdam	1–0
19/10/35	Ireland	Belfast	3–1
4/12/35	Germany	White Hart Lane	3–0
5/2/36	Wales	Wolverhampton	1–2
4/4/36	Scotland	Wembley	1–1
6/5/36	Austria	Vienna	1–2
9/5/36	Belgium	Brussels	2–3
17/10/36	Wales	Cardiff	1–2
18/11/36	Ireland	Stoke	3–1
2/12/36	Hungary	Highbury	6–2
17/4/37	Scotland	Glasgow	1–3
14/5/37	Norway	Oslo	6–0
17/5/37	Sweden	Stockholm	4–0
20/5/37	Finland	Helsinki	8–0
23/10/37	Ireland	Belfast	5–1
17/11/37	Wales	Middlesbrough	2–1
1/12/37	Czechoslovakia	White Hart Lane	5–4
9/4/38	Scotland	Wembley	0–1
14/5/38	Germany	Berlin	6–3
21/5/38	Switzerland	Zurich	1–2
26/5/38	France	Paris	4–2
22/10/38	Wales	Cardiff	2–4
26/10/38	FIFA	Highbury	3–0
9/11/38	Norway	Newcastle	4–0
16/11/38	Ireland	Manchester	7–0
15/4/39	Scotland	Glasgow	2–1
13/5/39	Italy	Milan	2–2
18/5/39	Yugoslavia	Belgrade	1–2
24/5/39	Romania	Bucharest	2–0

1940–49

Date	Opponent	Venue	Score
28/9/46	N Ireland	Belfast	7–2
30/9/46	Rep of Ireland	Dublin	1–0
19/10/46	Wales	Maine Road	3–0
27/11/46	Holland	Huddersfield	8–2
12/4/47	Scotland	Wembley	1–1
3/5/47	France	Highbury	3–0
18/5/47	Switzerland	Zurich	0–1
27/5/47	Portugal	Lisbon	10–0
21/9/47	Belgium	Brussels	5–2
18/10/47	Wales	Cardiff	3–0
5/11/47	N Ireland	Goodison Park	2–2
19/11/47	Sweden	Highbury	4–2
10/4/48	Scotland	Glasgow	2–0
16/5/48	Italy	Turin	4–0
26/9/48	Denmark	Copenhagen	0–0
9/10/48	N Ireland	Belfast	6–2
10/11/48	Wales	Villa Park	1–0
1/12/48	Switzerland	Highbury	6–0
9/4/48	Scotland	Wembley	1–3
13/5/49	Sweden	Stockholm	1–3
18/5/49	Norway	Oslo	4–1
22/5/49	France	Paris	3–1
21/9/49	Rep of Ireland	Goodison Park	0–2
15/10/49	Wales	Cardiff	4–1 (WCQ)
16/11/49	N Ireland	Maine Road	9–2 (WCQ)
30/11/49	Italy	White Hart Lane	2–0

1950

Date	Opponent	Venue	Score
15/4	Scotland	Glasgow	1–0 (WCQ)
14/5	Portugal	Lisbon	5–3
18/5	Belgium	Brussels	4–1
15/6	Chile	Rio de Janeiro	2–0 (WCF)
29/6	USA	Belo Horizonte	0–1 (WCF)
2/7	Spain	Rio de Janeiro	0–1 (WCF)
7/10	N Ireland	Belfast	4–1
15/11	Wales	Sunderland	4–2
22/11	Yugoslavia	Highbury	2–2

1951

Date	Opponent	Venue	Score
14/4	Scotland	Wembley	2–3
9/5	Argentina	Wembley	2–1
9/5	Portugal	Goodison Park	5–2
3/10	France	Highbury	2–2
20/10	Wales	Cardiff	1–1
14/11	N Ireland	Villa Park	2–0
28/11	Austria	Wembley	2–2

1952

Date	Opponent	Venue	Score
5/4	Scotland	Glasgow	2–1
18/5	Italy	Florence	1–1
25/5	Austria	Vienna	3–2
28/5	Switzerland	Zurich	3–0
4/10	N Ireland	Belfast	2–2
12/11	Wales	Wembley	5–2
26/11	Belgium	Wembley	5–0

1953

Date	Opponent	Venue	Score
18/4	Scotland	Wembley	2–2
17/5	Argentina	Buenos Aires	0–0
	(abandoned after 21 minutes)		
24/5	Chile	Santiago	2–1
31/5	Uruguay	Montevideo	1–2
8/6	USA	New York	6–3
10/10	Wales	Cardiff	4–1 (WCQ)
21/10	Rest of Europe	Wembley	4–4
11/11	N Ireland	Goodison Pk	3–1 (WCQ)
25/11	Hungary	Wembley	3–6

1954

Date	Opponent	Venue	Score
3/4	Scotland	Glasgow	4–2 (WCQ)
16/5	Yugoslavia	Belgrade	0–1
23/5	Hungary	Budapest	1–7
17/6	Belgium	Basle	4–4* (WCF)
20/6	Switzerland	Berne	2–0 (WCF)
26/6	Uruguay	Basle	2–4 (WCF)
2/10	N Ireland	Belfast	2–0
10/11	Wales	Wembley	3–2
1/12	W Germany	Wembley	3–1

1955

Date	Opponent	Venue	Score
2/4	Scotland	Wembley	7–2
18/5	France	Paris	0–1
18/5	Spain	Madrid	1–1
22/5	Portugal	Oporto	1–3
2/10	Denmark	Copenhagen	5–1
22/10	Wales	Cardiff	1–1
2/11	N Ireland	Wembley	3–0
30/11	Spain	Wembley	4–1

1956

Date	Opponent	Venue	Score
14/4	Scotland	Glasgow	1–1
9/5	Brazil	Wembley	4–2
16/5	Sweden	Stockholm	0–0
20/5	Finland	Helsinki	5–1
26/5	West Germany	Berlin	3–1
6/10	N Ireland	Belfast	1–1
14/11	Wales	Wembley	3–1
28/11	Yugoslavia	Wembley	3–0
5/12	Denmark	Wolverhampton	5–2 (WCQ)

1957

Date	Opponent	Venue	Score
6/4	Scotland	Wembley	2–1
8/5	Rep of Ireland	Wembley	5–1 (WCQ)
15/5	Denmark	Copenhagen	4–1 (WCQ)
19/5	Rep of Ireland	Dublin	1–1 (WCQ)
19/10	Wales	Cardiff	4–0
6/11	N Ireland	Wembley	2–3
27/11	France	Wembley	4–0

1958

Date	Opponent	Venue	Score
19/4	Scotland	Glasgow	4–0
7/5	Portugal	Wembley	2–1
11/5	Yugoslavia	Belgrade	0–5
18/5	USSR	Moscow	1–1
8/6	USSR	Gothenburg	2–2 (WCF)
11/6	Brazil	Gothenburg	0–0 (WCF)
15/6	Austria	Boras	2–2 (WCF)
17/6	USSR	Gothenburg	0–1 (WCF)
4/10	N Ireland	Belfast	3–3
22/10	USSR	Wembley	5–0
26/11	Wales	Villa Park	2–2

1959

Date	Opponent	Venue	Score
11/4	Scotland	Wembley	1–0
6/5	Italy	Wembley	2–2
13/5	Brazil	Rio de Janeiro	0–2
17/5	Peru	Lima	1–4
24/5	Mexico	Mexico C	1–2
28/5	USA	Los Angeles	8–1
17/10	Wales	Cardiff	1–1

28/10	Sweden	Wembley	2–3
18/11	N Ireland	Wembley	2–1

1960

19/4	Scotland	Glasgow	1–1
11/5	Yugoslavia	Wembley	3–3
15/5	Spain	Madrid	0–3
22/5	Hungary	Budapest	0–2
8/10	N Ireland	Belfast	5–2
19/10	Luxembourg	Luxembourg	9-0 (WCQ)
26/10	Spain	Wembley	4–2
23/11	Wales	Wembley	5–1

1961

15/4	Scotland	Wembley	9–3
10/5	Mexico	Wembley	8–0
21/5	Portugal	Lisbon	1–1 (WCQ)
24/5	Italy	Rome	3–2
27/5	Austria	Vienna	1–3
28/9	Luxembourg	Highbury	4–1 (WCQ)
14/10	Wales	Cardiff	1–1
25/10	Portugal	Wembley	2–0 (WCQ)
22–11	N Ireland	Wembley	1–1

1962

4/4	Austria	Wembley	3–1
14/4	Scotland	Glasgow	0–2
9/5	Switzerland	Wembley	3–1
20/5	Peru	Lima	4–0
31/5	Hungary	Rancagua	1–2 (WCF)
2/6	Argentina	Rancagua	3–1 (WCF)
7/6	Bulgaria	Rancagua	0–0 (WCF)
10/6	Brazil	Vina del Mar	1–3 (WCF)
3/10	France	Hillsborough	1–1 (ECQ)
20/10	N Ireland	Belfast	3–1
21/11	Wales	Wembley	4–0

1963

27/2	France	Paris	2–5 (ECQ)
6/4	Scotland	Wembley	1–2
8/5	Brazil	Wembley	1–1
20/5	Czechoslovakia	Bratislava	4–2
2/6	East Germany	Leipzig	2–1
5/6	Switzerland	Basle	8–1
12/10	Wales	Cardiff	4–0
23/10	Rest of World	Wembley	2–1
20/11	N Ireland	Wembley	8–3

1964

11/4	Scotland	Glasgow	0–1
6/5	Uruguay	Wembley	2–1
17/5	Portugal	Lisbon	4–3
24/5	Rep of Ireland	Dublin	3–1
27/5	USA	New York	10–0
30/5	Brazil	Rio de Janeiro	1–5 (BJT)
4/6	Portugal	São Paulo	1–1 (BJT)
6/6	Argentina	Rio de Janeiro	0–1 (BJT)
3/10	N Ireland	Belfast	4–3
21/10	Belgium	Wembley	2–2
18/11	Wales	Wembley	2–1
9/12	Holland	Amsterdam	1–1

1965

10/4	Scotland	Wembley	2–2
5/5	Hungary	Wembley	1–0
9/5	Yugoslavia	Belgrade	1–1
12/5	W Germany	Nuremberg	1–0
16/5	Sweden	Gothenburg	2–1
2/10	Wales	Cardiff	0–0
20/10	Austria	Wembley	2–3
10/11	N Ireland	Wembley	2–1
8/12	Spain	Madrid	2–0

1966

5/1	Poland	Anfield	1–1
23/2	W Germany	Wembley	1–0
2/4	Scotland	Glasgow	4–3
4/5	Yugoslavia	Wembley	2–0
26/6	Finland	Helsinki	3–0
29/6	Norway	Oslo	6–1

3/7	Denmark	Copenhagen	2–0
5/7	Poland	Chorzow	1–0
11/7	Uruguay	Wembley	0–0 (WCF)
16/7	Mexico	Wembley	2–0 (WCF)
20/7	France	Wembley	2–0 (WCF)
23/7	Argentina	Wembley	1–0 (WCF)
26/7	Portugal	Wembley	2–1 (WCF)
30/7	W Germany	Wembley	4–2* (WCF)
22/10	N Ireland	Belfast	2–0 (ECQ)
2/11	Czechoslovakia	Wembley	0–0
16/11	Wales	Wembley	5–1 (ECQ)

1967

15/4	Scotland	Wembley	2–3 (ECQ)
24/5	Spain	Wembley	2–0
27/5	Austria	Vienna	1–0
21/10	Wales	Cardiff	3–0 (ECQ)
22/11	N Ireland	Wembley	2–0 (ECQ)
6/12	USSR	Wembley	2–2

1968

24/2	Scotland	Glasgow	1–1 (ECQ)
3/4	Spain	Wembley	1–0 (ECQ)
8/5	Spain	Madrid	2–1 (ECQ)
22/5	Sweden	Wembley	3–1
1/6	W Germany	Hanover	0–1
5/6	Yugoslavia	Florence	0–1 (ECF)
8/6	USSR	Rome	2–0 (ECF)
6/11	Romania	Bucharest	0–0
11/12	Bulgaria	Wembley	1–1

1969

15/1	Romania	Wembley	1–1
12/3	France	Wembley	5–0
3/5	N Ireland	Belfast	3–1
7/5	Wales	Wembley	2–1
10/5	Scotland	Wembley	4–1
1/6	Mexico	Mexico C	0–0
8/6	Uruguay	Montevideo	2–1
12/6	Brazil	Rio de Janeiro	1–2
5/11	Holland	Amsterdam	1–0
10/12	Portugal	Wembley	1–0

1970

14/1	Holland	Wembley	0–0
25/2	Belgium	Brussels	3–1
18/4	Wales	Cardiff	1–1
21/4	N Ireland	Wembley	3–1
25/4	Scotland	Glasgow	0–0
20/5	Colombia	Bogota	4–0
24/5	Ecuador	Quito	2–0
2/6	Romania	Guadalajara	1–0 (WCF)
7/6	Brazil	Guadalajara	0–1 (WCF)
11/6	Czechoslovakia	Guadalajara	1–0 (WCF)
14/6	W Germany	Leon	2–3* (WCF)
25/11	E Germany	Wembley	3–1

1971

3/2	Malta	Valletta	1–0 (ECQ)
21/4	Greece	Wembley	4–0 (ECQ)
12/5	Malta	Wembley	5–0 (ECQ)
15/5	N Ireland	Belfast	1–0
19/5	Wales	Wembley	0–0
22/5	Scotland	Wembley	3–1
13/10	Switzerland	Basle	3–2 (ECQ)
10/11	Switzerland	Wembley	1–1 (ECQ)
1/12	Greece	Athens	2–0 (ECQ)

1972

29/4	W Germany	Wembley	1–3 (ECQ)
13/5	W Germany	Berlin	0–0 (ECQ)
20/5	Wales	Cardiff	3–0
23/5	N Ireland	Wembley	0–1
27/5	Scotland	Glasgow	1–0
11/10	Yugoslavia	Wembley	1–1
15/11	Wales	Cardiff	1–0 (WCQ)

1973

24/1	Wales	Wembley	1–1 (WCQ)
14/2	Scotland	Glasgow	5–0

12/5	N Ireland	Anfield	2–1
15/5	Wales	Wembley	3–0
19/5	Scotland	Wembley	1–0
27/5	Czechoslovakia	Prague	1–1
6/6	Poland	Chorzow	0–2 (WCQ)
10/6	USSR	Moscow	2–1
14/6	Italy	Turin	0–2
26/9	Austria	Vienna	7–0
17/10	Poland	Wembley	1–1 (WCQ)
14/11	Italy	Wembley	0–1

1974

3/4	Portugal	Lisbon	0–0
11/5	Wales	Cardiff	2–0
15/5	N Ireland	Wembley	1–0
18/5	Scotland	Glasgow	0–2
22/5	Argentina	Wembley	2–2
29/5	East Germany	Leipzig	1–1
1/6	Bulgaria	Sofia	1–0
5/6	Yugoslavia	Belgrade	2–2
30/10	Czechoslovakia	Wembley	3–0 (ECQ)
20/11	Portugal	Wembley	0–0 (ECQ)

1975

12/3	W Germany	Wembley	2–0
16/4	Cyprus	Wembley	5–0 (ECQ)
11/5	Cyprus	Limassol	1–0 (ECQ)
17/5	N Ireland	Belfast	0–0
21/5	Wales	Wembley	2–2
24/5	Scotland	Wembley	5–1
3/9	Switzerland	Basle	2–1
30/10	Czechoslovakia	Bratislava	1–2 (ECQ)
19/11	Portugal	Lisbon	1–1 (ECQ)

1976

24/3	Wales	Wrexham	2–1
8/5	Wales	Cardiff	1–0
11/5	N Ireland	Wembley	4–0
15/5	Scotland	Glasgow	1–2
23/5	Brazil	Los Angeles	0–1 (USBT)
28/5	Italy	New York	3–2 (USBT)
13/6	Finland	Helsinki	4–1 (WCQ)
8/9	Rep of Ireland	Wembley	1–1
13/10	Finland	Wembley	2–1 (WCQ)
17/11	Italy	Rome	0–2 (WCQ)

1977

9/2	Holland	Wembley	0–2
30/3	Luxembourg	Wembley	5–0 (WCQ)
28/5	N Ireland	Belfast	2–1
31/5	Wales	Wembley	0–1
4/6	Scotland	Wembley	1–2
8/6	Brazil	Rio de Janeiro	0–0
12/6	Argentina	Buenos Aires	1–1
15/6	Uruguay	Montevideo	0–0
7/9	Switzerland	Wembley	0–0
12/10	Luxembourg	Luxembourg	2–0 (WCQ)
16/11	Italy	Wembley	2–0 (WCQ)

1978

22/2	W Germany	Munich	1–2
19/4	Brazil	Wembley	1–1
13/5	Wales	Cardiff	3–1
16/5	N Ireland	Wembley	1–0
20/5	Scotland	Glasgow	1–0
24/5	Hungary	Wembley	4–1
20/9	Denmark	Copenhagen	4–3 (ECQ)
25/10	Rep of Ireland	Dublin	1–1 (ECQ)
29/11	Czechoslovakia	Wembley	1–0

1979

7/2	N Ireland	Wembley	4–0 (ECQ)
19/5	N Ireland	Belfast	2–0
23/5	Wales	Wembley	0–0
26/5	Scotland	Wembley	3–1
6/6	Bulgaria	Sofia	3–0 (ECQ)
10/6	Sweden	Stockholm	0–0
13/6	Austria	Vienna	3–4
12/9	Denmark	Wembley	1–0 (ECQ)
17/10	N Ireland	Belfast	5–1 (ECQ)

22/11	Bulgaria	Wembley	2–0 (ECQ)

1980

6/2	Rep of Ireland	Wembley	2–0 (ECQ)
26/3	Spain	Barcelona	2–0
13/5	Argentina	Wembley	3–1
17/5	Wales	Wrexham	1–4
20/5	N Ireland	Wembley	1–1
24/5	Scotland	Glasgow	2–0
31/5	Australia	Sydney	2–1
12/6	Belgium	Turin	1–1 (ECF)
15/6	Italy	Turin	0–1 (ECF)
18/6	Spain	Naples	2–1 (ECF)
10/9	Norway	Wembley	4–0 (WCQ)
15/10	Romania	Bucharest	1–2 (WCQ)
19/11	Switzerland	Wembley	2–1 (WCQ)

1981

25/3	Spain	Wembley	1–2
29/4	Romania	Wembley	0–0 (WCQ)
12/5	Brazil	Wembley	0–1
20/5	Wales	Wembley	0–0
23/5	Scotland	Wembley	0–1
30/5	Switzerland	Basle	1–2 (WCQ)
6/6	Hungary	Budapest	3–1 (WCQ)
9/9	Norway	Oslo	1–2 (WCQ)
18/11	Hungary	Wembley	1–0 (WCQ)

1982

23/2	N Ireland	Wembley	4–0
25/5	Holland	Wembley	2–0
29/5	Scotland	Glasgow	1–0
2/6	Iceland	Reykjavik	1–1
3/6	Finland	Helsinki	4–1
16/6	France	Bilbao	3–1 (WCF)
20/6	Czechoslovakia	Bilbao	2–0 (WCF)
25/6	Kuwait	Bilbao	1–0 (WCF)
29/6	W Germany	Madrid	0–0 (WCF)
5/7	Spain	Madrid	0–0 (WCF)
22/9	Denmark	Copenhagen	2–2 (ECQ)
13/10	W Germany	Wembley	1–2
17/11	Greece	Salonika	3–0 (ECQ)
15/12	Luxembourg	Wembley	9–0 (ECQ)

1983

23/2	Wales	Wembley	2–1
30/3	Greece	Wembley	0–0 (ECQ)
27/4	Hungary	Wembley	2–0 (ECQ)
28/5	N Ireland	Belfast	0–0
1/6	Scotland	Wembley	2–0
12/6	Australia	Sydney	0–0
15/6	Australia	Brisbane	1–0
19/6	Australia	Melbourne	1–1
21/9	Denmark	Wembley	0–1 (ECQ)
12/10	Hungary	Budapest	3–0 (ECQ)
16/11	Luxembourg	Luxembourg	4–0 (ECQ)

1984

29/2	France	Paris	0–2
4/4	N Ireland	Wembley	1–0
2/5	Wales	Wrexham	0–1
26/5	Scotland	Glasgow	1–1
2/6	USSR	Wembley	0–2
10/6	Brazil	Rio de Janeiro	2–0
13/6	Uruguay	Montevideo	0–2
17/6	Chile	Santiago	0–0
12/9	E Germany	Wembley	1–0
17/10	Finland	Wembley	5–0 (WCQ)
14/11	Turkey	Istanbul	8–0 (WCQ)

1985

27/2	N Ireland	Belfast	1–0 (WCQ)
26/3	Rep of Ireland	Wembley	2–1
1/5	Romania	Bucharest	0–0 (WCQ)
22/5	Finland	Helsinki	1–1 (WCQ)
25/5	Scotland	Glasgow	0–1
6/6	Italy	Mexico C	1–2
9/6	Mexico	Mexico C	0–1
12/6	W Germany	Mexico C	3–0
16/6	USA	Los Angeles	5–0

11/9	Romania	Wembley	1–1 (WCQ)
16/10	Turkey	Wembley	5–0 (WCQ)
13/11	N Ireland	Wembley	0–0 (WCQ)

1986

29/1	Egypt	Cairo	4–0
26/2	Israel	Ramat Gan	2–1
26/3	USSR	Tbilisi	1–0
23/4	Scotland	Wembley	2–1
17/5	Mexico	Los Angeles	3–0
24/5	Canada	Burnaby	1–0
3/6	Portugal	Monterrey	0–1 (WCF)
6/6	Morocco	Monterrey	0–0 (WCF)
11/6	Poland	Monterrey	3–0 (WCF)
18/6	Paraguay	Mexico C	3–0 (WCF)
22/6	Argentina	Mexico C	1–2 (WCF)
10/9	Sweden	Stockholm	0–1
15/10	N Ireland	Wembley	3–0 (ECQ)
12/11	Yugoslavia	Wembley	2–0 (ECQ)

1987

10/2	Spain	Madrid	4–2
1/4	N Ireland	Belfast	2–0 (ECQ)
29/4	Turkey	Izmir	0–0 (ECQ)
19/5	Brazil	Wembley	1–1
23/5	Scotland	Glasgow	0–0
9/9	W Germany	Düsseldorf	1–3
14/10	Turkey	Wembley	8–0 (ECQ)
11/11	Yugoslavia	Belgrade	4–1 (ECQ)

1988

17/2	Israel	Tel Aviv	0–0
23/3	Holland	Wembley	2–2
27/4	Hungary	Budapest	0–0
21/5	Scotland	Wembley	1–0
24/5	Colombia	Wembley	1–1
28/5	Switzerland	Lausanne	1–0
12/6	Rep of Ireland	Stuttgart	0–1 (ECF)
15/6	Holland	Düsseldorf	1–3 (ECF)
18/6	USSR	Frankfurt	1–3 (ECF)
14/9	Denmark	Wembley	1–0
19/10	Sweden	Wembley	0–0 (WCQ)
16/11	Saudi Arabia	Riyadh	1–1

1989

8/2	Greece	Athens	2–1
8/3	Albania	Tirana	2–0 (WCQ)
26/4	Albania	Wembley	5–0 (WCQ)
23/5	Chile	Wembley	0–0
27/5	Scotland	Glasgow	2–0
3/6	Poland	Wembley	3–0 (WCQ)
7/6	Denmark	Copenhagen	1–1
6/9	Sweden	Stockholm	0–0 (WCQ)
11/10	Poland	Katowice	0–0 (WCQ)
15/11	Italy	Wembley	0–0
13/12	Yugoslavia	Wembley	2–1

1990

28/3	Brazil	Wembley	1–0
25/4	Czechoslovakia	Wembley	4–2
15/5	Denmark	Wembley	1–0
22/5	Uruguay	Wembley	1–2
2/6	Tunisia	Tunis	1–1
11/6	Rep of Ireland	Cagliari	1–1 (WCF)
16/6	Holland	Cagliari	0–0 (WCF)
21/6	Egypt	Cagliari	1–0 (WCF)
26/6	Belgium	Bologna	1–0 (WCF)
1/7	Cameroon	Naples	3–2 (WCF)
4/7	W Germany	Turin	1–1* (WCF)
	(England lost 3–4 on penalties)		
7/7	Italy	Bari	1–2 (WCF)
12/9	Hungary	Wembley	1–0
17/10	Poland	Wembley	2–0 (ECQ)
14/11	Rep of Ireland	Dublin	1–1 (ECQ)

1991

6/2	Cameroon	Wembley	2–0
27/3	Rep of Ireland	Wembley	1–1 (ECQ)
1/5	Turkey	Izmir	1–0 (ECQ)
21/5	USSR	Wembley	3–1

25/5	Argentina	Wembley	2–2
1/6	Australia	Sydney	1–0
3/6	New Zealand	Auckland	1–0
8/6	New Zealand	Wellington	2–0
12/6	Malaysia	Kuala Lumpur	4–2
11/9	Germany	Wembley	0–1
16/10	Turkey	Wembley	1–0 (ECQ)
13/11	Poland	Poznan	1–1 (ECQ)

1992

19/2	France	Wembley	2–0
25/3	Czechoslovakia	Prague	2–2
29/4	CIS	Moscow	2–2
12/5	Hungary	Budapest	1–0
17/5	Brazil	Wembley	1–1
3/6	Finland	Helsinki	2–1
11/6	Denmark	Malmo	0–0 (ECF)
14/6	France	Malmo	0–0 (ECF)
17/6	Sweden	Stockholm	1–2 (ECF)
9/9	Spain	Santander	0–1
14/10	Norway	Wembley	1–1 (WCQ)
18/11	Turkey	Wembley	4–0 (WCQ)

1993

17/2	San Marino	Wembley	6–0 (WCQ)
31/3	Turkey	Izmir	2–0 (WCQ)
28/4	Holland	Wembley	2–2 (WCQ)
29/5	Poland	Katowice	1–1 (WCQ)
2/6	Norway	Oslo	0–2 (WCQ)
9/6	USA	Boston	0–2 (USC)
13/6	Brazil	Washington	1–1 (USC)
19/6	Germany	Detroit	1–2 (USC)
8/9	Poland	Wembley	3–0 (WCQ)
13/10	Holland	Rotterdam	0–2 (WCQ)
17/11	San Marino	Bologna	7–1 (WCQ)

1994

9/3	Denmark	Wembley	1–0
17/5	Greece	Wembley	5–0
22/5	Norway	Wembley	0–0
7/9	United States	Wembley	2–0
16/11	Nigeria	Wembley	1–0

1995

15/2	Rep of Ireland	Dublin	0–1
	(abandoned after 21 minutes)		
29/3	Uruguay	Wembley	0–0
3/6	Japan	Wembley	2–1 (UT)
8/6	Sweden	Leeds	3–3 (UT)
11/6	Brazil	Wembley	1–3 (UT)
6/9	Colombia	Wembley	0–0
11/10	Norway	Oslo	0–0
15/11	Switzerland	Wembley	3–1
12/12	Portugal	Wembley	1–1

1996

27/3	Bulgaria	Wembley	1–0
24/4	Croatia	Wembley	0–0
18/5	Hungary	Wembley	3–0
23/5	China	Beijing	3–0
8/6	Switzerland	Wembley	1–1 (ECF)
15/6	Scotland	Wembley	2–0 (ECF)
18/6	Holland	Wembley	4–1 (ECF)
22/6	Spain	Wembley	0–0 (ECF)
	(England won 4–2 on penalties)		
26/6	Germany	Wembley	1–1 (ECF)
	(England lost 5–6 on penalties)		
1/9	Moldova	Chisinau	3–0 (WCQ)
9/10	Poland	Wembley	2–1 (WCQ)
9/11	Georgia	Tbilisi	2–0 (WCQ)

1997

12/2	Italy	Wembley	0–1 (WCQ)
29/3	Mexico	Wembley	2–0
30/4	Georgia	Wembley	2–0 (WCQ)
24/5	South Africa	Old Trafford	2–1
31/5	Poland	Chorzow	2–0 (WCQ)
4/6	Italy	Nantes	2–0 (TDF)
7/6	France	Montpellier	1–0 (TDF)
10/6	Brazil	Paris	0–1 (TDF)

SCOTLAND

Nobody knows just when football was introduced to Scotland. There is reference to it being played there in the early seventeenth century, but no further record of it until a report of a challenge match staged between a team of Highlanders and the YMCA on the Queen's Park Recreation Ground (with 20 men a side) in 1867.

That game so caught the participants' imagination that on July 9, 1867, a meeting was organized at 3 Eglinton Terrace, Glasgow, for the purpose of forming a football club. Thus the famous Queen's Park club came into existence. They did not concede a single goal in their first five years, and they represented Scotland in the very first official international against England in 1872.

Before that Queen's Park had enrolled in the (English) Football Association and participated in the inaugural FA Cup competition, gaining a bye to the semi-final. Here they met the Wanderers in London and surprised everyone south of the border by forcing a goalless draw. Unfortunately funds did not stretch to a replay and Queen's Park were forced to scratch.

The visit to London nevertheless stimulated Scottish enthusiasm, and early in 1873 a move to form their own Association was set in progress. Seven clubs attended this historic gathering in Glasgow on March 13, and the Queen's Park officials had little difficulty persuading their colleagues of the good sense of the proposition on the table.

The founder members alongside Queen's Park were Third Lanark, Vale of Leven, Clydesdale, Eastern, Dumbreck and Granville. All were eventually persuaded to adopt the FA rules, but only after considerable argument over the offside rule.

The initial Scottish Cup competition was patronized by 16 clubs. Predictably, Queen's Park won it without conceding a goal, beating Clydesdale 2–0 in the final.

Religion and Rivalry

Having maintained their dominance in this competition for two more years, Queen's Park then found their pre-eminence in Scottish football gradually fading. Other names began to appear on the silverware: the Vale of Leven, Dumbarton, Renton – and then Hibernian, a club run by Roman Catholics and based in Edinburgh.

Hibs' SFA Cup Final win over Dumbarton in 1887 was considered sensational and created such a wave of enthusiasm among fellow religionists in Glasgow that the Celtic club was born. Celtic's success was immediate. Their first official game was a friendly with Rangers in May 1888. It was the first of the "Old Firm" clashes which have been the centre-piece of the Scottish domestic calendar ever since, and the beginning of a rivalry, both sporting and religious, which has been exploited to the full.

Rangers, as Queen's Park had done, entered the English FA Cup and in 1886–87 were eliminated by Aston Villa at the semi-final stage at Crewe. This was the last time a Scottish team competed in the English Cup. The Scottish FA disapproved and at their annual meeting on May 10, 1887, decreed that all Scottish clubs must withdraw their memberships of the FA. They were compensated for the loss of games by the popularity of the Glasgow Cup.

A League of Their Own

Scottish football, however, was losing ground. The administrators, still strongly influenced by amateur Queen's Park, repeatedly refused to accept professionalism and many of the best players were tempted to English clubs.

The practice of illegal payments through "boot money" became an open secret, but clubs needed revenue to finance their subterfuge. The success of the Football League in England had not gone unnoticed, and in 1890–91 Rangers, Celtic, Third Lanark, Hearts, St Mirren, Dumbarton, Renton, Cowlairs, Cambuslang, Vale of Leven and Abercorn formed the Scottish League. Three years later the SFA reluctantly bowed to professionalism and this coincided with Rangers winning the Scottish Cup for the first time. Their opponents? Celtic, who were beaten 3–1.

Scottish football entered the twentieth century on a firm footing. Their national side had won 15 and drawn six of the 29 games against England, and it was widely accepted that the Scots had applied a more scientific mind to their game.

In contrast with England, where the early protaganists on the field were mainly drawn from the gentry, the majority of players north of the border were recruited from working-class backgrounds. Their concept of the game was totally different.

The English persisted in a dribbling game, with individuals taking on opponents one after the other until they lost possession. The Scots, on the other hand, developed the passing game, attacking in groups and moving the ball one to the other. The slightly built inside-forward who could throw an opponent with a shrug of the shoulders, the flick of a hip, the precise pass, became symbolic of the artistry of Scottish football.

Over the years the Scottish game produced a galaxy of great individualists who never lost sight of their role in the team pattern.

From players of this type, it was said, most of Scotland's greatness in the game was measured. These included Bobby Walker of Hearts and later Jimmy Mason, Jimmy Williamson, Willie Buchan and Tommy Walker; then came "Slim" Jim Baxter in the 1960s; the impish brilliance of Denis Law and Gordon Strachan.

The "Old Firm"
In the 32 years from 1900 the dominance of Rangers and Celtic became almost suffocating. Third Lanark had won the Championship flag in 1904, but after that the "Old Firm" left the rest in their wake. Celtic reeled off

six successive titles, and Rangers responded with three. So it went on, Rangers stringing five more Championships together in consecutive seasons before Motherwell intervened to disturb the pattern in 1932. The game had overcome its blackest day: April 5, 1902, the day of the Ibrox disaster. A terrace of wooden steps supported by pillars collapsed during an international with England, plunging hundreds of fans into a chasm; 25 died and more than 500 were injured, yet the game continued – the players, officials, and indeed majority of fans, unaware of the tragedy in their midst.

The alteration to the offside law in 1925 significantly altered the Scottish style of play. The stopper centre-half was introduced, a more cautious approach leading to negative play. Even the new defensive formula, however, could not contain Jimmy McCrory, the Celtic centre-forward, who in January 1928 set a Scottish First Division record when he scored eight goals in one match against Dunfermline Athletic.

The Scottish League Cup was born in 1946 out of the wartime Southern Cup competition, and following the war there was also an attempt to reorganize the League itself. The concept was very similar to the Premiership, introduced in England in 1992. The idea was for the more powerful clubs to break away and invite others to join them in a 16-club competition under the banner of the "Super-League".

It was all about the distribution of wealth. The big clubs did not want to continue to support the smaller clubs. However, at a special meeting Clyde, opponents of such a split, received backing from a most unexpected source when both Celtic and Rangers supported them.

The Super-League was dead
On the playing front Hibernian were to emerge as one of the most attractive and effective combinations since the mid-thirties. They won three Championships in 1948, 1951 and 1952. Aberdeen, Hearts, Dundee and Kilmarnock also enjoyed League success before Celtic set a record with nine successive League

Championship wins between 1966 and 1974.

Billy McNeill and company also gained universal acclaim as Celtic became the first British side to win the European Cup. A 2–1 win over Internazionale in Lisbon on 25 May, 1967, provided the Parkhead faithful's greatest hour-and-a-half.

In 1975 the Premier Division was introduced and Rangers ran away with the honours, finishing a clear six points ahead of Celtic. The Ibrox Park club established yet another record in 1993, claiming their fifth Premiership title in a row after never looking like being caught.

The Rangers revival was instigated by manager Graeme Souness, who set a new trend by looking to England for players. He took England goalkeeper Chris Woods, centre-forward Mark Hateley, midfielder Ray Wilkins, right-back Gary Stevens and many more.

Dundee United, winners in 1983, and Aberdeen, winners in 1984 and 1985, under manager Alex Ferguson, had stimulated public interest by breaking the "Old Firm" monopoly. But it was only a brief interruption.

Dundee United won the 109th Cup Final in 1994, to end Rangers' dream of landing successive trebles for the first time in Scottish history. It was United's first victory in seven Final appearances.

Scots on the World Stage
At international level Scotland had remained an enigma. Capable of beating the best, they have usually tripped up against "easy" opponents. Scotland remained unbeaten against foreign opposition until 1931 when, lacking the players of Rangers and Celtic, they were heavily beaten in Vienna and Rome. Austria did manage a 2–2 draw in Glasgow in 1933, but had to wait till 1950 before they could shatter Scotland's proud home record.

The withdrawal of the British Associations from FIFA in 1928 no doubt hampered the Scots' development at international level, but there were no hints of this on March 31 of that year at Wembley.

Scotland took England apart with football as delightful as any which had been seen. Their slick combina-

tion play, speed of thought and precision passing were all too much for England, and the 5–1 scoreline emphasized the gulf between the two teams. This team were hailed as the "Wembley Wizards": Harkness in goal, full-backs Nelson and Law, half-backs Gibson, Bradshaw and McMullen and forwards Jackson, Dunn, Gallacher, James and Morton. In 1950 Scotland qualified for the World Cup Finals in Brazil by finishing second to England in the Home Championship. But the SFA had declared they would go only if they finished first, and a golden opportunity to test the world waters was wasted – to their cost, as Scotland discovered four years later. They did compete in the finals in Switzerland but had a disastrous time, losing 1–0 to Austria and 7–0 to Uruguay. It was a similar tale in the 1958 tournament in Sweden, when a 1–1 draw with Yugoslavia was followed by defeats by Paraguay (3–2) and France (2–1).

Not until 1974 did Scotland qualify again for the World Cup Finals, an achievement they were to repeat for the next four competitions – with consequent nightmares which included winger Willie Johnston failing a dope test in Argentina in 1978 and defeat by the unrated minnows of Costa Rica in 1990.

Failure to qualify for the 1994 finals was a bitter blow at a turbulent time in Scotland, with the competitive structure under permanent review. At least they qualified for the finals of the 1992 and 1996 European Championship, but at club level, none have made an impression.

This was not for a lack of investment. The Rangers hierarchy spent heavily on international superstars including Denmark's Brian Laudrup and England's Paul Gascoigne. Each man, in turn, inspired Rangers to maintain their dominance of the league championship to the continuing disappointment of Celtic. In 1997 Rangers emulated Celtic's feat of the 1960s and 1970s by winning their ninth consecutive league title.

At Celtic there were signs of a return to better days, thanks to imports such as Germany's Andreas Thom, Portugal's Jorge Cadete and Italy's Paolo Di Canio.

SCOTTISH LEAGUE CHAMPIONS

FIRST DIVISION

Season	Champions	Pts	Runners-up	Pts
1890–91	Dumbarton	29	Rangers	29 +
1891–92	Dumbarton	37	Celtic	35
1892–93	Celtic	29	Rangers	28
1893–94	Hearts	29	Celtic	26
1894–95	Hearts	31	Celtic	26
1895–96	Celtic	30	Rangers	26
1896–97	Hearts	28	Hibernian	26
1897–98	Celtic	33	Rangers	29
1898–99	Rangers	36	Hearts	26
1899–1900	Rangers	32	Celtic	25
1900–01	Rangers	35	Celtic	29
1901–02	Rangers	28	Celtic	26
1902–03	Hibernian	37	Dundee	31
1903–04	Third Lanark	43	Hearts	39
1904–05	Celtic	41	Rangers	41+
1905–06	Celtic	49	Hearts	43
1906–07	Celtic	55	Dundee	48
1907–08	Celtic	55	Falkirk	51
1908–09	Celtic	51	Dundee	50
1909–10	Celtic	54	Falkirk	52
1910–11	Rangers	52	Aberdeen	48
1911–12	Rangers	51	Celtic	45
1912–13	Rangers	53	Celtic	49
1913–14	Celtic	65	Rangers	59
1914–15	Celtic	65	Hearts	61
1915–16	Celtic	67	Rangers	56
1916–17	Celtic	64	Morton	54
1917–18	Rangers	56	Celtic	55
1918–19	Celtic	58	Rangers	57
1919–20	Rangers	71	Celtic	68
1920–21	Rangers	76	Celtic	66
1921–22	Celtic	67	Rangers	66
1922–23	Rangers	55	Airdrieonians	50
1923–24	Rangers	59	Airdrieonians	50
1924–25	Rangers	60	Airdrieonians	57
1925–26	Celtic	58	Airdrieonians*	50
1926–27	Rangers	56	Motherwell	51
1927–28	Rangers	60	Celtic*	55
1928–29	Rangers	67	Celtic	51
1929–30	Rangers	60	Motherwell	55
1930–31	Rangers	60	Celtic	58
1931–32	Motherwell	66	Rangers	61
1932–33	Rangers	62	Motherwell	59
1933–34	Rangers	66	Motherwell	62
1934–35	Rangers	55	Celtic	52
1935–36	Celtic	66	Rangers*	61
1936–37	Rangers	61	Aberdeen	54
1937–38	Celtic	61	Hearts	58
1938–39	Rangers	59	Celtic	48
1946–47	Rangers	46	Hibernian	44
1947–48	Hibernian	48	Rangers	46
1948–49	Rangers	46	Dundee	45
1949–50	Rangers	50	Hibernian	49
1950–51	Hibernian	48	Rangers*	38
1951–52	Hibernian	45	Rangers	41
1952–53	Rangers*	43	Hibernian	43
1953–54	Celtic	43	Hearts	38
1954–55	Aberdeen	49	Celtic	46
1955–56	Rangers	52	Aberdeen	46
1956–57	Rangers	55	Hearts	53
1957–58	Hearts	62	Rangers	49
1958–59	Rangers	50	Hearts	48
1959–60	Hearts	54	Kilmarnock	50
1960–61	Rangers	51	Kilmarnock	50
1961–62	Dundee	54	Rangers	51
1962–63	Rangers	57	Kilmarnock	48
1963–64	Rangers	55	Kilmarnock	49
1964–65	Kilmarnock*	50	Hearts	50
1965–66	Celtic	57	Rangers	55
1966–67	Celtic	58	Rangers	55
1967–68	Celtic	63	Rangers	61
1968–69	Celtic	54	Rangers	49
1969–70	Celtic	57	Rangers	45
1970–71	Celtic	56	Aberdeen	54
1971–72	Celtic	60	Aberdeen	50
1972–73	Celtic	57	Rangers	56
1973–74	Celtic	53	Hibernian	49
1974–75	Rangers	56	Hibernian	49

PREMIER DIVISION

Season	Champions	Pts	Runners-up	Pts
1975–76	Rangers	54	Celtic	48
1976–77	Celtic	55	Rangers	46
1977–78	Rangers	55	Aberdeen	53
1978–79	Celtic	48	Rangers	45
1979–80	Aberdeen	48	Celtic	47
1980–81	Celtic	56	Aberdeen	49
1981–82	Celtic	55	Aberdeen	53
1982–83	Dundee Utd	56	Celtic*	55
1983–84	Aberdeen	57	Celtic	50
1984–85	Aberdeen	59	Celtic	52
1985–86	Celtic*	50	Hearts	50
1986–87	Rangers	69	Celtic	63
1987–88	Celtic	72	Hearts	62
1988–89	Rangers	56	Aberdeen	50
1989–90	Rangers	51	Aberdeen*	44
1990–91	Rangers	55	Aberdeen	53
1991–92	Rangers	72	Hearts	63
1992–93	Rangers	73	Aberdeen	64
1993–94	Rangers	58	Aberdeen	55
1994–95	Rangers	69	Motherwell	54
1995–96	Rangers	87	Celtic	83
1996–97	Rangers	80	Celtic	75

Notes:* On goal average/difference; + Championship held jointly

SCOTTISH LEAGUE CUP

Season	Winners	Runners-up	Score
1946–47	Rangers	Aberdeen	4–0
1947–48	East Fife	Falkirk	0–0, 4–1
1948–49	Rangers	Raith Rovers	2–0
1949–50	East Fife	Dunfermline Ath	3–0
1950–51	Motherwell	Hibernian	3–0
1951–52	Dundee	Rangers	3–2
1952–53	Dundee	Kilmarnock	2–0
1953–54	East Fife	Partick T	3–2
1954–55	Hearts	Motherwell	4–2
1955–56	Aberdeen	St Mirren	2–1
1956–57	Celtic	Partick T	0–0, 3–0
1957–58	Celtic	Rangers	7–1
1958–59	Hearts	Partick T	5–1
1959–60	Hearts	Third Lanark	2–1
1960–61	Rangers	Kilmarnock	2–0
1961–62	Rangers	Hearts	1–1, 3–1
1962–63	Hearts	Kilmarnock	1–0
1963–64	Rangers	Morton	5–0
1964–65	Rangers	Celtic	2–1
1965–66	Celtic	Rangers	2–1
1966–67	Celtic	Rangers	1–0
1967–68	Celtic	Dundee	5–3
1968–69	Celtic	Hibernian	6–2
1969–70	Celtic	St Johnstone	1–0
1970–71	Rangers	Celtic	1–0
1971–72	Partick T	Celtic	4–1
1972–73	Hibernian	Celtic	2–1
1973–74	Dundee	Celtic	1–0
1974–75	Celtic	Hibernian	6–3
1975–76	Rangers	Celtic	1–0
1976–77	Aberdeen	Celtic	2–1
1977–78	Rangers	Celtic	2–1
1978–79	Rangers	Aberdeen	2–1
1979–80	Dundee Utd	Aberdeen	0–0, 3–0
1980–81	Dundee Utd	Dundee	3–0
1981–82	Rangers	Dundee Utd	2–1
1982–83	Celtic	Rangers	2–1
1983–84	Rangers	Celtic	3–2
1984–85	Rangers	Dundee Utd	1–0
1985–86	Aberdeen	Hibernian	3–0
1986–87	Rangers	Celtic	2–1
1987–88	Rangers	Aberdeen	3–3
	Rangers won 5–3 on penalties		
1988–89	Rangers	Aberdeen	3–2
1989–90	Aberdeen	Rangers	2–1
1990–91	Rangers	Celtic	2–1
1991–92	Hibernian	Dunfermline A	2–0
1992–93	Rangers	Aberdeen	2–1
1993–94	Rangers	Hibernian	2–1
1994–95	Raith Rovers	Celtic	0–0
	(Raith Rovers won 6–5 on penalties)		
1995–96	Aberdeen	Dundee	2–0
1996–97	Rangers	Hearts	4–3

SCOTTISH FA CUP

Year	Winners	Runners-up	Score
1874	Queen's Park	Clydesdale	2–0
1875	Queen's Park	Renton	3–0
1876	Queen's Park	Third Lanark	1–1, 2–0
1877	Vale of Leven	Rangers	0–0, 1–1, 3–2
1878	Vale of Leven	Third Lanark	1–0
1879	Vale of Leven	Rangers	
	Rangers failed to appear for replay after 1–1 draw. Vale awarded Cup		
1880	Queen's Park	Thornlibank	3–0
1881	Queen's Park	Dumbarton	3–1
1882	Queen's Park	Dumbarton	2–2, 4–1
1883	Dumbarton	Vale of Leven	2–2, 2–1
1884	Queen's Park	Vale of Leven	
	Vale of Leven failed to appear. Queen's Park awarded Cup		
1885	Renton	Vale of Leven	0–0, 3–1
1886	Queen's Park	Renton	3–1
1887	Hibernian	Dumbarton	2–1
1888	Renton	Cambuslang	6–1
1889	Third Lanark	Celtic	3–0+, 2–1
	+Replay ordered because of playing conditions in the first game		
1890	Queen's Park	Vale of Leven	1–1, 2–1
1891	Hearts	Dumbarton	1–0
1892	Celtic	Queen's Park	5–1
	After mutually protested game which Celtic won 1–0		
1893	Queen's Park	Celtic	2–1
1894	Rangers	Celtic	3–1
1895	St Bernard's	Renton	2–1
1896	Hearts	Hibernian	3–1
1897	Rangers	Dumbarton	5–1
1898	Rangers	Kilmarnock	2–0
1899	Celtic	Rangers	2–0
1900	Celtic	Queen's Park	4–3
1901	Hearts	Celtic	4–3
1902	Hibernian	Celtic	1–0
1903	Rangers	Hearts	1–1, 0–0, 2–0
1904	Celtic	Rangers	3–2
1905	Third Lanark	Rangers	0–0, 3–1
1906	Hearts	Third Lanark	1–0
1907	Celtic	Hearts	3–0
1908	Celtic	St Mirren	5–1
1909	Owing to riot, the cup was withheld after two drawn games		
	Celtic vs. Rangers		2–2, 1–1
1910	Dundee	Clyde	2–2, 0–0, 2–1
1911	Celtic	Hamilton A	0–0, 2–0
1912	Celtic	Clyde	2–0
1913	Falkirk	Raith R	2–0
1914	Celtic	Hibernian	0–0, 4–1
1920	Kilmarnock	Albion R	3–2
1921	Partick T	Rangers	1–0
1922	Morton	Rangers	1–0
1923	Celtic	Hibernian	1–0
1924	Airdrieonians	Hibernian	2–0
1925	Celtic	Dundee	2–1
1926	St Mirren	Celtic	2–0
1927	Celtic	East Fife	3–1
1928	Rangers	Celtic	4–0
1929	Kilmarnock	Rangers	2–0
1930	Rangers	Partick T	0–0, 2–1
1931	Celtic	Motherwell	2–2, 4–2
1932	Rangers	Kilmarnock	1–1, 3–0
1933	Celtic	Motherwell	1–0
1934	Rangers	St Mirren	5–0
1935	Rangers	Hamilton A	2–1
1936	Rangers	Third Lanark	1–0
1937	Celtic	Aberdeen	2–1
1938	East Fife	Kilmarnock	1–1, 4–2
1939	Clyde	Motherwell	4–0
1947	Aberdeen	Hibernian	2–1
1948	Rangers	Morton	1–1, 1–0
1949	Rangers	Clyde	4–1
1950	Rangers	East Fife	3–0
1951	Celtic	Motherwell	1–0
1952	Motherwell	Dundee	4–0
1953	Rangers	Aberdeen	1–1, 1–0
1954	Celtic	Aberdeen	2–1
1955	Clyde	Celtic	1–1, 1–0
1956	Hearts	Celtic	3–1
1957	Falkirk	Kilmarnock	1–1, 2–1
1958	Clyde	Hibernian	1–0
1959	St Mirren	Aberdeen	3–1
1960	Rangers	Kilmarnock	2–0
1961	Dunfermline A	Celtic	0–0, 2–0
1962	Rangers	St Mirren	2–0
1963	Rangers	Celtic	1–1, 3–0
1964	Rangers	Dundee	3–1
1965	Celtic	Dunfermline A	3–2
1966	Rangers	Celtic	0–0, 1–0
1967	Celtic	Aberdeen	2–0
1968	Dunfermline A	Hearts	3–1
1969	Celtic	Rangers	4–0
1970	Aberdeen	Celtic	3–1
1971	Celtic	Rangers	1–1, 2–1
1972	Celtic	Hibernian	6–1
1973	Rangers	Celtic	3–2
1974	Celtic	Dundee Utd	3–0
1975	Celtic	Airdrieonians	3–1
1976	Rangers	Hearts	3–1
1977	Celtic	Rangers	1–0
1978	Rangers	Aberdeen	2–1
1979	Rangers	Hibernian	0–0, 0–0, 3–2
1980	Celtic	Rangers	1–0
1981	Rangers	Dundee Utd	0–0, 4–1
1982	Aberdeen	Rangers	4–1*
1983	Aberdeen	Rangers	1–0*
1984	Aberdeen	Celtic	2–1*
1985	Celtic	Dundee Utd	2–1
1986	Aberdeen	Hearts	3–0
1987	St Mirren	Dundee Utd	1–0 *
1988	Celtic	Dundee Utd	2–1
1989	Celtic	Rangers	1–0
1990	Aberdeen	Celtic	0–0*
	(Aberdeen won 9–8 on penalties)		
1991	Motherwell	Dundee Utd	4–3*
1992	Rangers	Airdrieonians	2–1
1993	Rangers	Aberdeen	2–1
1994	Dundee Utd	Rangers	1–0
1995	Celtic	Airdrieonians	1–0
1996	Rangers	Hearts	5–1
1997	Kilmarnock	Falkirk	1–0

INTERNATIONAL RESULTS 1872–1899

Date	Opponents	Venue	F–A
30/11/72	England	Glasgow	0–0
8/3/73	England	London	2–4
7/3/74	England	Glasgow	2–1
6/3/75	England	London	2–2
4/3/76	England	Glasgow	3–0
25/3/76	Wales	Glasgow	4–0
3/3/77	England	London	3–1
5/3/77	Wales	Wrexham	2–0
2/3/78	England	Glasgow	7–2
23/3/78	Wales	Glasgow	9–0
7/4/79	Wales	Wrexham	3–0
5/4/79	England	London	4–5
13/3/80	England	Glasgow	5–4
27/3/80	Wales	Glasgow	5–1
12/3/81	England	London	6–1
14/3/81	Wales	Wrexham	5–1
11/3/82	England	Glasgow	5–1

25/3/82	Wales	Glasgow	5–0	1/3/09	Wales	Wrexham	2–3	6/4/35	England	Glasgow	2–0	14/4/56	England	Glasgow	1–1

Date	Team	Venue	Score
25/3/82	Wales	Glasgow	5–0
10/3/83	England	Sheffield	3–2
12/3/83	Wales	Wrexham	3–0
26/1/84	Ireland	Belfast	5–0
15/3/84	England	Glasgow	1–0
29/3/84	Wales	Glasgow	4–1
14/3/85	Ireland	Glasgow	8–2
21/3/85	England	London	1–1
23/3/85	Wales	Wrexham	8–1
20/3/86	Ireland	Belfast	7–2
31/3/86	England	Glasgow	1–1
10/4/86	Wales	Glasgow	4–4
19/2/87	Ireland	Glasgow	4–1
19/3/87	England	Blackburn	3–2
21/3/87	Wales	Wrexham	2–0
10/3/88	Wales	Edinburgh	5–1
17/3/88	England	Glasgow	0–5
24/3/88	Ireland	Belfast	10–2
9/3/89	Ireland	Glasgow	7–0
13/4/89	England	London	3–2
15/4/89	Wales	Wrexham	0–0
22/3/90	Wales	Glasgow	5–0
29/3/90	Ireland	Belfast	4–1
5/4/90	England	Glasgow	1–1
21/3/91	Wales	Wrexham	4–3
28/3/91	Ireland	Glasgow	2–1
6/4/91	England	Blackburn	1–2
19/3/92	Ireland	Belfast	3–2
26/3/92	Wales	Edinburgh	6–1
2/4/92	England	Glasgow	1–4
18/3/93	Wales	Wrexham	8–0
25/3/93	Ireland	Glasgow	6–1
1/4/93	England	Richmond	2–5
24/3/94	Wales	Kilmarnock	5–2
31/3/94	Ireland	Belfast	2–1
7/4/94	England	Glasgow	2–2
23/3/95	Wales	Wrexham	2–2
30/3/95	Ireland	Glasgow	3–1
6/4/95	England	Liverpool	0–3
21/3/96	Wales	Dundee	4–0
28/3/96	Ireland	Belfast	3–3
4/4/96	England	Glasgow	2–1
20/3/97	Wales	Wrexham	2–2
27/3/97	Ireland	Glasgow	5–1
3/4/97	England	London	2–1
19/3/98	Wales	Motherwell	5–2
26/3/98	Ireland	Belfast	3–0
2/4/98	England	Glasgow	1–3
18/3/99	Wales	Wrexham	6–0
25/3/99	Ireland	Glasgow	9–1
8/4/99	England	Birmingham	1–2

1900–1909

3/2/00	Wales	Aberdeen	5–2
3/3/00	Ireland	Belfast	3–0
7/4/00	England	Glasgow	4–1
23/2/01	Ireland	Glasgow	11–0
2/3/01	Wales	Wrexham	1–1
30/3/01	England	London	2–2
1/3/02	Ireland	Belfast	5–1
15/3/02	Wales	Greenock	5–1
3/5/02	England	Birmingham	2–2
9/3/03	Wales	Cardiff	1–0
21/3/03	Ireland	Glasgow	0–2
4/4/03	England	Sheffield	2–1
12/3/04	Wales	Dundee	1–1
26/3/04	Ireland	Dublin	1–1
9/4/04	England	Glasgow	0–1
6/3/05	Wales	Wrexham	1–3
18/3/05	Ireland	Glasgow	4–0
1/4/05	England	London	0–1
3/3/06	Wales	Edinburgh	0–2
17/3/06	Ireland	Dublin	1–0
7/4/06	England	Glasgow	2–1
4/3/07	Wales	Wrexham	0–1
16/3/07	Ireland	Glasgow	3–0
6/4/07	England	Newcastle	1–1
7/3/08	Wales	Dundee	2–1
14/3/08	Ireland	Dublin	5–0
4/4/08	England	Glasgow	1–1

1/3/09	Wales	Wrexham	2–3
15/3/09	Ireland	Glasgow	5–0
3/4/09	England	London	0–2

1910–1914

5/3/10	Wales	Kilmarnock	1–0
19/3/10	Ireland	Belfast	0–1
2/4/10	England	Glasgow	2–0
6/3/11	Wales	Cardiff	2–2
18/3/11	Ireland	Glasgow	2–0
1/4/11	England	Liverpool	1–1
2/3/12	Wales	Edinburgh	1–0
16/3/12	Ireland	Belfast	4–1
23/3/12	England	Glasgow	1–1
3/3/13	Wales	Wrexham	0–0
15/3/13	Ireland	Dublin	2–1
5/4/13	England	Stamford Bridge	0–1
28/2/14	Wales	Glasgow	0–0
14/3/14	Ireland	Belfast	1–1
4/4/14	England	Glasgow	3–1

1920–1929

26/2/20	Wales	Cardiff	1–1
13/3/20	Ireland	Glasgow	3–0
10/4/20	England	Sheffield	4–5
12/2/21	Wales	Aberdeen	2–1
26/2/21	Ireland	Belfast	2–0
9/4/21	England	Glasgow	3–0
4/2/22	Wales	Wrexham	1–2
4/3/22	Ireland	Glasgow	2–1
8/4/22	England	Birmingham	1–0
3/3/23	Ireland	Belfast	1–0
17/3/23	Wales	Glasgow	2–0
14/4/23	England	Glasgow	2–2
16/2/24	Wales	Cardiff	0–2
1/3/24	Ireland	Glasgow	2–0
12/4/24	England	Wembley	1–1
14/2/25	Wales	Edinburgh	3–1
28/2/25	Ireland	Belfast	3–0
4/4/25	England	Glasgow	2–0
31/10/25	Wales	Cardiff	3–0
27/2/26	Ireland	Glasgow	4–0
17/4/26	England	Manchester	1–0
30/10/26	Wales	Glasgow	3–0
26/2/27	Ireland	Belfast	2–0
2/4/27	England	Glasgow	1–2
29/10/27	Wales	Wrexham	2–2
25/2/28	Ireland	Glasgow	0–1
31/3/28	England	Wembley	5–1
27/10/28	Wales	Glasgow	4–2
23/2/29	Ireland	Belfast	7–3
13/4/29	England	Glasgow	1–0
26/5/29	Norway	Bergen	7–3
1/6/29	Germany	Berlin	1–1
4/6/29	Holland	Amsterdam	2–0
26/10/29	Wales	Cardiff	4–2

1930–1939

22/2/30	Ireland	Glasgow	3–1
5/4/30	England	Wembley	2–5
18/5/30	France	Paris	2–0
25/10/30	Wales	Glasgow	1–1
21/2/31	Ireland	Belfast	0–0
28/3/31	England	Glasgow	2–0
16/5/31	Austria	Vienna	0–5
20/5/31	Italy	Rome	0–3
24/5/31	Switzerland	Geneva	3–2
19/9/31	Ireland	Glasgow	3–1
31/10/31	Wales	Wrexham	3–2
9/4/32	England	Wembley	0–3
8/5/32	France	Paris	3–1
19/9/32	Ireland	Belfast	4–0
26/10/32	Wales	Edinburgh	2–5
1/4/33	England	Glasgow	2–1
16/9/33	Ireland	Glasgow	1–2
4/10/33	Wales	Cardiff	2–3
29/11/33	Austria	Glasgow	2–2
14/4/34	England	Wembley	0–3
20/10/34	Ireland	Belfast	1–2
21/11/34	Wales	Aberdeen	3–2

6/4/35	England	Glasgow	2–0
5/10/35	Wales	Cardiff	1–1
13/11/35	Ireland	Edinburgh	2–1
4/4/36	England	Wembley	1–1
14/10/36	Germany	Glasgow	2–0
31/10/36	Ireland	Belfast	3–1
2/12/36	Wales	Dundee	1–2
17/4/37	England	Glasgow	3–1
9/5/37	Austria	Vienna	1–1
22/5/37	Czechoslovakia	Prague	3–1
30/10/37	Wales	Cardiff	1–2
10/11/37	Ireland	Aberdeen	1–1
8/12/37	Czechoslovakia	Glasgow	5–0
9/4/38	England	Wembley	1–0
21/5/38	Holland	Amsterdam	3–1
8/10/38	Ireland	Belfast	2–0
9/11/38	Wales	Edinburgh	3–2
7/12/38	Hungary	Glasgow	3–1
15/4/39	England	Glasgow	1–2

1940–1949

19/10/46	Wales	Wrexham	1–3
27/11/46	N Ireland	Glasgow	0–0
12/4/47	England	Wembley	1–1
18/5/47	Belgium	Brussels	1–2
24/5/47	Luxembourg	Luxembourg	6–0
4/10/47	N Ireland	Belfast	0–2
12/11/47	Wales	Glasgow	1–2
10/4/48	England	Glasgow	0–2
28/4/48	Belgium	Glasgow	2–0
17/5/48	Switzerland	Berne	1–2
23/5/48	France	Paris	0–3
23/10/48	Wales	Cardiff	3–1
17/11/48	N Ireland	Glasgow	3–2
9/4/49	England	Wembley	3–1
27/4/49	France	Glasgow	2–0
1/10/49	N Ireland	Belfast	8–2 (WCQ)
9/11/49	Wales	Glasgow	2–0 (WCQ)

1950–1959

15/4/50	England	Glasgow	0–1 (WCQ)
26/4/50	Switzerland	Glasgow	3–1
25/5/50	Portugal	Lisbon	2–2
27/5/50	France	Paris	1–0
21/10/50	Wales	Cardiff	3–1
1/11/50	N Ireland	Glasgow	6–1
13/12/50	Austria	Glasgow	0–1
14/4/51	England	Wembley	3–2
12/5/51	Denmark	Glasgow	3–1
16/5/51	France	Glasgow	1–0
20/5/51	Belgium	Brussels	5–0
27/5/51	Austria	Vienna	0–4
6/10/51	N Ireland	Belfast	3–0
28/11/51	Wales	Glasgow	0–1
5/4/52	England	Glasgow	1–2
30/4/52	USA	Glasgow	6–0
25/5/52	Denmark	Copenhagen	2–1
30/5/52	Sweden	Stockholm	1–3
15/10/52	Wales	Cardiff	2–1
5/11/52	N Ireland	Glasgow	1–1
18/4/53	England	Wembley	2–2
6/5/53	Sweden	Glasgow	1–2
3/10/53	N Ireland	Belfast	3–1 (WCQ)
4/11/53	Wales	Glasgow	3–3 (WCQ)
3/4/54	England	Glasgow	2–4 (WCQ)
5/5/54	Norway	Glasgow	1–0
19/5/54	Norway	Oslo	1–1
25/5/54	Finland	Helsinki	2–1
16/6/54	Austria	Zurich	0–1 (WCF)
19/6/54	Uruguay	Basle	0–7 (WCF)
16/10/54	Wales	Cardiff	1–0
3/11/54	N Ireland	Glasgow	2–2
8/12/54	Hungary	Glasgow	2–4
2/4/55	England	Wembley	2–7
16/5/55	Portugal	Glasgow	3–0
15/5/55	Yugoslavia	Belgrade	2–2
19/5/55	Austria	Vienna	4–1
29/5/55	Hungary	Budapest	1–3
8/10/55	N Ireland	Belfast	1–2
9/11/55	Wales	Glasgow	2–0

14/4/56	England	Glasgow	1–1
2/5/56	Austria	Glasgow	1–1
20/10/56	Wales	Cardiff	2–2
7/11/56	N Ireland	Glasgow	1–0
21/11/56	Yugoslavia	Glasgow	2–0
6/4/57	England	Wembley	1–2
8/5/57	Spain	Glasgow	4–2 (WCQ)
19/5/57	Switzerland	Basle	2–1 (WCQ)
22/5/57	W Germany	Stuttgart	3–1
26/5/57	Spain	Madrid	1–4 (WCQ)
5/10/57	N Ireland	Belfast	1–1
6/11/57	Switzerland	Glasgow	3–2 (WCQ)
13/11/57	Wales	Glasgow	1–1
19/4/58	England	Glasgow	0–4
7/5/58	Hungary	Glasgow	1–1
1/6/58	Poland	Warsaw	2–1
8/6/58	Yugoslavia	Vasteras	1–1 (WCF)
11/6/58	Paraguay	Norrköping	2–3 (WCF)
15/6/58	France	Örebro	1–2 (WCF)
18/10/58	Wales	Cardiff	3–0
5/11/58	N Ireland	Glasgow	2–2
11/4/59	England	Wembley	0–1
6/5/59	W Germany	Glasgow	3–2
27/5/59	Holland	Amsterdam	2–1
3/6/59	Portugal	Lisbon	0–1
3/10/59	N Ireland	Belfast	4–0
14/11/59	Wales	Glasgow	1–1

1960–69

9/4/60	England	Glasgow	1–1
4/5/60	Poland	Glasgow	2–3
29/5/60	Austria	Vienna	1–4
5/6/60	Hungary	Budapest	3–3
8/6/60	Turkey	Ankara	2–4
22/10/60	Wales	Cardiff	0–2
9/11/60	N Ireland	Glasgow	5–2
15/4/61	England	Wembley	3–9
3/5/61	Rep of Ireland	Glasgow	4–1 (WCQ)
7/5/61	Rep of Ireland	Dublin	3–0 (WCQ)
14/5/61	Czechoslovakia	Bratislava	0–4 (WCQ)
26/9/61	Czechoslovakia	Glasgow	3–2 (WCQ)
7/10/61	N Ireland	Belfast	6–1
8/11/61	Wales	Glasgow	2–0
29/11/61	Czechoslovakia	Brussels	2–4 (WCQ)
14/4/62	England	Glasgow	2–0
2/5/62	Uruguay	Glasgow	2–3
20/10/62	Wales	Cardiff	3–2
7/11/62	N Ireland	Glasgow	5–1
6/4/63	England	Wembley	2–1
8/5/63	Austria	Glasgow	4–1
4/6/63	Norway	Bergen	3–4
9/6/63	Rep of Ireland	Dublin	0–1
13/6/63	Spain	Madrid	6–2
12/10/63	N Ireland	Belfast	1–2
7/11/63	Norway	Glasgow	6–1
20/11/63	Wales	Glasgow	2–1
11/4/64	England	Glasgow	1–0
12/5/64	W Germany	Hanover	2–2
3/10/64	Wales	Cardiff	2–3
21/10/64	Finland	Glasgow	3–1 (WCQ)
25/11/64	N Ireland	Glasgow	3–2
10/4/65	England	Wembley	2–2
8/5/65	Spain	Glasgow	0–0
23/5/65	Poland	Chorzow	1–1 (WCQ)
27/5/65	Finland	Helsinki	2–1 (WCQ)
2/10/65	N Ireland	Belfast	2–3
13/10/65	Poland	Glasgow	1–2 (WCQ)
9/11/65	Italy	Glasgow	1–0 (WCQ)
24/11/65	Wales	Glasgow	4–1
7/12/65	Italy	Naples	0–3 (WCQ)
2/4/66	England	Glasgow	3–4
11/5/66	Holland	Glasgow	0–3
18/6/66	Portugal	Glasgow	0–1
25/6/66	Brazil	Glasgow	1–1
22/10/66	Wales	Cardiff	1–1 (ECQ)
16/11/66	N Ireland	Glasgow	2–1 (ECQ)
15/4/67	England	Wembley	3–2 (ECQ)
10/5/67	USSR	Glasgow	0–2
21/10/67	N Ireland	Belfast	0–1 (ECQ)
22/11/67	Wales	Glasgow	3–2 (ECQ)

Date	Opponent	Venue	Result
24/2/68	England	Glasgow	1–1 (ECQ)
30/5/68	Holland	Amsterdam	0–0
16/10/68	Denmark	Copenhagen	1–0
6/11/68	Austria	Glasgow	2–1 (WCQ)
11/12/68	Cyprus	Nicosia	5–0 (WCQ)
16/4/69	W Germany	Glasgow	1–1 (WCQ)
3/5/69	Wales	Wrexham	5–3
6/5/69	N Ireland	Glasgow	1–1
10/6/69	England	Wembley	1–4
12/5/69	Cyprus	Glasgow	8–0 (WCQ)
21/9/69	Rep of Ireland	Dublin	1–1
22/10/69	W Germany	Hamburg	2–3 (WCQ)
5/11/69	Austria	Vienna	0–2 (WCQ)

1970

Date	Opponent	Venue	Result
18/4	N Ireland	Belfast	1–0
22/4	Wales	Glasgow	0–0
25/4	England	Glasgow	0–0
11/11	Denmark	Glasgow	1–0 (ECQ)

1971

Date	Opponent	Venue	Result
3/2	Belgium	Liège	0–3 (ECQ)
21/4	Portugal	Lisbon	0–2 (ECQ)
15/5	Wales	Cardiff	0–0
18/5	N Ireland	Glasgow	0–1
22/5	England	Wembley	1–3
9/6	Denmark	Copenhagen	0–1 (ECQ)
14/6	USSR	Moscow	0–1
13/10	Portugal	Glasgow	2–1 (ECQ)
10/11	Belgium	Aberdeen	1–0 (ECQ)
1/12	Holland	Rotterdam	1–2

1972

Date	Opponent	Venue	Result
26/4	Peru	Glasgow	2–0
20/5	N Ireland	Glasgow	2–0
24/5	Wales	Glasgow	1–0
27/5	England	Glasgow	0–1
29/6	Yugoslavia	Belo Horizonte	2–2
2/7	Czechoslovakia	Porto Alegre	0–0
5/7	Brazil	Rio de Janeiro	0–1
18/10	Denmark	Copenhagen	4–1 (WCQ)
15/11	Denmark	Glasgow	2–0 (WCQ)

1973

Date	Opponent	Venue	Result
14/2	England	Glasgow	0–5
12/5	Wales	Wrexham	2–0
16/5	N Ireland	Glasgow	1–2
19/5	England	Wembley	0–1
22/6	Switzerland	Berne	0–1
30/6	Brazil	Glasgow	0–1
26/9	Czechoslovakia	Glasgow	2–1 (WCQ)
17/10	Czechoslovakia	Bratislava	0–1 (WCQ)
14/11	W Germany	Glasgow	1–1

1974

Date	Opponent	Venue	Result
27/3	W Germany	Frankfurt	1–2
11/5	N Ireland	Glasgow	0–1
14/5	Wales	Glasgow	2–0
18/5	England	Glasgow	2–0
2/6	Belgium	Brussels	1–2
6/6	Norway	Oslo	2–1
14/6	Zaïre	Dortmund	2–0 (WCF)
18/6	Brazil	Frankfurt	0–0 (WCF)
22/6	Yugoslavia	Frankfurt	1–1 (WCF)
30/10	E Germany	Glasgow	3–0
20/11	Spain	Glasgow	1–2 (ECQ)

1975

Date	Opponent	Venue	Result
5/2	Spain	Valencia	1–1 (ECQ)
16/4	Sweden	Gothenburg	1–1
13/5	Portugal	Glasgow	1–0
17/5	Wales	Cardiff	2–2
20/5	N Ireland	Glasgow	3–0
24/5	England	Wembley	1–5
1/6	Romania	Bucharest	1–1 (ECQ)
3/9	Denmark	Copenhagen	1–0 (ECQ)
29/10	Denmark	Glasgow	3–1 (ECQ)
17/12	Romania	Glasgow	1–1 (ECQ)

1976

Date	Opponent	Venue	Result
7/4	Switzerland	Glasgow	1–0
6/5	Wales	Glasgow	3–1
8/5	N Ireland	Glasgow	3–0
15/5	England	Glasgow	2–1
8/9	Finland	Glasgow	6–0
13/10	Czechoslovakia	Prague	0–2 (WCQ)
17/11	Wales	Glasgow	1–0 (WCQ)

1977

Date	Opponent	Venue	Result
27/4	Sweden	Glasgow	3–1
28/5	Wales	Wrexham	0–0
1/6	N Ireland	Glasgow	3–0
4/6	England	Wembley	2–0
15/6	Chile	Santiago	4–2
18/6	Argentina	Buenos Aires	1–1
23/6	Brazil	Rio de Janeiro	0–2
7/9	E Germany	E Berlin	0–1
21/9	Czechoslovakia	Glasgow	3–1 (WCQ)
12/10	Wales	Liverpool	2–0 (WCQ)

1978

Date	Opponent	Venue	Result
22/2	Bulgaria	Glasgow	2–1
13/5	N Ireland	Glasgow	1–1
17/5	Wales	Glasgow	1–1
20/5	England	Glasgow	0–1
3/6	Peru	Cordoba	1–3 (WCF)
7/6	Iran	Cordoba	1–1 (WCF)
11/6	Holland	Mendoza	3–2 (WCF)
20/9	Austria	Vienna	2–3 (ECQ)
25/10	Norway	Glasgow	3–2 (ECQ)
29/11	Portugal	Lisbon	0–1 (ECQ)

1979

Date	Opponent	Venue	Result
19/5	Wales	Cardiff	0–3
22/5	N Ireland	Glasgow	1–0
26/5	England	Wembley	1–3
2/6	Argentina	Glasgow	1–3
7/6	Norway	Oslo	4–0 (ECQ)
12/9	Peru	Glasgow	1–1
17/10	Austria	Glasgow	1–1 (ECQ)
21/11	Belgium	Brussels	0–2 (ECQ)
19/12	Belgium	Glasgow	1–3 (ECQ)

1980

Date	Opponent	Venue	Result
26/3	Portugal	Glasgow	4–1 (ECQ)
16/5	N Ireland	Belfast	0–1
21/5	Wales	Glasgow	1–0
24/5	England	Glasgow	0–2
28/5	Poland	Poznan	0–1
31/5	Hungary	Budapest	1–3
10/9	Sweden	Stockholm	1–0 (WCQ)
15/10	Portugal	Glasgow	0–0 (WCQ0

1981

Date	Opponent	Venue	Result
25/2	Israel	Tel Aviv	1–0 (WCQ)
25/3	N Ireland	Glasgow	1–1 (WCQ)
28/4	Israel	Glasgow	3–1 (WCQ)
16/5	Wales	Swansea	0–2
19/5	N Ireland	Glasgow	2–0
23/5	England	Wembley	1–0
9/9	Sweden	Glasgow	2–0 (WCQ)
14/10	N Ireland	Belfast	0–0 (WCQ)
18/11	Portugal	Lisbon	1–2 (WCQ)

1982

Date	Opponent	Venue	Result
24/2	Spain	Valencia	0–3
23/3	Holland	Glasgow	2–1
28/4	N Ireland	Belfast	1–1
24/5	Wales	Glasgow	1–0
29/5	England	Glasgow	0–1
15/6	New Zealand	Malaga	5–2 (WCF)
18/6	Brazil	Seville	1–4 (WCF)
22/6	USSR	Malaga	2–2 (WCF)
13/10	E Germany	Glasgow	2–0 (ECQ)
17/11	Switzerland	Berne	0–2 (ECQ)
15/12	Belgium	Brussels	2–3 (ECQ)

1983

Date	Opponent	Venue	Result
30/3	Switzerland	Glasgow	2–2 (ECQ)
24/5	N Ireland	Glasgow	0–0
28/5	Wales	Cardiff	2–0
1/6	England	Wembley	0–2
12/6	Canada	Vancouver	2–0
16/6	Canada	Edmonton	3–0
20/6	Canada	Toronto	2–0
21/9	Uruguay	Glasgow	2–0
12/10	Belgium	Glasgow	1–1 (ECQ)
16/11	E Germany	Halle	1–2 (ECQ)
13/12	N Ireland	Belfast	0–2

1984

Date	Opponent	Venue	Result
28/2	Wales	Glasgow	2–1
26/5	England	Glasgow	1–1
1/6	France	Marseille	0–2
12/9	Yugoslavia	Glasgow	6–1
17/10	Iceland	Glasgow	3–0 (WCQ)
14/11	Spain	Glasgow	3–1 (WCQ)

1985

Date	Opponent	Venue	Result
27/2	Spain	Seville	0–1 (WCQ)
27/3	Wales	Glasgow	0–1 (WCQ)
25/5	England	Glasgow	1–0
28/5	Iceland	Reykjavik	1–0 (WCQ)
10/9	Wales	Cardiff	1–1 (WCQ)
16/10	E Germany	Glasgow	0–0
20/11	Australia	Glasgow	2–0 (WCQ)
4/12	Australia	Melbourne	0–0 (WCQ)

1986

Date	Opponent	Venue	Result
28/1	Israel	Tel Aviv	1–0
26/3	Romania	Glasgow	3–0
23/4	England	Wembley	1–2
29/4	Holland	Eindhoven	0–0
4/6	Denmark	Nezahualcoyot	0–1 (WCF)
8/6	W Germany	Queretaro	1–2 (WCF)
13/6	Uruguay	Nezahualcoyot	0–0 (WCF)
10/9	Bulgaria	Glasgow	0–0 (ECQ)
15/10	Rep of Ireland	Dublin	0–0 (ECQ)
12/11	Luxembourg	Glasgow	3–0 (ECQ)

1987

Date	Opponent	Venue	Result
18/2	Rep of Ireland	Glasgow	0–1 (ECQ)
1/4	Belgium	Brussels	1–4 (ECQ)
6/5	Brazil	Glasgow	0–2
23/5	England	Glasgow	0–0
9/9	Hungary	Glasgow	2–0
14/10	Belgium	Glasgow	2–0 (ECQ)
11/11	Bulgaria	Sofia	1–0 (ECQ)
2/12	Luxembourg	Esch	0–0 (ECQ)

1988

Date	Opponent	Venue	Result
17/2	Saudi Arabia	Riyadh	2–2
22/3	Malta	Valletta	1–1
27/4	Spain	Madrid	0–0
17/5	Colombia	Glasgow	0–0
21/5	England	Wembley	0–1
14/9	Norway	Oslo	2–1 (WCQ)
19/10	Yugoslavia	Glasgow	1–1 (WCQ)
22/12	Italy	Perugia	0–2

1989

Date	Opponent	Venue	Result
8/2	Cyprus	Limassol	3–2 (WCQ)
8/3	France	Glasgow	2–0 (WCQ)
26/4	Cyprus	Glasgow	2–1 (WCQ)
27/5	England	Glasgow	0–2
30/5	Chile	Glasgow	2–0
6/9	Yugoslavia	Zagreb	1–3 (WCQ)
11/10	France	Paris	0–3 (WCQ)
15/11	Norway	Glasgow	1–1 (WCQ)

1990

Date	Opponent	Venue	Result
28/3	Argentina	Glasgow	1–0
25/4	E Germany	Glasgow	0–1
19/5	Poland	Glasgow	1–1
28/5	Malta	Valletta	2–1
11/6	Costa Rica	Genoa	0–1 (WCF)
16/6	Sweden	Genoa	2–1 (WCF)
20/6	Brazil	Turin	0–1 (WCF)
12/9	Romania	Glasgow	2–1 (ECQ)
17/10	Switzerland	Glasgow	2–1 (ECQ)
14/11	Bulgaria	Sofia	1–1 (ECQ)

1991

Date	Opponent	Venue	Result
6/2	USSR	Glasgow	0–1
27/3	Bulgaria	Glasgow	1–1 (ECQ)
1/5	San Marino	Serravalle	2–0 (ECQ)
11/9	Switzerland	Berne	2–2 (ECQ)
16/10	Romania	Bucharest	0–1 (ECQ)
13/11	San Marino	Glasgow	4–0 (ECQ)

1992

Date	Opponent	Venue	Result
25/3	Finland	Glasgow	1–1
17/5	USA	Denver	1–0
21/5	Canada	Toronto	3–1
3/6	Norway	Oslo	0–0
12/6	Holland	Gothenburg	0–1 (ECF)
15/6	Germany	Gothenburg	0–2 (ECF)
18/6	CIS	Norrkoping	3–0 (ECF)
9/9	Switzerland	Berne	1–3 (WCQ)
14/10	Portugal	Glasgow	0–0 (WCQ)
18/11	Italy	Glasgow	0–0 (WCQ)

1993

Date	Opponent	Venue	Result
17/2	Malta	Glasgow	3–0 (WCQ)
24/3	Germany	Glasgow	0–1
28/4	Portugal	Lisbon	0–5 (WCQ)
19/5	Estonia	Tallinn	3–0 (WCQ)
2/6	Estonia	Aberdeen	3–1 (WCQ)
8/9	Switzerland	Glasgow	1–1 (WCQ)
13/10	Italy	Rome	1–3 (WCQ)
17/11	Malta	Sliema	2–0 (WCQ)

1994

Date	Opponent	Venue	Result
23/3	Holland	Glasgow	0–1
20/4	Austria	Vienna	2–1
27/5	Holland	Utrecht	1–3
7/9	Finland	Helsinki	2–0 (ECQ)
12/10	Faroe Islands	Glasgow	5–1 (ECQ)
16/11	Russia	Glasgow	1–1 (ECQ)
19/12	Greece	Athens	0–1 (ECQ)

1995

Date	Opponent	Venue	Result
29/3	Russia	Moscow	0–0 (ECQ)
26/4	San Marino	Serravalle	2–0 (ECQ)
21/5	Japan	Hiroshima	0–0
24/5	Ecuador	Toyama, Japan	2–1
7/6	Faroe Islands	Toftir	2–0 (ECQ)
16/8	Greece	Glasgow	1–0 (ECQ)
6/9	Finland	Glasgow	1–0 (ECQ)
8/10	Sweden	Stockholm	0–2
15/11	San Marino	Glasgow	5–0 (ECQ)

1996

Date	Opponent	Venue	Result
27/3	Australia	Glasgow	1–0
24/4	Denmark	Copenhagen	0–2
26/5	United States	New Britain, Conn	1–2
29/5	Colombia	Miami	0–1
10/6	Holland	Birmingham	0–0 (ECF)
15/6	England	Wembley	0–2 (ECF)
18/6	Switzerland	Birmingham	1–0 (ECF)
31/8	Austria	Vienna	0–0 (WCQ)
5/10	Latvia	Riga	2–0 (WCQ)
9/10	Estonia	Tallinn	0–0 (WCQ)
(abandoned because Estonia did not arrive)			
10/11	Sweden	Glasgow	1–0 (WCQ)

1997

Date	Opponent	Venue	Result
11/2	Estonia	Monaco	0–0 (WCQ)
29/3	Estonia	Kilmarnock	2–0 (WCQ)
2/4	Austria	Glasgow	2–0 (WCQ)
30/4	Sweden	Gothenburg	1–2 (WCQ)
27/5	Wales	Kilmarnock	0–1
1/6	Malta	Valletta	3–2
8/6	Belarus	Minsk	1–0 (WCQ)

WALES

At the close of the 1992–93 season Cwmbran became the first Konica-sponsored League of Wales champions, finishing four points ahead of Inter Cardiff.

Until then the participation of the principality's senior clubs, Cardiff City, Swansea City, Newport County and Wrexham, in the Football League meant that the senior tournament under the auspices of the FA of Wales was always the Welsh Cup.

This competition celebrated its 100th anniversary in 1977, the first Cup tie between Newtown and Druids having kicked-off on October 30, 1877 with Wrexham winning 1–0. Druids were captained by Llewelyn Kenrick, the founder of the FA of Wales, and Wrexham played with three half-backs. This was the first occasion such a formation was adopted.

The Village That Grew Footballers

In the formative years of the Welsh Cup the little village of Chirk figured prominently. Chirk was the home club of the great Billy Meredith, Charlie Morris of Derby, Lot Jones of Manchester City, Dai Jones of Bolton and many others. Not surprising then that between 1886 and 1894 Chirk appeared in six finals, winning five. Meredith played in two finals, against Wrexham and Westminster Rovers, and it was then that he was snapped up by Manchester City. Consequently Meredith became the first Welsh player to win Welsh Cup and FA Cup medals.

In modern times the competition has gained more significance with entry into the European Cup-Winners Cup as the prize for the winners. Entry into European competition has also been granted to to the champions of the new league.

The FA of Wales was formed in 1876 and on March 25 the national team lost 4–0 to Scotland in their first international. In 1907 they won the British Championship for the first time and they qualified for the World Cup Finals in 1958, when they surprised everyone by reaching the quarter-finals, losing 1–0 to Brazil – by a deflected goal from Pele.

LEAGUE OF WALES

1993	Cwmbran Town
1994	Bangor C
1995	Bangor C
1996	Barry T
1997	Barry T

LEAGUE OF WALES CUP

Year	Winners	Runners-up	Score
1993	Caersws	Afan Lido	Penalties
1994	Afan Lido	Bangor	1–0
1995	Llansantffraid	Ton Pentre	2–1
1996	Connah's Quay	Ebbw Vale	1–0
1997	Barry Town	Bangor City	2–2
	(Barry Town won 4–2 on penalties)		

WELSH CUP FINALS

Year	Winners	Runners-up	Score
1878	Wrexham	Druids	1–0
1879	Newtown	Wrexham	1–0
1880	Druids	Ruthin	2–1
1881	Druids	Newtown White Stars	2–0
1882	Druids	Northwich	2–1
1883	Wrexham	Druids	1–0
1884	Oswestry	Druids	3–2
1885	Druids	Oswestry	2–0
1886	Druids	Newtown	5–0
1887	Chirk	Davenham	4–2
1888	Chirk	Newtown	5–0
1889	Bangor	Northwich	2–1
1890	Chirk	Wrexham	1–0
1891	Shrewsbury T	Wrexham	5–2
1892	Chirk	Westminster R	2–1
1893	Wrexham	Chirk	2–1
1894	Chirk	Westminster R	2–0
1895	Newtown	Wrexham	3–2
1896	Bangor	Wrexham	3–1
1897	Wrexham	Newtown	2–0
1898	Druids	Wrexham	1–1, 2–1
1899	Druids	Wrexham	2–2, 1–0
1900	Aberystwyth	Druids	3–0
1901	Oswestry	Druids	1–0
1902	Wellington	Wrexham	1–0
1903	Wrexham	Aberaman	8–0
1904	Druids	Aberdare	3–2
1905	Wrexham	Aberdare	3–0
1906	Wellington	Whitchurch	3–2
1907	Oswestry	Whitchurch	2–0
1908	Chester	Connah's Quay	3–1
1909	Wrexham	Chester	1–0
1910	Wrexham	Chester	2–1

1911	Wrexham	Connah's Quay	6–1
1912	Cardiff C	Pontypridd	0–0, 3–0
1913	Swansea	Pontypridd	0–0, 1–0
1914	Wrexham	Llanelly	1–1, 3–0
1915	Wrexham	Swansea	0–0, 1–0
1920	Cardiff C	Wrexham	2–1
1921	Wrexham	Pontypridd	1–1, 3–1
1922	Cardiff C	Ton Pentre	2–0
1923	Cardiff C	Aberdare	3–2
1924	Wrexham	Merthyr	2–2, 1–0
1925	Wrexham	Flint	3–1
1926	Ebbw Vale	Swansea	3–2
1927	Cardiff C	Rhyl	0–0, 4–2
1928	Cardiff C	Bangor	2–0
1929	Connah's Quay	Cardiff C	3–0
1930	Cardiff C	Rhyl	0–0, 4–2
1931	Wrexham	Shrewsbury	7–0
1932	Swansea	Wrexham	1–1, 2–0
1933	Chester	Wrexham	2–0
1934	Bristol C	Tranmere R	1–1, 3–0
1935	Tranmere R	Chester	1–0
1936	Crewe	Chester	2–0
1937	Crewe	Rhyl	1–1, 3–1
1938	Shrewsbury	Swansea	2–1
1939	S Liverpool	Cardiff C	2–1
1940	Welling T	Swansea	4–0
1947	Chester	Merthyr Tydfil	0–0, 5–1
1948	Lovells Ath	Shrewsbury T	3–0
1949	Merthyr Tydfil	Swansea T	2–0
1950	Swansea T	Wrexham	4–1
1951	Merthyr Tydfil	Cardiff C	1–1, 3–2
1952	Rhyl	Merthyr Tydfil	4–3
1953	Rhyl	Chester	2–1
1954	Flint T Utd	Chester	2–0
1955	Barry T	Chester	1–1, 4–3
1956	Cardiff C	Swansea T	3–2
1957	Wrexham	Swansea T	2–1
1958	Wrexham	Chester	1–1, 2–0
1959	Cardiff C	Lovells Ath	2–0
1960	Wrexham	Cardiff C	0–0, 1–0
1961	Swansea T	Bangor C	3–1
1962	Bangor C	Wrexham	3–1
1963	Borough Utd	Newport Co	2–1 *
1964	Cardiff C	Bangor C	5–3 *
1965	Cardiff C	Wrexham	8–2 *
1966	Swansea T	Chester	2–1
1967	Cardiff C	Wrexham	2–1 *
1968	Cardiff C	Hereford Utd	6–1 *
1969	Cardiff C	Swansea T	5–1 *
1970	Cardiff C	Chester	5–0
1971	Cardiff C	Wrexham	4–1 *
1972	Wrexham	Cardiff C	3–2 *

1973	Cardiff C	Bangor C	5–1 *
1974	Cardiff C	Stourbridge	2–0 *
1975	Wrexham	Cardiff C	5–2 *
1976	Cardiff C	Hereford Utd	6–5 *
1977	Shrewsbury T	Cardiff C	4–2 *
1978	Wrexham	Bangor C	3–1 *
1979	Shrewsbury T	Wrexham	2–1 *
1980	Newport Co	Shrewsbury T	5–1 *
1981	Swansea C	Hereford Utd	2–1 *
1982	Swansea C	Cardiff C	2–1 *
1983	Swansea C	Wrexham	4–1 *
1984	Shrewsbury T	Wrexham	2–0 *
1985	Shrewsbury T	Bangor C	5–1 *
1986	Kidderminster H	Wrexham	1–1, 2–1
1987	Merthyr Tydfil	Newport Co	2–2, 1–0
1988	Cardiff C	Wrexham	1–0
1989	Swansea C	Kidderminster H	5–0
1990	Hereford Utd	Wrexham	2–1
1991	Swansea C	Wrexham	2–0
1992	Cardiff C	Hednesford T	1–0
1993	Cardiff C	Rhyl	5–0
1994	Barry T	Cardiff C	2–1
1995	Wrexham	Cardiff C	2–1
1996	Llansantffraid	Barry T	3–3
	(Llansantffraid won 3–2 on penalties)		
1997	Barry T	Cwmbran T	2–1
* Aggregate score			

INTERNATIONAL RESULTS
1876–1899

Date	Opponents	Venue	F–A
25/3/76	Scotland	Glasgow	0–4
5/3/77	Scotland	Wrexham	0–2
23/3/78	Scotland	Glasgow	0–9
18/1/79	England	London	1–2
7/4/79	Scotland	Wrexham	0–3
15/3/80	England	Wrexham	2–3
27/3/80	Scotland	Glasgow	1–5
26/2/81	England	Blackburn	1–0
14/3/81	Scotland	Wrexham	1–5
25/2/82	Ireland	Wrexham	7–1
13/3/82	England	Wrexham	5–3
25/3/82	Scotland	Glasgow	0–5
3/2/83	England	London	0–5
12/3/83	Scotland	Wrexham	0–3
17/3/83	Ireland	Belfast	1–1
9/2/84	Ireland	Wrexham	6–0
17/3/84	England	Wrexham	0–4
29/3/84	Scotland	Glasgow	1–4
14/3/85	England	Blackburn	1–1

23/3/85	Scotland	Wrexham	1–8
11/4/85	Ireland	Belfast	8–2
27/2/86	Ireland	Wrexham	5–0
29/3/86	England	Wrexham	1–3
10/4/86	Scotland	Glasgow	1–4
26/2/87	England	London	0–4
12/3/87	Ireland	Belfast	1–4
21/3/87	Scotland	Wrexham	0–2
4/2/88	England	Crewe	1–5
3/3/88	Ireland	Wrexham	11–0
10/3/88	Scotland	Edinburgh	1–5
23/2/89	England	Stoke	1–4
15/4/89	Scotland	Wrexham	0–0
27/4/89	Ireland	Belfast	3–1
8/2/90	Ireland	Shrewsbury	5–2
15/3/90	England	Wrexham	1–3
22/3/90	Scotland	Glasgow	0–5
7/2/91	Ireland	Belfast	2–7
7/3/91	England	Sunderland	1–4
21/3/91	Scotland	Wrexham	3–4
27/2/92	Ireland	Bangor	1–1
5/3/92	England	Wrexham	0–2
26/3/92	Scotland	Edinburgh	1–6
13/3/93	England	Stoke-on-Trent	0–6
18/3/93	Scotland	Wrexham	0–8
5/4/93	Ireland	Belfast	3–4
24/2/94	Ireland	Swansea	4–1
12/3/94	England	Wrexham	1–5
24/3/94	Scotland	Kilmarnock	2–5
16/3/95	Ireland	Belfast	2–2
18/3/95	England	London	1–1
23/3/95	Scotland	Wrexham	2–2
29/2/96	Ireland	Wrexham	6–1
16/3/96	England	Cardiff	1–9
21/3/96	Scotland	Dundee	0–4
6/3/97	Ireland	Belfast	3–4
20/3/97	Scotland	Wrexham	2–2
29/3/97	England	Sheffield	0–4
19/2/98	Ireland	Llandudno	0–1
19/3/98	Scotland	Motherwell	2–5
28/3/98	England	Wrexham	0–3
4/3/99	Ireland	Belfast	0–1
18/3/99	Scotland	Wrexham	0–6
20/3/99	England	Bristol	0–4

1900–1919

3/2/00	Scotland	Aberdeen	2–5
24/2/00	Ireland	Llandudno	2–0
26/3/00	England	Cardiff	1–1
2/3/01	Scotland	Wrexham	1–1
18/3/01	England	Newcastle	0–6
23/3/01	Ireland	Belfast	1–0

Date	Opponent	Venue	Score
22/2/02	Ireland	Cardiff	0–3
3/3/02	England	Wrexham	0–0
15/3/02	Scotland	Greenock	1–5
2/3/03	England	Portsmouth	1–2
9/3/03	Scotland	Cardiff	0–1
28/3/03	Ireland	Belfast	0–2
29/2/04	England	Wrexham	2–2
12/3/04	Scotland	Dundee	1–1
21/3/04	Ireland	Bangor	0–1
6/3/05	Scotland	Wrexham	3–1
27/3/05	England	Liverpool	1–5
8/4/05	Ireland	Belfast	2–2
3/3/06	Scotland	Edinburgh	2–0
19/3/06	England	Cardiff	0–1
2/4/06	Ireland	Wrexham	4–4
23/2/07	Ireland	Belfast	3–2
4/3/07	Scotland	Wrexham	1–0
18/3/07	England	Fulham	1–1
7/3/08	Scotland	Dundee	1–2
16/3/08	England	Wrexham	1–7
11/4/08	Ireland	Aberdare	0–1
1/3/09	Scotland	Wrexham	3–2
15/3/09	England	Nottingham	0–2
20/3/09	Ireland	Belfast	3–2
5/3/10	Scotland	Kilmarnock	0–1
14/3/10	England	Cardiff	0–1
11/4/10	Ireland	Wrexham	4–1
28/1/11	Ireland	Belfast	2–1
6/3/11	Scotland	Cardiff	2–2
13/3/11	England	London	0–3
2/3/12	Scotland	Edinburgh	0–1
11/3/12	England	Wrexham	0–2
13/4/12	Ireland	Cardiff	2–3
18/1/13	Ireland	Belfast	1–0
3/3/13	Scotland	Wrexham	0–0
17/3/13	England	Bristol	3–4
19/1/14	Ireland	Wrexham	1–2
28/2/14	Scotland	Glasgow	0–0
16/3/14	England	Cardiff	0–2

1920–1929

Date	Opponent	Venue	Score
14/2/20	Ireland	Belfast	2–2
26/2/20	Scotland	Cardiff	1–1
15/3/20	England	London	2–1
12/2/21	Scotland	Aberdeen	1–2
16/3/21	England	Cardiff	0–0
9/4/21	Ireland	Swansea	2–1
4/2/22	Scotland	Wrexham	2–1
13/3/22	England	Liverpool	0–1
1/4/22	Ireland	Belfast	1–1
5/3/23	England	Cardiff	2–2
17/3/23	Scotland	Glasgow	0–2
14/4/23	Ireland	Wrexham	0–3
16/2/24	Scotland	Cardiff	2–0
3/3/24	England	Blackburn	2–1
15/3/24	Ireland	Belfast	1–0
14/2/25	Scotland	Edinburgh	1–3
28/2/25	England	Swansea	1–2
18/4/25	Ireland	Wrexham	0–0
31/10/25	Scotland	Cardiff	0–3
13/2/26	Ireland	Belfast	0–3
1/3/26	England	London	3–1
30/10/26	Scotland	Glasgow	0–3
14/2/27	England	Wrexham	3–3
9/4/27	Ireland	Cardiff	2–2
29/10/27	Scotland	Wrexham	2–2
28/11/27	England	Burnley	2–1
4/2/28	Ireland	Belfast	2–1
27/10/28	Scotland	Glasgow	2–4
17/11/28	England	Swansea	2–3
2/2/29	Ireland	Wrexham	2–2
26/10/29	Scotland	Cardiff	2–4
20/11/29	England	London	0–6

1930–1939

Date	Opponent	Venue	Score
1/2/30	Ireland	Belfast	0–7
25/10/30	Scotland	Glasgow	1–1
22/11/30	England	Wrexham	0–4
22/4/31	Ireland	Wrexham	3–2
31/10/31	Scotland	Wrexham	2–3
18/11/31	England	Liverpool	1–3
5/12/31	Ireland	Belfast	0–4
26/10/32	Scotland	Edinburgh	5–2
16/11/32	England	Wrexham	0–0
7/12/32	Ireland	Wrexham	4–1
25/5/33	France	Paris	1–1
4/10/33	Scotland	Cardiff	3–2
4/11/33	Ireland	Belfast	1–1
15/11/33	England	Newcastle	2–1
29/9/34	Ireland	Cardiff	0–4
21/11/34	Scotland	Aberdeen	2–3
27/3/35	Ireland	Wrexham	3–1
5/10/35	Scotland	Cardiff	1–1
5/2/36	England	Wolverhampton	2–1
11/3/36	Ireland	Belfast	2–3
17/10/36	England	Cardiff	2–1
2/12/36	Scotland	Dundee	2–1
17/3/37	Ireland	Wrexham	4–1
30/10/37	Scotland	Cardiff	2–1
17/11/37	England	Middlesbrough	1–2
16/3/38	Ireland	Belfast	0–1
22/10/38	England	Cardiff	4–2
9/11/38	Scotland	Edinburgh	2–3
15/3/39	Ireland	Wrexham	3–1
20/5/39	France	Paris	1–2

1940–1949

Date	Opponent	Venue	Score
19/10/46	Scotland	Wrexham	3–1
13/11/46	England	Manchester	0–3
16/4/47	N Ireland	Belfast	1–2
18/10/47	England	Cardiff	0–3
12/11/47	Scotland	Glasgow	2–1
10/3/48	N Ireland	Wrexham	2–0
23/10/48	Scotland	Cardiff	1–3
10/11/48	England	Villa Park	0–1
9/3/49	N Ireland	Belfast	2–0
15/5/49	Portugal	Lisbon	2–3
23/5/49	Belgium	Liege	1–3
26/5/49	Switzerland	Berne	0–4
15/10/49	England	Cardiff	1–4 (WCQ)
9/11/49	Scotland	Glasgow	0–2 (WCQ)
23/11/49	Belgium	Cardiff	5–1

1950–1959

Date	Opponent	Venue	Score
8/3/50	N Ireland	Wrexham	0–0 (WCQ)
21/10/50	Scotland	Cardiff	1–3
15/11/50	England	Sunderland	2–4
7/3/51	N Ireland	Belfast	2–1
12/5/51	Portugal	Cardiff	2–1
16/5/51	Switzerland	Wrexham	3–2
20/10/51	England	Cardiff	1–1
20/11/51	Scotland	Glasgow	1–0
5/12/51	Rest of UK	Cardiff	3–2
19/3/52	N Ireland	Swansea	3–0
18/10/52	Scotland	Cardiff	1–2
12/11/52	England	Wembley	2–5
15/4/53	N Ireland	Belfast	3–2
14/5/53	France	Paris	1–6
21/5/53	Yugoslavia	Belgrade	2–5
10/10/53	England	Cardiff	1–4 (WCQ)
4/11/53	Scotland	Glasgow	3–3 (WCQ)
31/3/54	N Ireland	Wrexham	1–2 (WCQ)
9/5/54	Austria	Vienna	0–2 (WCQ)
22/9/54	Yugoslavia	Cardiff	1–3
16/10/54	Scotland	Cardiff	0–1
10/11/54	England	Wembley	2–3
20/4/55	N Ireland	Belfast	3–2
22/10/55	England	Cardiff	2–1
9/11/55	Scotland	Glasgow	0–2
23/11/55	Austria	Wrexham	1–2 (ECQ)
11/4/56	N Ireland	Cardiff	1–1
20/10/56	Scotland	Cardiff	2–2
14/11/56	England	Wembley	1–3
10/4/57	N Ireland	Belfast	0–0
1/5/57	Czechoslovakia	Cardiff	1–0 (WCQ)
19/5/57	E Germany	Leipzig	1–2 (WCQ)
26/5/57	Czechoslovakia	Prague	0–2 (W
25/9/57	E Germany	Cardiff	4–1 (WCQ)
19/10/57	England	Cardiff	0–4
13/11/57	Scotland	Glasgow	1–1
15/1/58	Israel	Tel Aviv	2–0 (WCQ)
5/2/58	Israel	Cardiff	2–0 (WCQ)
16/4/58	N Ireland	Cardiff	1–1
8/6/58	Hungary	Sandviken	1–1 (WCF)
11/6/58	Mexico	Stockholm	1–1 (WCF)
15/6/58	Sweden	Stockholm	0–0 (WCF)
17/6/58	Hungary	Stockholm	2–1 (WCF)
19/6/58	Brazil	Gothenburg	0–1 (WCF)
18/10/58	Scotland	Cardiff	0–3
26/11/58	England	Villa Park	2–2
22/4/59	N Ireland	Belfast	1–4
17/10/59	England	Cardiff	1–1
4/11/59	Scotland	Glasgow	1–1

1960–69

Date	Opponent	Venue	Score
6/4/60	N Ireland	Wrexham	3–2
28/9/60	Rep of Ireland	Dublin	3–2
22/10/60	Scotland	Cardiff	2–0
23/11/60	England	Wembley	1–5
12/4/61	N Ireland	Belfast	5–1
19/4/61	Spain	Cardiff	1–2 (WCQ)
18/5/61	Spain	Madrid	1–1 (WCQ)
28/5/61	Hungary	Budapest	2–3
14/10/61	England	Cardiff	1–1
8/11/61	Scotland	Glasgow	0–2
11/4/62	N Ireland	Cardiff	4–0
12/5/62	Brazil	Rio de Janeiro	1–3
16/5/62	Brazil	São Paulo	1–3
22/5/62	Mexico	Mexico City	1–2
20/10/62	Scotland	Cardiff	2–3
7/11/62	Hungary	Budapest	1–3 (ECQ)
21/11/62	England	Wembley	0–4
20/3/63	Hungary	Cardiff	1–1 (ECQ)
3/4/63	N Ireland	Belfast	4–1
12/10/63	England	Cardiff	0–4
20/11/63	Scotland	Glasgow	1–2
15/4/64	N Ireland	Swansea	2–3
3/10/64	Scotland	Cardiff	3–2
21/10/64	Denmark	Copenhagen	0–1 (WCQ)
18/11/64	England	Wembley	1–2
9/12/64	Greece	Athens	0–2 (WCQ)
17/2/65	Greece	Cardiff	4–1 (WCQ)
31/3/65	N Ireland	Belfast	5–0
1/5/65	Italy	Florence	1–4
30/5/65	USSR	Moscow	1–2 (WCQ)
2/10/65	England	Cardiff	0–0
27/10/65	USSR	Cardiff	2–1 (WCQ)
24/11/65	Scotland	Glasgow	1–4 (ECQ)
1/12/65	Denmark	Wrexham	4–2 (WCQ)
30/3/66	N Ireland	Cardiff	1–4
14/5/66	Brazil	Rio de Janeiro	1–3
18/5/66	Brazil	Belo Horizonte	0–1
22/5/66	Chile	Santiago	0–2
22/10/66	Scotland	Cardiff	1–1 (ECQ)
16/11/66	England	Wembley	1–5 (ECQ)
12/4/67	N Ireland	Belfast	0–0 (ECQ)
21/10/67	England	Cardiff	0–3 (ECQ)
22/11/67	Scotland	Glasgow	2–3 (ECQ)
28/2/68	N Ireland	Wrexham	2–0 (ECQ)
8/5/68	W Germany	Cardiff	1–1
23/10/68	Italy	Cardiff	0–1 (WCQ)
26/3/69	W Germany	Frankfurt	1–1
16/4/69	E Germany	Dresden	1–2 (WCQ)
3/5/69	Scotland	Wrexham	3–5
7/5/69	England	Wembley	1–2
10/5/69	N Ireland	Belfast	0–0
28/7/69	Rest of UK	Cardiff	0–1
22/10/69	E Germany	Cardiff	1–3 (WCQ)
4/11/69	Italy	Rome	1–4 (WCQ)

1970

Date	Opponent	Venue	Score
18/4	England	Cardiff	1–1
22/4	Scotland	Glasgow	0–0
25/4	N Ireland	Swansea	1–0
11/11	Romania	Cardiff	0–0 (ECQ)

1971

Date	Opponent	Venue	Score
21/4	Czechoslovakia	Swansea	1–3 (ECQ)
15/5	Scotland	Cardiff	0–0
18/5	England	Wembley	0–0
22/5	N Ireland	Belfast	0–1
26/5	Finland	Helsinki	1–0 (ECQ)
13/10	Finland	Swansea	3–0 (ECQ)
27/10	Czechoslovakia	Prague	0–1 (ECQ)
24/11	Romania	Bucharest	0–2 (ECQ)

1972

Date	Opponent	Venue	Score
20/5	England	Cardiff	0–3
24/5	Scotland	Glasgow	0–1
27/5	N Ireland	Wrexham	0–0
15/11	England	Cardiff	0–1 (WCQ)

1973

Date	Opponent	Venue	Score
24/1	England	Wembley	1–1 (WCQ)
28/3	Poland	Cardiff	2–0 (WCQ)
12/5	Scotland	Wrexham	0–2
15/5	England	Wembley	0–3
19/5	N Ireland	Liverpool	0–1
26/9	Poland	Chorzow	0–3 (WCQ)

1974

Date	Opponent	Venue	Score
11/5	England	Cardiff	0–2
14/5	Scotland	Glasgow	0–2
18/5	N Ireland	Wrexham	1–0
4/9	Austria	Vienna	1–2 (ECQ)
30/10	Hungary	Cardiff	2–0 (ECQ)
20/11	Luxembourg	Swansea	5–0 (ECQ)

1975

Date	Opponent	Venue	Score
16/4	Hungary	Budapest	2–1 (ECQ)
1/5	Luxembourg	Luxembourg	3–1 (ECQ)
17/5	Scotland	Cardiff	2–2
21/5	England	Wembley	2–2
23/5	N Ireland	Belfast	0–1
19/11	Austria	Wrexham	1–0 (ECQ)

1976

Date	Opponent	Venue	Score
24/3	England	Wrexham	1–2
24/4	Yugoslavia	Zagreb	0–2 (ECQ)
6/5	Scotland	Glasgow	1–3
8/5	England	Cardiff	0–1
14/5	N Ireland	Swansea	1–0
22/5	Yugoslavia	Cardiff	1–1 (ECQ)
6/10	W Germany	Cardiff	0–2
17/11	Scotland	Glasgow	0–1 (WCQ)

1977

Date	Opponent	Venue	Score
30/3	Czechoslovakia	Wrexham	3–0 (WCQ)
28/5	Scotland	Wrexham	0–0
31/5	England	Wembley	1–0
3/6	N Ireland	Belfast	1–1
6/9	Kuwait	Wrexham	0–0
20/9	Kuwait	Kuwait	0–0
12/10	Scotland	Liverpool	0–2 (WCQ)
16/11	Czechoslovakia	Prague	0–1 (WCQ)
14/12	W Germany	Dortmund	1–1

1978

Date	Opponent	Venue	Score
18/4	Iran	Teheran	1–0
13/5	England	Cardiff	1–3
17/5	Scotland	Glasgow	1–1
19/5	N Ireland	Wrexham	1–0
25/10	Malta	Wrexham	7–0 (ECQ)
29/11	Turkey	Wrexham	1–0 (ECQ)

1979

Date	Opponent	Venue	Score
2/5	W Germany	Wrexham	0–2 (ECQ)
19/5	Scotland	Cardiff	3–0
23/5	England	Wembley	0–0
25/5	N Ireland	Belfast	1–1
2/6	Malta	Valetta	2–0 (ECQ)
11/9	Rep of Ireland	Swansea	2–1
17/10	W Germany	Cologne	1–5 (ECQ)
21/11	Turkey	Izmir	0–1 (ECQ)

1980

17/5	England	Wrexham	4–1
21/5	Scotland	Glasgow	0–1
23/5	N Ireland	Cardiff	0–1
2/6	Iceland	Reykjavic	4–0 (WCQ)
15/10	Turkey	Cardiff	4–0 (WCQ)
19/11	Czechoslovakia	Cardiff	1–0 (WCQ)

1981

24/2	Rep of Ireland	Dublin	3–1
25/3	Turkey	Ankara	1–0 (WCQ)
16/5	Scotland	Swansea	2–0
20/5	England	Wembley	0–0
30/5	USSR	Wrexham	0–0 (WCQ)
9/9	Czechoslovakia	Prague	0–2 (WCQ)
14/10	Iceland	Swansea	2–2 (WCQ)
18/11	USSR	Tbilisi	0–3 (WCQ)

1982

24/3	Spain	Valencia	1–1
27/4	England	Cardiff	0–1
24/5	Scotland	Glasgow	0–1
27/5	N Ireland	Wrexham	3–0
2/6	France	Toulouse	1–0
22/9	Norway	Swansea	1–0 (ECQ)
15/12	Yugoslavia	Titograd	4–4 (ECQ)

1983

23/2	England	Wembley	1–2
27/4	Bulgaria	Wrexham	1–0 (ECQ)
28/5	Scotland	Cardiff	0–2
31/5	N Ireland	Belfast	1–0
12/6	Brazil	Cardiff	1–1
21/9	Norway	Oslo	0–0 (ECQ)
12/10	Romania	Wrexham	5–0
16/11	Bulgaria	Sofia	0–1 (ECQ)
14/12	Yugoslavia	Cardiff	1–1 (ECQ)

1984

28/2	Scotland	Glasgow	1–2
2/5	England	Wrexham	1–0
22/5	N Ireland	Swansea	1–1
6/6	Norway	Trondheim	0–1
10/6	Israel	Tel Aviv	0–0
12/9	Iceland	Reykjavik	0–1 (WCQ)
17/10	Spain	Seville	0–3 (WCQ)
14/11	Iceland	Cardiff	2–1 (WCQ)

1985

26/2	Norway	Wrexham	1–1
27/3	Scotland	Glasgow	1–0 (WCQ)
30/4	Spain	Wrexham	3–0 (WCQ)
5/6	Norway	Bergen	2–4
10/9	Scotland	Cardiff	1–1 (WCQ)
16/10	Hungary	Cardiff	0–3

1986

25/2	Saudi Arabia	Dhahran	2–1
26/3	Rep of Ireland	Dublin	1–0
21/4	Uruguay	Cardiff	0–0
10/5	Canada	Toronto	0–2
20/5	Canada	Vancouver	3–0
10/9	Finland	Helsinki	1–1 (ECQ)

1987

18/2	USSR	Swansea	0–0
1/4	Finland	Wrexham	4–0 (ECQ)
29/4	Czechoslovakia	Wrexham	1–1 (ECQ)
9/9	Denmark	Cardiff	1–0 (ECQ)
14/10	Denmark	Copenhagen	0–1 (ECQ)
11/11	Czechoslovakia	Prague	0–2 (ECQ)

1988

23/3	Yugoslavia	Swansea	1–2
27/4	Sweden	Stockholm	1–4
1/6	Malta	Valletta	3–2
4/6	Italy	Brescia	1–0
14/9	Holland	Amsterdam	0–1 (WCQ)
19/10	Finland	Swansea	2–2 (WCQ)

1989

8/2	Israel	Tel Aviv	3–3
26/4	Sweden	Wrexham	0–2
31/5	W Germany	Cardiff	0–0 (WCQ)
6/9	Finland	Helsinki	0–1 (WCQ)
11/10	Holland	Wrexham	1–2 (WCQ)
15/11	W Germany	Cologne	1–2 (WCQ)

1990

28/3	Rep of Ireland	Dublin	0–1
25/4	Sweden	Stockholm	2–4
20/5	Costa Rica	Cardiff	1–0
1/9	Denmark	Copenhagen	0–1
17/10	Belgium	Cardiff	3–1 (ECQ)
14/11	Luxembourg	Luxembourg	1–0 (ECQ)

1991

6/2	Rep of Ireland	Wrexham	0–3
27/3	Belgium	Brussels	1–1 (ECQ)
1/5	Iceland	Cardiff	1–0
29/5	Poland	Radom	0–0
5/6	W Germany	Cardiff	1–0 (ECQ)
11/9	Brazil	Cardiff	1–0
16/10	W Germany	Nüremberg	1–4 (ECQ)
13/11	Luxembourg	Cardiff	1–0 (ECQ)

1992

19/2	Rep of Ireland	Dublin	1–0
29/4	Austria	Vienna	1–1
20/5	Romania	Bucharest	1–5 (WCQ)
30/5	Holland	Utrecht	0–4
3/6	Argentina	Tokyo	0–1
7/6	Japan	Matsuyama	1–0
9/9	Faeroes	Cardiff	6–0 (WCQ)
14/10	Cyprus	Limassol	1–0 (WCQ)
18/11	Belgium	Brussels	0–2 (WCQ)

1993

17/2	Rep of Ireland	Dublin	1–2
31/3	Belgium	Cardiff	2–0 (WCQ)
28/4	Czechoslovakia	Ostrava	1–1 (WCQ)
6/6	Faeroes	Toftir	3–0 (WCQ)
8/9	RCS*	Cardiff	2–2 (WCQ)
13/10	Cyprus	Cardiff	2–0 (WCQ)
17/11	Romania	Cardiff	1–2 (WCQ)

* Representation of Czechs & Slovaks (was Czechoslovakia).

1994

9/3	Norway	Cardiff	1–3
20/4	Sweden	Wrexham	0–2
23/5	Estonia	Tallinn	2–1
7/9	Albania	Cardiff	2–0 (ECQ)
12/10	Moldova	Chislau	2–3 (ECQ)
16/11	Georgia	Tbilisi	0–5 (ECQ)
14/12	Bulgaria	Cardiff	0–3 (ECQ)
7/9	Albania	Cardiff	2–0 (ECQ)

1995

29/3	Bulgaria	Sofia	1–3 (ECQ)
26/4	Germany	Düsseldorf	1–1 (ECQ)
7/6	Georgia	Cardiff	0–1 (ECQ)
6/9	Moldova	Cardiff	1–0 (ECQ)
11/10	Germany	Cardiff	1–2 (ECQ)
15/11	Albania	Tirana	1–1 (ECQ)

1996

24/1	Italy	Terni	0–3
24/4	Switzerland	Lugano	0–2
2/6	San Marino	Sarravalle	5–0 (WCQ)
31/8	San Marino	Cardiff	6–0 (WCQ)
5/10	Holland	Cardiff	1–3 (WCQ)
9/11	Holland	Eindhoven	1–7 (WCQ)
14/12	Turkey	Cardiff	0–0 (WCQ)

1997

11/2	Rep of Ireland	Cardiff	0–0
29/3	Belgium	Cardiff	1–2 (WCQ)
27/5	Scotland	Kilmarnock	1–0

NORTHERN IRELAND

The story of Irish football runs parallel to that of mainland Britain. The start is familiar ground, with the founding of the Irish Football Association on November 18, 1880, and the launching of the Irish Cup by the pioneering J. M. McAlery. Entry cost seven participants ten shillings each, and though Knock beat Distillery 11–0 in the opening round, it was Cliftonville – the first club formed in Ireland in 1879 – who took on the Castledawson team Moyola Park in the inaugural final.

That Moyola Park, the underdogs, should become the winners amply demonstrated the magic of the knockout competition. A single goal from outside-left Morrow was the decisive strike.

Thirteen clubs figured in the Cup in its second season, Queen's Island proving successful with a 2–1 final victory over Cliftonville. At last, Cliftonville won the trophy at their third successive attempt, convincingly disposing of Ulster by 5–0.

Distillery became the first club to win the Cup three years in a row. Their initial success in 1883–84, when they thrashed Wellington Park 5–0, followed by victories over Limavady (2–0) in 1895 and by 1–0 a year later.

Alas, a protest lodged by Limavady on the conduct of some Distillery players who, they claimed, had intimidated them, was upheld by the Association, who decreed "that the Cup and medals be witheld for the year owing to the conduct of players of both teams". Such were the trials and tribulations of those formative years.

Regiments of British troops were then stationed throughout Ireland, and military sides entered the Irish Cup from time to time. Only one won it, however, the Gordon Highlanders in 1890, a season in which the Black Watch and the East Lancashire Regiment also participated.

An important change was made in the rules allowing players from Great Britain to play if they had three months' residence in Ireland. Linfield reached the final for the fifth year in succession in 1895, celebrating with a 10–1 win over Bohemians, who opened the scoring.

By the turn of the century Dublin was hosting the finals. The first, in 1903, between Distillery and Bohemians, attracted 6,000 spectators to Dalymount Park. In 1905 Shelbourne became the first Dublin side to win the trophy, but in the season of 1911–12 a serious split parted the Dubliners from Belfast. The Belfast clubs withdrew their support and organized a new Irish Cup, with a trophy made of gold. Belfast Celtic beat Glentoran 2–0 in the final, but the rift was healed before the start of the next season.

Another oddity occurred in 1920, when Shelbourne were awarded the trophy without kicking a ball in the final. Unprecedented scenes at the semi-final between Glentoran and Belfast Celtic resulted in both teams being expelled from the competition.

Meanwhile Ireland was heading for political division, and that was formalized in football by a split within the game's administration. The Irish Football Association continued to run the game in the North while the new Football Association of Ireland controlled soccer in the Irish Free State, now the Republic of Ireland.

Domestic football in the North has been dominated by Linfield, who first made headlines in 1958 by signing England centre-forward Jackie Milburn from Newcastle United. He gained only a runners-up medal in the Irish Cup that year, being not fully fit after injuring a knee while playing for the Irish League against the League of Ireland at Cliftonville. But "Wor Jackie", now player-coach, steered Linfield to another League title in 1959.

Overseas Campaigns

On the international front, Northern Ireland's most memorable year was 1957, when they beat England 3–2 at Wembley for the first time and qualified, also for the first time, for the World Cup Finals in Italy – beating Italy, of all people, on the way with a fine team inspired by Harry Gregg in goal, Danny Blanchflower and Jimmy McIlroy in midfield, and Billy Bingham and Peter McParland.

Little Wilbur Cush scored the goal which defeated Czechoslovakia in Northern Ireland's opening game at the finals in Sweden, but a 3–1 defeat by Argentina and a 2–2 draw with Germany left Irish hopes resting on a play-off, again against Czechoslovakia. Two goals from McParland clinched a brilliant 2–1 win in Malmo. Northern Ireland were through to the quarter-finals, but the fatigue and injuries carried over from the first round play-off proved too much and they went down 4–0 to the France of Raymond Kopa and Just Fontaine.

Bingham was to enjoy more World Cup glory in 1982 and 1986 as manager. In 1982, in Spain, Norman Whiteside became the youngest player ever to appear in the finals (at 17 years and 42 days). His youthful talent, mixed with the experience of Martin O'Neill and Pat Jennings, saw Northern Ireland create a sensation by defeating hosts Spain 1–0 through a goal by Gerry Armstrong. In the second round, however, it was France – orchestrated by Platini – who again ended Irish dreams, this time 4–1. In 1986 Bingham, undaunted, brought Northern Ireland again to the finals in Mexico, where goalkeeper Jennings played, in the game lost to Brazil, his 119th and last international – then a world record – on his 41st birthday. It was, of course, a British goalkeeping colleague in Peter Shilton who broke the Jennings record four years later in the 1990 World Cup finals in Italy.

Bingham retired at 62, waving farewell to Windsor Park in the final World Cup qualifying tie against the Republic of Ireland in November 1993. He had been in charge for 14 years and was by far his country's most successful manager. His highlights were winning the 1980 British Championship, and beating West Germany in Hamburg in 1983 – a challenging standard for his successor, Bryan Hamilton.

LEAGUE CHAMPIONS

1891–1899

1891	Linfield	1892	Linfield
1893	Linfield	1894	Glentoran
1895	Linfield	1896	Distillery
1897	Glentoran	1898	Glenfield
1899	Distillery		

1900–1909

1900	Belfast Celtic	1901	Distillery
1902	Linfield	1903	Distillery
1904	Linfield	1905	Glentoran
1906	Cliftonville/Distillery	1907	Linfield
1908	Linfield	1909	Linfield

1910–1915

1910	Cliftonville	1911	Linfield
1912	Glentoran	1913	Glentoran
1914	Linfield	1915	Belfast Celtic

1920–1929

1920	Belfast Celtic	1921	Glentoran
1922	Linfield	1923	Linfield
1924	Queen's Island	1925	Glentoran
1926	Belfast Celtic	1927	Belfast Celtic
1928	Belfast Celtic	1929	Belfast Celtic

1930–1939

1930	Linfield	1931	Glentoran
1932	Linfield	1933	Belfast Celtic
1934	Linfield	1935	Linfield
1936	Belfast Celtic	1937	Belfast Celtic
1938	Belfast Celtic	1939	Belfast Celtic

1940–1949

1940	Belfast Celtic	1948	Belfast Celtic
1949	Linfield		

1950–1959

1950	Linfield	1951	Glentoran
1952	Glenavon	1953	Glentoran
1954	Linfield	1955	Linfield
1956	Linfield	1957	Glentoran
1958	Ards	1959	Linfield

1960–1969

1960	Glenavon	1961	Linfield
1962	Linfield	1963	Distillery
1964	Glentoran	1965	Derry City
1966	Linfield	1967	Glentoran
1968	Glentoran	1969	Linfield

1970–1979

1970	Glentoran	1971	Linfield
1972	Glentoran	1973	Crusaders
1974	Coleraine	1975	Linfield
1976	Crusaders	1977	Glentoran
1978	Linfield	1979	Linfield

1980–1989

1980	Linfield	1981	Linfield
1982	Linfield	1983	Linfield
1984	Linfield	1985	Linfield
1986	Linfield	1987	Linfield
1988	Glentoran	1989	Linfield

1990–1997

1990	Portadown	1991	Portadown
1992	Glentoran	1993	Linfield
1994	Linfield	1995	Crusaders
1996	Portadown	1997	Crusaders

IRISH CUP FINALS

Year	Winners	Runners-up	Result
1881	Moyola Park	Cliftonville	1–0
1882	Queen's Island	Cliftonville	2–1
1883	Cliftonville	Ulster	5–0
1884	Distillery	Ulster	5–0
1885	Distillery	Limavady	2–0
1886	Distillery	Limavady	1–0
1887	Ulster	Cliftonville	3–1
1888	Cliftonville	Distillery	2–1
1889	Distillery	YMCA	5–4
1890	Gordon Highlanders	Cliftonville	2–2, 3–0
1891	Linfield	Ulster	4–2
1892	Linfield	The Black Watch	7–0
1893	Linfield	Cliftonville	5–1
1894	Distillery	Linfield	2–2, 3–2
1895	Linfield	Bohemians	10–1
1896	Distillery	Glentoran	3–1
1897	Cliftonville	Sherwood Foresters Curragh	3–1
1898	Linfield	St Columbs Hall Celtic Derry	2–0
1899	Linfield	Glentoran	1–0
1900	Cliftonville	Bohemians	2–1
1901	Cliftonville	Freebooters, Dublin	1–0
1902	Linfield	Distillery	5–1
1903	Distillery	Bohemians	3–1
1904	Linfield	Derry Celtic	5–0
1905	Distillery	Shelbourne	3–0
1906	Shelbourne	Belfast Celtic	2–0
1907	Cliftonville	Shelbourne	0–0, 1–0
1908	Bohemians	Shelbourne	1–1, 3–1
1909	Cliftonville	Bohemians	0–0, 2–1
1910	Distillery	Cliftonville	1–0
1911	Shelbourne	Bohemians	0–0, 2–1
1912	Not played: Linfield awarded cup		
1913	Linfield	Glentoran	2–0
1914	Glentoran	Linfield	3–1
1915	Linfield	Belfast Celtic	1–0
1916	Linfield	Glentoran	1–0
1917	Glentoran	Belfast Celtic	2–0
1918	Belfast Celtic	Linfield	0–0, 0–0, 2–0
1919	Linfield	Glentoran	1–1, 0–0, 2–1
1920	Not played: Shelbourne awarded cup		
1921	Glentoran	Glenavon	2–0
1922	Linfield	Glenavon	2–0
1923	Linfield	Glentoran	2–0
1924	Queen's Island	Willowfield	1–0
1925	Distillery	Glentoran	2–1
1926	Belfast Celtic	Linfield	3–2
1927	Ards	Cliftonville	3–2
1928	Willowfield	Larne	1–0
1929	Ballymena Utd	Belfast Celtic	2–1
1930	Linfield	Ballymena United	4–3
1931	Linfield	Ballymena United	3–0
1932	Glentoran	Linfield	2–1
1933	Glentoran	Distillery	1–1, 1–1, 3–1
1934	Linfield	Cliftonville	5–0
1935	Glentoran	Larne	0–0, 0–0, 1–0
1936	Linfield	Derry City	0–0, 2–1
1937	Belfast Celtic	Linfield	3–0
1938	Belfast Celtic	Bangor	0–0, 2–0
1939	Linfield	Ballymena Utd	2–0
1940	Ballymena Utd	Glenavon	2–0
1941	Belfast Celtic	Linfield	1–0
1942	Linfield	Glentoran	3–1
1943	Belfast Celtic	Glentoran	1–0
1944	Belfast Celtic	Linfield	3–1
1945	Linfield	Glentoran	4–2
1946	Linfield	Distillery	3–0
1947	Belfast Celtic	Glentoran	1–0
1948	Linfield	Coleraine	3–0
1949	Derry City	Glentoran	3–1
1950	Linfield	Distillery	2–1
1951	Glentoran	Ballymena Utd	3–1
1952	Ards	Glentoran	1–0
1953	Linfield	Coleraine	5–0
1954	Derry City	Glentoran	1–0
1955	Dundela	Glenavon	3–0
1956	Distillery	Glentoran	1–0
1957	Glenavon	Derry City	2–0
1958	Ballymena Utd	Linfield	2–0
1959	Glenavon	Ballymena Utd	2–0
1960	Linfield	Ards	5–1
1961	Glenavon	Linfield	5–1
1962	Linfield	Portadown	4–0
1963	Linfield	Distillery	2–1
1964	Derry City	Glentoran	2–0
1965	Coleraine	Glenavon	2–1
1966	Glentoran	Linfield	2–0
1967	Crusaders	Glentoran	3–1
1968	Crusaders	Linfield	2–0
1969	Ards	Distillery	4–2
1970	Linfield	Ballymena Utd	2–1
1971	Distillery	Derry City	3–0
1972	Coleraine	Portadown	2–1
1973	Glentoran	Linfield	3–2
1974	Ards	Ballymena Utd	2–1
1975	Coleraine	Linfield	1–1, 0–0, 1–0
1976	Carrick Rangers	Linfield	2–1
1977	Coleraine	Linfield	4–1
1978	Linfield	Ballymena Utd	3–1
1979	Cliftonville	Portadown	3–2
1980	Linfield	Crusaders	2–0
1981	Ballymena Utd	Glenavon	1–0
1982	Linfield	Coleraine	2–1
1983	Glentoran	Linfield	1–1, 2–1
1984	Ballymena Utd	Garrick Rangers	4–1
1985	Glentoran	Linfield	1–1, 1–0
1986	Glentoran	Coleraine	2–1
1987	Glentoran	Larne	1–0
1988	Glentoran	Glenavon	1–0
1989	Ballymena Utd	Larne	1–0
1990	Glentoran	Portadown	3–0
1991	Portadown	Glenavon	2–1
1992	Glenavon	Linfield	2–1
1993	Bangor	Ards	1–1, 1–1, 1–0
1994	Linfield	Bangor	2–0
1995	Linfield	Carrick Rangers	3–1
1996	Glentoran	Glenavon	1–0
1997	Glenavon	Cliftonville	1–0

INTERNATIONAL RESULTS

Date	Opponents	Venue	F–A
1882			
18/2/82	England	Belfast	0–13
25/2/82	Wales	Wrexham	1–7
1883			
24/2/83	England	Liverpool	0–7
17/3/83	Wales	Belfast	1–1
1884			
26/1/84	Scotland	Belfast	0–5
9/2/84	Wales	Wrexham	0–6
23/2/84	England	Belfast	1–8
1885			
28/2/85	England	Manchester	0–4
14/3/85	Scotland	Glasgow	2–8
11/4/85	Wales	Belfast	2–8
1886			
27/2/86	Wales	Wrexham	0–5
13/3/86	England	Belfast	1–6
20/3/86	Scotland	Belfast	2–7
1887			
5/2/87	England	Sheffield	0–7
19/2/87	Scotland	Glasgow	1 4
12/3/87	Wales	Belfast	4–1
1888			
3/3/88	Wales	Wrexham	0–11
24/3/88	Scotland	Belfast	2–10
7/4/88	England	Belfast	1–5
1889			
2/3/89	England	Liverpool	1–6
9/3/89	Scotland	Glasgow	0–7
27/4/89	Wales	Belfast	1–3

1890
8/2 Wales Shrewsbury 2–5
15/3 England Belfast 1–9
29/3 Scotland Belfast 1–4

1891
7/2 Wales Belfast 7–2
7/3 England Wolverhampton 1–6
28/3 Scotland Glasgow 1–2

1892
27/2 Wales Bangor 1–1
5/3 England Belfast 0–2
19/3 Scotland Belfast 2–3

1893
25/2 England Birmingham 1–6
25/3 Scotland Glasgow 1–6
5/4 Wales Belfast 4–3

1894
24/2 Wales Swansea 1–4
3/3 England Belfast 2–2
31/3 Scotland Belfast 1–2

1895
9/3 England Derby 0–9
16/3 Wales Belfast 2–2
30/3 Scotland Glasgow 1–3

1896
29/2 Wales Wrexham 1–6
7/3 England Belfast 0–2
28/3 Scotland Belfast 3–3

1897
20/2 England Nottingham 0–6
6/3 Wales Belfast 4–3
27/3 Scotland Glasgow 1–5

1898
19/2 Wales Llandudno 1–0
5/3 England Belfast 2–3
26/3 Scotland Belfast 0–3

1899
18/2 England Sunderland 2–13
4/3 Wales Belfast 1–0
25/3 Scotland Glasgow 1–9

1900
24/2 Wales Llandudno 0–2
3/3 Scotland Belfast 0–3
17/3 England Dublin 0–2

1901
23/2 Scotland Glasgow 0–11
9/3 England Southampton 0–3
23/3 Wales Belfast 0–1

1902
22/2 Wales Cardiff 3–0
1/3 Scotland Belfast 1–3
22/3 England Belfast 0–1

1903
14/2 England Wolverhampton 0–4
21/3 Scotland Glasgow 2–0
28/3 Wales Belfast 2–0

1904
12/3 England Belfast 1–3
21/3 Wales Bangor 1–0
26/3 Scotland Dublin 1–1

1905
25/2 England Middlesbrough 1–1
18/3 Scotland Glasgow 0–4
8/4 Wales Belfast 2–2

1906
17/2 England Belfast 0–5
17/3 Scotland Dublin 0–1
2/4 Wales Wrexham 4–4

1907
16/2 England Liverpool 0–1
23/2 Wales Belfast 2
16/3 Scotland Glasgow 0–3

1908
15/2 England Belfast 1–3
14/3 Scotland Dublin 0–5
11/4 Wales Aberdare 1–0

1909
13/2 England Bradford 0–4
15/3 Scotland Glasgow 0–5
20/3 Wales Belfast 2–3

1910
12/2 England Belfast 1–1
19/3 Scotland Belfast 1–0
11/4 Wales Wrexham 1–4

1911
28/1 Wales Belfast 1–2
11/2 England Derby 1–2
18/3 Scotland Glasgow 0–2

1912
10/2 England Dublin 1–6
16/3 Scotland Belfast 1–4
13/4 Wales Cardiff 3–2

1913
18/1 Wales Belfast 0–1
15/2 England Belfast 2–1
15/3 Scotland Dublin 1–2

1914
19/1 Wales Wrexham 2–1
14/2 England Middlesbrough 3–0
14/3 Scotland Belfast 1–1

1919
25/10 England Belfast 1–1

1920
14/2 Wales Belfast 2–2
13/3 Scotland Glasgow 0–3
23/10 England Sunderland 0–2

1921
26/2 Scotland Belfast 0–2
9/4 Wales Swansea 1–2
22/10 England Belfast 1–1

1922
4/3 Scotland Glasgow 1–2
1/4 Wales Belfast 1–1
21/10 England West Bromwich 0–2

1923
3/3 Scotland Belfast 0–1
14/4 Wales Wrexham 3–0
20/10 England Belfast 2–1

1924
1/3 Scotland Glasgow 0–2
15/3 Wales Belfast 0–1
22/10 England Liverpool 1–3

1925
28/2 Scotland Belfast 0–3
18/4 Wales Wrexham 0–0
24/10 England Belfast 0–0

1926
13/2 Wales Belfast 3–0
27/2 Scotland Glasgow 0–4
20/10 England Liverpool 3–3

1927
26/2 Scotland Belfast 0–2
19/4 Wales Cardiff 2–2
22/10 England Belfast 2–0

1928
4/2 Wales Belfast 1–2
25/2 Scotland Glasgow 1–0
22/10 England Liverpool 1–2

1929
2/2 Wales Wrexham 2–2
23/2 Scotland Belfast 3–7
19/10 England Belfast 0–3

1930
1/2 Wales Belfast 0–7
22/2 Scotland Glasgow 1–3
20/10 England Sheffield 1–5

1931
21/2 Scotland Belfast 0–0
22/4 Wales Wrexham 2–3
19/9 Scotland Glasgow 1–3
17/10 England Belfast 2–6
5/12 Wales Belfast 4–0

1932
12/9 Scotland Belfast 0–4
17/10 England Blackpool 0–1
7/12 Wales Wrexham 1–4

1933
16/9 Scotland Glasgow 2–1
14/10 England Belfast 0–3
4/11 Wales Belfast 1–1

1934
20/10 Scotland Belfast 2–1

1935
6/2 England Liverpool 1–2
27/3 Wales Wrexham 1–3
19/10 England Belfast 1–3
13/11 Scotland Edinburgh 1–2

1936
11/3 Wales Belfast 3–2
31/10 Scotland Belfast 1–3
18/11 England Stoke–on–Trent 1–3

1937
17/3 Wales Wrexham 1–4
23/10 England Belfast 1–5
10/11 Scotland Aberdeen 1–1

1938
16/3 Wales Belfast 1–0
8/11 Scotland Belfast 0–2
16/11 England Manchester 0–7

1939
15/3 Wales Wrexham 1–3

1940
28/9 England Belfast 2–7
27/11 Scotland Glasgow 0–0

1947
16/4 Wales Belfast 2–1
4/10 Scotland Belfast 2–0
5/11 England Everton 2–2

1948
10/3 Wales Wrexham 0–2
9/10 England Belfast 2–6
17/11 Scotland Glasgow 2–3

1949
9/3 Wales Belfast 0–2
1/10 Scotland Belfast 2–8 (WCQ)
6/11 England Manchester 2–9 (WCQ)

1950
8/3 Wales Wrexham 0–0 (WCQ)
7/10 England Belfast 1–4
1/11 Scotland Glasgow 1–6

1951
7/3 Wales Belfast 1–2
12/5 France Belfast 2–2
6/10 Scotland Belfast 0–3
20/11 England Villa Park 0–2

1952
19/3 Wales Swansea 0–3
4/10 England Belfast 2–2
5/11 Scotland Glasgow 1–1
11/11 France Paris 1–3

1953
15/4 Wales Belfast 2–3
3/10 Scotland Belfast 1–3 (WCQ)
11/11 England Everton 1–3 (WCQ)

1954
31/3 Wales Wrexham 2–1 (WCQ)
2/10 England Belfast 0–2
3/11 Scotland Glasgow 2–2

1955
20/4 Wales Belfast 2–3
8/10 Scotland Belfast 2–1
2/11 England Wembley 0–3

1956
11/4 Wales Cardiff 1–1
6/10 England Belfast 1–1
7/11 Scotland Glasgow 0–1

1957
16/1 Portugal Lisbon 1–1 (WCQ)
10/4 Wales Belfast 0–0
25/4 Italy Rome 0–1 (WCQ)
1/5 Portugal Belfast 3–0 (WCQ)
5/10 Scotland Belfast 1–1
6/11 England Wembley 3–2
4/12 Italy Belfast 2–2

1958
15/1 Italy Belfast 2–1 (WCQ)
16/4 Wales Cardiff 1–1
8/10 Czechoslovakia Halmstad 1–0 (WCF)
11/6 Argentina Halmstad 1–3 (WCF)
15/6 West Germany Malmo 2–2 (WCF)
17/6 Czechoslovakia Malmo 2–1 (WCF)
19/6 France Norrkoping 0–4 (WCF)
4/10 England Belfast 3–3
15/10 Spain Madrid 2–6
5/11 Scotland Glasgow 2–2

1959
22/4 Wales Belfast 4–1
3/10 Scotland Belfast 0–4
18/11 England Wembley 1–2

1960
6/4 Wales Wrexham 2–3
8/10 England Belfast 2–5
26/10 W Germany Belfast 3–4 (WCQ)
9/11 Scotland Glasgow 2–5

1961
Date	Opponent	Venue	Score	
12/4	Wales	Belfast	1–5	
25/4	Italy	Bologna	2–3	
3/5	Greece	Athens	1–2	(WCQ)
10/5	W Germany	Berlin	1–2	(WCQ)
7/10	Scotland	Belfast	1–6	
17/10	Greece	Belfast	2–0	(WCQ)
22/11	England	Wembley	1–1	

1962
11/4	Wales	Cardiff	0–4	
9/5	Holland	Rotterdam	0–4	
10/10	Poland	Katowice	2–0	(ECQ)
20/10	England	Belfast	1–3	
7/11	Scotland	Glasgow	1–5	
28/11	Poland	Belfast	2–0	(ECQ)

1963
3/4	Wales	Belfast	1–4	
30/5	Spain	Bilbao	1–1	
12/10	Scotland	Belfast	2–1	
30/10	Spain	Belfast	0–1	
20/11	England	Wembley	3–8	

1964
15/4	Wales	Swansea	3–2	
29/4	Uruguay	Belfast	3–0	
3/10	England	Belfast	3–4	
14/10	Switzerland	Belfast	1–0	(WCQ)
14/11	Switzerland	Lausanne	1–2	(WCQ)
25/11	Scotland	Glasgow	2–3	

1965
17/3	Holland	Belfast	2–1	(WCQ)
31/3	Wales	Belfast	0–5	
7/4	Holland	Rotterdam	0–0	(WCQ)
7/5	Albania	Belfast	4–1	(WCQ)
2/10	Scotland	Belfast	3–2	
10/11	England	Wembley	1–2	
24/11	Albania	Tirana	1–1	(WCQ)

1966
30/3	Wales	Cardiff	4–1	
7/5	W Germany	Belfast	0–2	
22/6	Mexico	Belfast	4–1	
22/10	England	Belfast	0–2	(ECQ)
16/11	Scotland	Glasgow	1–2	

1967
12/4	Wales	Belfast	0–0	(ECQ)
21/10	Scotland	Belfast	1–0	
22/11	England	Wembley	0–2	(ECQ)

1968
28/2	Wales	Wrexham	0–2	(ECQ)
10/9	Israel	Jaffa	3–2	
23/10	Turkey	Belfast	4–1	(WCQ)
11/12	Turkey	Istanbul	3–0	(WCQ)

1969
3/5	England	Belfast	1–3	
6/5	Scotland	Glasgow	1–1	
10/5	Wales	Belfast	0–0	
10/9	USSR	Belfast	0–0	(WCQ)
22/10	USSR	Moscow	0–2	(WCQ)

1970
18/4	Scotland	Belfast	0–1	
21/4	England	Wembley	1–3	
25/4	Wales	Swansea	0–1	
11/11	Spain	Seville	0–3	(ECQ)

1971
3/2	Cyprus	Nicosia	3–0	(ECQ)
21/4	Cyprus	Belfast	5–0	(ECQ)
15/5	England	Belfast	0–1	
18/5	Scotland	Glasgow	1–0	
22/5	Wales	Belfast	1–0	
22/9	USSR	Moscow	0–1	(ECQ)
13/10	USSR	Belfast	1–1	(ECQ)

1972
16/2	Spain	Hull	1–1	(ECQ)
20/5	Scotland	Glasgow	0–2	
23/5	England	Wembley	1–0	
27/5	Wales	Wrexham	0–0	
18/10	Bulgaria	Sofia	0–3	(WCQ)

1973
14/2	Cyprus	Nicosia	0–1	(WCQ)
28/3	Portugal	Coventry	1–1	(WCQ)
8/5	Cyprus	London	3–0	(WCQ)
12/5	England	Liverpool	1–2	
16/5	Scotland	Glasgow	2–1	
19/5	Wales	Liverpool	1–0	
26/9	Bulgaria	Hillsborough	0–0	(WCQ)
14/11	Portugal	Lisbon	1–1	(WCQ)

1974
11/5	Scotland	Glasgow	1–0	
15/5	England	Wembley	0–1	
18/5	Wales	Wrexham	0–1	
4/9	Norway	Oslo	1–2	(ECQ)
30/10	Sweden	Solna	2–0	(ECQ)

1975
16/3	Yugoslavia	Belfast	1–0	(ECQ)
17/5	England	Belfast	0–0	
20/5	Scotland	Glasgow	0–3	
23/5	Wales	Belfast	1–0	
3/9	Sweden	Belfast	1–2	(ECQ)
29/10	Norway	Belfast	3–0	(ECQ)
19/11	Yugoslavia	Belgrade	0–1	(ECQ)

1976
24/3	Israel	Tel Aviv	1–1	
8/5	Scotland	Glasgow	0–3	
11/5	England	Wembley	0–4	
14/5	Wales	Swansea	0–1	
13/10	Holland	Rotterdam	2–2	(WCQ)
10/11	Belgium	Liège	0–2	(WCQ)

1977
27/4	W Germany	Cologne	0–5	
28/5	England	Belfast	1–2	
1/6	Scotland	Glasgow	0–2	
3/6	Wales	Belfast	1–1	
11/6	Iceland	Reykjavik	0–1	(WCQ)
21/9	Iceland	Belfast	2–0	(WCQ)
12/10	Holland	Belfast	0–1	(WCQ)
16/11	Belgium	Belfast	3–0	(WCQ)

1978
13/5	Scotland	Glasgow	1–1	
16/5	England	Wembley	0–1	
19/5	Wales	Wrexham	0–1	
20/9	Rep of Ireland	Dublin	0–0	(ECQ)
25/10	Denmark	Belfast	2–1	(ECQ)
29/11	Bulgaria	Sofia	2–0	(ECQ)

1979
7/2	England	Wembley	0–4	(ECQ)
2/5	Bulgaria	Belfast	2–0	(ECQ)
19/5	England	Belfast	0–2	
22/5	Scotland	Glasgow	0–1	
25/5	Wales	Belfast	1–1	
6/6	Denmark	Copenhagen	0–4	(ECQ)
17/10	England	Belfast	1–5	(ECQ)
21/11	Rep of Ireland	Belfast	1–0	(ECQ)

1980
26/3	Israel	Tel Aviv	0–0	(WCQ)
16/5	Scotland	Belfast	1–0	
20/5	England	Wembley	1–1	
23/5	Wales	Cardiff	1–0	
11/6	Australia	Sydney	2–1	
15/6	Australia	Melbourne	1–1	
18/6	Australia	Adelaide	2–1	
15/10	Sweden	Belfast	3–0	(WCQ)
19/11	Portugal	Lisbon	0–1	(WCQ)

1981
25/3	Scotland	Glasgow	1–1	(WCQ)
29/4	Portugal	Belfast	1–0	(WCQ)
19/5	Scotland	Glasgow	0–2	
3/6	Sweden	Stockholm	0–1	(WCQ)
14/10	Scotland	Belfast	0–0	(WCQ)
18/11	Israel	Belfast	1–0	(WCQ)

1982
23/2	England	Wembley	0–4	
24/3	France	Paris	0–4	
28/4	Scotland	Belfast	1–1	
27/5	Wales	Wrexham	0–3	
17/6	Yugoslavia	Zaragoza	0–0	(WCF)
21/6	Honduras	Zaragoza	1–1	(WCF)
25/6	Spain	Valencia	1–0	(WCF)
1/7	Austria	Madrid	2–2	(WCF)
4/7	France	Madrid	1–4	(WCF)
13/10	Austria	Vienna	0–2	(ECQ)
17/11	W Germany	Belfast	1–0	(ECQ)
15/12	Albania	Tirana	0–0	(ECQ)

1983
30/3	Turkey	Belfast	2–1	(ECQ)
27/4	Albania	Belfast	1–0	(ECQ)
24/5	Scotland	Glasgow	0–0	
28/5	England	Belfast	0–0	
31/5	Wales	Belfast	0–1	
21/9	Austria	Belfast	3–1	(ECQ)
12/10	Turkey	Ankara	0–1	(ECQ)
16/11	W Germany	Hamburg	1–0	(ECQ)
13/12	Scotland	Belfast	2–0	

1984
4/4	England	Wembley	0–1	
22/5	Wales	Swansea	1–1	
27/5	Finland	Pori	0–1	(WCQ)
12/9	Romania	Belfast	3–2	(WCQ)
16/10	Israel	Belfast	3–0	
14/11	Finland	Belfast	2–1	(WCQ)

1985
27/2	England	Belfast	0–1	(WCQ)
27/3	Spain	Palma	0–0	
1/5	Turkey	Belfast	2–0	(WCQ)
11/9	Turkey	Izmir	0–0	(WCQ)
16/10	Romania	Bucharest	1–0	(WCQ)
13/11	England	Wembley	0–0	(WCQ)

1986
26/2	France	Paris	0–0	
26/3	Denmark	Belfast	1–1	
23/4	Morocco	Belfast	2–1	
3/6	Algeria	Guadalajara	1–1	(WCF)
7/6	Spain	Guadalajara	1–2	(WCF)
12/6	Brazil	Guadalajara	0–3	(WCF)
15/10	England	Wembley	0–3	(ECQ)
12/11	Turkey	Izmir	0–0	(ECQ)

1987
18/2	Israel	Tel Aviv	1–1	
1/4	England	Belfast	0–2	(ECQ)
29/4	Yugoslavia	Belfast	1–2	(ECQ)
14/10	Yugoslavia	Sarajevo	0–3	(ECQ)
11/11	Turkey	Belfast	1–0	(ECQ)

1988
17/2	Greece	Athens	2–3	
23/3	Poland	Belfast	1–1	
27/4	France	Belfast	0–0	
21/5	Malta	Belfast	3–0	(WCQ)
14/9	Rep of Ireland	Belfast	0–0	(WCQ)
19/10	Hungary	Budapest	0–1	(WCQ)
21/12	Spain	Seville	0–4	(WCQ)

1989
8/2	Spain	Belfast	0–2	(WCQ)
26/4	Malta	Valletta	2–0	(WCQ)
26/5	Chile	Belfast	0–1	
6/9	Hungary	Belfast	1–2	(WCQ)
11/10	Rep of Ireland	Dublin	0–3	(WCQ)

1990
27/3	Norway	Belfast	2–3	
18/5	Uruguay	Belfast	1–0	
12/9	Yugoslavia	Belfast	0–2	(ECQ)
17/10	Denmark	Belfast	1–1	(ECQ)
14/11	Austria	Vienna	0–0	(ECQ)

1991
5/2	Poland	Belfast	3–1	
27/3	Yugoslavia	Belgrade	1–4	(ECQ)
1/5	Faeroes	Belfast	1–1	(ECQ)
11/9	Faeroes	Landsrona	5–0	(ECQ)
16/10	Austria	Belfast	2–1	(ECQ)
13/11	Denmark	Odense	1–2	(ECQ)

1992
28/4	Lithuania	Belfast	2–2	(WCQ)
2/6	Germany	Bremen	1–1	
9/9	Albania	Belfast	3–0	(WCQ)
14/10	Spain	Belfast	0–0	(WCQ)
18/11	Denmark	Belfast	0–1	(WCQ)

1993
17/2	Albania	Tirana	2–1	(WCQ)
31/3	Rep of Ireland	Dublin	0–3	(WCQ)
28/4	Spain	Seville	1–3	(WCQ)
25/5	Lithuania	Vilnius	1–0	(WCQ)
2/6	Latvia	Riga	2–1	(WCQ)
8/9	Latvia	Belfast	2–0	(WCQ)
13/10	Denmark	Copenhagen	0–1	(WCQ)
17/11	Rep of Ireland	Belfast	1–1	(WCQ)

1994
20/4	Liechtenstein	Belfast	4–1	(ECQ)
3/6	Colombia	Boston	0–2	
12/6	Mexico	Miami	0–3	
7/9	Portugal	Belfast	1–2	(ECQ)
12/10	Austria	Vienna	2–1	(ECQ)
16/11	Rep of Ireland	Belfast	0–4	(ECQ)

1995
29/3	Rep of Ireland	Dublin	1–1	(ECQ)
26/4	Latvia	Riga	1–0	(ECQ)
22/5	Canada	Edmonton	0–2	
25/5	Chile	Edmonton	1–2	
7/6	Latvia	Belfast	1–2	(ECQ)
26/4	Latvia	Riga	1–0	(ECQ)
3/9	Portugal	Lisbon	1–1	(ECQ)
11/10	Liechtenstein	Eschen	4–0	(ECQ)
15/11	Austria	Belfast	5–3	(ECQ)

1996
27/3	Norway	Belfast	0–2	
24/4	Sweden	Belfast	1–2	
29/5	Germany	Belfast	1–1	
31/8	Ukraine	Belfast	0–1	(WCQ)
5/10	Armenia	Belfast	1–1	(WCQ)
9/11	Germany	Nüremburg	1–1	(WCQ)
14/12	Albania	Belfast	2–0	(WCQ)

1997
29/3	Portugal	Belfast	0–0	(WCQ)
2/4	Ukraine	Kiev	1–2	(WCQ)
30/4	Armenia	Yerevan	0–0	(WCQ)
21/5	Thailand	Bangkok	0–0	

REPUBLIC OF IRELAND

The Irish Republic developed as an independent international soccer entity after partition and the creation of the Irish Free State in the early 1920s. They competed in the World Cup qualifiers of 1934 and 1938, and the clubs founded before partition lived on and gained new strength.

However, many old links survived. Several players appeared for both Irelands, and an interesting fact of which few are aware is that the first foreign nation to beat England in England was the Irish Republic – who won 2–0 at Goodison Park, Liverpool in September 1949. England, that day, included the likes of Wright, Franklin, Finney and Mannion.

The Republic Comes Into Its Own

Almost all the best players raised in the Republic were quickly sold to English and Scottish clubs. Ironically, it was not until the advent of an Englishman, Jack Charlton, as a national manager prepared to take full advantage of the parental qualification loophole, that the Irish Republic eventually gained international prestige. Equally importantly, Charlton brought organization and discipline to the Irish play, and by 1988 had proved his worth by leading the Republic to their first appearance in the European Championship Finals. Better still, they beat England 1–0 in their opening game.

Two years later the Irish were experiencing their first World Cup Finals. Again they were to face England, this time forcing a 1–1 draw in Cagliari. A second round victory on penalties over Romania took the Irish into the quarter-finals where hosts Italy proved too strong.

Charlton's men were back at the finals in 1994 and beat Italy 1–0 in their opening game at Giants Stadium in New Jersey, before falling to Holland in the second round. Holland repeated their 2–0 victory in the qualifying play-off for the 1996 European Championship. This defeat at Anfield proved the end of the road for Charlton. His former defensive mainstay, Mick McCarthy, succeeded him as manager.

FAI LEAGUE CHAMPIONS

Year	Champions	Runners-up
1922	St James's Gate	Bohemians
1923	Shamrock R	Shelbourne
1924	Bohemians	Shelbourne
1925	Shamrock R	Bohemians
1926	Shelbourne	Shamrock R
1927	Shamrock R	Shelbourne
1928	Bohemians	Shelbourne
1929	Shelbourne	Bohemians
1930	Bohemians	Shelbourne
1931	Shelbourne	Dundalk
1932	Shamrock R	Cork
1933	Dundalk	Shamrock R
1934	Bohemians	Cork
1935	Dolphin	St James's Gate
1936	Bohemians	Dolphin
1937	Sligo R	Dundalk
1938	Shamrock R	Waterford
1939	Shamrock R	Sligo R
1940	St James's Gate	Shamrock R
1941	Cork Utd	Waterford
1942	Cork Utd	Shamrock R
1943	Cork Utd	Dundalk
1944	Shelbourne	Limerick
1945	Cork Utd	Limerick
1946	Cork Utd	Drumcondra
1947	Shelbourne	Drumcondra
1948	Drumcondra	Dundalk
1949	Drumcondra	Shelbourne
1950	Cork Ath	Drumcondra
1951	Cork Ath	Shelbourne
1952	St Patrick's Ath	Sligo R
1953	Shelbourne	Evergreen Utd
1954	Shamrock R	Drumcondra
1955	St Patrick's Ath	Waterford
1956	St Patrick's Ath	Shamrock R
1957	Shamrock R	Drumcondra
1958	Drumcondra	Shamrock R
1959	Shamrock R	Evergreen Utd
1960	Limerick	Cork Celtic
1961	Drumcondra	St Patrick's Ath
1962	Shelbourne	Cork Celtic
1963	Dundalk	Waterford
1964	Shamrock R	Dundalk
1965	Drumcondra	Shamrock R
1966	Waterford	Shamrock R
1967	Dundalk	Bohemians
1968	Waterford	Dundalk
1969	Waterford	Shamrock R
1970	Waterford	Shamrock R
1971	Cork Hibs	Shamrock R
1972	Waterford	Cork Hibs
1973	Waterford	Finn Harps
1974	Cork Celtic	Bohemians
1975	Bohemians	Athlone T
1976	Dundalk	Finn Harps
1977	Sligo R	Bohemians
1978	Bohemians	Finn Harps
1979	Dundalk	Bohemians
1980	Limerick	Dundalk
1981	Athlone T	Dundalk
1982	Dundalk	Shamrock R
1983	Athlone T	Drogheda Utd
1984	Shamrock R	Bohemians
1985	Shamrock R	Bohemians
1986	Shamrock R	Galway Utd
1987	Shamrock R	Dundalk
1988	Dundalk	St Patrick's Ath
1989	Derry City	Dundalk
1990	St Patrick's Ath	Derry City
1991	Dundalk	Cork City
1992	Shelbourne	Derry City
1993	Cork City	Bohemians
1994	Shamrock R	Cork City
1995	Dundalk	Shelbourne
1996	St Patrick's Ath	Bohemians
1997	Derry City	Bohemians

FAI SENIOR CHALLENGE CUP

Year	Winners	Runners-up	Score
1922	St James's Gate	Shamrock R	1–1, 1–0
1923	Alton Utd	Shelbourne	1–0
1924	Athlone T	Fordsons	1–0
1925	Shamrock R	Shelbourne	2–1
1926	Fordsons	Shamrock R	3–2
1927	Drumcondra	Brideville	1–1, 1–0
1928	Bohemians	Drumcondra	1–0
1929	Shamrock R	Bohemians	0–0, 3–0
1930	Shamrock R	Brideville	1–0
1931	Shamrock R	Dundalk	1–1, 1–0
1932	Shamrock R	Dolphin	1–0
1933	Shamrock R	Dolphin	3–3, 3–0
1934	Cork	St James's Gate	2–1
1935	Bohemians	Dundalk	4–3
1936	Shamrock R	Cork	2–1
1937	Waterford	St James's Gate	2–1
1938	St James's Gate	Dundalk	2–1
1939	Shelbourne	Sligo R	1–1, 1–0
1940	Shamrock R	Sligo R	3–0

Year			Score
1941	Cork Utd	Waterford	2–2, 3–1
1942	Dundalk	Cork Utd	3–1
1943	Drumcondra	Cork Utd	2–1
1944	Shamrock R	Shelbourne	3–2
1945	Shamrock R	Bohemians	1–0
1946	Drumcondra	Shamrock R	2–1
1947	Cork Utd	Bohemians	2–2, 2–0
1948	Shamrock R	Drumcondra	2–1
1949	Dundalk	Shelbourne	3–0
1950	Transport	Cork Ath	2–2, 2–2, 3–1
1951	Cork Ath	Shelbourne	1–0
1952	Dundalk	Cork Ath	1–1, 3–0
1953	Cork Ath	Evergreen Utd	2–2, 2–1
1954	Drumcondra	St Patrick's Ath	1–0
1955	Shamrock R	Drumcondra	1–0
1956	Shamrock R	Cork Ath	3–2
1957	Drumcondra	Shamrock R	2–0
1958	Dundalk	Shamrock R	1–0
1959	St Patrick's Ath	Waterford	2–2, 2–1
1960	Shelbourne	Cork Hibs	2–0
1961	St Patrick's Ath	Drumcondra	2–1
1962	Shamrock R	Shelbourne	4–1
1963	Shelbourne	Cork Hibs	2–0
1964	Shamrock R	Cork Celtic	1–1, 2–1
1965	Shamrock R	Limerick	1–1, 1–0
1966	Shamrock R	Limerick	2–0
1967	Shamrock R	St Patrick's Ath	3–2
1968	Shamrock R	Waterford	3–0
1969	Shamrock R	Cork Celtic	1–1, 4–1
1970	Bohemians	Sligo R	0–0, 0–0, 2–1
1971	Limerick	Drogheda	0–0, 3–0
1972	Cork Hibs	Waterford	3–0
1973	Cork Hibs	Shelbourne	0–0, 1–0
1974	Finn Harps	St Patrick's Ath	3–1
1975	Home Farm	Shelbourne	1–0
1976	Bohemians	Drogheda Utd	1–0
1977	Dundalk	Limerick	2–0
1978	Shamrock R	Sligo R	1–0
1979	Dundalk	Waterford	2–0
1980	Waterford	St Patrick's Ath	1–0
1981	Dundalk	Sligo R	2–0
1982	Limerick Utd	Bohemians	1–0
1983	Sligo R	Bohemians	2–1
1984	University College	Shamrock R	2–1
1985	Shamrock R	Galway Utd	1–0
1986	Shamrock R	Waterford Utd	2–0
1987	Shamrock R	Dundalk	3–0
1988	Dundalk	Derry City	1–0
1989	Derry City	Cork City	0–0, 1–0
1990	Bray W	St Francis	3–0
1991	Galway Utd	Shamrock R	1–0
1992	Bohemians	Cork City	1–0
1993	Shelbourne	Dundalk	1–0
1994	Sligo R	Derry City	1–0
1995	Derry City	Shelbourne	1–0
1996	Shelbourne	St Patrick's Ath	1–1, 2–1
1997	Shelbourne	Derry City	2–0

INTERNATIONAL RESULTS 1920–1959

Date	Opponents	Venue	F–A
21/3/26	Italy	Turin	0–3
23/4/27	Italy	Dublin	1–2
12/2/28	Belgium	Liège	4–2
30/4/29	Belgium	Dublin	4–0
11/5/30	Belgium	Brussels	3–1
26/4/31	Spain	Barcelona	1–1
13/12/31	Spain	Dublin	0–5
8/5/32	Holland	Amsterdam	2–0
25/2/34	Belgium	Dublin	4–4 (WCQ)
8/4/34	Holland	Amsterdam	2–5 (WCQ)
15/12/34	Hungary	Dublin	2–4
5/5/35	Switzerland	Basle	0–1
8/5/35	Germany	Dortmund	1–3
8/12/35	Holland	Dublin	3–5
17/3/36	Switzerland	Dublin	1–0
3/5/36	Hungary	Budapest	3–3
9/5/36	Luxembourg	Luxembourg	5–1
17/10/36	Germany	Dublin	5–2
6/12/36	Hungary	Dublin	2–3
17/5/37	Switzerland	Berne	1–0
23/5/37	France	Paris	2–0
10/10/37	Norway	Oslo	2–3 (WCQ)
7/11/37	Norway	Dublin	3–3 (WCQ)
18/5/38	Czechoslovakia	Prague	2–2
22/5/38	Poland	Warsaw	0–6
18/9/38	Switzerland	Dublin	4–0
13/11/38	Poland	Dublin	3–2
19/3/39	Hungary	Cork	2–2
18/5/39	Hungary	Budapest	2–2
23/5/39	Germany	Bremen	1–1
16/6/46	Portugal	Lisbon	1–3
23/6/46	Spain	Madrid	1–0
30/9/46	England	Dublin	0–1
2/3/47	Spain	Dublin	3–2
4/5/47	Portugal	Dublin	0–2
23/5/48	Portugal	Lisbon	0–2
30/5/48	Spain	Barcelona	1–2
5/12/48	Switzerland	Dublin	0–1
24/4/49	Belgium	Dublin	0–2

Date	Opponent	Venue	Result
22/5/49	Portugal	Dublin	1–0
2/6/49	Sweden	Stockholm	1–3 (WCQ)
12/6/49	Spain	Dublin	1–4
8/9/49	Finland	Dublin	3–0 (WCQ)
21/9/49	England	Everton	2–0
9/10/49	Finland	Helsinki	1–1 (WCQ)
13/11/49	Sweden	Dublin	1–3 (WCQ)
10/5/50	Belgium	Brussels	1–5
26/11/50	Norway	Dublin	2–2
13/5/51	Argentina	Dublin	0–1
30/5/51	Norway	Oslo	3–2
17/10/51	W Germany	Dublin	3–2
4/5/52	W Germany	Cologne	0–3
7/5/52	Austria	Vienna	0–6
1/6/52	Spain	Madrid	0–6
25/3/53	Austria	Dublin	4–0
4/10/53	France	Dublin	3–5 (WCQ)
28/10/53	Luxembourg	Dublin	4–0 (WCQ)
25/11/53	France	Paris	0–1 (WCQ)
7/3/54	Luxembourg	Luxembourg	1–0 (WCQ)
8/11/54	Norway	Dublin	2–1
1/5/55	Holland	Dublin	1–0
25/5/55	Norway	Oslo	3–1
28/5/55	W Germany	Hamburg	1–2
19/9/55	Yugoslavia	Dublin	1–4
27/11/55	Spain	Dublin	2–2
10/5/56	Holland	Rotterdam	4–1
3/10/56	Denmark	Dublin	2–1 (WCQ)
25/11/56	Denmark	Dublin	3–0
8/5/57	England	Wembley	1–5 (WCQ)
19/5/57	England	Dublin	1–1 (WCQ)
2/10/57	Denmark	Copenhagen	2–0 (WCQ)
14/3/58	Austria	Vienna	1–3
11/5/58	Poland	Katowice	2–2
5/10/58	Poland	Dublin	2–2
5/4/59	Czechoslovakia	Dublin	2–0 (ECQ)
10/5/59	Czechoslovakia	Bratislava	0–4 (ECQ)
1/11/59	Sweden	Dublin	3–2

1960–1969

Date	Opponent	Venue	Result
30/3/60	Chile	Dublin	2–0
11/5/60	W Germany	Düsseldorf	1–0
18/5/60	Sweden	Malmö	1–4
28/9/60	Wales	Dublin	2–3
6/11/60	Norway	Dublin	3–1
3/5/61	Scotland	Glasgow	1–4 (WCQ)
7/5/61	Scotland	Dublin	0–3 (WCQ)
8/10/61	Czechoslovakia	Dublin	1–3 (WCQ)
29/10/61	Czechoslovakia	Prague	1–7 (WCQ)
8/4/62	Austria	Dublin	2–3
12/8/62	Iceland	Dublin	4–2 (ECQ)
2/9/62	Iceland	Reykjavik	1–1 (ECQ)
9/6/63	Scotland	Dublin	1–0
25/9/63	Austria	Vienna	0–0 (ECQ)
13/10/63	Austria	Dublin	3–2 (ECQ)
11/3/64	Spain	Seville	1–5 (ECQ)
8/4/64	Spain	Dublin	0–2 (ECQ)
10/5/64	Poland	Cracow	1–3
13/5/64	Norway	Oslo	4–1
24/5/64	England	Dublin	1–3
25/10/64	Poland	Dublin	3–2
24/3/65	Belgium	Dublin	0–2
5/5/65	Spain	Dublin	1–0 (WCQ)
27/10/65	Spain	Seville	1–4 (WCQ)
10/11/65	Spain	Paris	0–1 (WCQ)
4/5/66	W Germany	Dublin	0–4
22/5/66	Austria	Vienna	0–1
25/5/66	Belgium	Liège	3–2
23/10/66	Spain	Dublin	0–0 (ECQ)
16/11/66	Turkey	Dublin	2–1 (ECQ)
7/12/66	Spain	Valencia	0–2 (ECQ)
22/2/67	Turkey	Ankara	1–2 (ECQ)
21/5/67	Czechoslovakia	Dublin	0–2 (ECQ)
22/11/67	Czechoslovakia	Prague	2–1 (ECQ)
15/5/68	Poland	Dublin	2–2
30/10/68	Poland	Katowice	0–1
10/11/68	Austria	Dublin	2–2
4/12/68	Denmark	Dublin	1–1 (WCQ)
	(abandoned after 51 minutes)		
4/5/69	Czechoslovakia	Dublin	1–2 (WCQ)

Date	Opponent	Venue	Result
27/5/69	Denmark	Copenhagen	0–2 (WCQ)
8/6/69	Hungary	Dublin	1–2 (WCQ)
21/9/69	Scotland	Dublin	1–1
7/10/69	Czechoslovakia	Prague	0–3 (WCQ)
15/10/69	Denmark	Dublin	1–1 (WCQ)
5/11/69	Hungary	Budapest	0–4 (WCQ)

1970–1984

Date	Opponent	Venue	Result
6/5/70	Poland	Dublin	1–2
9/5/70	W Germany	Berlin	1–2
23/9/70	Poland	Dublin	0–2
14/10/70	Sweden	Dublin	1–1 (ECQ)
28/10/70	Sweden	Malmö	0–1 (ECQ)
8/12/71	Italy	Rome	0–3 (ECQ)
10/5/71	Italy	Dublin	1–2 (ECQ)
30/5/71	Austria	Dublin	1–4 (ECQ)
10/10/71	Austria	Linz	0–6 (ECQ)
18/6/72	Iran	Recife	2–1
19/6/72	Ecuador	Natal	3–2
21/6/72	Chile	Recife	1–2
25/6/72	Portugal	Recife	1–2
18/10/72	USSR	Dublin	1–2 (WCQ)
15/11/72	France	Dublin	2–1 (WCQ)
13/5/73	USSR	Moscow	0–1 (WCQ)
16/5/73	Poland	Wroclaw	0–2
19/5/73	France	Paris	1–1 (WCQ)
6/6/73	Norway	Oslo	1–1
21/10/73	Poland	Dublin	1–0
8/5/74	Uruguay	Montevideo	0–2
12/5/74	Chile	Santiago	2–1
30/10/74	USSR	Dublin	3–0 (ECQ)
20/11/74	Turkey	Izmir	1–1 (ECQ)
1/3/75	W Germany	Dublin	1–0 +
	(+ W Germany 'B' side)		
11/5/75	Switzerland	Dublin	2–1 (ECQ)
18/5/75	USSR	Kiev	1–2 (ECQ)
29/10/75	Turkey	Dublin	4–0 (ECQ)
24/3/76	Norway	Dublin	3–0
26/5/76	Poland	Prosjan	2–0
8/9/76	England	Wembley	1–1
13/10/76	Turkey	Ankara	3–3
17/11/76	France	Paris	0–2 (WCQ)
9/2/77	Spain	Dublin	0–1
30/3/77	France	Dublin	1–0 (WCQ)
24/4/77	Poland	Dublin	0–0
1/6/77	Bulgaria	Sofia	1–2 (WCQ)
12/10/77	Bulgaria	Dublin	0–0 (WCQ)
5/4/78	Turkey	Dublin	4–2
12/4/78	Poland	Lodz	0–3
21/5/78	Norway	Oslo	0–0
24/5/78	Denmark	Copenhagen	3–3 (ECQ)
20/9/78	N Ireland	Dublin	0–0 (ECQ)
25/10/78	England	Dublin	1–1 (ECQ)
2/5/79	Denmark	Dublin	2–0 (ECQ)
19/5/79	Bulgaria	Sofia	0–1 (ECQ)
22/5/79	W Germany	Dublin	1–3
11/9/79	Wales	Swansea	1–2
26/9/79	Czechoslovakia	Prague	1–4
17/10/79	Bulgaria	Dublin	3–0 (ECQ)
29/10/79	USA	Dublin	3–2
21/11/79	N Ireland	Belfast	0–1 (ECQ)
6/2/80	England	Wembley	0–2 (ECQ)
26/3/80	Cyprus	Nicosia	3–2 (WCQ)
30/4/80	Switzerland	Dublin	2–0
16/5/80	Argentina	Dublin	0–1
10/9/80	Holland	Dublin	2–1 (WCQ)
15/10/80	Belgium	Dublin	1–1 (WCQ)
28/10/80	France	Paris	0–2 (WCQ)
19/11/80	Cyprus	Dublin	6–0 (WCQ)
24/2/81	Wales	Dublin	1–3
25/3/81	Belgium	Brussels	0–1 (WCQ)
29/4/81	Czechoslovakia	Dublin	3–1
21/5/81	W Germany	Bremen	0–3
	(W Germany 'B' side)		
23/5/81	Poland	Bydgoszcz	0–3
9/9/81	Holland	Rotterdam	2–2 (WCQ)
14/10/81	France	Dublin	3–2 (WCQ)
22/5/82	Chile	Santiago	0–1
27/5/82	Brazil	Vberlandia	0–7
30/5/82	Trinidad & Tobago	Port Of Spain	1–2

Date	Opponent	Venue	Result
22/9/82	Holland	Rotterdam	1–2 (ECQ)
17/11/82	Spain	Dublin	3–3 (ECQ)
30/3/83	Malta	Valletta	1–0 (ECQ)
27/4/83	Spain	Zaragoza	0–2 (ECQ)
12/10/83	Holland	Dublin	2–3 (ECQ)
16/11/83	Malta	Dublin	8–0 (ECQ)
4/4/84	Israel	Tel Aviv	0–3
23/5/84	Poland	Dublin	0–0
3/6/84	China	Sapporo	1–0
8/8/84	Mexico	Dublin	0–0
12/9/84	USSR	Dublin	1–0 (WCQ)
17/10/84	Norway	Oslo	0–1 (WCQ)
14/11/84	Denmark	Copenhagen	0–3

1985

Date	Opponent	Venue	Result
5/2	Italy	Dublin	1–2
26/3	England	Wembley	1–2
1/5	Norway	Dublin	0–0 (WCQ)
21/5	Israel	Tel Aviv	0–0
26/5	Spain	Cork	0–0 (WCQ)
2/6	Switzerland	Dublin	3–0 (WCQ)
11/9	Switzerland	Berne	0–0 (WCQ)
16/10	USSR	Moscow	0–2 (WCQ)
13/11	Denmark	Dublin	1–4 (WCQ)

1986

Date	Opponent	Venue	Result
26/3	Wales	Dublin	0–1
23/4	Uruguay	Dublin	1–1
25/5	Iceland	Reykjavik	2–1
27/5	Czechoslovakia	Reykjavik	1–0
10/9	Belgium	Brussels	2–2 (ECQ)
15/10	Scotland	Dublin	0–0 (ECQ)
12/11	Poland	Warsaw	0–1

1987

Date	Opponent	Venue	Result
18/2	Scotland	Glasgow	1–0 (ECQ)
1/4	Bulgaria	Sofia	1–2 (ECQ)
29/4	Belgium	Dublin	0–0 (ECQ)
23/5	Brazil	Dublin	1–0
28/5	Luxembourg	Luxembourg	2–0 (ECQ)
9/9	Luxembourg	Dublin	2–1 (ECQ)
14/10	Bulgaria	Dublin	2–0 (ECQ)
10/11	Israel	Dublin	5–0

1988

Date	Opponent	Venue	Result
23/3	Romania	Dublin	2–0
27/4	Yugoslavia	Dublin	2–0
22/5	Poland	Dublin	3–1
1/6	Norway	Oslo	0–0
12/6	England	Stuttgart	1–0 (ECF)
15/6	USSR	Hanover	1–1 (ECF)
18/6	Holland	Gelsenkirchen	0–1 (ECF)
14/9	N Ireland	Belfast	0–0 (WCQ)
19/10	Tunisia	Dublin	4–0
16/11	Spain	Seville	0–2 (WCQ)

1989

Date	Opponent	Venue	Result
7/2	France	Dublin	0–0
8/3	Hungary	Budapest	0–0 (WCQ)
26/4	Spain	Dublin	1–0 (WCQ)
28/5	Malta	Dublin	2–0 (WCQ)
4/6	Hungary	Dublin	2–0 (WCQ)
6/9	W Germany	Dublin	1–1
11/10	N Ireland	Dublin	3–0 (WCQ)
15/11	Malta	Valetta	2–0 (WCQ)

1990

Date	Opponent	Venue	Result
12/1	Morocco	Dublin	1–0
28/3	Wales	Dublin	1–0
25/4	USSR	Dublin	1–0
16/5	Finland	Dublin	1–1
27/5	Turkey	Izmir	0–0
3/6	Malta	Valetta	3–0
11/6	England	Cagliari	1–1 (WCF)
17/6	Egypt	Palermo	0–0 (WCF)
21/6	Holland	Palermo	1–1 (WCF)
25/6	Romania	Genoa	0–0 (WCF)
	(Rep of Ireland won on penalties: 5–4)		
30/6	Italy	Rome	0–1 (WCF)

Date	Opponent	Venue	Result
17/10	Turkey	Dublin	5–0 (ECQ)
14/11	England	Dublin	1–1 (ECQ)

1991

Date	Opponent	Venue	Result
6/2	Wales	Wrexham	3–0
27/3	England	Wembley	1–1 (ECQ)
1/5	Poland	Dublin	0–0 (ECQ)
22/5	Chile	Dublin	1–1
2/6	USA	Foxboro	1–1
11/9	Hungary	Gyor	2–1
16/10	Poland	Poznan	3–3 (ECQ)
13/11	Turkey	Istanbul	3–1 (ECQ)

1992

Date	Opponent	Venue	Result
19/2	Wales	Dublin	0–1
25/3	Switzerland	Dublin	2–1
29/4	USA	Dublin	4–1
26/5	Albania	Dublin	2–0 (WCQ)
30/5	USA	Washington	1–3
4/6	Italy	Foxboro	0–2
7/6	Portugal	Foxboro	2–0
9/9	Latvia	Dublin	4–0 (WCQ)
14/10	Denmark	Copenhagen	0–0 (WCQ)
18/11	Spain	Seville	0–0 (WCQ)

1993

Date	Opponent	Venue	Result
17/2	Wales	Dublin	2–1
31/3	N Ireland	Dublin	3–0 (WCQ)
28/4	Denmark	Dublin	1–1 (WCQ)
26/5	Albania	Tirana	2–1 (WCQ)
2/6	Latvia	Riga	2–1 (WCQ)
16/6	Lithuania	Vilnius	1–0 (WCQ)
8/9	Lithuania	Dublin	2–0 (WCQ)
13/10	Spain	Dublin	1–3 (WCQ)
17/11	N Ireland	Belfast	1–1 (WCQ)

1994

Date	Opponent	Venue	Result
23/3	Russia	Dublin	0–0
20/4	Holland	Tilburg	1–0
24/5	Bolivia	Dublin	1–0
29/5	Germany	Hannover	2–0
4/6	Czech Republic	Dublin	1–3
18/6	Italy	New York	1–0 (WCF)
24/6	Mexico	Orlando	1–2 (WCF)
28/6	Norway	New York	0–0 (WCF)
4/7	Holland	Orlando	0–2 (WCF)
7/9	Latvia	Riga	3–0 (ECQ)
12/10	Liechtenstein	Dublin	4–0 (ECQ)
16/11	N Ireland	Belfast	4–0 (ECQ)

1995

Date	Opponent	Venue	Result
15/2	England	Dublin	1–0
	(abandoned after 21 minutes)		
29/3	N Ireland	Dublin	1–1 (ECQ)
26/4	Portugal	Dublin	1–0 (ECQ)
3/6	Liechtenstein	Vaduz	0–0 (ECQ)
11/6	Austria	Dublin	1–3 (ECQ)
6/9	Austria	Vienna	1–3 (ECQ)
11/10	Latvia	Dublin	2–1 (ECQ)
15/11	Portugal	Lisbon	0–3 (ECQ)
13/12	Holland	Liverpool	0–2 (ECQ)

1996

Date	Opponent	Venue	Result
27/3	Russia	Dublin	0–2
24/4	Czech Republic	Prague	0–2
29/5	Portugal	Dublin	0–1
31/8	Liechtenstein	Vaduz	5–0 (WCQ)
9/10	FYR Macedonia	Dublin	3–0 (WCQ)
10/11	Iceland	Dublin	0–0 (WCQ)

1997

Date	Opponent	Venue	Result
11/2	Wales	Cardiff	0–0
2/4	FYR Macedonia	Skopje	2–3 (WCQ)
30/4	Romania	Bucharest	0–1 (WCQ)
21/5	Liechtenstein	Dublin	5–0 (WCQ)

SOCCER CHRONOLOGY

1848: First code of rules compiled at Cambridge University

1855: Sheffield FC, world's oldest club, formed

1862: Notts County, world's oldest league club, formed

1863: FA formed, Oct 26

1871: FA Cup inaugurated

1872: Size of ball fixed

1872: Scotland draw 0–0 with England in first official international at West of Scotland cricket ground

1873: Scottish FA and Cup launched

1874: Shinguards introduced by Sam Weller Widdowson of Nottingham Forest and England

1875: Crossbar replaces tape

1876: FA of Wales formed

1878: Referee's whistle used for first time at Nottingham Forest's ground

1878: Almost 20,000 people watch first floodlit match, between two Sheffield teams, with lighting provided by four lamps on 30ft wooden towers

1882: International Board formed

1883: Two-handed throw-in introduced

1885: Professionalism legalized

1888: Football League, brainchild of Aston Villa director, William McGregor, founded, and first matches played on Sept 8

1888: Scottish Cup winners Renton beat English FA Cup winners West Bromwich for the "Championship of the World"

1889: Unbeaten Preston, "The Invincibles", become first club to win League and Cup double

1890: Scottish and Irish Leagues formed

1891: Goal nets and penalties introduced

1891: Referees and linesman replace umpires and referees

1892: Football League Second Division formed

1893: Genoa, oldest Italian League club, formed

1895: FA Cup, held by Aston Villa, stolen from Birmingham shop window and never seen again

1897: Players' Union formed

1897: Juventus formed

1898: Promotion and relegation introduced

1899: Barcelona formed

1901: Maximum wage rule in force

1901: Southern League Tottenham Hotspur become first professional club to take FA Cup south

1901: First 100,000 attendance (110,802) at Cup Final, venue Crystal Palace

1901: Argentina beat Uruguay 3–2 in first international between South American countries

1902: Ibrox Park disaster: 25 killed when part of new wooden stand collapses at Scotland vs. England match

1902: Real Madrid formed

1902: Austria beat Hungary 5–0 in Vienna, the first international between teams outside the home countries

1904: FIFA formed with seven members

1905: England join FIFA

1905: Goalkeepers ordered to stay on goal-line at penalties

1905: First £1,000 transfer: Alf Common, from Sunderland to Middlesbrough

1908: Transfer limit of £350 introduced in January, withdrawn in April

1908: UK beat Denmark to win first Olympic title at Shepherds Bush

1908: England travel to Vienna to beat Austria 6–1 in their first international on foreign soil

1910: Argentina win the first South American Championship

1919: League extended to 44 clubs

1920: Third Division South formed

1921: Third Division North formed

1923: Football pools introduced

1923: First Wembley FA Cup final: Bolton 2 West Ham 0

1924: First Wembley international: England 1 Scotland 1

1924: Goal can be scored direct from corner kick

1925: Offside rule change: a player needs two, not three, players between him and goal to stay onside

1926: Huddersfield complete first hat-trick of championships

1927: Hughie Ferguson's goal against Arsenal makes Cardiff first club to take FA Cup out of England

1928: The four home countries withdraw from FIFA

1928: Bill "Dixie" Dean scores 60 First Division goals, still a record

1929: Goalkeepers ordered to stay on goal-line until penalty is kicked

1930: Uruguay win first World Cup

1933: Numbered shirts worn in the FA cup final for first time, winners Everton wearing 1–11, Manchester City 12–22

1934: Sudden death of Arsenal manager Herbert Chapman on Jan 6

1936: Joe Payne's 10-goal record (Luton 12 Bristol Rovers 0)

1938: First live TV transmission of Cup Final (Preston 1 Huddersfield 0)

1939: Compulsory numbering of players in Football League

1939: All normal competitions suspended because of war

1946: British Associations rejoin FIFA

1946: 33 killed and 500 injured as wall and crowd barriers collapse at Bolton vs. Stoke FA Cup tie

1947: First £20,000 transfer: Tommy Lawton, from Chelsea to Notts County

1949: England's first home defeat by a non-Home nation (0–2 vs. Republic of Ireland at Goodison Park, Liverpool)

1949: Entire Torino team wiped out when aircraft taking them home from Lisbon crashes near Turin

1950: League extended from 88 to 92 clubs

1950: England humbled 1–0 by US in

GOAL GLUT

Arbroath beat Bon-Accord 36–0 on September 5, 1885 in the first round of the Scottish FA Cup, which is still a record score for a British first-class match. But it was little wonder the visitors went down by a cricket score, for the Aberdonians from 30 miles up the coast were actually cricketers, playing in their working clothes and not possessing a pair of boots between them. Their goalkeeper, who had never played football before, was injured and replaced at half-time by a half-back. The Arbroath goalkeeper was not called upon to touch the ball, and winger John Petrie scored 13 goals – a record for an individual. It was not a good day for Aberdeen: Dundee Harp beat Aberdeen Rovers 35–0.

World Cup group match, and world record crowd (203,500) see Uruguay beat Brazil 2–1 in the Final in Rio

1950: Scotland first beaten at home by foreign team (Austria, 1–0)

1951: White ball comes into use

1951: First official match under floodlights played at Highbury: between Arsenal and Hapoel Tel Aviv

1952: Newcastle become first to win successive FA Cup finals at Wembley

1953: Hungary beat England 6–3 at Wembley

1954: Hungary beat England 7–1 in Budapest

1955: First floodlit FA Cup tie (replay): Kidderminster vs. Brierley Hill Alliance

1956: First floodlit League match: Portsmouth vs. Newcastle

1956: Real Madrid, from an entry of 16 teams, win first European Cup

1956: South Korea defeat Israel to win first Asian Cup

1957: First African Nations Cup final: Egypt 4 Ethiopia 1

1958: Electrified pitch used by Everton to beat frost

1958: Munich air disaster kills 19, including eight Manchester United players

1958: English League restructured into four divisions

1958: Barcelona beat a London Select team 8–2 over two games to win first Inter City Fairs Cup

1959: Billy Wright of Wolves, first man to reach 100 caps for England, retires on 105

1960: FA recognizes Sunday football

1960: Football League Cup introduced

1960: European champions Real Madrid win first World Club Championship, beating South American champions Penarol over two legs

1960: Soviet Union win the first European Championship

1960: Penarol of Uruguay win first Copa Libertadores

1961 Tottenham complete first League and Cup double this century

1961: Maximum wage (£20) abolished

1961: First British £100-a-week wage paid to Johnny Haynes by Fulham

1961: Spurs pay £99,999 for striker Jimmy Greaves from Torino

1961: First £100,000 British transfer: Denis Law, from Manchester City to Torino

1961: Fiorentina beat Rangers 4–2 over

two games to win first European Cup-winners' Cup

1961: Hapoel Tel Aviv defeat Selangor of Malaysia 2–1 to win first Asian Champions Cup

1962: Manchester United pay record £115,000 to bring Law back from Italy

1963: Tottenham beat Atletico Madrid 5–1 in Cup-winners' Cup Final to become first British club to win European trophy

1963 FA centenary

1963: First Pools Panel

1964: First televised Match of the Day (BBC 2, Liverpool 3 Arsenal 2, August 22)

1964: 318 die and 500 injured in crowd riot over disallowed goal during Peru vs. Argentina Olympic tie in Lima

1964: Oryx Douala of Cameroon defeat Stade Malien of Mali 2–1 to win first African Champions Club Cup

1965: Ten Football League players jailed and banned for life for match-fixing

1965: Stanley Matthews knighted

1965: Substitutes allowed for injured players in League matches

1966: England win World Cup, beating West Germany 4 2 after extra time at Wembley

1967: Alf Ramsey, England manager, knighted

1967: Celtic beat Internazionale 2–1 to become first British winners of European Cup and complete unprecedented grand slam: European Cup, Scottish League, League Cup, Scottish Cup and Glasgow Cup

1967: First substitutes in Cup final (Chelsea vs. Tottenham), but neither is used

1968: 74 die at Nunez, Buenos Aires, when panic breaks out during River Plate vs. Boca Juniors match

1968: Alan Mullery becomes first England player sent off, vs. Yugoslavia in European Championship

1968: Manchester United become first English winners of European Cup beating Benfica 4–1 after extra time

1970: Brazil beat Italy 4–1 to capture World Cup for third time and win Jules Rimet trophy outright

1971: 66 fans trampled to death and 100 injured in second Ibrox disaster, as they tumbled down stairway just before end of Rangers vs. Celtic New Year's Day game

1972: Fairs Cup becomes UEFA Cup and is won by Tottenham, who defeat Wolves 3–2 over two games

1974: League football played on Sunday for first time

1974: Last FA Amateur Cup Final

1974: Joao Havelange succeeds Sir Stanley Rous as FIFA president

1977: Liverpool win League Championship and European Cup

1978: Freedom of contract accepted for League players

1978: Liverpool first English club to win successive European Cups

1978: Ban on foreign players in English football lifted

1979: First all-British £500,000 transfer: David Mills, from Middlesbrough to West Bromwich

1979: First £1m British transfer: Trevor Francis, from Birmingham City to Nottingham Forest

1981: Tottenham win 100th Cup Final

1981: Liverpool win European Cup, becoming first British side to hold it three times

1981: Three points for a win introduced in Football League

1981: Record British transfer: Bryan Robson, from WBA to Manchester United for £1.5m

1981: QPR install first artificial pitch in English football

1982: 340 fans crushed to death during Spartak Moscow vs. Haarlem UEFA Cup tie at Lenin Stadium

1982: Aston Villa become sixth consecutive English winners of European Cup

1982: Tottenham retain FA Cup, first time since Spurs in 1961–62

1982 League Cup becomes Milk Cup

1982: Italy defeat West Germany 3–1 in Madrid to complete third World Cup triumph

1983: Football League sponsored by Canon for three years

1984: Aberdeen take Scottish Cup for third successive season and win championship

1984: Liverpool win European Cup in penalty shoot-out and complete unique treble for an English club, with Milk Cup and League title

1984: Northern Ireland win last British Home Championship

1984: France win their first honour – the European Championship

1984: Britain's biggest score this century: Stirling Albion beat Selkirk 20–0 in

Scottish Cup

1985: Bradford City fire disaster kills 56

1985: Kevin Moran (Manchester United) becomes first player sent off in Cup Final

1985: Heysel disaster: 39 die as a result of rioting at Liverpool vs. Juventus European Cup Final in Brussels. UEFA ban English clubs indefinitely from European competition

1986: Sir Stanley Rous dies, aged 91

1986: Wales FA move HQ from Wrexham to Cardiff after 110 years

1986: Luton ban all visiting supporters as a measure against hooliganism

1986: Two substitutes allowed in FA and League Cups

1987: Play-offs introduced for last promotion place; re-election abolished; automatic promotion for winners of Conference

1987: The 18-strong squad plus youth players and officials of Alianza Lima die in plane crash

1989: Hillsborough disaster: 95 crushed to death at Liverpool vs. Nottingham Forest FA Cup semi-final

1990: International Board amends offside law (player level no longer offside); FIFA make professional foul a sending-off offence

1990: English clubs (Manchester United and Aston Villa) restored to European competition

1990 Guiseppe Lorenzo of Bologna creates world record by being sent off after 10 seconds for striking Parma opponent

1991: End of artificial pitches in Division One (Oldham and Luton)

1992: Premier League of 22 clubs launched; Football League reduced to 71 clubs in three divisions

1992: 15 killed and 1,300 injured when temporary stand collapses at Bastia, Corsica, during Bastia vs. Marseille in French Cup semi-final

1993: Marseille are the first French team to win European Cup, but cannot defend their trophy following bribery scandal

1994: Manchester United win "double"

1994: Brazil become first country to win the World Cup on a penalty shoot-out, beating Italy after 0–0 draw

1996: Manchester United become first club to win English "double" twice

1996: English host the European Championship finals for the first time

MAJOR SOCCER AWARDS

FOOTBALLER OF THE YEAR

FIFA WORLD FOOBALLER OF THE YEAR

1991	Lothar Matthäus (Germany)
1992	Marco Van Basten (Holland)
1993	Roberto Baggio (Italy)
1994	Romario (Brazil)
1995	George Weah (Liberia)
1996	Ronaldo (Brazil)

WORLD FOOTBALLER OF THE YEAR (WORLD SOCCER MAGAZINE)

1982	Paolo Rossi (Juventus & Italy)
1983	Zico (Udinese & Brazil)
1984	Michel Platini (Juventus & France)
1985	Michel Platini (Juventus & France)
1986	Diego Maradona (Napoli & Argentina)
1987	Ruud Gullit (Milan & Holland)
1988	Marco Van Basten (Milan & Holland)
1989	Ruud Gullit (Milan & Holland)
1990	Lothar Matthäus (Internazionale & West Germany)
1991	Jean-Pierre Papin (Marseille & France)
1992	Marco Van Basten (Milan & Holland)
1993	Roberto Baggio (Juventus & Italy)
1994	Paolo Maldini (Milan & Italy)
1995	Gianluca Vialli (Juventus & Italy)
1996	Ronaldo (Barcelona & Brazil)

EUROPEAN FOOTBALLER OF THE YEAR (FRANCE FOOTBALL MAGAZINE)

1956	Stanley Matthews (Blackpool)
1957	Alfredo Di Stefano (Real Madrid)
1958	Raymond Kopa (Real Madrid)
1959	Alfredo Di Stefano (Real Madrid)
1960	Luis Suarez (Barcelona)
1961	Omar Sivori (Juventus)
1962	Josef Masopust (Dukla Prague)
1963	Lev Yashin (Moscow Dynamo)
1964	Denis Law (Manchester Utd)
1965	Eusebio (Benfica)
1966	Bobby Charlton (Manchester U)
1967	Florian Albert (Ferencvaros)
1968	George Best (Manchester U)
1969	Gianni Rivera (Milan)
1970	Gerd Müller (Bayern Munich)
1971	Johan Cruyff (Ajax)
1972	Franz Beckenbauer (B Munich)
1973	Johan Cruyff (Barcelona)
1974	Johan Cruyff (Barcelona)
1975	Oleg Blokhin (Dynamo Kiev)
1976	Franz Beckenbauer (B Munich)
1977	Allan Simonsen (Borussia MG)
1978	Kevin Keegan (Hamburg)
1979	Kevin Keegan (Hamburg)
1980	Karl-Heinz Rumenigge (B Munich)
1981	Karl-Heinz Rumenigge (B Munich)
1982	Paolo Rossi (Juventus)
1983	Michel Platini (Juventus)
1984	Michel Platini (Juventus)
1985	Michel Platini (Juventus)
1986	Igor Belanov (Dynamo Kiev)
1987	Ruud Gullit (Milan)
1988	Marco Van Basten (Milan)
1989	Marco Van Basten (Milan)
1990	Lothar Matthäus (Inter)
1991	Jean-Pierre Papin (Marseilles)
1992	Marco Van Basten (Milan)
1993	Roberto Baggio (Juventus)
1994	Hristo Stoichkov (Barcelona)
1995	George Weah (Milan)
1996	Matthias Sammer (B Dortmund)

SOUTH AMERICAN FOOTBALLER OF THE YEAR

1971	Tostao (Brazil)
1972	Teofilio Cubillas (Peru)
1973	Pele (Brazil)
1974	Elias Figueroa (Chile)
1975	Elias Figueroa (Chile)
1976	Elias Figueroa (Chile)
1977	Zico (Brazil)
1978	Mario Kempes (Argentina)
1979	Diego Maradona (Argentina)
1980	Diego Maradona (Argentina)
1981	Zico (Brazil)
1982	Zico (Brazil)
1983	Socrates (Brazil)
1984	Enzo Francescoli (Uruguay)
1985	Romero (Brazil)
1986	Alzamendi (Uruguay)
1987	Carlos Valderrama (Colombia)
1988	Ruben Paz (Uruguay)
1989	Bebeto (Brazil)
1990	Raul Amarilla (Paraguay)
1991	Oscar Ruggeri (Argentina)
1992	Rai (Brazil)

1993   Carlos Valderrama (Colombia)
1994   Cafu (Brazil)
1995   Enzo Francescoli (Uruguay)
1996   Jose Luis Chilavert (Paraguay)

AFRICAN FOOTBALLER OF THE YEAR (FRANCE FOOTBALL MAGAZINE)

1970   Salif Keita (Mali)
1971   Ibrahim Sunday (Ghana)
1972   Cherif Souleymane (Guinea)
1973   Tshimen Bwanga (Zaïre)
1974   Paul Moukila (Congo)
1975   Ahmed Faras (Morocco)
1976   Roger Milla (Cameroon)
1977   Tarak Dhiab (Tunisia)
1978   Karim Abdoul Razak (Ghana)
1979   Thomas N'Kono (Cameroon)
1980   Manga Onguene (Cameroon)
1981   Lakhdar Belloumi (Algeria)
1982   Thomas N'Kono (Cameroon)
1983   Mahmoud Al Khatib (Egypt)
1984   Theophile Abega (Cameroon)
1985   Mohamed Timoumi (Morocco)
1986   Badou Zaki (Morocco)
1987   Rabah Madjer (Algeria)
1988   Kalusha Bwalya (Zambia)
1989   George Weah (Liberia)
1990   Roger Milla (Cameroon)
1991   Abedi Pele (Ghana)
1992   Abedi Pele (Ghana)
1993   Abedi Pele (Ghana)
1994   George Weah (Liberia)
1995   George Weah (Liberia)
1996   Nwankwo Kanu (Nigeria)

The African Confederation player of the year award has been awarded to:

1993   Rashidi Yekini (Nigeria)
1994   Emanuel Amunike (Nigeria)
1995   George Weah (Liberia)
1996   Nwankwo Kanu (Nigeria)

ASIAN FOOTBALLER OF THE YEAR

1990   Kim Joo-sung (South Korea)
1991   Kim Joo-sung (South Korea)
1992   *no award*
1993   Kazu Miura (Japan)
1994   Said Al-Owairan (Saudi Arabia)
1995   Masami Ihara (Japan)
1996   Kholdad Azizi (Iran)

OCEANIA FOOTBALLER OF THE YEAR

1990   Robby Slater (Australia)
1991   Wynton Rufer (New Zealand)
1992   Wynton Rufer (New Zealand)

1993   Robby Slater (Australia)
1994   Aurelio Vidmar (Australia)
1995   Christian Karembeu (New Caledonia & France)

ENGLISH FOOTBALLER OF THE YEAR FOOTBALL WRITERS' ASSOCIATION)

1948   Stanley Matthews (Blackpool)
1949   Johnny Carey (Manchester U)
1950   Joe Mercer (Arsenal)
1951   Harry Johnston (Blackpool)
1952   Billy Wright (Wolves)
1953   Nat Lofthouse (Bolton W)
1954   Tom Finney (Preston North End)
1955   Don Revie (Manchester C)
1956   Bert Trautmann (Manchester C)
1957   Tom Finney (Preston North End)
1958   Danny Blanchflower (Tottenham H)
1959   Syd Owen (Luton Town)
1960   Bill Slater (Wolverhampton W)
1961   Danny Blanchflower (Tottenham H)
1962   Jimmy Adamson (Burnley)
1963   Stanley Matthews (Stoke City)
1964   Bobby Moore (West Ham United)
1965   Bobby Collins (Leeds United)
1966   Bobby Charlton (Manchester U)
1967   Jackie Charlton (Leeds United)
1968   George Best (Manchester United)
1969   Dave Mackay (Derby County) *and* Tony Book (Manchester City)
1970   Billy Bremner (Leeds United)
1971   Frank McLintock (Arsenal)
1972   Gordon Banks (Stoke City)
1973   Pat Jennings (Tottenham H)
1974   Ian Callaghan (Liverpool)
1975   Alan Mullery (Fulham)
1976   Kevin Keegan (Liverpool)
1977   Emlyn Hughes (Liverpool)
1978   Kenny Burns (Nottingham Forest)
1979   Kenny Dalglish (Liverpool)
1980   Terry McDermott (Liverpool)
1981   Frans Thijssen (Ipswich Town)
1982   Steve Perryman (Tottenham H)
1983   Kenny Dalglish (Liverpool)
1984   Ian Rush (Liverpool)
1985   Neville Southall (Everton)
1986   Gary Lineker (Everton)
1987   Clive Allen (Tottenham H)
1988   John Barnes (Liverpool)
1989   Steve Nicol (Liverpool)
1990   John Barnes (Liverpool)
1991   Gordon Strachan (Leeds United)
1992   Gary Lineker (Tottenham H)
1993   Chris Waddle (Sheffield W)
1994   Alan Shearer (Blackburn Rovers)
1995   Jürgen Klinsmann (Tottenham H)
1996   Eric Cantona (Manchester U)
1997   Gianfranco Zola (Chelsea)

SCOTTISH FOOTBALLER OF THE YEAR

1965   Billy McNeill (Celtic)
1966   John Greig (Rangers)
1967   Ronnie Simpson (Celtic)
1968   Gordon Wallace (Raith Rovers)
1969   Bobby Murdoch (Celtic)
1970   Pat Stanton (Hibernian)
1971   Martin Buchan (Aberdeen)
1972   Dave Smith (Rangers)
1973   George Connelly (Celtic)
1974   Scotland World Cup squad
1975   Sandy Jardine (Rangers)
1976   John Greig (Rangers)
1977   Danny McGrain (Celtic)
1978   Derek Johnstone (Rangers)
1979   Andy Ritchie (Morton)
1980   Gordon Strachan (Aberdeen)
1981   Alan Rough (Partick Thistle)
1982   Paul Sturrock (Dundee United)
1983   Charlie Nicholas (Celtic)
1984   Willie Miller (Aberdeen)
1985   Hamish McAlpine (Dundee United)
1986   Sandy Jardine (Hearts)
1987   Brian McClair (Celtic)
1988   Paul McStay (Celtic)
1989   Richard Gough (Rangers)
1990   Alex McLeish (Aberdeen)
1991   Maurice Malpas (Dundee United)
1992   Ally McCoist (Rangers)
1993   Andy Goram (Rangers)
1994   Mark Hateley (Rangers)
1995   Brian Laudrup (Rangers)
1996   Paul Gascoigne (Rangers)
1997   Brian Laudrup (Rangers)

LEADING GOAL SCORERS IN EUROPE — EUROPEAN GOLDEN BOOT

Year	Player	Club	Goals
1968	Eusebio	Benfica	42
1969	Petar Jekov	CSKA Sofia	36
1970	Gerd Müller	Bayern Munich	38
1971	Josip Skoblar	Olympique Marseille	44
1972	Gerd Müller	Bayern Munich	40
1973	Eusebio	Benfica	40
1974	Hector Yazalde	Sporting Lisbon	46
1975	Dudu Georgescu	Dinamo Bucharest	33
1976	Sotiris Kaiafas	Omonia Nicosia	39
1977	Dudu Georgescu	Dinamo Bucharest	47
1978	Hans Krankl	Rapid Vienna	41
1979	Kees Kist	AZ Alkmaar	34
1980	Erwin Vandenburgh	Lierse	39
1981	Georgi Slavkov	Trakia Plovdiv	31
1982	Wim Kieft	Ajax	32
1983	Fernando Gomes	Porto	36
1984	Ian Rush	Liverpool	32
1985	Fernando Gomes	Porto	39
1986	Marco Van Basten	Ajax	37
1987	Rodion Camataru	Dinamo Bucharest	44
1988	Tanju Colak	Galatasaray	39
1989	Dorin Mateut	Dinamo Bucharest	43
1990	Hugo Sanchez	Real Madrid	38
	Hristo Stoichkov	CSKA Sofia	38
1991	Darko Pancev	Red Star Belgrade	34

Note: The Golden Boot award was interrupted between 1991 and 1996, when sponsors and promoters decided irregularities in some countries had reduced the credibility of the award. It was revived in 1996–97 with a "secure" format based on a points system.

INDEX
& ACKNOWLEDGEMENTS

PHOTO CREDITS

The Publishers would like to thank the following sources for their kind permission to reproduce the pictures used in this publication:

Allsport/Shaun Botterill, Clive Brunskill, Simon Bruty, David Cannon, Chris Cole, Stu Forster, Mike Hewitt, David Leah, Gray Mortimore, Ben Radford; NS Barrett; Colorsport/Gadoffre, Rick Rickman, David Rogers, Norbert Rzepka, SIPA, Mark Thompson, Varley, Zabci; Empics; Mary Evans Picture Library; Hulton Deutsch Collection; Illustrated London News; Mirror Syndication International; Popperfoto Russell Boyce/Reuters; Sporting Pictures (UK) Ltd; Bob Thomas/Shaun Botterill, Clive Brunskill, Tony Feeder, Stuart Forster, Gamma-Barrault, David Joyner, Dave Rogers, Tempsport, Mark Thompson.

Thanks are also due to Matthew Impey at Colorsport and Andrew Wrighting at Bob Thomas.

In addition a number of individuals very kindly loaned their memorabilia from their collections for special photography:
    p.207 tl P. Stacey – 1909 FA Cup Final shirt
    p.207 cl Charlie Mitten – 1948 FA Cup Final shirt
    p.207 bl Frank Stapleton – Brazil shirt
    p.207 tr Mrs I. Beevers – 1911 England Trials shirt
    p.207 cr Harry Gregg – 1960 Real Madrid goalkeeper's shirt
    p.208 t   Mrs I. Beevers – boots
    p.208 cl Alf Kirchen – 1936 socks
    p.209 tr Alf Kirchen – 1936 shin pads
    p.211 bl Mrs M. Whittaker – ball, 1958 FA Cup game
    p.211 tr Dennis Viollet – 1961 England cap
    p.211 cr George Wall – 1910 England cap
    p.211 br Tony Hurley – 1930 FA Cup-winner's medal

040–732